Willi Münzenberg

WILLI MÚNZENBERG:

A Political Biography

by

Babette Gross

Translated by Marian Jackson

MICHIGAN STATE UNIVERSITY PRESS

1974

★
★
★
★
★

Willi Münzenberg

Contents

Contents

Prologue

On 20 June 1940, several hundred German refugees interned by the French when the Germans attacked France, camped under the trees of the hamlet of Charmes, some ninety-four miles south-east of Lyon and twelve and one half miles from the Tournon bridgehead. They had left the camp of Chambaran, south-east of Lyon, on the previous evening. The German army was advancing relentlessly southwards, and the refugees were filled with barely concealed emotion. Almost without exception they had fled from those into whose hands they were now in danger of falling. Was there still any chance of escape? The goal of the march was the small town of Le Cheylard, about twenty-eight miles to the west of the Rhône, where yet another camp awaited them. But, if the German advance continued at its present pace, how long would it be before they reached Le Cheylard? And where would these people seek refuge then? A terrible fate, even death, was in store for most of these men if the Germans caught them.

There exists evidence of a discussion between six men, perched on tree trunks, about the uncertain future and the danger which it held in store. One of these six was Willi Münzenberg, who urged that they should not just drift. He believed that they should press on under their own steam, and that the French guards were unlikely to put any obstacles in their way. The Germans were getting nearer and nearer and the French would probably be glad to have a few less men on their hands. Alone or in small groups they would still have a chance of reaching the south.

Leopold Schwarzschild, the distinguished journalist and editor of the journal *Das Neue Tagebuch,* who did not share Münzenberg's view wondered where they could go. Münzenberg suggested the Mediterranean, preferably Marseilles. From Marseilles it would still be possible to catch a boat to North Africa. But he regarded the prospects of a successful mass escape as minimal. Le Cheylard was no good to them. They gained nothing by going there. The Germans were bound to come. He certainly had no intention of letting himself be caught like a mouse in a trap. He would try to pick up a car which would get him to the south. In vain Schwarzschild counselled caution. The chances of getting anywhere alone were small. Where would he find a car? In the general chaos he was safest among a crowd. If he went on alone he exposed himself too much.

The publisher Kurt Wolff and the art historian Paul Westheim agreed. But Münzenberg refused to listen. The all pervading sense of helplessness was particularly irksome to a man who had always been active, who in the most trying circumstances had always struggled to master the situation. He was adamant: the only chance lay in individual escape.

Evening came and preparations were made to spend the night under the trees of Charmes. But as if to confirm Münzenberg's fears the French commandant suddenly ordered the prisoners to prepare to march as the enemy had made a new breakthrough. To the best of anyone's knowledge that was the last day any of his friends saw him.

On 20 October 1940 a French newspaper carried a report of Münzenberg's final fate:

> At the foot of an oak tree in the forest of Caugnet two chasseurs discovered a male body. Death appears to have occurred several months previously. The unknown man is presumed to have hanged himself as part of a rope was still around his neck. Having investigated the case the Saint Marcellin gendarmerie established that the body was that of a certain 51-year old Willi Münzenberg, a writer born in Erfurt.

Twenty-four years later, on 13 October 1964, the journalist Clément Korth, one of the six participants in the discussion at Charmes, wrote to me: "After our session on the tree trunk . . . we four [Kurt Wolff, Leopold Schwarzschild, Paul Westheim and Korth] at any rate never saw Willi again."

Among the political activists of the nineteen-twenties and thirties Münzenberg was undoubtedly one of the most controversial. Who was this almost insignificant, nervy man, this bundle of energy with brown eyes and thick, dishevelled, dark-brown hair? Was he an adventurer who used whatever means he could find to satisfy his lust for power or was he a political leader whom fate refused the fulfilment of his dreams? Was he the brilliant creator of the "front organisations" which carried the influence of Communism so far that an American senator once described him as a "genius of organisation?" Or was he merely a conspirator, a cynical political gambler, perhaps even the willing tool of secret bodies?

All these conflicting verdicts have at some time or other been passed on Willi Münzenberg. Throughout his life his opponents and sometimes even his friends puzzled about him. Many were fascinated by him although he made them feel uneasy. His impact on people of totally different character and origin was such that he often succeeded in persuading them to serve a cause which they ordinarily would not have approved of, let alone supported.

Münzenberg was neither a party functionary in the accepted meaning of the word, a man who was given clearly defined tasks and who worked as an agitator within the limits of these tasks, nor was he a secret agent. He was the "red millionaire"—so called without in fact ever being a millionaire—the creator and the driving power of a vast concern whose activities were plain to all, albeit their effect benefited a political cause which frequently and wisely shunned the limelight. A man of contradictions, condemned often and harshly but also highly praised by very different people; a man who was the equal of a Joseph Goebbels in Goebbels' own sphere of totalitarian propaganda, who opened up this sphere to his party long before Goebbels helped the National Socialists to political victory by the same method.

Recent history has shown that behind really effective propaganda there is not just polished technique and virtuosity but a daemonic spirit. There was a daemon in Willi Münzenberg. Perhaps he was even a daemonic man, which need not be the same thing. This obsessive quality certainly helped to give his portrait the iridescence, the intangible character, that have led to such flagrant misjudgments—both negative and positive. But this daemonic quality quite apart, Münzenberg's life, devoted to politics as it was from an early age, provides ideal material for a political biography. His career in the Socialist movement, his close—often stormy—encounters with the most brilliant members of this movement, his manifold activities as a Socialist organiser and agitator, his journalistic ventures, are part of a typical but individualistic life and illustrate a hectic period of contemporary German and international history. The dramatic end of his adventurous career and the resulting speculations add a mysterious touch to the story of his life. But it is more than this colourfulness, this exciting proximity to history, that tempts one to drag Münzenberg's figure from semi-obscurity. There is almost no mention of him in works on contemporary German history.[1] His name does not appear in the *Grosse Brockhaus*. Historians behind the Iron Curtain are even less aware of Münzenberg, the former companion of Lenin and the founder of the Communist Youth International. For thirty years, since he parted with Stalin, he has been con-

[1] A few biographical studies of Münzenberg have appeared in recent years in English. Carew Hunt, "Willi Münzenberg," in *St. Antony's Papers,* No. 9 (International Communism, ed. by David Footman), London 1960, pp. 72–87. Jorgen Schleimann, "The Life and Work of Willi Münzenberg," in *Survey* (London), No. 55 (April 1965). Helmut Gruber, "Willi Münzenberg. Propagandist For and Against the Comintern," in *International Review of Social History,* Vol. X (1965), Part 2, pp. 188–210.

demned to oblivion. But the political biographer can do more than recreate the past, he can also establish some direct links with the present.

Münzenberg's later activities, which were of extreme importance to the Communist Party, were wholly directed at bringing under Communist influence a group that was always regarded as politically unstable, the intellectuals. Motivated by emotion instead of reasoned political opinions they remained uncommitted, frequently filled by a desire to participate actively in the struggle for what depending on their particular political views, they regarded as right or wrong, as justice or oppression. Rarely did they realize that the calculating—or fanatical—functionary, the cynical manipulator of political calculations, the Marxist "expert," the conservative or fascist—namely, the type who on the right and the left but particularly among the extremist groups formed the nucleus of a political party, usually viewed them with disapproval or at best an ironical superiority feeling. Apart from a few, if notable, exceptions these writers, artists and scientists were romantics who at times were capable of grotesquely quixotic acts, although they were almost always imbued with good will—idealists who lacked the basis of solid political knowledge. But they were also people who had influence, whose word was listened to—and not only in the sphere in which they were known to be authorities. The poet, the painter, the musician can be as sure of an attentive audience when pronouncing on politics as when he speaks about his art. The more extreme his utterances the more likely this is to be true. Because of the all pervading sense of crisis, the "golden" twenties and early thirties in which Münzenberg's activity reached its peak provided a particularly suitable climate for political dilettantism.

Münzenberg recognized early that here there was suitable material with which to help his party. Let the writers and artists who sympathized with the cause sign countless petitions, appeals and manifestos. Let them be more or less loquacious extras always protesting at some congress or other. They were usually tractable, and if there was any hesitancy Münzenberg was the right man to overcome it.

The phenomenon of the non-political fellow-travellers and their political exploitation, developed into a fine art by Münzenberg did not cease with his death; it is still an important technique in our political society.

For over ten years I have been intending to write the story of Münzenberg's life. That I did not do so earlier was due largely to the extreme difficulty of finding the necessary material. Everything behind the Iron Curtain was inaccessible. There the "renegade" Münzenberg continues to be ignored or dismissed in footnotes even by scholars. In the Leipzig dissertation by Walter Sieger on "The first decade of the German Workers' Youth Movement" (Berlin 1958) Münzenberg's name was subsequently deleted.[1]

Of private documents, evidence, letters etc. almost nothing remains. This material was lost in three different places at three different times: the letters of the young Socialist, and above all the evidence of his early collaboration with Lenin and the Bolsheviks—lost during his arrest in Zurich in 1917;[2] the personal documents of the twenties and early thirties—lost in Berlin after Münzenberg had left Germany in March 1933; and the later documents on his work as an émigré—lost in 1940 in Paris where they were confiscated by the Gestapo.

This may have been one of the reasons why many of Münzenberg's former friends and collaborators asked me, soon after I returned in 1947 from exile in Mexico, to write the story of his life. I met Münzenberg in 1922 and spent the remaining years until his death with him. These were probably the decisive years of his life. I not only shared his life with him but also worked with him in a position which enabled me to gain considerable insight into his varied activities. I was able to observe him during negotiations and frequently acted as his interpreter; after 1925 I accompanied him on almost every trip to Moscow. Our intimate relationship made him talk about many things more frankly to me than to any other person. Born in Potsdam in 1898 and brought up in a middle class home I became a Communist in the winter of 1920, although partly because of my middle class origin but mainly because of my temperament I always remained somewhat of an outsider. I was incapable of the total personality surrender demanded by Communism and in spite of all my faith I managed in some respects to remain objective, not least as far as Münzenberg was concerned who—for very different reasons and although he came from a very different background—was also an outsider.

The special nature of my relationship with Münzenberg perhaps justified the faith which his friends placed in me, enabling me as it did to complete the picture from personal experience wherever authentic documentation was lacking. However, I have fallen back on personal reminiscences only when there were no other sources. Münzenberg himself has described his early formative years in *Die Dritte Front*. The first part of my book is based largely on his description with such rectifi-

---

[1]It is characteristic of even the immediate past that the July 1966 number of the Soviet historical journal *Voprosi Istorii* contained a long article on the International Workers' Aid from 1921–27 without mentioning Münzenberg.
[2]The Swiss authorities have told me that the papers that were confiscated from Münzenberg in 1917 are kept under lock and key in the Public Prosecutor's Office and are not available for examination.

cations as the passing of time and the emergence of new viewpoints
have demanded. It was impossible to write Münzenberg's biography
without describing the happenings in the Socialist/Communist camp
which motivated him. Here, after so many years, subjective experience
inevitably becomes inextricably mixed up with historical evidence. In
case of doubt I have relied on the latter.

I

The Young Socialist

1. Childhood

Willi Münzenberg was born in Erfurt, Thuringia, on 14 August 1889. His early youth was spent in the village of Friemar on the Nesse, five miles northeast of Gotha. Münzenberg's father, who came from Nebra on the Unstrut, was the illegitimate child of a shepherdess and Baron von Seckendorf.

The Seckendorfs are an ancient family with branches in Germany and Austria. It was the wish of old Seckendorf that his son should choose a military career. But this did not happen. After leaving the army as a warrant officer, Münzenberg's father became a game-keeper through Seckendorf's good offices. Later he married the daughter of a Friemar farmer and took over the management of a hostelry, but found it hard to settle in one place or occupation. This may have been because he was restless, but partly it was the result of an effort to earn more money to keep his growing family.

Münzenberg's mother was a delicate, ailing woman who died after a long illness when Willi, the youngest of four children, was not yet five. From then onwards responsibility for the education of the child rested solely with the father and Willi's elder sister, Emmy, who from time to time took charge of the household. Two much older brothers had left home long ago; both had served in the army for twelve years. Karl, the eldest, now worked as a minor civil servant in Mülhausen in Thuringia. He looked as one imagines an old Prussian soldier to look; and, having indeed been a soldier, was now an honest, totally unpolitical *pater familias.* Hermann, the other brother, after leaving the army had like his father gone into the inn-keeping business, first in Thuringia and later in Berlin. In the years before 1933 he was in charge of an old people's home in Rüdersdorf, near Berlin. Hermann too was a completely non-political, lower middle class person, although to please his famous brother he became a member of the International Workers' Aid.

There were disagreements very early between the father and his youngest son. The father had a quick temper. Discontent with his life made him restless and he increasingly gave way to the temptation to drink. The only pleasure left to him was hunting and he often roamed through the forests for days on end.

His youngest son must have been a puzzle to the old Münzenberg. The other children had been healthy and industrious. They had not presented any problems. The youngest was a weakly boy who seemed to take after his mother. But from an early age this frail child exhibited a will of iron. It first found expression in the stubborn determination with which the young Münzenberg sought to escape as much as possible from parental control and from the continuous work in the inn. Later, at the beginning of his years in Switzerland, Willi Münzenberg wrote a number of plays and violent stories on the father-son problem for his youth organization. One might deduce from these that he had hated his father. But these out-pourings are largely indicative of a theme which was then current. He did not hate his father. On the contrary when he talked of his childhood one felt that he had kept a curious respect for the stubborn old man whom he so much resembled in vitality and restlessness.

Nevertheless there was the occasional violent outburst. One of Willi Münzenberg's most painful childhood memories was in connection with his duty of cleaning the oil lamps which lit the tables in the bar. Whenever possible he avoided this chore. One day when the lamps were dirty the drunken father attacked the boy with a stick and hit a lamp by mistake. In a fit of fury he blamed the boy for the broken lamp and threw a rope at him, asking him to go away and hang himself with it. The child fled in tears to the attic where he was found, after hours of searching, asleep with the rope in his hands.

But such scenes were not frequent. Willi learned at an early age how to handle his father. Whereas he had few recollections of his schooling in Friemar and close-by Eberstadt, he vividly remembered in later life the events in the inn. There he helped to serve the guests, and wash glasses and plates. He learned to talk to the peasants and artisans, read them the daily news from the local paper, listened to their comments and tried to join in their discussions. If a third man was required for a game of *Skat* Willi came to the rescue. Before he could even read and write he knew the rules of this and other card games, and as he grew older he became something of an expert. Later in the hectic Berlin years he could sit down with friends after a ten hour working day and play *Skat* for hours. In this he revealed himself as a wild gambler. I was only accepted into the fraternity after I had learned to play the complicated game tolerably well. The day after the Reichstag fire we happened to be in Frankfurt am Main, Münzenberg having only just escaped arrest. We left Frankfurt precipitately and found ourselves fleeing we knew not where. We spent the night in a small hotel between Frankfurt and Darmstadt where he played his last game of *Skat* on German soil with Emil, the factotum and driver, and myself. He did this to calm our nerves and his therapy was entirely successful.

Willi Münzenberg was eleven years old when the Boer War broke out. Young and old in Germany were delighted at the Boers' first victories. Vent was given to pent-up hatred of Britain. People were delighted to see "perfidious Albion" humiliated. For the young Germans this war was the liberation struggle of a small people against a powerful, rich country which presumed to rule the earth. At the time there was hardly a youngster in Germany who did not admire Pieter Maritz, the hero of a much read novel about the war. Young Willi Münzenberg read everything he could lay his hands on about the Boers. Even then he revealed a quality which was to determine his later life, the urge to translate theory into practice. Secretly he planned to leave home to join the Boers, and when he did start out it took several days before gendarmes found him on the road to Eisenach. He tried to explain to his angry father that he had wanted to become a soldier, to join the Boers in Africa. This was the first, but also the last, time that Münzenberg wanted to become a soldier.

He does not seem to have attended the village school very regularly. Lessons took place in a crowded school room where one teacher taught the youth of the village from the first to the eighth year. As Münzenberg wrote later, he was merely taught the three R's. Münzenberg's handwriting must have defied all efforts of the teacher. The clever, restless boy was bored in school and tried to absent himself as often as possible to read in a quiet corner.

Old Münzenberg's end was dramatic. One day, about two years after

Willi's unsuccessful flight from home, the old man was drunk once again. Trying to clean one of his guns he shot himself in the head. The accident does not seem to have made a great impression on the thirteen year old Willi. Asked in later years whether his father might have committed suicide he said that the old man had not the slightest suicidal tendencies but that he had as always been totally drunk and careless with his gun.

After his father's death, Willi Münzenberg moved to his sister's home in Gotha where he attended primary school for another year. This was probably the only year that he attended school regularly and with interest. In 1904 he left school in order to acquire a trade. He was apprenticed to a barber because it seemed the most suitable occupation for a delicate boy.

2. Apprenticeship

Life was not easy for Münzenberg in the Gotha barber's shop. Later he wrote:

> Conditions for apprentices in Imperial Germany defied description. For many apprentices, for example cooks, waiters, bakers, pastry-cooks, barbers and hairdressers, hours of work were not regulated. Many apprentices were made to work twelve, fourteen, sixteen and even more hours a day. Under the terms of the apprenticeship the 'master' was entitled to chastise the apprentice and made liberal use of this right.[1]

Münzenberg worked fourteen hours a day and on Sundays from 7 a.m. to 1 p.m. He had no free day and no midday break. Saturday afternoon was spent at the old age home in Gotha where the apprentices could practice on the residents. For every man shaved, the city paid five pfennig into the Guild chest. These funds were used to defray the costs of the annual feast of Master Barbers. One day an argument developed between Münzenberg and another apprentice during which the other man threw a brick at Münzenberg, who was hospitalized with a concussion. This was the end of his barber's apprenticeship because he refused to return to the shop.

The Socialists had long been concerned about the inhuman conditions under which young people in Germany learned their trade. As Münzenberg started his apprenticeship, in October 1904, the Apprentices and Young Workers Association was founded in Berlin. Eduard

[1] Willi Münzenberg, *Die Dritte Front. Aufzeichnungen aus 15 Jahren proletarischer Jugendbewegung*, Berlin 1930, p. 24.

Bernstein, in the Social Democratic *Neue Monatsblatt* which he published, provided space for fierce attacks on ill-treatment of apprentices. The cause for this campaign was the suicide of a locksmith apprentice, Paul Nehring, whose body, covered with blood and weals, had been found in the Grünewald. Bernstein called upon the young to protect and defend themselves. An engraver's apprentice, Max Peters, founded the Association without adult assistance.[1] The right-wing press at once violently attacked the "red apprentices association." In 1905, Peters began to publish a paper, *Die arbeitende Jugend*, contributions to which came exclusively from young workers. As the result of his initiative, Socialist apprentices associations mushroomed all over north Germany. People were not idle in southern Germany either. Almost at the same time as Peters established his organization in Berlin the Social Democratic lawyer and Reichstag Deputy, Dr. Ludwig Frank, founded the "Association of Young Workers" in Mannheim, rechristened in 1906 the "Association of Young Workers of Germany," whose crusading organ was *Die junge Garde*. Whereas the north German association concentrated almost exclusively on the fight of the young for better working conditions, Frank's south German association had a political and anti-militaristic note. Frank was a follower of Lassalle and an admirer of Jaurès; he was killed as a volunteer in France in 1914.

Münzenberg knew nothing of all this when his sister moved to Erfurt taking him with her. Erfurt was in the throes of becoming an important industrial town with metal works and lamp and shoe factories. It was in one of these shoe factories, Lingel's, that the young Münzenberg started to work as an unskilled labourer. His horizon continued to be very limited. Although he read a lot and frequented the city's lending library, his tastes were immature. He loved wild west stories, particularly those of Karl May, and preferred the cinema to the theatre. Yet it was then that Münzenberg came into contact with politics for the first time. The worker for whom Münzenberg acted as mate in the factory belonged to the Social Democratic Party (SPD) and was a man who thought much about social and political matters. He could not bear to see the young apprentices waste their time hanging about in bars and dance halls, and he began to educate them politically. Münzenberg liked the older man and confided in him. The worker told him about the party and about an educational association called "Propaganda" which met weekly in a bar and would certainly be happy to have him as a member.

The chairman of the association was Georg Schumann, who was four years Münzenberg's senior. A toolmaker from the vicinity of Leipzig,

[1]Max Peters, *Neuer Vorwärts*, 8 October 1954.

Schumann was self-taught. He was an excellent teacher and could explain clearly and factually difficult concepts of Socialist teaching to uninitiated young workers. Münzenberg soon formed a close attachment to Schumann, who stimulated him.[1]

When he joined the Workers Educational Association Propaganda in the summer of 1906 a whole new world opened up for Münzenberg. He spent every free hour reading and debating with his new friends. He read whatever he could find, mainly but not exclusively books on politics: Karl Kautsky, Friedrich Engels, Lassalle but also Haeckel's *Die Welträtsel*, Darwin, the Swiss psychiatrist Forel and last but not least the poetry of Freiligrath, Herwegh and Heine. It was characteristic of Münzenberg that he was not content to enjoy this rich fare alone. Others had to share it with him. He saw his fellow workers in the factory with new eyes. He invited them to come with him to meetings of Propaganda. Here another characteristic of Münzenberg revealed itself. He did in fact persuade many of his fellow workers to join Propaganda, even though they were completely opposed to the idea of changing their usual way of life. The Educational Association, which consisted of about twenty members between nineteen and twenty-eight years of age when Münzenberg joined it, was suddenly overrun by sixteen and seventeen year old workers and within a short time underwent a complete change of character. The debating club Propaganda became the germ cell of Erfurt's first proletarian youth organization. The driving force behind this development was Münzenberg who was sympathetically assisted by the head of the association, Georg Schumann, and when Schumann left Erfurt early in 1907 Münzenberg, after being a member for less than a year, became Propaganda's chairman. Münzenberg had found his element. In the course of this one year he not only acquired a certain amount of general knowledge, he also, if only superficially, became acquainted with the basic ideas of Socialism. And he understood that it was impossible to achieve tangible results as

[1]Schumann had a remarkable career. He started in 1907 in Jena as leader of the Socialist Youth Organization of Thuringia; after a spell in 1912 at the SPD party school in Berlin and after meeting Karl Liebknecht, he became editor in Hof and at the *Leipziger Volkszeitung*. During the war he was twice sentenced to imprisonment for 'opposition to the war and inciting the troops to sedition'; in 1919 he helped to found the KPD and edited the *Rote Fahne;* in 1921 he was elected to the Prussian Landtag and in 1928 to the Reichstag. At the end of 1933 Schumann was arrested in Breslau for illegally working for the KPD and sentenced to three years imprisonment followed by detention in the concentration camp at Sachsenhausen; in 1939 he was released. About Schumann's last years the political writer and physician, Dr. Josef Scholmer (who wrote *Die Toten kehren zurück*, Cologne 1954) told the author that while in detention during the summer of 1944 he met Schumann who was waiting to be tried by the People's Court. Schumann told him that after 1939 he had been in touch with persons who had spied for the Russians in Leipzig armaments factories. He expected to be sentenced to death and was indeed executed on 11 January 1945 in Dresden.

long as the Erfurt association remained isolated.

Münzenberg was anxious to establish connections with Frank's south German "Association of German Workers," although the Erfurt Association could not affiliate officially because it was proscribed in Prussia for its radical—and above all its anti-militaristic—tendencies. However, its organ, *Die junge Garde,* which was also prohibited in Prussia, could be illegally distributed by the Erfurt Association. Ludwig Frank, an unselfish idealist from a bourgeois family, published the paper with great material sacrifice. Among the contributors, who generally gave their services free, was the idol of Socialist youth, Karl Liebknecht, who had just, in 1907, been sentenced to eighteen months imprisonment for his pamphlet *Militarismus und Anti-Militarismus.*

Although the north German Youth Association, founded by Peters, was less radical the Erfurt group could affiliate with it because it was permitted in Prussia. This happened and henceforth the group called itself "Free Youth Erfurt." A photograph taken in 1907 at a meeting of the Jena Youth Educational Association shows the delicate, seemingly child-like Münzenberg beside the tall Schumann who, although only a few years older, appears much more adult. But Münzenberg's childish face reflects his awareness of the dignity of a "chairman." Fritz Altwein, who was present at this meeting, recalls that Münzenberg displayed considerable verve when making a speech. He attacked the football unions which made it so difficult for the associations to interest the young in political problems.

But more dangerous opposition came from another side. Max Peters says in his memoirs:

> "War to the knife" [*sic*] was declared in writing on the 'Social Democratic Printers Association' by the seemingly gentle evangelical youth association led by the court preacher and Reichstag Deputy Stöcker and his brother-in-law, Lizentiat Mumm. The Catholic Youth Association worked in secret. The Master craftsmen with their Guilds and tradesmen's Chambers and the employers recommended that organized apprentices should be proceeded against and invited the police and the Public Prosecutor to act. Over each one of our meetings hung the threat of dissolution.[1]

3. Socialist Youth Activity in Prussia

It would have been much easier for the Young Socialists if they could have turned for understanding, and if necessary help, to the Social Democratic Party and the trade unions. But the reverse was the case.

[1] Max Peters, *Neuer Vorwärts,* 8 October 1954.

The trade unions adopted a very reserved attitude towards the youth associations. At the Trade Union Congress of 1908, the trade union leader and Reichstag Deputy, Robert Schmidt, said that the independent youth organizations were "playing at association" and that "the apprentices would do better to buy themselves a slice of sausage for their penny subscription to the association."[1] A year previously Schmidt had said of the independent youth associations that "romanticism had driven them into the arms of anti-militarism" and that it was intolerable "that young men bash their heads against the steely armour of militarism." This trade union official was convinced that "this political form of the military system will wither away when the economic formations change".[2] But the trade unionists also attacked the youth associations over a more concrete issue. They maintained that it was their task—not the youth associations'—to concern themselves with matters such as work permits, protection for young workers and similar matters, or to intervene in economic disputes.

The Social Democratic Party faced a dilemma. At the Reichstag elections of 1907 it had suffered its first serious defeat since the collapse of the anti-Socialist law. Although it gained votes it lost many seats and there were only forty-three Socialist Deputies in the new Reichstag instead of eighty-one. Chancellor Bülow used this weakened Socialist position to push through a number of reactionary laws, including the new Anti-Association Law, aimed at curtailing the political activity of juveniles. This law made it a punishable offence for persons under eighteen years of age to join political organizations or to attend political meetings. The purpose of these provisions was to check the anti-militaristic trend among the young generation and to prevent workers from being given socialist indoctrination before their military service.

On the one hand the SPD was bound to oppose this law, on the other the Party Executive watched with suspicion and dismay the appearance of a radical youth movement. In the Reichstag and the press the Social Democratic Party strongly attacked the law. But within the Party the future shape of the youth groups was extensively discussed. The Party, still smarting from its electoral defeat, was afraid that unnecessary difficulties might be created by the imprudent, radical attitude of the youth groups. The majority demanded that the youngsters should be placed under the control of the Party and restricted to cultural activities, to sport and entertainment.

Münzenberg had no intention of confining himself to cultural work or diverting his young friends with games. Although the new Anti-

[1]As quoted by Peters. Ibid.
[2]Quoted in *Die Dritte Front*, p. 31.

Association Law which had come into force on 15 May 1908 gave the police far greater opportunities than before to keep an eye on the activity of youth groups, Münzenberg organized public meetings for apprentices to make even non-members feel that they could at any time turn to the group for help. Handbills were printed and distributed in the streets and outside factory gates. During this campaign Münzenberg was arrested for the first time. He did not allow himself to be intimidated, but he was told in the shoe factory, where his arrest had not remained unknown, that he would be dismissed if such an incident were to recur.

The young chairman of the "Erfurt Free Youth" knew little about the political background and the controversies of the Social Democrats. It is characteristic that later, in his reminiscences written as literature for young Communists, he described the disagreements of those years as the beginning of the struggle against the "reformists," that in retrospect he invented differences between an embryonic revolutionary group and a party bureaucracy ruthlessly opposed to all progress. In reality, however, the conflict arose out of the general process of authority. Practical political considerations aside from these disputes were undoubtedly aggravated by the clash between the generations, a problem which during those years became increasingly important in all spheres of life. Although the questions which worried the young workers and which they sought to solve had little to do with the determination of bourgeois youth to preserve its individuality, both groups were firm in their opposition to the older generation. Never before had a young generation been so convinced that it was turning a new page in the book of history, that it was the herald and pioneer of a new era totally different from the past. But like the middle class fathers who refused to abandon their way of life without a struggle, the old Socialists were determined to defend the security they had fought to attain.

A conference of youth group representatives was convened at Berlin in September 1908. The resolutions adopted there were to be submitted to the Socialist Party Congress. In spite of police opposition, approximately one hundred and seven local groups of socialist youth associations with roughly 12,400 members had been formed in the Reich in the course of two years. Münzenberg went to represent the Erfurt group. He was given two days leave from the factory, having killed off a nonexistent aunt for the purpose.[1]

Between one hundred and one hundred and twenty participants attended the conference, including Robert Danneberg from Vienna who represented the International Socialist Youth Bureau set up in

[1] *Die Dritte Front,* p. 35.

August 1907 at the Congress of the Second International at Stuttgart.
Danneberg was to become Münzenberg's collaborator and also his rival.
Karl Liebknecht, another member of this Bureau, was still in prison.

An important decision faced the delegates: Was the Party Executive
to be told that the youth organizations were not prepared to give up
their independence? Münzenberg completely agreed with Max Peters'
statement that

> . . . our opponents are using every form of pressure against us. This is
> where the class-conscious working class should give us strong support
> instead of bullying us. Youth is worthless unless it puts honour above all.[1]

In the end, however, Münzenberg voted for a resolution which was as
tortuous as it was meaningless and which did much to hasten the end
of the independent youth groups. Twenty years later Münzenberg said:

> At the time we were rather naive, put our faith in congress resolutions
> and were firmly convinced that everyone would risk his life to save the
> proletarian youth organizations.

Two weeks later the fate of the proletarian youth groups was finally
determined at the Nuremberg Party Congress. It was decided that they
must cease to exist as independent political associations. If they wished
to continue their work, they must renounce all political activity and
invite older comrades to collaborate with them—a collaboration which
amounted to supervision. They were replaced by a "Central Authority
for Germany's Working Youth." The north German association under
Max Peters was dissolved; Frank's Mannheim association had already
voluntarily dissolved before the Party Congress.

The Erfurt group was not dissolved immediately. It kept its name and
tried to preserve its old freedom of action. But it gradually lost its
independence. Party officials came to give lectures and to whittle away
its influence. Finally the Party Executive formed a Youth Committee.
The "old hands," headed by Münzenberg, gathered for discussions and
attended meetings and demonstrations. The year 1908 was characterized by unrest. Internationally, the first Morocco crisis intensified the
differences between world powers, while internally there was an economic crisis with strikes, lockouts and unemployment. Prussia was
preoccupied with the struggle to abolish the three tier electoral system,
a struggle during which there were repeated demonstrations and
clashes between demonstrators and police. Rosa Luxemburg had re-

[1] *Ibid.*, p. 38 et seq. (also for the subsequent account).

peatedly but without success demanded a mass strike against this electoral law.

Even though street demonstrations had been forbidden, the Erfurt Social Democrats gathered at the edge of the town to march to the centre. The police had closed the bridges leading across the Gera and party and trade union secretaries implored the demonstrators not to attempt a crossing. The Young Socialists at the head of the march did not heed the advice, broke through the cordon and invaded Erfurt's parade square where the public was listening to a Sunday military band concert. The Young Socialists sang one forbidden song after another until the police appeared, sealed off the square and proceeded to beat up all of those present. Münzenberg and his friends went home "in a state of intoxication."[1]

Shortly afterwards Helmut von Gerlach, the chairman of the German Peace Society, made a speech against the three tier electoral system at a Progressive Liberal meeting. He demanded the introduction of an equal, secret and direct ballot for all Germans over the age of twenty-five. Münzenberg gave the aged chairman a scrap of paper with his name on it. The chairman, under the impression that the young man wished to announce another speaker, was very surprised when Münzenberg himself stepped onto the rostrum and made a speech demanding the vote for twenty year olds who after all had "the right" to die on the battlefield. The following day the *Erfurter Allgemeine Anzeiger* noted: "The bull's-eye at the meeting was hit by seventeen year old Willi Münzenberg."[2]

He continued to work between ten and twelve hours a day at Lingel's. But the end was now in sight. One day as he circulated a list in the factory asking for support for the Swedish general strike he was denounced to the management by a colleague. The manager arrived and said to the foreman: "His speech at the meeting means war and war means: out."[3] The management had long been waiting for an opportunity to rid itself of the agitator. Münzenberg suddenly found himself on the streets at a period of great unemployment. No other Erfurt factory was prepared to employ him.

Summer was coming to an end when Münzenberg decided to "tramp the country" with a friend. At the start he had all of three marks in his pocket, but the world seemed open to him. In the period before 1914 many unmarried young workers took to the road in this fashion. Such travels had long ceased to be motivated by the romanticism of previous decades. Necessity as well as restlessness drove these apprentices to the

[1] *Ibid.* p. 47.
[2] *Ibid.* p. 49.
[3] *Ibid.*

road. Although Münzenberg set out because there was no suitable outlet for his energy in Erfurt, he was undoubtedly attracted by the unknown, by the prospect of an easy, unfettered existence.

The crusaders of those years were poor wretches who rarely found
work and who were often looked upon with suspicion as vagabonds. By
the time they reached Offenbach, Münzenberg's companion had had
enough and went back. Münzenberg continued alone along the Rhine,
upstream and downstream, without finding work. Then he turned west-
wards first to Pirmasens where there were many shoe factories. Here
his clothes were stolen one night in the hostel by a young apprentice.
After persuading the hostel keeper to give him an old pair of trousers
and boots that were much too big for him he decided to return home.
In forced marches he returned to the Rhine, arriving sick in Heidelberg
where he had a haemorrhage at the police station. A week later he was
back at Erfurt; his first attempt to escape had failed.

His sister kept him for some weeks, then he found work again. He
returned to political work with great enthusiasm and tried to revive the
youth group, writing a long letter to Fritz Ebert, the then chairman of
the Central Youth Committee, only to be referred laconically to the
Erfurt Party organization. During this winter he met Otto Rühle and
Hermann Duncker, two of the SPD's most active young "itinerant
teachers" who were giving lectures at Erfurt on Marxist topics. But the
call of the outside world had not lost its attraction. In the summer of
1910 he gave notice and set out southwards, alone and better prepared,
moving in slow stages through the forests of Thuringia, through Fran-
conia to the Black Forest and across the Swiss border.

4. Radicals in Zurich

Münzenberg arrived in Zurich at the beginning of July 1910, without
friends, without connections and above all without money. Initially he
regarded Zurich and Switzerland as a stage on the road further south.
Little did he suspect that his arrival in Zurich began a period which was
to be of great importance in his own development and, beyond that,
constituted an eventful and fruitful epoch in the history of the Swiss
Workers' Movement.

Shortly after his arrival Münzenberg visited the offices of the Social
Democratic Youth Organization. His experiences in Germany had not
filled him with great expectations. But the wanderer, who had nothing
to recommend him except his membership in the Erfurt "Free Youth,"
was accepted immediately and without reservation. This may have
been due partially to the frank, uncomplicated manner in which he
reported on his Erfurt experiences.

The chairman of the Swiss Youth Organization was a German, Max Bock, a trade union secretary. In him Münzenberg found a friend who remained loyal through the years. But to start with it was less a question of politics than of earning a living in Zurich. Münzenberg needed a job and even his new friends could not find that for him. So he moved on, first southwards to Zug, Lucerne, Interlaken, Thun and from there to Berne, this time supplied with addresses of the Swiss Youth Organization. He found a job in Berne in the hotel *Zum Stern* where he worked for four weeks. Then he received a letter from Bock telling him that there was work for him at Zurich. After a long discussion with a friend who had joined him in Berne and who, like Münzenberg, wanted to move on to Marseilles and perhaps from there to America, Münzenberg made the decision that was to determine the course of his life: he gave notice.

Münzenberg started work in August as an assistant in the *Josefsapotheke* in Zurich. The pharmacist, a Pole by birth, sympathised with the young Socialists. On Bock's insistence he had agreed to employ the young man even though he was completely inexperienced in pharmacy. The following day, with an advance of ten francs in his pocket, Münzenberg joined the Social Democratic Youth Organization.

The Swiss Socialist Workers Movement was born later than its German counterpart, because the industrialization of Switzerland proceeded at a slower pace. But the Socialist Youth Movement developed earlier in Switzerland and with less opposition than in Germany. Although they dissolved themselves shortly afterwards, the first Social Democratic Youth Associations were formed in the nineties. In 1901 Pastor Paul Pflüger founded an "association of like-minded working youths for the purpose of education and friendship" in the Johanniskirche in Zurich. However baroque the title of this organization—it soon became popularly known as the *Jungburschenverein* (Young Apprentices Association)—its founder was remarkable. Until 1923 Paul Pflüger was one of the most striking leaders of the right-wing of the Swiss Workers' Movement. At the beginning of the century his main purpose had been to offer young workers—who came mostly from the countryside and lived alone in the city—a home as well as intellectual stimulus. Pflüger wrote a number of highly individualistic articles on social questions. He listened readily to those who had complaints and was not afraid to speak out to the city and cantonal administration. He was a hot-headed, hard-drinking independent who inspired the masses, and about whom stories were legion.

The city of Zurich put at the disposal of the *Jungburschen* a one-story house with two large rooms, situated in the midst of a large meadow in the Aussersihl district.

Chicherin, later Foreign Minister of the Soviet Union, was no longer a young man when he frequented the premises of the Youth Movement. In 1919 his *Sketches from the History of the Youth Movement* appeared in Berlin; they contain the following description:

> After only a year Paul Pflüger's movement began to be taken over by others and after the first Russian Revolution came to be dominated by anarchists, semi-anarchists and anarcho-syndicalists. The mainstay of the Swiss socialist youth was the Zurich organization. It was an interesting institution. Its meetings were attended by more old men than young ones. The anarchists who had come to Switzerland from every country under the rule of the elderly Frenchmen with long beards, Germans and Austrians, and who found it difficult to adjust to the pressure of local semi-absolutism dominated the young generation. At the meetings one could see boys thinking silently in the background without taking much part in what was happening before their very eyes, while adults, even old men, treated the so-called youth organization as their own debating club.

In 1920, during the Second Comintern Congress, when Münzenberg was invited one morning to meet People's Commissar Chicherin at the Kremlin and started to introduce himself, the latter, as Münzenberg later recounted, slapped him on the back and reminded him that they knew each other from the days of the Zurich Youth Movement.

This curious atmosphere of freedom, of internationally orientated anarchism, characterised the youth movement even in 1910 when Münzenberg joined it. It was a world which differed sharply from the provincial atmosphere of the Erfurt Youth Association and also, a few exceptions apart, from the whole German Socialist Youth Movement as Münzenberg had known it. He took root in this world at once.

In 1905 an anti-militaristic league had been formed in Zurich which for a time published a journal, *Der Vorposten.* Members of this league often addressed meetings of local youth organization groups among whom they found a warm response. By and by these youth groups moved towards syndicalism and anarchism. In February 1907 they began to publish their own paper, *Der Skorpion,* the fighting organ of a young generation which "strives towards the light from the darkest depths."[1] *Skorpion* enthused over individual terror and praised the Russian social revolutionaries who practiced it as the only way to liberate the working class. When the social revolutionary, Tatiana Leontiev, shot a Swiss at Interlaken because she mistook him for a Russian minister, *Skorpion* celebrated the fatal misunderstanding as an heroic act.

[1] *Die Dritte Front,* p. 68.

"We believe that a good deed or the intention to do a good deed—whatever the result might be—cannot be punished," the paper said. "We further believe that it is unimportant if by some chance an outsider is hit."[1] The urge for freedom was so great among some members that they refused to commit their thoughts to paper because they refused to limit themselves to a certain direction. When Münzenberg arrived in Switzerland he knew nothing about anarchism as a philosophical and political movement but he threw himself wholeheartedly into the adventure. His pharmacist employer was generous and sympathetic and allowed him much freedom. Later Münzenberg was able to take off days at a time to lecture to other youth groups. For the moment he devoured any piece of anarchist literature that he could lay hands on. The anarchist tradition was an old one among the Swiss workers, particularly in western Switzerland and in intellectual circles. Contemporaries of Michael Bakunin, the great opponent of Karl Marx and romantic revolutionary who had died in Berne in 1876, were still living. One of the co-founders of the First International, the teacher Guillaume, now aged seventy, lived in Lucerne. He had been a leading member of the Jura Federation and was among the prominent proponents of the Bakunin line in Switzerland. He, with Bakunin, had been expelled from the First International.

Like most young men and women of his circle Münzenberg soon fell under the spell of a fascinating anarchist figure. The Russian prince, Peter Kropotkin, had found asylum in Lugano. His words, in which the originality of the ideas was matched by the daring of the conclusions and a brilliant style, fascinated the young readers. Soon after *Mutual Aid* appeared it became one of the most influential books of the period. In 1911, on his trip to Italy, Münzenberg like so many of his friends wanted to make the pilgrimage to Kropotkin but he had just been handed over to the Russians by the Swiss authorities.

Apart from Kropotkin there was of course Max Stirner, whose book *Der Einzige und sein Eigentum* seemed to convey new knowledge, but Münzenberg was not experienced enough to be aware of its dubious nature. The pamphlets of Johannes Most which August Bebel and Wilhelm Liebknecht had strongly disapproved of because they advocated terrorist methods also left their mark.

Münzenberg later said that what had attracted him in these books was above all their anti-authoritarianism, anti-militarism and the "propaganda for action." Without then being in a position to evaluate Bakunin's criticism of Marxist Socialism he felt instinctively attracted by Bakunin's belief in the independence of man. He shared Bakunin's

[1] *Ibid.*

profound distaste for public authority, all restriction of freedom of thought and rebelled against bourgeois morality which to the anarchists was nothing but hypocrisy. By saying that Marxist Socialism represented the greatest threat to man by making him a tool of authoritarian forces, Bakunin not only advanced a devastating criticism of the teaching to which Münzenberg himself subscribed but attacked the very roots of Marxist doctrine. But this the young man failed to appreciate at the time.

The person who undoubtedly had a decisive influence on Münzenberg and his intellectual development during those years was Dr. Fritz Brupbacher. Born in 1874 Brupbacher had joined the Social Democratic *Bildungsverein* (educational association) in Zurich in 1898. He had not come into contact with a single worker until he was twenty-three. But then he settled in the industrial district of Zurich, founded the journal *Die Junge Schweiz* and shortly afterwards met Pfarrer Pflüger.

Although Brupbacher was nominally a member of the Social Democratic Party when Münzenberg met him he had long rebelled against the bureaucracy that existed within the party and the trade unions and become an anarchist. He was on friendly terms with Kropotkin and all the well-known French and Spanish anarchists. Later, in 1905, through his Russian wife, Lydia Petrovna, he came into close contact with the Russian revolutionary Socialists.

As doctor to the poor he knew the cares and needs of the underprivileged and was not afraid to communicate them to the public. He was in favour—an enormous step at the time—of birth control and published a pamphlet, *Kindersegen und kein Ende* (Children and Evermore Children). The whole of Switzerland was scandalized. He viewed with horror complete Socialism where everything would be "regulated down to a plaster of Paris coffin." Brupbacher, a tall, stooping, delicately boned man, had a great appreciation of art and literature. He liked the poetry of Rilke and admired Peter Altenberg and Maeterlinck. In his essay *Die Psychologie des Dekadenten* (Zurich, 1904) he defended decadence as being the enemy of false morality. Brupbacher met Münzenberg at a meeting at which the doctor gave a lecture. He liked the intelligent, lively young man. Subsequently Münzenberg attended a course of lectures given by Brupbacher who was a brilliant speaker, and gradually the young worker became involved with these radical intellectuals, was invited to Brupbacher's home and there met a whole new group of revolutionaries. Once more a different world opened up to him, more tempting and exciting than that of the Zurich Youth Group and above all more stimulating intellectually. Brupbacher points a vivid picture of this world. The Zurich of those days, he says, harboured

> . . . against a background of about 200,000 respectable citizens and God-fearing workers a thousand characters from all over the world: Russian Mensheviks and Bolsheviks, revolutionary syndicalists and anarchists from Italy, Poland, Germany, Russia and Austria. The infectious ideas of Marx, Bakunin, Kropotkin and Stirner pervaded the air. All the ferment in Europe was represented at the Red League of Nations at Zurich.[1]

At last young Münzenberg, described by Brupbacher as "a sort of émigré," had found an older man who respected him, who criticized him good humouredly, who tore his poetry to shreds and who stimulated him. Brupbacher followed Münzenberg's development with interest. Later he wrote of him:

> With the lack of scruple of a "Marquis von Keith" in the service of Communism he managed, wherever he happened to stand, to mobilize the philosopher as well as the horse-thief for the idea. Contempt for men and their fecklessness was accompanied in Willi by a great urge to serve the idea and to place everything in the world at its service.[2]

From Brupbacher, who had visited Lydia Petrovna in 1910 in exile near Archangel, Münzenberg heard for the first time of conditions in Tzarist Russia, of the plight of the peasants, the corruption of officials and the oppressive atmosphere that pervaded public life. He met Russian politicians and intellectuals who had spent years in exile in Siberia —Ustinov, a nephew of Stolypin, Chernov, Boris Savinkov and others. The Russian students, of whom there were many in Switzerland, were mostly very poor. They lived together, they were unconventional and they spoke of the revolutionary working class. For a time Vera Figner, the famous social revolutionary, stayed with Brupbacher and his sister.

The heroic figures who were the models of the young generation lived right in their midst: Vera Figner, Lydia Petrovna, and the aged Guillaume who had been ostracized by the Marxists and who in 1912 was ostentatiously made an honorary member of the *Jungburschenverein* as a snub to the Social Democratic Party.

5. The Jungburschen Move into Action

In the spring of 1911 Münzenberg visited Italy, accompanied by a friend from the youth organization, Heinrich Frisch. In Milan they

---

[1] *Die Dritte Front*, Preface by Brupbacher, p. 7 *et seq.*
[2] Fritz Brupbacher, *60 Jahre Ketzer*, Zurich 1935, p. 237.

were hospitably received by the workers' organization. In the evening Münzenberg addressed the Milan Socialists on anti-militaristic tactics.

Münzenberg found a very different type of Socialist Youth Movement in Italy, well organized, purposeful and unsentimental. Unlike the German and the Swiss movements it had become an effective fighting organ, particularly in the field of anti-militarism. The Italian Socialist Party, which viewed the radicalism of the young with as much distaste as its German and Swiss counterparts, had tried in vain to disband the youth organization. Milan was a stronghold of the left wing of the party under the leadership of Benito Mussolini which in 1912 overthrew the Reformist Party leadership and thus finally saved the youth organization from dissolution.

Münzenberg's visit to Italy represents a clear dividing line in his life and activity. Even before the start of his journey, early fascination with the unreserved worship of freedom, and the anarchists' unfettered individualism, gradually lost its hold on him. He began to realize that obstinate negation could do little either for the economic well-being of the young workers or for their enlightenment and political education. His healthy realism got the better of him and he gathered around him a minority who sought to rise above the motley crowd of socialist oriented bohemians. There were serious, in part physical, clashes with the anarchist majority. In Italy he suddenly found a youth organization which spread across the entire country and which in 1911 had eighty-two local groups with approximately six thousand members. Was it not possible to create a similar organization in Switzerland, an association that was not merely a debating club, but a factor of political importance? The frantic individualism of the genuine anarchists and the pseudo-anarchists had brought the *Jungburschenverein* to the brink of disintegration. After his return from Italy Münzenberg set about, "occasionally with extremely forceful direction," as one of his then collaborators put it years later—welding the group together again.

The Swiss Social Democrats before the First World War sought to change the social order not by revolutionary means but by evolution and reform. Opposed to this line, which was set out in the Party's programme, was a left wing which demanded more forceful methods —particularly in wage struggles and the use of the military against strikes. In Zurich this opposition was headed by Fritz Platten. Born in 1883 the son of a worker he had done his apprenticeship as a blacksmith in the metal factory of Escher, Wyss and Co. and had been quick to join the trade unions and the Social Democratic Party. When revolution broke out in Russia in 1905 nothing could keep him in Zurich. He went to Riga, which was Russian at the time, in order to join the Latvian Socialists who, because the revolution had meanwhile collapsed, had been forced underground. But he made contacts and worked there until his arrest by the Tzarist secret police in May 1907. He faced the prospect of a long prison sentence but his friends succeeded in having him released on bail. They smuggled him onto a German ship which brought him back to the west.

In 1911 the Zurich opposition and Platten wanted the left-wing Socialist Robert Grimm to be elected to the National Council, an objective in which they were given valuable support by the young generation led by Münzenberg. For Münzenberg it was of extreme importance to establish contact with the left wing of the Party. The majority of the Social Democratic Party failed to show any understanding for the youth organization and the fight against opponents within the Party continued for years with varying success. In 1913 it ended with the recognition of the independence of the youth groups.

On 17 June 1911 the *Jungburschenverein* and the association *Eintracht*, whose members were mostly German workers living in Switzerland, convened a mass meeting which was addressed by Karl Liebknecht. Münzenberg had met him shortly before the international meeting at Arbon on Lake Constance. Liebknecht's subject was "Militarism and Anti-Militarism," the theme of a pamphlet with the same title which he had published in 1906 and which in 1907 had brought him an eighteen months prison sentence. He addressed himself particularly to the young generation. The soldiers of the future needed to be told early about the nature and effect of militarism. Desertion was undesirable because it exhausted itself in individual actions. The aim was to make the army red.

Münzenberg, who had meanwhile become the head of the Zurich-Aussersihl group, soon found himself and his followers at odds with the Central Committee of the Swiss Youth Organization under Max Bock. He accused the workers' secretary, who had called him to Zurich a year previously, of being too much under the thumb of the Party Executive. Even Fritz Platten had become the spokesman of the Executive and demanded the establishment of youth committees on the German model. The idea did not appeal at all to Münzenberg who opposed it with his characteristic vehemence. In the Zurich group which he dominated almost without opposition he introduced a revolutionary innovation which aroused some criticism but which was soon adopted by the Swiss Youth Organization as a whole. Whereas membership had hitherto been confined to boys, Münzenberg created a girls' section. The association's name was changed to "Zurich Socialist Youth Organization." With the aim of strengthening the girls' group, Münzenberg had handbills distributed announcing a public lecture on "Whom should the working girl marry?" Münzenberg himself addressed the meeting.

Fifty girls attended, half of whom left the hall having listened uncom-
prehendingly for fifteen minutes to what the young man was saying;
two took part in the discussion and eight joined the group.

> Our handbill with the interesting topic continued to make the rounds of
> the bourgeois press and was taken as proof of our irresponsibility.[1]

In the Zurich girls' section was a young bookbinder named Adèle who
came from the Valais. She was a graceful, black-haired, high-spirited
girl, imbued with the common sense which usually characterises
French Swiss girls of working class origin. Soon after her arrival in
Zurich she became Münzenberg's girl-friend and remained so until the
mid-twenties. She looked after him to the extent that he allowed it and
developed all the good qualities of a capable housewife. Münzenberg's
relationship with her was based not so much on great passion as on
genuine affection. Soon after making Adèle's acquaintance he met the
great love of his youth. Fanny had been sent from the Winterthur girls'
section as a delegate to the Zurich Central Executive. Night after night
when the meetings were over Münzenberg travelled from Zurich to
Winterthur to spend a few hours with Fanny. She gave him a gold
engagement ring, the only piece of jewelry he ever possessed. In later
life Münzenberg, who was usually very secretive about matters of the
heart, frequently spoke of his love for Fanny. After many years he, who
otherwise had no eyes for the appearance of the women around him,
could describe the dresses and hats that Fanny had worn when they
hiked together or visited the theatre. The break with Fanny came in
November 1918 when Münzenberg was expelled to Germany. Fanny
had hoped that he would marry her and it was probably beyond her
strength to share the dangerous life of a professional revolutionary with
him.
    Even his closest collaborators in the Youth Organization knew noth-
ing about this liaison. However free Münzenberg wished his private life
to be he was convinced that he must set an example to his Young
Socialists, politically and morally.
    During the whole period of his friendship with Fanny, Adèle re-
mained tactfully in the background. She did not complain, she made no
demands, she was always even-tempered and happy; working with
indefatigable energy in the secretariat she soon became a familiar
figure to the Young Socialists of Europe who came to Zurich during the
war to attend conferences. It was in fact her restraint and her modesty
that made her an indispensable companion to Münzenberg who was

[1] *Die Dritte Front*, p. 89.

almost neurotically afraid, probably stemming from his anarchist days, of any close ties resembling however remotely the hated institutions of marriage or family. Adèle followed him to Germany where she continued to work for him. When she died in Berlin in the mid-thirties her old Communist friends gathered at her graveside. If the Gestapo had known of this and stepped in, it could have made an important coup.

Despite Adèle's various activities in the secretariat, she was not politically minded and this fact was largely responsible for the durability of her relationship with Münzenberg. He did not like women with political ambitions. At every opportunity he later made vicious jibes at his female Communist comrades. In this he merely followed the customs and prejudices of the Communist Party. Fundamentally the CP was an association of men. Women had little say in it, although some of them, like Ruth Fischer, Helene Hoernle, Hertha Sturm or Rosi Wolfstein, rose to leading positions in the early years of the Weimar Republic. Klara Zetkin alone occupied a special position as a sort of monument from the heroic age. Even Münzenberg respected her.

Fritz Brupbacher, tired of the ever-lasting controversy with the party bureaucracy, decided to concentrate in future on the intellectual education, the psychological and literary training of a number of hand-picked young socialists. He founded the "Schwänli Club," named after the hostelry in which it met. Later the club achieved a certain fame. It was frequented by writers and painters of great repute, the German contingent including Leonhard Frank, Richard Huelsenbeck, Erich Mühsam and Gustav Landauer and the painter Max Oppenheimer, who under the pseudonym MOPP was well known for his portraits of famous personalities in the Berlin of the twenties.

Brupbacher invited Münzenberg and some of his friends, among them the young Russian painter Margulies (Julius Lyss) and Heinrich Frisch who had accompanied Münzenberg on his Italian trip, to join the "Schwänli Club." In accordance with the taste of the age and Brupbacher's personal inclination the club began by studying Russian literature. Münzenberg recalled later:

> To begin with we were fascinated by Russian literature, we read Gogol, Turgenev, Dostoyevsky, Herzen, Tolstoi and Gorki. For nights on end we discussed the subject matter, particular characters, the intentions of the writer, the significance of the books in relation to our propaganda and our movement . . . Every participant examined a book in detail and gave a lecture on it. I was given Dostoyevsky's *Crime and Punishment*. I worked industriously at it for several months and was given a reasonable mark on my lecture by Brupbacher.[1]

---

[1] *Die Dritte Front*, p. 92 *et seq.*

Another idol of the age, Henrik Ibsen, soon replaced the Russians. Nora still held undisputed sway as the ideal "modern" woman and the problems raised by Ibsen were still as topical as at the end of the previous century. After Ibsen came the discovery which had, as one would say today, an "existentialist" effect and which almost proved disastrous: August Strindberg. Surprisingly Münzenberg succumbed immediately to the magic of this brilliant mystic and out and out pessimist. As a result he missed expulsion from the Workers Union by a hair's breadth because a few religiously inclined Socialists considered his preoccupation with Strindberg a sign of extreme depravity. But what was more serious was the emotional shock which Münzenberg received from reading some of Strindberg's works, particularly *The Confessions of a Fool*. The book depressed him profoundly. Everything suddenly seemed futile—the goal unobtainable and hope in vain. Some of his friends succumbed so to this world weariness that they toyed with the idea of suicide. Was not Socialism making headway too slowly? Were the sceptics not right who viewed the efforts put into the struggle for the future well-being of the proletariat with a compassionate amusement? This was the time when some of Münzenberg's friends abandoned the youth movement. In later life Münzenberg, the Communist, thought back with mixed feelings to this disquieting interlude in his life. In his autobiography he describes this phase of despair as a "set back." Given his strong urge for practical action he may have seen it thus in retrospect but he was using Communist clichés when he later wrote about this period:

> Possessed by the urge to do something positive I put Strindberg aside and took up the works of Engels, Marx and Mehring; above all I read Lassalle.[1]

He was back in the fold of the Socialist Youth Movement but literature continued to have a hold on him for a long time to come.

In 1912 Max Barthel, the poet factory worker from Dresden whose first collection of verse, *Von unten auf* (From below) had been published by Diederichs, came to Zurich. His mentor and friend was Alfons Paquet who later also became one of Münzenberg's close friends. Barthel persuaded Münzenberg to produce an anthology of poems and stories by worker poets. It appeared in the autumn of 1912 under the title *Weihnachts-glocken* (Christmas Bells). "This volume started the rot", Münzenberg confessed.

---

[1] *Ibid.*, p. 95.

The quick sale of the book had made us think that as proletarian poets we could arouse the masses . . . During the next months I began to write plays, producing in quick succession several so-called 'plays for workers' stages' including the piece of social realism, *Kinder der Tiefe* (Children of the Deep). My purpose had been to have as my main theme the life and suffering of apprentices. The play was performed too many times . . . It did not enrich proletarian literature but led to an increase in our organization's funds.[1]

Münzenberg's *Die Kommune* had a success of a special kind. It contained much drilling of soldiers, building of barricades and above all plenty of shooting. For the opening night one of Münzenberg's friends had procured the services of twelve Swiss reservists who fired three salvoes offstage for the execution of the communards. This caused a panic in the crowded theatre because people thought that an explosion had taken place.

Although Brupbacher pulled Münzenberg's plays to pieces they survived and many years later he discovered his poems in Swedish, Norwegian and Russian translations. When he visited Russia for the first time in 1920 he was repeatedly welcomed as the "workers' poet". He himself fortunately soon realized that his talents did not lie in this direction.

Meanwhile he was confronted by so many practical tasks that he completely overcame his *Weltschmerz*. In the autumn of 1912 a centre for young people was set up in Zurich where apprentices and adolescents could congregate until eleven o'clock at night. Other towns followed the example. When the French League for Human Rights appealed for help for the countless exiles in distant Siberia an association for the relief of political prisoners in Russia was set up in Winterthur with assistance from the young.

In the summer of 1912 a general strike was proclaimed in Zurich following several weeks of striking by painters and metal-workers. They had not been able to come to terms with the employers who had simply gone to neighbouring Germany to hire workers to come to Zurich as strike-breakers. Serious clashes resulted in which the youth groups participated. A striking painter was killed, another seriously injured. The town council, on which the Social Democrats were represented, decided on brutal measures against the strikers. It prohibited picketing, an order which infuriated the Zurich workers. The Workers' Union called for a twenty-four hour protest strike. This was how the strike day went according to Brupbacher:

[1] *Ibid.*, p. 120.

The strike was a great success. Almost all industrial workers, van drivers, electricity workers, gas and railway workers downed tools . . . Some of those who went to work only pretended to be going and were delighted not to be allowed in by the pickets . . . Deputations were sent to the shopkeepers in the Bahnhofstrasse advising them to shut up shop, advice which they quickly obeyed . . . The worker bicyclists rendered us splendid service. They cycled to all places of work to see where work still went on and telephoned us at the House of the People to tell us how many people were needed to bring out those who were still at work. Cinemas were closed, but food shops were allowed to stay open. Many shops telephoned to enquire humbly, as one enquires from the police, whether they should stay open or close . . .[1]

Under Münzenberg's leadership the youth organizations threw themselves whole-heartedly into the fray. Münzenberg rushed from one centre of conflict to the next on the pharmacy bicycle. The government's reply to the general strike was to occupy the House of the People and arrest several workers' leaders including Max Bock, the Secretary of the Zurich Workers' Union and Chairman of the Socialist Youth Organization. When Bock was expelled the party approached Münzenberg and asked him to change his mind and join the Central Executive. The decision was not an easy one but he realized that he could be far more effective if he accepted the offer. At the same time he was entrusted with the publication of the monthly journal *Freie Jugend*.

The first numbers of *Freie Jugend* under his editorship were devoted primarily to propaganda against militarism and war. The fourth number provoked one of the biggest scandals that has ever shaken the Swiss Social Democratic Party. He printed an article by Brupbacher entitled "For What We Would Die" in which the author said that although democracy was better than absolutism he would not pay more than five Rappen to ensure that democracy was preserved. Brupbacher went on to attack mercilessly a Social Democratic teacher for having commanded a guard of honour during a visit of Wilhelm II to Switzerland and for having accepted a diamond pin as a gift from the Kaiser. The article which was full of insults to Social Democratic officials finished with the words:

Everyone who advises us to defend the bourgeois Fatherland is a 'traitor' to our Fatherland, to Socialism. Long live the International. Long live the general strike of all armed and unarmed proletarians of all countries.

[1]Fritz Brupbacher, *Erinnerungen eines Revoluzzers*, Zurich 1927, p. 60 et seq.

The reaction of the Social Democrats was indescribable. The remark about the "five Rappen" was the ultimate insult. Here was a Social Democrat who preached anarchist ideas. Brupbacher's expulsion from the party was immediately demanded and the issue was thrashed out at a public meeting. Brupbacher's defence was welcomed enthusiastically and his expulsion rejected by an overwhelming majority. Although the Party Executive tried to ignore this majority decision and expel Brupbacher regardless, in the end it was forced to give up these efforts because of fear of criticism from the rank and file of the party.

In November 1912 the Second International convened at Basle in the mediaeval building Basle Minster. Once more the Socialist parties of the world swore a joint oath never to allow their peoples to be dragged into a war. This Congress, whose historic significance today lies primarily in the fact that it took place shortly before the outbreak of the war, had originally been convened as a protest against the Balkan War. Hence the German Social Democrat Hugo Haase began his speech which subsequently became famous with the words: "War ravages the Balkan fields". Europe was on fire in the south east and the conflagration threatened to engulf the whole continent. Everyone of note in the International was present at Basle Minster, the Germans August Bebel and Klara Zetkin, Kamenev for the Bolsheviks, Martov for the Mensheviks, Trotsky, the Italians Mussolini and Turati, Victor Adler and many others. Münzenberg had gone as youth delegate to Basle where Jean Jaurès probably impressed him most.

A few weeks earlier Münzenberg, after reading an announcement of the Congress in the papers, had gone out and hired the biggest hall in Zurich for a youth organization meeting. He then sent express letters to Rosa Luxemburg and Karl Liebknecht inviting them to address the meeting. The Party Executive was furious because such a meeting was a matter for the party not for the youth organization. The Executive forbade the meeting and reported this to the two speakers who immediately refused to attend. But Münzenberg was not put off. As several hundred delegates were meeting in Basle it was still likely that some prominent Socialists could be persuaded to address the meeting.

Friedrich Adler, then an editor of the Zurich *Volksrecht,* also sought to persuade the Young Socialists to abandon their plan. But Münzenberg stood firm. Sunday came—the meeting was planned for Monday evening—and still no speakers of international repute with sufficient pull to fill three thousand seats had been found. In the end he obtained as his first speaker an unknown but strikingly attractive woman, Alexandra Kollontai, from Petersburg, who was living in exile in Norway at the time. On Sunday night an acceptance arrived from Paris, from Gustave

Hervé, then still a fanatical anti-militarist. On Monday morning Münzenberg had ten thousand bright red leaflets printed which members
of his organization distributed outside the factory gates. In the afternoon news arrived that Hervé was not coming and was sending an
unknown replacement. Hervé probably had learned meanwhile of the
Party Executive's opposition to the meeting. The Young Socialists reconciled themselves to the inevitable and went to the station to meet the
Frenchman. Arriving at the same time was the Bulgarian Socialist
Deputy Sakasoff, who had been the only person in the Bulgarian Parliament to vote against the Balkan War. As soon as the *Jungburschen* had
recognized him, they tried to persuade him that he must address their
meeting, although he had only intended to change trains at Zurich. He
was taken to a hotel and guarded until the meeting, where he saved the
evening with a first-hand description of the horrors of war in the Balkans.

6. *Münzenberg as Swiss Youth Secretary*

To strengthen the youth organization in the smaller Swiss localities,
Münzenberg suggested the establishment of a Socialist Youth Secretariat. Although his proposal resulted in lengthy and heated discussions
because the Executive was afraid of the extra expense, a Secretariat was
eventually established on 1 January 1914 and Münzenberg was unanimously elected Secretary. He left his pharmacy and became a paid
party official.

Münzenberg thus moved closer to his ambition. A few years earlier
he had remarked to Fritz Brupbacher: "One must refuse the small
cakes and aim for the final goal."[1] This single-mindedness had greatly
impressed Brupbacher at the time and it was certainly typical of Münzenberg's attitude not only towards life but also towards his task as an
official of Socialist youth.

The difficulties which accompanied the establishment of the Youth
Secretariat and the continued publication of *Freie Jugend* show that this
step forward was not an easy one. A few days before New Year's Eve
the firm which printed the paper and which was run by a Social Democrat, Couzett, presented *Freie Jugend* with an ultimatum. The Youth
Organization owed the firm fifteen hundred francs and they refused to
continue to print *Freie Jugend* unless four hundred francs of this debt
was paid by 2 January 1914. The idea that the paper might cease
publication had never occurred to Münzenberg and his most active
supporters, Edy Meyer, Willy Trostel and Julius Mimiola, and they were

[1] *Die Dritte Front*, Brupbacher's Preface, p. 5.

desperate to raise the money. Then Münzenberg had an idea: it was New Year's Eve and the population of Zurich was in a festive mood. So the *Junggenossen* trooped from one place of public entertainment to the next shamelessly begging from friends and members. On New Year's Day they continued the efforts with a house to house collection. By evening they had collected four hundred and thirty francs. *Freie Jugend* could continue to appear. Above all Münzenberg had ensured that his activities as Youth Secretary did not begin with an embarrassing fiasco.

The Secretariat began its work in extremely modest circumstances. Münzenberg's room in the Werdstrasse served as office, dispatch room, and youth hostel. Many years later Ernst Christiansen, who was then leader of the Socialist Youth Organization of Denmark, told me that when he passed through Zurich in 1915 he was naturally put up in this room. With his customary energy Münzenberg spent almost every hour of the day and frequently a considerable part of the night at his job, for which he received one hundred francs a month. Apart from some files there was no office equipment so Münzenberg wrote every letter and circular by hand. As his handwriting was practically illegible it was a miracle that the members of the Swiss Youth Organization ever understood what their Secretary was telling them or what he wanted from them.

And he always wanted something. From the moment he took office he was indefatigable. It was as though he sensed that he had only a short time before the Youth Organization's entire activity would be directed into new channels as the result of a world shaking event.

At the beginning of 1914, Münzenberg's ideas were still dominated by Socialist maxims unheard at the turn of the century. The catch-phrase which for years had influenced the Socialist movement, and which had introduced Münzenberg to a whole new world during his Erfurt days, still seemed to him a suitable motto for his work as Secretary: Knowledge is power. To him the most important of his tasks as Secretary was education. Within the framework of this educational activity it was curiously enough opposition to the cinema which preoccupied Münzenberg. In his adolescence he had been among the enthusiastic audiences at thrillers and wild west films. He was therefore fully aware of the extent to which youngsters could be influenced by such spectacles. Also, a young person who spent his or her time in a dark cinema auditorium was a difficult target for Socialist propaganda. Münzenberg succeeded in persuading a number of cinema owners to put on special performances of cultural films or documentaries, as well as filmed versions of great works of literature. The school authorities were also asked their advice on each of these films. Münzenberg's fight against the triviality of the cinema grew into a "cinematic reform movement." Middle class and church youth leaders denounced the educational activities of the Socialist youth movement as the spread of semi-education. Münzenberg firmly rejected the accusation. He was undoubtedly seriously concerned in giving young Socialists as solid an educational basis as possible, since Socialist educational work had been of tremendous importance to him. Moreover this aspect of his youth work appealed to the markedly pedagogic trait in his character.

But his preoccupation with education did not make Münzenberg neglect the day-to-day demands of Socialist youth. At the head of the list was the fight for a federal apprentices' law. Even in the war years that followed this fight continued.

The Swiss Youth Organization had hitherto largely been confined to the few big cities. In the smaller towns or the countryside the organization had few members. Münzenberg now embarked on extensive recruiting campaigns throughout Switzerland. He was careful not to appear as a political agitator to young people as yet unaccustomed to revolutionary ideas. Even on these propaganda trips his main emphasis was on education. As a result he achieved an extraordinary personal popularity among the young workers everywhere in Switzerland. It was certainly partly because of this popularity that within a few years the number of active members rose from about one thousand to over six thousand, the number of passive members to over three thousand—an important factor because these passive members paid graduated contributions according to their income—and the number of sections from twenty to one hundred and fifty. Under Münzenberg's editorship *Freie Jugend* reached a circulation of eight thousand copies. The "Year Book of the Swiss Youth Organization for 1914/15" contains a report ("A week in the life of the Secretary") which shows that in 1914 alone Münzenberg organized three hundred and thirty-six meetings all over Switzerland "although the outbreak of war made travel almost impossible for weeks." The following extract is taken from the Year Book:[1]

Saturday 15.1: Lecture in Altdorf.
Sunday 16.1: Attended executive meeting in Richterswil.
Monday 17.1: Before noon dealt with Saturday and Sunday correspondence, about 40 letters and a few circulars; afternoon: examination of material for and preparation of No. 3 of *Freie Jugend*, settled some business; evening: directed discussion in Dietikon; at night: dealt with afternoon and evening correspondence, about 15 letters.
Tuesday 18.1: Before noon visited some comrades to persuade them to

[1] *Jahrbuch der Schweizerischen Jugendorganisation für die Jahre 1914/15*, in the Sozialarchiv, Zurich.

speak at lecture course, correspondence, approx. 10 letters, circular to sections prepared and duplicated, preparations for Central Executive meeting scheduled for the evening; afternoon: despatch of *Freie Jugend* No. 2 to subscribers, 1,000 copies, and to about 150 addresses abroad; evening: Central Executive meeting; at night: correspondence and work for International Bureau [the direction of which had meanwhile been entrusted to Münzenberg].

Wednesday 19.1: Before noon circular to advertisers drafted, duplicated and despatched to 40 addresses, dealt with correspondence, checked subscribers' lists and enquiries, visited post office, bookbinder and book shop; afternoon: attended management meeting; evening: lecture in Olten.

Thursday 20.1: In the morning went to Frauenfeld, consultation with workers' secretary on apprentices' law for the canton of Thurgau; afternoon: dealt with correspondence, approximately 40 letters, 2 circulars to the sections; evening: meeting with cashier and settlement of the annual accounts; at night: 3 letters for the International Bureau.

Friday 21.1: Before noon edited *Freie Jugend;* afternoon: correspondence, approximately 30 letters, filing of letters etc., evening: lecture in Wettingen.

Saturday 22.1: Before noon correspondence, provision of speakers, 10 a.m. journey to Geneva; evening: lecture in Geneva.

In addition trade union papers and party papers were to be read, numerous visits paid to the post office, the printers and the stationer and many Secretariat visitors received.

Under Münzenberg's intensely active leadership the Socialist Youth Organization in Switzerland rapidly developed from a relatively small, poorly organized group, noted solely for the occasional revolt motivated by youthful exuberance rather than political radicalism, into a well directed, enlightened movement—a factor to be reckoned with in the political life of the country. Soon even the Social Democratic Party of Switzerland realized this, however much its leading officials—a few exceptions apart—had hitherto opposed the Youth Organization because of its alleged lack of obedience and respect.

At Whitsun 1914, a delegation of the Swiss Youth Organization went to Stuttgart to attend the Württemberg Youth Rally. The group, consisting of fifty-four young people under Münzenberg's leadership, arrived in Stuttgart with definite propagandist intentions. They had smuggled a hundred copies of Karl Liebknecht's pamphlet *Militarismus und Anti-Militarismus* and fifty copies of Hervé's book *The Fatherland of the Rich* across the frontier. These books were forbidden in Germany and the Stuttgart delegates fought to obtain copies. The speech which Münzenberg made was in many ways characteristic. Above all it showed a passionately held belief in internationalism. Many of Liebknecht's and Hervé's ideas also appeared. He repeatedly introduced markedly anti-militaristic sentiments into this speech, made not so long before the outbreak of the war. The whole oration was a passionate appeal to the great international brotherhood of the workers and his language rose to an almost religious symbolism:

> Legend has it that two thousand years ago the Holy Spirit filled Jesus' disciples so that they went forth and taught all nations. A legend perhaps but I know that this spirit of Pentecost must be with us today and always. We shall go forth to all nations, to all brothers and sisters and fire them with enthusiasm for Socialism.

Towards the end of his speech Münzenberg became positively rhapsodic:

> Have you ever stood on the shore and watched the sea surge against the rocks which bar its waves entry to the land beyond? . . . In the course of the years hundreds of waves beat against the rocks and each one carries something away with it, a few stones, some bits of rock . . . One day a storm will break that will churn up the sea in its deepest depths and throw a great tidal wave against the hollow rock, sweeping it away and opening up the path to the land beyond . . . The rigid, lifeless rocks are capitalism, but the sea, my young friends—you will have felt it already—are we, the working class.[1]

During this visit to Stuttgart and the subsequent trip to Thuringia and Saxony, Münzenberg saw familiar parts of Germany from a new angle. For the first time he met politically active young people with whom he could exchange views and experiences. The Whitsun days in Stuttgart in particular marked the beginnings of friendships which came to fruition years later. Among others Münzenberg met Jakob Walcher, Fritz Rück, Edwin Hoernle and Arthur Crispien, a determined left-wing radical whose energy and passionate single-mindedness almost rivalled Münzenberg's. The friendships which he struck up then certainly influenced him in 1918, after his expulsion from Switzerland, to go to Stuttgart where he became embroiled in the Spartacist uprising.

[1] *Die Dritte Front*, p. 136.

II

Lenin's Pupil

1. The First War Casualty—The Second International

A few weeks after Münzenberg's return to Switzerland, Gavrilo Princip's shots in Bosnian Sarajevo abruptly aroused the world. The news of the attempt on the lives of the Austrian Crown Prince Francis Ferdinand and his wife led to excited discussions between Münzenberg and his friends. But not one of them could at first believe that war between the nations of Europe was now inevitable. War in Europe? In 1914? A serious conflict between Austria and Serbia was conceivable, but not a European war. Two considerations seemed to eliminate this possibility. The international interests of capital were far too extensive to permit a war. And also the times were surely passed when wars could be started by the rulers and the people must prepare to be slaughtered without protest. In the age of socialism the people would have their say. The leaders of European Social Democracy would naturally oppose this lunacy, supported by the members of the workers' parties who were sufficiently numerous to prevent the worst. Only two years before the leading Social Democrats of Europe had sworn a solemn oath at the

Basle Congress to do everything in their power to oppose war. No, Münzenberg and his friends could not believe in a European war, let alone in a world war.

Then the assassination was followed by the Austrian ultimatum, and the ultimatum by Austria's declaration of war on Serbia. Day after day Austrian citizens resident in Zurich swarmed down the Bahnhofstrasse towards the station to report for military service at home. Most of them were workers, many were Socialists, but they went not merely willingly but for the most part with exuberant enthusiasm. Each departing party was accompanied to the station by crowds of compatriots and Swiss.

When a few days later the spectre of a world war became a terrible reality with Germany's declaration of war on France, enthusiasm rose even higher. Now it was the Germans who left Switzerland. And they went no less willingly than the Austrians. Socialists or not, they rushed to the colours. The congestion on the Zurich Bahnhofstrasse was such that the police had to intervene to keep the crowds in check. Münzenberg and his Young Socialists suddenly found themselves on the side of their old enemies, the Zurich police, whom they helped to the best of their abilities. A negligible group of Social Democrats and a few anarchist intellectuals apart, all Germans left Switzerland. They would not abandon their Kaiser.

Münzenberg was thunderstruck. What about the reasoning which even after the murder at Sarajevo had made war among the peoples of Europe seem improbable? What of the oath of Basle? That the Socialist leaders in the belligerent countries had not kept it became clear immediately after the outbreak of war. What the attitude of the Social Democrats in neutral Switzerland would be Münzenberg was to learn shortly. A few days after the outbreak of war the Workers' Union held a rally at the Velodrome, the Zurich cycle racing track. The first speaker to come to the rostrum was the Swiss Social Democrat Johann Sigg. He deplored the slaughter but thought that anti-war action was impossible. The only hope was that an opportunity to rebuild the International would come at the end of the war. Münzenberg leapt onto the podium and angrily attacked Sigg's fatalistic attitude. On the contrary, he said, the war must be opposed by every means, and as a last resort there was still the general strike. The young people whom he represented had no intention of going to war for the capitalists. Their only aim was to fight for the Socialist movement. This vehement attack brought the Nestor of Swiss Social Democracy, the party chairman, Hermann Greulich, to the scene. He conceded that Münzenberg had spoken in good faith but felt compelled "to pour some water into the tempestuous young man's wine."[1] Like his party friend Sigg, Greulich also admitted that it was

[1] *Die Dritte Front*, p. 143.

impossible to oppose the war. The Socialists were too weak to do so. The individual was swept along by the machine.

These words expressed more than a passing feeling of resignation that might have been explained by saying that the shock of the declaration of war had not yet worn off. They went much further. At the outset of the war Greulich laid down the line that the Socialist parties of the neutral countries followed for the whole of the war. Hot-headed and convinced of the correctness of his point of view Münzenberg might well have rebelled against this line but he must have realized that on this point most of the members of his own party were definitely opposed to his position.

Even more disappointing for a dedicated anti-militarist than the resigned attitude of the Social Democrats in the neutral countries, was the nationalism of the Social Democratic majority in the belligerent countries. These Socialists realized that what they had always assumed to be their innermost convictions were being put to the test, and that they were first and foremost citizens of their country and only in the second place international Socialists. The most intransigent opponents of the war understandably overlooked the bitterness with which many Social Democrats capitulated to nationalism. They accused the "traitors" of being nothing but fanatical chauvinists. Many responsible leaders of European Social Democracy certainly did not find it easy to resign themselves to what they believed to be the inevitable. Victor Adler, the great Viennese Socialist, according to an eye-witness, looked ten years older overnight when on 28 July 1914 at a session of the Bureau of the Second International at Brussels he spoke about the conflict which even then he regarded as inevitable. A man like Adler certainly did not face the threatening catastrophe with indifference. But even the "War on War" mass rally also held on that date in Brussels could not mitigate the realities of the situation. Three days later, on 31 July, Jean Jaurès was murdered. Two days later still the majority of French and German Socialists voted in favour of war credits. In his *History of the International* Julius Braunthal later said that the Second International was the first war casualty.

Did it then fall victim to traitors and renegades within its own ranks? And what had internationalism accomplished in the decades preceding the outbreak of the war? There is no doubt that anti-militarist, anti-chauvinist educational work went on, particularly among young workers. These ideas came mainly from France. Among their most influential protagonists was Gustave Hervé, whose book *Leur Patrie* (1906) had provided the bourgeois enemies of Socialism with the contemptuous phrase "unpatriotic riff-raff." But even such a determined anti-militarist as Karl Liebknecht always wanted the movement to remain "within

legal bounds", never to "ask anywhere for military insubordination."
Hervé on the other hand was a much more consistent anti-militarist.
For him there was only unconditional war on war. He even denied the
existence of any difference between aggressive and defensive wars.
War was *ipso facto* wicked. With equal eloquence he championed unconditional internationalism. This attitude was deeply rooted in the
French tradition. It was the direct continuation of the anarchist credo
of men like Proudhon. It also had its parallels in several points of the
First International programme. Fundamentally it was the necessary
consequence of the demand: "Proletarians of the world unite." But the
theory of unconditional internationalism, of the need to abolish the
nation as an obstacle to the unification of the working class, did not
remain without opponents. Even Jean Jaurès who later paid for his
pacifism with his life often and clearly expressed himself against destroying the nation.

During the first ten years of the century militarism was one of the
main topics of all workers' movement congresses. The leaders of the
German Social Democrats had plenty of opportunity to voice their
views on this topic. They did so unequivocally and by no means always
in the sense obviously expected of them in 1914. At the Stuttgart International Socialist Congress in 1907, August Bebel opposed a French
resolution which demanded the prevention of war by means of mass
strikes and revolt:

> This is impossible in Germany because six million men, two million of
> whom are Social Democrats, will be called up immediately. Who then can
> take part in the general strike?

The idea that those who were called up might strike never occurred to
him. It was at this congress that Bebel said: "If there should be a war
with Russia even I shall shoulder a rifle in my old age." Although Bebel's
remark may have been meant to convey the idea that it was the oppressive absolutist monarchy in Russia that was the enemy it does not exactly exude dedicated anti-militarism. Also at Stuttgart, Noske said: "If
Germany is attacked, if there is a serious threat, the Social Democrats
will rush to defend their country." At the last pre-war Party Congress
which took place in Jena in 1913, the left wing submitted the following
resolution:

> Militarism must be fought to the utmost as it is the strongest weapon of
> the ruling classes. All draft legislation submitted to the Reichstag for the
> purpose of strengthening militarism, as well as all proposals for taxation
> intended to cover the costs of militarism whether direct or indirect taxes,
> must be thrown out.

This resolution was rejected by 333 votes to 142. Instead the SPD voted in favour of increasing the defence budget by one milliard because the proposal was linked with a graduated wealth tax.

The Congress at Basle which had given rise to so much romantic hope had in reality been a demonstration,—no doubt passionate—but nevertheless noncommittal, against the Balkan War. The great nations were not involved in this war and there was therefore no need for the leaders of their workers' movements to declare themselves—for or against their countries. The vow of peace remained an abstract vow; although certainly made with conviction it was, as time showed, unrealistic.

The attitude of the Socialist majority in the belligerent countries, and also in the neutral states, should not have come as a shock to those who had followed the reactions of the spokesmen of the European workers' movement in the pre-war period. Moreover it was not only the leaders of the workers' movement who could not shed their nationalist prejudices. What was much more important was that the overwhelming mass of their supporters were not willing to sacrifice their patriotism for a noble ideal which, contrary to the view of some Socialists, was not yet part and parcel of the Socialist way of life. When their country was threatened the workers decided without hesitation to defend it. Nor were the French, the originators of the idea of anti-militarism and anti-nationalism, an exception.

And what about the radicals, the intransigents? Kurt Geyer certainly had a point when years later he wrote to Ruth Fischer:[1]

> On reflection I find that Münzenberg and I and others of my generation were not motivated by animosity towards the 'Reich'. Ours was a theoretical internationalism which was at the same time a violent, hate-filled anti-imperialism directed against 'greater' Germany and expansion. Fundamentally during the war we were the most orthodox *status quo* politicians imaginable.

But for Münzenberg and many of his generation "theoretical internationalism," as Geyer rightly called it with hindsight, was a reality which determined their life, just as their anti-militarism was a reality. These realities strengthened their hatred of the "traitors" in the Second International and caused them to ignore the fact that it was not so much that they had been betrayed by fellow members of the movement as that an illusion nurtured with intense love had proved false.

However energetically Münzenberg and his close collaborators among the Zurich group campaigned against the war, most other sections of the Socialist youth movement in Switzerland seemed unaware

[1]Made available to the author by Kurt Geyer.

of the world crisis. Even though the first number of *Freie Jugend* to
appear after the outbreak of the war was given over to the theme of
"war on war" and contained a violent attack on the "capitalist war" by
its editor, Münzenberg, reports from the sections were largely confined
to the usual routine. They dealt with general and regional problems of
youth work and either ignored the outbreak of the war altogether or
mentioned it only in passing. In young officials like Trostel, Meyer, and
Mimiola, Münzenberg had certainly found collaborators who supported
his anti-war propaganda with a conviction and an enthusiasm equal to
his. But what is also certain is that it was his driving force which in the
end roused not only the activists and the sympathizers but also the
majority of Young Socialists in Switzerland.

2. *The Berne Youth Conference*

Like the Bureau of the Second International at Brussels, the Vienna
Bureau of the International Association of Socialist Youth Organizations
had closed down at the outbreak of war. This Bureau had been founded
in 1907 at the Stuttgart Congress. Later, having long since become a
Communist, Münzenberg observed that the Bureau's activity even
before the war had been confined to "an inefficient exchange of letters"
and the "publication of a pathetic bulletin which appeared at very
irregular intervals."[1] If it did nothing else, however, the Bureau, whose
chief, Robert Danneberg, was also Secretary of the well organized
Austrian Socialist Youth, maintained close ties with all other independent Socialist youth associations in Europe. When the war broke out,
Danneberg was in the midst of preparations for an international youth
meeting at Vienna.

Shortly after the outbreak of the war the Socialist youth associations,
particularly those of the neutral states, asked that the Vienna Bureau
be transferred to a neutral country. They wanted to meet to discuss
such issues as the *Burgfrieden* (party truce), national defence and disarmament, and, of course, ways and means of ending the war as quickly
as possible. Zega Hoeglund, the chairman of the Swedish Youth Organization, and the Italians asked Münzenberg to get in touch with Danneberg and persuade him to agree to an international conference in
Switzerland. A lively exchange of letters followed.[2] On 10 November
1914 Münzenberg suggested that Danneberg should arrange for an
international youth conference to meet in Switzerland at Whitsun
1915. Danneberg replied unenthusiastically that it was very uncertain

[1] *Die Dritte Front*, p. 153.
[2] The originals are in the International Institute for Social History, Amsterdam.

whether this would be possible. On 2 February 1915 Münzenberg informed him that at the request of the Italian and Northern youth organizations he had convened a conference in Berne for Easter 1915. He enclosed the agenda. The letter was signed W.M., "Bureau of International Socialist Youth Organizations." Danneberg immediately objected to Hoeglund in Stockholm; he was opposed to the whole conference and especially to the second point of the agenda which concerned the organization of international Socialist youth associations. A conference of this kind could not decide on a future programme. He also addressed a strongly worded letter to Münzenberg saying that the Vienna Bureau had complied with the request of the neutrals to play a bigger role in the Bureau by appointing Hoeglund to an official position. The German organization would not attend the conference, neither would the Belgian. The most the Berne meeting could accomplish would be a show of international solidarity. He demanded that the second point be deleted from the agenda and that Hoeglund send out the invitations. Münzenberg replied that his Central Executive had considered Danneberg's letter. It had decided not to delete the second item on the agenda. The conference would be of a consultative nature, it would not make binding decisions. As the Germans did not belong to the international association they could hardly come. However, individual representatives from German towns had already told him that they wished to attend. At the last minute Danneberg tried to prevent the conference from taking place. When Münzenberg telegraphed to Vienna on 31 March that Hoeglund was unable to come and asked Danneberg to attend so that the International Bureau might be represented, Danneberg replied that he could not come either and therefore suggested a postponement of the conference.

But the conference met from 4 to 6 April 1915 in Berne, the first public Socialist manifestation against the war. (An international women's conference which had met under Klara Zetkin's leadership from 26 to 28 March 1915, also in Berne, had been held in secret.) Sixteen elected youth delegates came to Berne from Italy, Holland, Scandinavia, Switzerland, the Balkan countries, Poland and Russia. A few young German Socialists who disagreed with the Party Executive had illegally crossed the frontier. No delegate had come from France, a fact welcomed by official French Socialist circles.[1]

Robert Grimm represented the Swiss Party, Angelica Balabanoff the Italian. Grimm made the main speech on "War and the Attitude of the Social Democratic Parties and the Socialist Youth Organizations to the War." He dismissed the national defence theory and attacked the *Burg-*

---

[1] A. Rosmer, *Le Mouvement Ouvrier Pendant la Guerre*, Paris 1927, p. 310.

frieden. He asked for opposition to war and militarism. A resolution which he submitted jointly with Angelica Balabanoff demanded complete disarmament.

The conference had begun with a clash with the Bolshevik delegates, Inessa Armand and G.S. Yegorov because, at Lenin's instigation, they demanded that every country present should have not one but two votes. When the proposal was rejected the Russians left the conference. After a heated discussion the dispute was settled in favour of the Russian proposal. Every country was given two votes and Poland was regarded as an independent country. The Russians returned. But soon there was further disagreement on the resolution submitted by Grimm and the conference organizers. Lenin, who was not allowed to attend the conference, sat in the *Volkshaus Café*, where one of the Bolshevik delegates reported to him frequently and received new directives. The Russians bitterly attacked Grimm's resolution because of its pacifist trend and submitted a text drafted by Lenin which condemned the Second International and called for a disarming of the bourgeoisie and for armed rebellion. The other delegates rejected this proposal but the Russians persisted. Time and again the conference was adjourned. Finally Friedrich Notz, a young Stuttgart Socialist, asked in despair what he should say to his comrades at the front and in the trenches if they failed to achieve unity among Socialists.

But the delegates remained firm and the Bolsheviks walked out for the second time. Grimm's resolution was adopted in their absence. Angelica Balabanoff recalls in her memoirs how representatives of both sides, accompanied by Robert Grimm, went to Lenin's home and there persuaded the Russian delegates to withdraw their proposal so that a unanimous resolution could be presented to the world. But Lenin insisted that the draft resolution should at least form part of the protocol of the session.[1] Münzenberg was not perturbed by these clashes. Some of the Swiss Socialists had warned him of Lenin, presenting him as a terrible sectarian and dogmatist—a man hopelessly caught up in absurd Asiatic ideas. Nevertheless the Bolsheviks were something completely new for Münzenberg. He had never come up against such an implacable, single-minded attitude in politics. Although he disagreed wholeheartedly with them on matters of fact, their determination impressed him. When the Scandinavian delegates deplored the withdrawal of the Russians from the Berne conference Münzenberg reassured them, as Ernst Christiansen, the Danish delegate, recalls with the following words:

[1]Angelica Balabanoff, *Erinnerungen und Erlebnisse*, Berlin 1927, p. 102.

They are good Socialists but they have no great movement behind them.
We must find a formula on which we can agree, we must make allowances
for them.[1]

One of the most important results of the Berne conference was undoubtedly that delegates had dared to proclaim the independence of
their youth organizations and to express unequivocably their opposition
to the Socialist parties of which they were part.

It was decided at Berne to found an International Youth Secretariat
and Münzenberg was unanimously elected Secretary. For the first time
he was given an opportunity to extend his activities beyond the frontiers of Switzerland. Immediately after the conference he approached
Danneberg in modest, almost subservient, terms for advice and help.
Danneberg was cold but being a responsible comrade he finally gave
Münzenberg detailed advice on how to conduct an International
Bureau. On 20 July Münzenberg reported to Vienna on his plan to
publish a new quarterly, to be called *Youth International*. The detailed
descriptions of the proposed format and number of copies of the journal, of how it would be financed and how he was in close contact with
every international organization were typically Münzenberg. The fact
that up to September 1916 Danneberg contributed regularly to *Youth
International* shows the extent to which he put the cause of Socialism
above all personal differences with Münzenberg.

The new International Youth Secretariat became very active quickly
and Münzenberg proved an able pupil who soon overtook his master.
The Socialist youth groups in the belligerent countries who were opposed to their party leaderships received a flood of illegal material—
manifestoes, pamphlets, journals, above all *Youth International*, the
first number of which appeared in September 1915. Every conceivable
means was used to smuggle prohibited material into Germany, France
or Italy. It was hidden in jam jars, cigar boxes and food parcels. A lively
courier service was organized. The Swiss Young Socialists Herzog and
Arnold went to Berlin where they established contact with the Spartacist League. A sixteen year old Rumanian student, Valeriu Marcu, distributed publications of the International Youth Secretariat in France
and his own country. Even a Vatican courier allowed himself to be
misused as postman. Some of these people did not travel exclusively in
Münzenberg's service; other oppositional Socialists, Lenin among
them, also frequently sent illegal mail with them. Arnold remembers
smuggling letters to Berlin from Robert Grimm to Hugo Haase in which
Grimm implored the Berlin Independents to intervene in the negotia-

[1]As told to the author by Ernst Christiansen.

tions of the Zimmerwald group and not to surrender to the Left without a struggle.[1]

It is surprising that travel on such a scale was possible during the war; it was certainly not without danger. Couriers were repeatedly arrested and given prison sentences. In November 1916 the young Socialist Toscani was sentenced to five years imprisonment in Rome for distributing the *Youth International*. In a trial which took place at the same time in Leipzig couriers were given prison sentences of between three and six months for the same offence.

But the work of the Swiss Youth Organization certainly did not suffer because of this international liaison activity. Although the meetings and rallies, the annual international youth congresses and anti-war demonstrations assumed an increasingly radical character politically, these Socialist youth group gatherings closely resembled that of their counterpart, the bourgeois youth movement in non-political activities. They went hiking, climbed mountains and, having little money, slept in deserted mountain huts. They admired the grandeur of the Swiss landscape, they danced and sang. Ferdi Böhny, a Zurich friend in whose house Münzenberg was then a frequent visitor, summarized his memories of the period as follows:

> I would almost say that as we became more radical we danced more folk dances.[2]

With the next meeting, the next demonstration in preparation in the city, the war seemed an overpowering political factor but under the shadow of the Swiss mountains it occasionally receded into an unreal distance.

3. First Contacts with Lenin

Münzenberg met Lenin in the spring of 1915 in Berne. He had met Trotsky, who had come to Zurich in 1914 and who was for a time a member of the Executive of the Workers' Educational Association *Eintracht*, earlier when they had jointly addressed an anti-war meeting in Berne. At the time there was great resentment between Lenin and Trotsky. In the autumn of 1914, Trotsky had published a pamphlet, *The War and the Second International*, in which he advocated peace without out annexations, without victors or vanquished, and the breakup of

---

[1]As told to the author by Emil Arnold.
[2]Ferdi Böhny, *Die sozialistische Jugendbewegung des Ersten Weltrieges als politischer Faktor*. Offprint from *Öffentlicher Dienst* (Zurich), 1964, No. 45–49, p. 3.

Austria-Hungary—views completely contrary to Lenin's and which Lenin dismissed as childish trivialities. Lenin made his first public statement on the war on 11 October in the *Volkshaus* in Lausanne where the Menshevik leader, Plekhanov, was giving a lecture attended by many Russian immigrants. The overwhelming majority of the audience were Mensheviks but there were also a few Bolsheviks. Plekhanov, who started by attacking German imperialism and thereby gained Lenin's support, went on to argue that the war was necessary to contain German imperialism. As an émigré of many years' standing in France, he invited Russian émigrés living in Switzerland to volunteer for service in the French army. Lenin, who was the only other person to speak, gave his view: the war was not an accident, it was the result of contradictions in the capitalist system. He reminded the audience of the peace resolutions of Stuttgart, Copenhagen and Basle, and said the war must be transformed into a war of the proletariat against the ruling classes. Lenin's first public appearance in war time ended in a defeat. Plekhanov, a brilliant speaker, replied and the great majority of the audience was on his side.

Three days later Lenin, lecturing in the same place on "The Proletariat and the War," went over to the attack. For the Bolsheviks it was clear who would win the war. Again he stressed that it was necessary to transform the imperialist war into a citizen's war—this was the central message of his political programme. He demanded a merciless fight against the former leaders of the Second International, and asked for the establishment of a new International ready to devote itself wholeheartedly to the realization of these demands. The Bolsheviks were by no means solidly behind him. Piatakov, Bukharin and others did not agree with his radical views, whilst Zinoviev and Radek, loyal and devoted collaborators, supported him without reservation. This small group of Russian émigrés soon exerted a notable influence on the left wing of Swiss Social Democracy.

Münzenberg quickly struck up a friendship with Polish-born Karl Radek, a brilliant, witty and resourceful journalist who had worked in Bremen before the war. They had the same temperament and the same talent for repartee but Radek had more political and journalistic experience than Münzenberg. He was an excellent adviser to the young editor of *Freie Jugend* and *Youth International,* and he soon gained a firm foothold in the Socialist press of Switzerland. Whole-heartedly in agreement with Lenin's views, Radek became their most capable propagandist.

It is understandable that Lenin, with his undisguised contempt for the leaders of the Second International, his aggressiveness and his radicalism, fascinated the energetic young elements of Swiss Social Democracy. It soon became clear that there was considerable difference be-

tween the Swiss Young Socialists' opposition to the war and Lenin's own
attitude. Münzenberg and his friends were by no means ready to adopt
Lenin's point of view without reservation. When Münzenberg submitted the resolution adopted at Berne to a meeting of Zurich delegates,
Lenin opposed it strongly but without success. The delegates unanimously agreed to the Berne resolution. To Lenin the attitude of the
Swiss Young Socialists must have seemed like simple, emotional pacifism. The west Swiss group expressed themselves strongly against
defending their country and appealed to prospective recruits to disobey
the call to arms. Under the leadership of Jules Humbert-Droz—whom
Lenin in a letter of 18 December 1916 to Inessa Armand was to describe as a "Tolstoyan Philistine"[1]—they used their organ, La Voix des
Jeunes, to oppose Lenin's idea of revolutionizing the army and trans-
forming the imperialist war into a civil war. Meanwhile the Young
Socialists of eastern Switzerland had gradually turned away from pacifism and were making more radical demands. This was due to constantly rising prices and increasing unemployment resulting from pro-
longation of the war. It was this growing crisis rather than the direct
influence of Lenin and the Bolsheviks, as the bourgeois press later liked
to claim, that gradually made the Swiss workers generally more radical.
There is no doubt that the Bolsheviks exploited the situation to the best
of their abilities.

In spite of differences of view on the question of the war, Lenin and
the Bolsheviks soon became a factor to be reckoned with. Their one
hundred year old tradition of political dialectics, coupled with a degree
of single-mindedness hitherto almost unknown, was to have its impact.

Münzenberg and many Young Socialists were attracted by Lenin
primarily because he was willing to let the youth organization form its
own political ideas and make independent decisions. Lenin was convinced that these young people had been given an important political
role to play, whereas the Social Democratic Party had hitherto only
tolerated them as troublesome mischief-makers. Lenin, on the other
hand, went to their discussions and always praised and criticized with
obvious sympathy. Ferdi Böhny later wrote:

> The way in which he debated with us resembled the Socratic discussion.
> And like some of Socrates' questions Lenin's questions were not without
> suggestive formulation and effect. With his constant questions he pushed
> us into a corner. Our own critical faculties only reappeared when we no
> longer felt his presence . . . Our enthusiasm for Lenin resulted from the
> fact that he took us young people seriously even if he did not agree with

[1]M. Pianzola, Lenin in der Schweiz, Berlin 1956, p. 134.

our views. At last we had met a grown-up, clever man who argued seriously with us . . .[1]

Later Münzenberg often described his discussions with "the old
man"—who was then just forty-five years old. He recalled that Lenin
was intensely interested in every party official—what he thought, how
he behaved and how he should be rated. He continually stressed the
importance of the individual, of his personal worth: "Men make history."

He was a firm advocate of an independent Youth International. On
2 December 1916 he wrote in *Socialdemokrat:*

> Without complete independence the young generation can neither be-
> come good Social Democrats nor prepare themselves to lead Socialism
> forward.

When Lenin moved from Berne to Zurich in February 1916, Münzenberg visited him in his small flat in the *Spiegelgasse,* forever permeated
by the smell of the sausage factory in the courtyard. Krupskaya cooked
and after the meal they sat in the kitchen. Lenin catechized Münzenberg with unending patience, trying to turn the emotional young rebel
into a conscious Marxist revolutionary.

Undoubtedly Lenin showed his best side to Münzenberg and the
Young Socialists whom he hoped to gain for his cause. But even those
who succumbed to his charm realized that there was more to this
"Socrates" than he was prepared to show: there was the ruthless, cold
manipulator of men who in 1904 in Geneva had said to the Russian
Socialist Valentinoff "Everything is permitted to a revolutionary provided it serves the cause of the revolutionary movement and the
party."[2] Lenin's political obsession could make him appear destructive.
Ferdi Böhny wrote in reminiscences of this Zurich period:

> Lenin gave me the impression of a man who was in permanent opposition
> to every existing thing and who will not be at rest until everything has
> been turned upside down; and who also constantly manoeuvres a small
> group of people into clashes.[3]

[1]Ferdi Böhny, *op. cit.,* p. 8 *et seq.*
[2]Paul Oberg in *Neue Zürcher Zeitung,* 17 January 1954 on Nikolai Valentinoff, *Vstrechi
s Leninom,* New York 1954.
[3]Ferdi Böhny, *op. cit.,* p. 8.

4. Lenin and the Zimmerwald Left

The one preoccupation of the Socialist parties of the neutral states was that their countries might be involved in the European war. Hence they urged that representatives of the Socialists of the belligerent countries meet with them to discuss the possibilities of ending the war as quickly as possible. Before Italy's entry into the war on 23 May 1915 the Italian Socialists had been the most energetic and indefatigable advocates of such a conference. As confirmed anti-militarists and internationalists they did not, however, wish to meet those representatives of the Second International who had agreed to the *Burgfrieden* and who had taken the side of their belligerent governments.

All attempts to revive the Second International, and to bring its representatives together at an international conference, failed because the French and the British Socialists refused to meet their German colleagues and vice versa. In France one of the most fanatic opponents of a joint conference with the Germans was Marcel Cachin, the future Communist Party leader. Soon after the outbreak of war the Party sent him to Milan with a large sum of money made available by the French Government. There he visited the editor-in-chief of *Avanti*, Benito Mussolini, who was one of the Italian Socialists advocating Italian intervention in the war. Forced to leave *Avanti* soon afterwards, Mussolini found this windfall from Paris very useful in founding his own chauvinist paper.

The Italians persisted in their efforts to arrange a peace conference between the Socialists of the belligerent countries and of the neutral states. On 27 September 1914, the Italian Socialists Turati, Lazzari, Serrati and Balabanoff met Robert Grimm and other Swiss delegates in Lugano. They held preliminary discussions and drew up a plan for a meeting which eventually took place a year later, from 5–8 September 1915, in Zimmerwald near Berne.

The Party Executive of the Swiss Social Democrats did not approve of the plan and the four Swiss delegates, Grimm, Naine, Graber and Platten, went to Zimmerwald as private individuals without a mandate from their party. Grimm obviously did not think it advisable that there should be another Zurich "radical" in addition to Platten. Therefore Münzenberg was not invited to Zimmerwald. He was deeply hurt and voiced his anger in *Youth International*. Thirty-eight Socialists—Russians, Germans, Frenchmen, Italians, Swiss, Dutchmen, Swedes, Rumanians and Bulgarians—gathered in the little resort in the Bernese Oberland. The British had been refused passports. Although the Party Executive strongly disapproved of the meeting, several well-known figures in the Second International appeared. The majority did not represent their party but small opposition groups which objected to the *Burgfrieden* and which regarded the struggle for peace as their most important task. The aims set for the Zimmerwald gathering, which had been formulated at a preliminary discussion on 11 July in Berne, were on the whole restrained and modest: the proletariat would be called upon to take part in a joint peace campaign. For this purpose a new centre would be established. And naturally the *Burgfrieden* would be opposed. The new centre, the "Bureau of the International Socialist Commission" was set up in Berne under the direction of Robert Grimm.

What happened in Zimmerwald was basically a repetition of what had happened at the International Youth Conference in Berne. The restrained demands of the participants met with violent opposition from Lenin and the Bolsheviks who submitted a resolution to the conference with their usual extreme terms and who found their proposal rejected by a substantial majority.

The Socialists assembled at Zimmerwald may not have agreed with the Second International on the war issue but the proceedings of the conference make it clear that their aim was not to achieve a break with the International, such as Lenin and the Bolsheviks were trying to bring about. On the contrary they sought to eliminate disagreements and to find ways of reviving the International. The planned Bureau of the International Socialist Commission was not intended as a threat to the Bureau of the Second International, which had meanwhile been transferred to The Hague, but was regarded as a provisional arrangement which would cease to exist as soon as the Hague Bureau could function again. The moderates won the day in Zimmerwald.

The manifesto agreed to after long and bitter quarrels reflects this moderation. In wordy, vague phrases it appeals to "the proletarians of Europe" to defend "their cause," the "sacred aims of Socialism." No sacrifice must be too great, no burden too heavy to "achieve the goal, peace among nations." The author of the manifesto, which lacked even the rudiments of a practical programme and which deeply aroused the Bolsheviks, was Leon Trotsky, with whom Lenin became reconciled at Zimmerwald. The Zimmerwald conference would no doubt have long been forgotten as were countless other conferences of other Socialist splinter groups, had not Lenin and the Bolsheviks formed a radical group which became known as the "Zimmerwald Left."

Münzenberg and several other members of the Youth Organization joined the Zimmerwald Left at once. The group met once a week for political discussions, at first at the Stüssihof, and later at the Café Adler. Outwardly it was disguised as a "skittles club." When the police appeared discussion stopped and the participants took up their game. After his move to Zurich, Lenin became a constant visitor to the "skittles club." Krupskaya's picture, used also by other Lenin biographers, of Lenin in 1915 in Zurich living in isolation, with practically no contact with the radical Socialist groups of Zurich, does not correspond to the facts. It is quite likely that Lenin did go to Zurich, as he stated in his application for a resident's permit of 18 April 1916, to write a book and to use the resources of the Zurich library. But he probably also hoped that this city, where Fritz Platten controlled the workers and Willi Münzenberg the Young Socialists, would most readily offer him a platform for his political ideas. The "skittles club" soon became the focal point of the radical elements of Swiss Social Democracy, and if Lenin had hoped for a receptive audience in Zurich he certainly found it. His influence on the Swiss Young Socialists became increasingly marked. The Executive of the Swiss Social Democrats, which Lenin had also joined, was not exactly happy about this radical influence. Zinoviev reported later that when Lenin began to organize young workers in Zurich against the war the Party demanded his expulsion for "criminal anti-war propaganda amongst the young."[1]

Münzenberg was not inactive in the months after Zimmerwald. In November 1915 he wrote to Robert Grimm expressing a desire for co-operation between his International Bureau and the International Socialist Commission in Berne. He informed Grimm that he was preparing for a meeting in December or January of the International Youth Bureau with Norwegian, Italian, Danish and German delegates. He asked Grimm for names of French comrades, as he was anxious to include them. In another letter to Grimm on 31 January 1916 he returned to the proposal and suggested a joint session with the International Socialist Commission. But Grimm's reply was cool. Münzenberg was undoubtedly one of the men whose insistence on yet more meetings and conferences finally resulted in a Second International Conference being held from 24–30 April at the Bear Hotel at Kienthal, not far from Zimmerwald. But there is also little doubt that, in addition to Münzenberg's ceaseless urge for action, Lenin and the Bolsheviks, after the defeat at Zimmerwald, wanted a new forum for their political ideas.

The Swiss Young Socialists were invited to Kienthal and Münzenberg went as a delegate. The leading men of the German anti-war group, Karl Kautsky, Hugo Haase and Eduard Bernstein, were also invited but refused to attend. Lenin's most determined opponents were therefore absent. But if he had thought that his ideas would be better received by those representatives of the Socialist opposition that were present he

[1]G. Zinoviev, *Histoire du Parti Communiste Russe*, Paris 1926, p. 172.

was mistaken. The two most important questions dealt with at Kienthal were the position of the proletariat on the peace issue, and the relationship of the Socialist organizations to the International Socialist Bureau at The Hague which was seeking to convene a plenary session of the Second International. On the first question the Bolshevik group in their draft resolution, refrained from insisting on incorporating a demand for an armed uprising of the proletariat, and the establishment of a new, Third International. Even so the Bolshevik resolution was not adopted. Although the wording of the resolutions and the appeal was more precise and radical than at Zimmerwald, resolutions finally agreed upon at Kienthal were the outcome of a compromise to which even the Bolsheviks had to agree to preserve the outward appearance of unanimity. Nor did the Bolsheviks and their supporters have their way on the issue of a final break with the Bureau at The Hague.

There are many legends about the conferences of Zimmerwald and Kienthal. Soviet historians like to claim that Zimmerwald was the birthplace of the Third Communist International. Occasionally it has been said that Lenin conquered the Russian Empire from Zimmerwald. Is this true? When Lenin realized that the majority of participants at Zimmerwald and Kienthal were not prepared to listen to him he concentrated on the Zimmerwald Left, some of whose members did indeed later become co-founders and active officials of the Communist parties of their respective countries. But Lenin did not succeed either at Zimmerwald or at Kienthal in finally breaking up the Second International. The so-called Third Zimmerwald Conference which met from 5th to 12th September 1917 at Stockholm he treated with contempt.

"The Zimmerwald bog can no longer be tolerated. We must not for the sake of the Zimmerwald 'Kautskyites' continue the semi-alliance with the chauvinist International of the Plekhanovs and Scheidemanns. We must break with this International immediately. We must remain in Zimmerwald only for the purpose of information," he wrote in the pamphlet *The Tasks of the Proletariat in Our Revolution* (April Theses).[1] When the Zimmerwald group met in Stockholm the game was over because Russia was on the eve of the October Revolution which is in fact the moment when the Third International was born.

The Zimmerwald Left, under Lenin's direction, tried ever more intensively to introduce revolutionary ideas into the Swiss Social Democratic Party. Lenin's efforts were resisted by Robert Grimm who had a strong following and who fought to prevent the Zimmerwald move-

[1] V. I. Lenin, *The Tasks of the Proletariat in Our Revolution, Collected Works*, London, Vol. 24, p. 82.

ment, of which he was secretary, from coming under Lenin's influence. A break with Grimm became imperative and the decision to make it was taken early in February 1917 in Münzenberg's flat at a meeting which was also the last meeting of the Zimmerwald Left in Zurich. It was the opinion of those present that unless such a break was made publicly it would have no effect. Only Fritz Platten who wanted Grimm to be "put on probation" opposed the open break. Lenin had his way of course and the press of the Zimmerwald Left, the Bremen *Arbeiterpolitik* and the Dutch *Vorboten*, published an article by Paul Levi expounding Lenin's view; simultaneously there appeared a violent anti-Grimm pamphlet written by Karl Radek immediately after the conference.

In the April Theses of 1917 Lenin drew the final dividing line:

> In January 1917 the chairman of the Zimmerwald and Kienthal conferences, Robert Grimm, joined the social chauvinists in his own party . . . against the true internationalists.[1]

Lenin went on to make it clear whom he regarded as the mainstay of his own group:

> At two conferences of Zimmerwaldists from various countries in January and February 1917 this equivocal, double-faced behaviour of the Zimmerwald majority was formally stigmatised by the Left internationalists of several countries: by Münzenberg, secretary of the international youth organization . . ., by Zinoviev, representative of the Central Committee of our Party, by K. Radek of the Polish Social Democratic Party . . . and by Hartstein [the pseudonym of Paul Levi], a German Social Democrat and member of the Spartacist group.

Even though they had not been collaborating long in the Zimmerwald Left, and in spite of all initial differences of opinion particularly on the question of opposition to the war, Lenin obviously felt that in Münzenberg he had found a supporter of his dream of a new International:

> It is we who must found, and right now, a new revolutionary, proletarian International, or rather, we must not fear to acknowledge publicly that this new International is already established and operating.
> This is the International of those internationalists in deed whom I precisely listed above. They and they alone are the representatives of the revolutionary internationalist mass and not its corrupters.[2]

[1] V. I. Lenin, *op. cit.*, p. 81.
[2] *Ibid.*, pp. 81 and 82.

But only a month later the quarrel with Grimm was pushed into the background. On 11 March 1917 revolution broke out in Russia and the Tzar was deposed. The newly formed provisional government issued an amnesty for all victims of political persecution. A "Russian Central Evacuation Committee" was formed in Zurich under the direction of the Menshevik, Professor Reichesberg. But for the Russian émigrés in Switzerland, particularly for the Bolsheviks, the return to St. Petersburg was not easy because France and Britain gave transit visas only to Russian émigrés sympathetic towards the Entente. Although Germany was still at war with Russia the Menshevik Martov proposed that the German government be asked to permit Russian émigrés resident in Switzerland to pass through Germany. As a *quid pro quo* there could be an exchange with Germans interned in Russia. The Milyukov Government was sent a telegram asking them to agree to this exchange but failed to respond.

Lenin was enormously excited by the news of the revolution in Russia. He recognized immediately that he and his party friends in Switzerland must return to Russia as quickly as possible. Normal diplomatic channels proceeded too slowly for him and, although he had only recently made the most vicious attacks on Grimm, he now approached him through the Russian members of the Zimmerwald movement and asked him to get in touch with the German Embassy. Grimm later told an investigation commission of Russian émigrés[1] that he was called on by Zinoviev, Martov and Bobrov who told him that they were proposing to travel to Russia via Germany. Grimm approached a member of the Swiss Government, Hofmann, who refused, however, to act officially as an intermediary since such a step might be regarded as an infringement of Switzerland's neutrality. But Hofmann called privately on the German Ambassador, Freiherr von Romberg. The two men agreed to set up a commission in Holland to organize the exchange of Russian émigrés for Germans interned in Russia. This proposal was rejected by the Russians in exile. Meanwhile Grimm had succeeded, with Hofmann's assistance, in obtaining from the German Government approval in principle for the Russians to travel through Germany. As Petrograd still had not responded to the request that they agree to this exchange, it was now suggested that Russian émigrés return anyway and once in Petrograd insist that the Germans interned in Russia be sent home. The German authorities agreed to this proposal and so did the representatives of the Bolsheviks but not the other émigrés. At this

[1] *Investigation Commission of Russian Émigrés in Switzerland on the Circumstances of the Departure of Lenin and his Comrades from Switzerland and Germany in the Spring of 1917.* Handwritten protocols in Russian and German, International Institute for Social History, Amsterdam.

point Grimm regarded his mission as completed. He did not intend to
renew his efforts until all groups were agreed.

Lenin suspected, certainly without justification, that Grimm was pur-
posely delaying their return. At any rate it was necessary to find another
Swiss go-between. Münzenberg recalls:

> One day I was rung up at lunch time and asked to come to the restaurant
> *Eintracht* at the Neumarkt . . . I was told that I was urgently expected
> in the small meeting room. There I found Lenin, Karl Radek and Fritz
> Platten. This was the only occasion when I saw Lenin excited and angry.
> He paced up and down the small room with short quick strides speaking
> in staccato sentences . . . We discussed what other means there were to
> obtain a favourable result more quickly and to achieve a speedier return
> home.[1]

According to Münzenberg Lenin foresaw even at this meeting the
possible political consequences for him and his group if they travelled
through Germany when Germany was at war with Russia. They would
be branded as bought German agents, as spies, as indeed they were
later on. Nevertheless, Lenin was determined to go even if they had to
pass through hell. In search of an intermediary he turned to Münzenberg who had to refuse as he was a German citizen. His next choice was
Fritz Platten who was particularly qualified because as Nationalrat he
had sufficient authority to negotiate with the Germans.[2] On the evening
of the same day he went with Lenin to Berne where he succeeded in

[1] *Die Dritte Front,* p. 235 et. seq.
[2] Fritz Platten took the same train as Lenin through Germany to Russia. But at the frontier
the provisional government refused him entry. Lenin reacted with angry protests. It was
only on the sixth émigré transport that Platten reached Petrograd after the October
Revolution. He was welcomed by Lenin at Smolny with the words: Every internationalist
will feel at home here. During an attack on Lenin's life on 14 January 1918 Platten was
wounded in the hand. Shortly afterwards he returned to Switzerland where he was
threatened with prosecution as one of the instigators of the general strike of November
1918. He avoided arrest by escaping to Moscow. Shortly afterwards he visited Finland,
Rumania, Latvia and Germany for the Bolsheviks. In July 1920 he was arrested in Zurich
and spent six months in prison. He played an important part in the foundation of the Swiss
Communist Party. In 1923 he finally settled with his family in the Soviet Union. In 1927
he was the head of the German Club in Moscow. In 1929 together with other Swiss
workers he took over for the International Workers' Aid the Vaskino estate near Moscow
to set up a 'model kolkhoz.' In 1931 he worked in the International Agrarian Institute.
In 1938 this passionate Socialist became a victim of the Great Purge. He was arrested and
died on 24 April 1942 in a prison hospital. After the XXth Party Congress of the CPSU
at which Khrushchev revealed the crimes in which he too had at the time had a hand,
A. Ivanov, a scientist member of the Moscow Marx-Lenin Institute of the Central Committee of the CPSU, published a biography of Platten in the journal *Ogonyok* in which
he said: "Platten who was wrongly sentenced loved our country and our people, he
believed in Lenin's ideas and his life was a daily struggle for the victory of these ideas."
Cf. A. Ivanov, *Fritz Platten,* Moscow 1963, p. 77 *et seq.*

coming to terms with the German Embassy. The Germans agreed to the conditions formulated by Lenin and submitted by Fritz Platten according to which "the carriage [would be] given extra-territorial status" and there would be "no passport control or personal control . . . either upon entering or upon leaving Germany."

Before the German Government agreed to let the Russians pass through Germany there had been a lively exchange of telegrams between the German Ambassador in Berne, von Romberg, the Foreign Office in Berlin and the German General Staff. On 23 March 1917 Secretary of State Zimmermann wired to the representative of the Foreign Office at Military Headquarters:

> As it is in our interest that the influence of the radical wing of the revolutionaries gains the upper hand in Russia consider transit permission desirable.

The political expert at Headquarters, Herr von Hülsen, also stated he was in favour of granting transit to the followers of Lenin's party, the Maximalists and Bolsheviks consisting in all of "approximately forty" persons.[1]

Münzenberg later expressed the view that the mysterious friend of the Bolsheviks, the Swiss social democrat Karl Moor, had made use of his contacts with the German General Staff to expedite matters.

On 9 April 1917 everything was ready. Münzenberg gives the following account of the farewell:

> The youth delegates and a handful of faithfuls stood by the train that was to take Lenin to Russia via Germany. I cannot recollect whether it was Lenin or Radek who said to me as they left: "Either we shall be swinging from the gallows within three months or we shall be in power."[2]

What Münzenberg omitted to say was that Lenin's departure was attended not only by his supporters but also by his enemies who had gathered to accuse him and his fellow travellers of being German spies delighted to return home at the Kaiser's expense. The police were finally forced to separate the two groups as the train pulled out of the station.

I was given an interesting eye-witness account of the trip through Germany by Fritz Picard, the well-known Paris antiquarian and bookseller:

[1]Werner Hahlweg, *Lenins Rückkehr nach Russland 1917,* Leiden 1957, pp. 65 and 72.
[2]W. Münzenberg, *Mit Lenin in der Schweiz, Inprecorr.* 27 August 1926, p. 1838

In the spring of 1917 when I was a soldier in Constance I and two others
were ordered to go at the crack of dawn the following morning by train
to Gottmardingen—at the Swiss frontier near Schaffhausen—to accompany a "Russian transport" to Sassnitz. The sergeant had obviously mis-
understood the orders of the Army Corps Command. At any rate we
arrived booted, spurred and armed early in the morning at Gottmardingen station. There we were received by an officer of the General Staff who
was in charge of the transport and who made us a short speech: "Gentle-
men [sic] you seem to have come here under a misconception. Get rid
of your rifles, do you have no decent shoes or caps? You are not here to
guard anybody but to accompany a number of civilians through Germany
. . ." and he finished by saying: "Be polite to the men, be chivalrous to the
women."

We soon discovered who the Russians were without being aware of the
importance of this transport.

The carriage was not sealed but there was obviously a tacit understanding that none of the passengers was allowed to leave the train even for
a moment and thus to put foot on German soil. I tried repeatedly to strike
up a conversation with someone who was obviously an important person
but it was as though I was speaking to a deaf man.

There was only one passenger whom I almost never saw during the two
day journey. He sat in a compartment with the blinds pulled down and
if the door happened to open in order to let in or let out a visitor one saw
nothing but an enormous heap of newspapers. This must have been Lenin's compartment. But even if he had been pointed out to me his name
would have meant nothing to me. The journey was fantastically highly
organized by the Germans. At every station at which the train stopped
during any hour of the day vast coppers with boiling water were kept in
readiness and our only task was to fetch this water and to pour it into
samovars.

5. Münzenberg—A "German Spy"?

A meeting of the International Youth Bureau which Münzenberg
intended to attend was slated for May 1917 at Stockholm. Encouraged
by the success of Lenin and the Russian émigrés, Münzenberg himself
now approached the German Embassy and—as a German citizen who
had not joined up but who, on the contrary, had loudly protested
against the war—applied for permission to travel through Germany to
Stockholm. The Ambassador in Berne, Freiherr von Romberg, telegraphed on 24 April 1917 to the Foreign Office:

Secretary of the International Association of Socialist Youth Organizations
Muenzenberg [sic] requests permission to pass through Germany to
Stockholm for imminent meeting of Association. Reliable informant

recommends approval of project as Münzenberg would work for peace. Request telegraphic reply whether visa should be granted.[1]

Initially there was considerable confusion at the German Consulate-General because Münzenberg, having played such a prominent role in the Swiss Socialist movement, was thought to be a Swiss. The reliable informant was, it later emerged, Sklarz, a colleague of Parvus-Helphand, who was in close contact with the German diplomatic service and the German General Staff. Exactly what reply came from Berlin is not known but Münzenberg was given a transit visa. He was somewhat ill at ease during the journey through Germany, afraid of being arrested at any moment. He was acutely conscious of the fate of Karl Liebknecht who had been arrested in 1916 because of his anti-militarist activity and sentenced to four years in prison. But he reached the Danish frontier without incident and arrived in the Swedish capital many hours later.

The meeting of the International Socialist Youth Bureau[2] in Stockholm coincided with the founding congress of the Left Wing Socialist Party of Sweden which later grew into the Swedish Communist Party. This congress was attended by Robert Grimm, Angelica Balabanoff and Karl Radek as representatives of the Zimmerwald group. Münzenberg made a short speech at the congress strongly attacking the centre element of the Zimmerwald group. It might be added in passing that he was surprised by the form of the Swedish meetings, by the complicated ceremonial and the band which "welcomed each speaker with a fanfare".

While Münzenberg was in Stockholm the second transport of Russian émigrés arrived there on its way to Petrograd. Together with Radek and Grimm, Münzenberg met them at the station. The Russians tried to persuade him to go on with them to Russia but he refused. His work in Switzerland for the International Youth Bureau seemed too important to him. Grimm on the other hand went on to Petrograd where his brief sojourn ended with a tragic misunderstanding. He was accused of having worked in the German interest for a separate peace between Germany and Russia. The reason for this was a telegram from Grimm to Hofmann, at the time Foreign Minister of Switzerland, in which he did speak of the possibility of a separate peace. Grimm was expelled from Russia by the pro-Entente Milyukov Government. He was also attacked by Lenin and the Bolsheviks who only a few months later, when they had come to power, did exactly what Grimm had proposed: they concluded a separate peace with Germany. Grimm's case was later

[1] Werner Hahlweg, op. cit., p. 58.
[2] W. Münzenberg, Die Sitzung des internationalen sozialistischen Jugendbüros, Sozialistische Jugendbibliothek Vol. 14, Zurich 1917.

examined by a special committee of the Zimmerwald group and the Swiss Socialist was completely cleared.

Münzenberg returned to Switzerland via Copenhagen in time to attend the extraordinary Party Congress of the Swiss Social Democrats on 9 and 10 June in Berne, convened to clear up the party's attitude to the Kienthal decisions and the military question. The Party Congress was characterized by an increased radical trend, vainly opposed by a right wing minority. The majority demanded "resistance to all military institutions and the refusal by the party of all military duties for the bourgeois class state."[1] Münzenberg's Youth Organization went even further and proposed that the anti-militarist approach of this demand should be brought more in line with Russian theory. The Berne Party Congress resulted in an overwhelming victory for the radicals and above all for their spokesmen, the Zimmerwald Left.

Meanwhile Münzenberg had become the centre of a vicious press campaign. The bourgeois press, particularly of pro-French western Switzerland, accused him, as they had accused Lenin and the Bolsheviks, of being a German agent. Otherwise, they asked why would the German Government allow a notorious pacifist, a man who had ignored his call-up orders, to pass through Germany in wartime without arresting him immediately after crossing the frontier? But in 1917 Münzenberg was not in the position of having ignored his call-up orders. In October 1916 he was asked to present himself personally at the German Consulate General and, after discussions with some Party friends, he decided to submit to a medical examination. As a result he was put on the deferred list as "employable." Therefore he had not disobeyed any call-up orders when he travelled through Germany. It was not until September 1917 that he ignored an order to report to the army. The bourgeois papers accused Münzenberg of being a German agent. The press of the right wing of the Social Democrats attacked him for clarifying his military status. Their line was that his loudly proclaimed anti-militarism and anti-patriotism was nothing but talk, a pose which it pleased him to assume, but that in reality he was patriotic and pro-militaristic.

Münzenberg took these attacks sufficiently seriously to reply to them in detail. The concern which the German Government had made to him, it had made to others, for example to Grimm, Kautsky and Haase, perhaps because it thought that the political activity of the Socialists might promote the cause of peace. As to the second accusation, Karl Liebknecht had spent eighteen months in prison for anti-militarist propaganda and yet he had not only enlisted when asked to do so but

[1] Protocol of the Extraordinary Party Congress of the SSP of 9–10 June 1917, p. 13 et seq.

had actually served in the army. Moreover he, Münzenberg, had never advocated individuals should disobey their call-up orders.

In the summer of 1917 tension grew among the Swiss workers and there was a succession of demonstrations against profiteering and demanding food rationing that clearly expressed general discontent. The Swiss workers took an increasing interest in developments in Russia after the February Revolution. The young generation particularly worked itself into a state of feverish expectation. This situation reached its climax on October 9 when the press first reported the victorious October Revolution. A number of small groups whose members almost all belonged to the Social Democratic Party called for direct action. The *Forderung* (demand) group included some anarchists and several "active" pacifists, led by Rotter, an Austrian who had refused to obey his call-up orders, and Dättwyler, who had spent some time in an asylum. Dättwyler's followers used a fairly simple, naive method to further the cause of peace: they appealed to the armaments workers, of whom there were about three thousand in Zurich alone at the beginning of 1917, asking them to strike. This simplicity and naivety was very effective with the workers. The Zurich police finally lost patience on 15 November when Dättwyler, at the head of a crowd of about a thousand, entered several munitions factories and closed them. A rally called by Dättwyler and Rotter, with the support of some of the members of the *Forderung* group, was scheduled for the evening of 16 November at the Helvetiaplatz. The police, following orders to arrest Dättwyler and Rotter, appeared and a mêlée followed in which many demonstrators were injured.

An action committee was established at once and a protest meeting was called for the next evening, 17 November. A large crowd responded by assembling once more at the Helvetiaplatz. Münzenberg and Platten had meanwhile lost control and the scene was dominated by the radicals and the anarchists. Münzenberg disapproved of the methods of the Dättwyler supporters and the *Forderung* group and had tried previously to restrain them. But the speakers at the Helvetiaplatz incited the crowd with their accusations against the police and the mob marched to the police barracks and the *Neue Zürcher Zeitung*. In the end there was a street battle which lasted until the early hours of the morning even after the military had been forced to intervene. Two demonstrators were killed, a policeman was shot, a stray bullet killed a woman spectator, and many were injured.

The events in Zurich aroused the entire country. The bourgeois press freely expressed its indignation and the authorities had no hesitation in calling to account those who in the opinion of the police had incited the crowd. Although Münzenberg had disapproved of the whole campaign and had tried to calm the mob it was undeniable that the Young Socialists had played a considerable part in the disturbances. Some of their leaders were arrested the following day; Münzenberg's own arrest, however, did not come until 19 November. He describes the incident as follows:

> I was arrested on Monday and on Wednesday, only two days later, the Swiss Government ordered my expulsion. The Government had not even waited for a report from the Zurich police and the judicial authorities. . . . For years the Swiss had waited for the opportunity to expel the awkward foreigner who had influenced thousands of their young compatriots by his anti-militarist youth propaganda.[1]

In the early days of his detention in the Zurich police barracks Münzenberg felt "numbed"; there were no meetings, no action committees, no correspondence to be dealt with and above all no friends and collaborators—nothing but the dreary silent seclusion of the cell. Later he recalled that what he had missed most was the postman in the morning. But the prison was a relatively pleasant one, without strict regimentation.

Meanwhile his friends at home and abroad agitated for his release. There was a flood of sympathetic telegrams, and the new Soviet Government even officially protested to the Swiss authorities against the proposed expulsion of Münzenberg.

After five months' detention he was released conditionally on bail. He threw himself immediately into his work, edited the estra numbo, *Brot, Friede, Freiheit,* which appeared in April 1918 in place of the banned *Youth International,* with contributions by Lenin and other Bolsheviks, in an edition of ten thousand copies which immediately sold out. Under the pseudonym E. Arnold he wrote the first article in German on the Bolshevik revolution in Russia.[2]

6. The Echo of the Russian Revolution in Switzerland

One of the first Bolshevik emissaries to reach Switzerland via France, a man named Holzmann, gave Münzenberg an eye-witness account of the Russian revolution. It was on this that Münzenberg based his de-

---

[1] *Die Dritte Front,* p. 249.
[2] Only the third edition of this publication (*Der Kampf und Sieg der Bolschewiki*) appeared in 1919 in Stuttgart under Münzenberg's name.

scription of the events of 7 November in *Der Kampf und Sieg der Bolschewiki* (The struggle and victory of the Bolsheviks), of those events that had taken place while he had been in prison. In Russia the revolutionary hopes in which he believed wholeheartedly seemed to have come true. It is this certainty that characterizes his account of the victory of the revolution. It was an account that did not ask reasons and could not ask them because its author had neither the detachment nor knowledge of the circumstances to do so. The decisive events which were eventually to shake the foundations of the Socialist Workers' Movement were not mentioned in his account.

But what had really happened in Russia? After Trotsky had overthrown the Kerensky Government, with the help of the units stationed in Petrograd, Lenin seized leadership of the country. It was the moment for which he had waited long—and often impatiently. Now at last elections for the Constituent Assembly were held. Before taking over the Bolsheviks had always clamoured for this. But the result was not what they expected—it gave the mass party of the Social Revolutionaries an overwhelming majority with 370 seats out of 707. The Bolsheviks had to be content with 175 seats. Lenin had no intention of accepting this, but what about the democratic manifestation of the wishes of the Russian people? There would surely have been no objection if the decision had favoured the Bolsheviks, but as it was the peoples' wishes must be ignored. When the Assembly finally met on 18 January 1918, the Tauride Palace was occupied by Latvian snipers loyal to the Bolsheviks. Although *Pravda* had exhorted the inhabitants of Petrograd to remain at home on that day "as no quarter would be given," a large number of workers and students shouting "Long live the Constituent Assembly" marched to the Tauride Palace where they were stopped by rifle salvoes. The Assembly disappeared amid scenes of indescribable tumult. Finally the Bolsheviks formulated their ultimatum: the Constituent Assembly must place itself under the Congress of Soviets which the Bolsheviks had hastily convened and which they controlled together with the left wing of the Social Revolutionaries. The deputies rejected the suggestion and the Constituent Assembly was dispersed by a commando of marines.

Lenin knew exactly what he had done. In a conversation with Trotsky he observed:

> The breaking up of the Constituent Assembly by the Soviet power is the complete and public liquidation of formal democracy in the name of the revolutionary dictatorship.

Trotsky's comment on this was:

"Thus theoretical generalization went hand in hand with the transfer of the Leftist guard regiment."[1] Meanwhile the Russian army was in a state of complete disarray. Afraid of losing out on the distribution of land, soldiers rushed back in large numbers to their villages. Lenin started at once to prepare armistice negotiations. What the German General Staff had hoped for had happened. Talks were held in Brest-Litovsk on a separate peace with Germany. Lenin faced heavy opposition—and not only from his opponents. At a meeting of the Bolshevik Central Committee on 22 February 1918 there were seven votes in favour of his proposal to conclude a peace treaty, four against and four abstentions. But at the plenary meeting of the All-Russian Central Executive Committee which took place two days later, Bolshevik party discipline prevailed and there were 126 votes in favour of the peace treaty against 85 votes of the left wing Social Revolutionaries and 26 abstentions. The dictated peace which separated Finland, the Ukraine and the Baltic provinces from Russia was signed on 3 March 1918. For Lenin only one thing mattered: the workers' republic must be preserved.

Meanwhile the Bolsheviks energetically pursued their efforts to consolidate their party's dictatorship. After the dissolution of the Constituent Assembly, many leading politicians of other parties were arrested. The next decisive step was the abolition of freedom of speech and the press. In May 1918 opposition newspapers were forbidden to publish. The Bolsheviks slowly won the day because there was no other political force as highly organized in Russia. Although as a party they were, if well organized, a relatively small minority they enjoyed at the start a certain mass support from the peasants for having given them "peace and land," and from the industrial workers who regarded themselves as the privileged class of the new state. But the opposition had not by any means been silenced. On 14 January 1918 the first attempt was made on Lenin's life. The bullet which missed him hit Fritz Platten injuring him in the hand.

The Extraordinary Commission of the Council of People's Commissars, popularly known as Cheka, had been set up on 7 December 1917. Its purpose was to fight counter-revolution, sabotage or any attempts to endanger the precarious rule of the Bolsheviks. Thereby Lenin had created an effective instrument of terror.

On 29 December 1917, in the midst of the chaotic birth of the Soviet state, an appeal had been issued for formation of a "Revolutionary People's Socialist Army," to be joined by all those "in whom beats the

[1] Leon Trotsky, *Lenin*, London 1925, p. 150.

heart of a revolutionary."[1] On 26 April 1918 with the introduction of military service, the Red Workers and Peasant Army was founded. The revolutionary left, which had rallied to the Spartacist League in Germany in 1916 and 1917, followed developments in Russia with the same close attention that Münzenberg devoted to them. Their interest was all the greater because of Lenin's conviction that the revolution in Russia was only a beginning and that revolution in Germany would be the next logical step on the road to world-wide social change. It was this group that Münzenberg, given his temperament and his political conviction, was bound to join after his return to Germany.

The most independent-minded member of the Spartacists was undoubtedly Rosa Luxemburg. She demonstrated an extraordinary clairvoyance as to the road that Lenin's revolution would take in Russia. The news of happenings in Russia after the October Revolution worried her. Without general elections, without freedom of the press and of assembly and without a free exchange of views, she wrote, no institution could live. She was apprehensive of dictatorship by a handful of politicians, which was a "dictatorship in the bourgeois sense, in the sense of the Jacobin rulers"[2] not a dictatorship of the proletariat.

"It is the historic task of the proletariat when it gains power to create Socialist democracy in the place of bourgeois democracy, not to do away with all democracy." The dictatorship of the proletariat lay "in the way of using democracy not in its abolition, in energetic, determined interference in the established rights of bourgeois society without which no Socialist change is possible." But that dictatorship was the work of the class as a whole not of a small minority acting in the name of that class. It must always be the result of the active participation of the masses, be directly influenced by them and be controlled by the community as a whole. She was deeply concerned about all that she had heard about the terror in Russia. It was true that she saw the "fearful pressure of the world war, of the German occupation and of the difficulties resulting therefrom" as the most important reasons preventing the Bolsheviks from building Socialist democracy in her sense. She emphasized that there was danger the moment the Bolsheviks made a virtue of necessity and presented their tactics necessitated by adverse circumstances, as models to the international proletariat. However, in spite of keeping a critical distance, in spite of genuine anxiety, Rosa Luxemburg concluded that the Bolsheviks' achievement was of enormous importance

[1]Decree of 29 December 1917 In: *Illustrierte Geschichte der Russischen Revolution*, Berlin 1928, p. 493.
[2]This and the following quotations are taken from: *Die russische Revolution. Eine kritische Würdigung*. Aus dem Nachlass von Rosa Luxemburg. Edited and introduced by Paul Levi, Berlin 1922.

to the fate of the Socialist workers' movement. It was not so much a matter of "detailed questions of tactics" as of the "ability of the proletariat to take action, the energy of the masses, the general determination of Socialism to achieve power." In that respect the Bolsheviks had shown what the proletarian masses were capable of. They had created a precedent without which a victory of the Socialist revolution was unthinkable. That, according to Rosa Luxemburg, was the historic role of the Bolsheviks.

It was for this reason that Rosa Luxemburg, with misgivings and without abandoning her critical attitude remained a Bolshevik ally until her assassination.

At first Münzenberg was unaware of these internal struggles. His reaction to the October and November events in Russia was relief. At last the decisive, long awaited step had been taken, and taken successfully. Above all this was an incentive to work even harder because Münzenberg now saw a real goal ahead. But he was not allowed to do so in freedom for long.

The bourgeois press of Switzerland became more indignant daily at the thought that Münzenberg was at large. The authorities therefore decided to intern him. Münzenberg assumed that he would be taken to some village in the centre of Switzerland. But instead he was taken to the isolated prison of Witzwil. He was allowed to receive visitors and many friends came to see him. One day, as the emissary of the Bolsheviks, Karl Moor called on him. Münzenberg struck up a friendship with him and described him as "at present probably the most interesting figure in the European workers' movement."[1] Karl Moor at that time was already in his sixties and there were many legends about him. Although his "official" father was a senior Austrian officer it was said that he was really the son of a member of the Bavarian aristocracy and an actress. Moor had come into contact with Socialist circles at an early age, meeting the "traitors" Wilhelm Liebknecht and August Bebel in the Hubertusburg fortress; later he went to Switzerland where he purchased Swiss citizenship and assumed the significant name Karl Moor.[2] In Berne he became Secretary of the Socialist Workers' Association and editor of *Tagwacht.* He was a member of the First International and later of the Second. In 1904 he met Lenin in Geneva and Radek in Berne and from then on was on the friendliest terms with the Russian Socialists. It was Karl Moor who paid the required guarantees when Lenin and his group came to Switzerland in 1914. Münzenberg later

[1] *Die Dritte Front,* p. 255.
[2] The hero in Schiller's *Die Räuber.* (Translator's note.)

hinted that Moor played an important role in the preparations for Lenin's journey through Germany and had paved the way for the Swiss negotiations with the German authorities. Heinrich Brandler thinks that Moor financed Lenin's and his companions' journey to Russia. Karl Moor was a picturesque figure in the workers' movement, a *grand seigneur* and an admirer of the opposite sex, a Bohemian whose radical views frequently brought him into conflict with his more cautious Swiss comrades. After the October Revolution, Moor was made an honorary citizen of Soviet Russia. Lenin liked to use him for delicate missions. He was one of the emissaries entrusted with the distribution of the vast sums that were given to various European revolutionary groups, including the Youth International, by the Bolsheviks immediately after they came to power.

Meanwhile the Public Prosecutor's office had advanced sufficiently in the proceedings against Münzenberg to transfer him for further questioning to the district prison of Meilen on Lake Zurich. Here he was given the so-called "best room", a spacious cell with a view of the lake. The bourgeois press complained, not altogether without justification, about Münzenberg's gay life in this prison run by the widow of the late prison director. The result of Münzenberg's interrogation, the report prepared by the Public Prosecutor, Brunner, was a remarkable document. Brunner analyzed the development of the Swiss Workers' Movement, the influences and changes to which it had been subject through the effect of Lenin's powerful personality and through the economic difficulties which the war had created for the workers, and his analysis was characterized by unusual objectivity and insight. Brunner's description of Münzenberg reveals his sympathy for the accused:

> What singled him out from the mass of those who thought like him was his many-sided, even literary, talent, his constant attempt to fill in the gaps in his education and thereby to help others, his limitless desire for action, his tremendous ability to work and his determination to pursue ruthlessly and cleverly his aims, a surprising trait in the seemingly delicate, youthful and gentle looking man. He was also a talented popular speaker who knew how to judge the mood of his audience, he was polite and possessed of a rare talent for organization and agitation. One must also acknowledge the selflessness of his activity in the interest of the youth movement as he sees it. The mixture of a talented teacher of youth, a convinced fighter for the improvement of the conditions of the young workers and a revolutionary who feels called to greater deeds is typical of Münzenberg.
>
> The first quality is probably his most characteristic trait whereas the second is acquired, developed and encouraged by his surroundings and conditions. That Münzenberg should attach greater importance to the

second quality is a consequence of the deception generally resulting from
an overestimate of one's own qualities.[1]

His enemies later accused Münzenberg of shamelessly seeking the
friendship of the "class enemy" Brunner. Münzenberg maintained that
by dialectics he had won over the Public Prosecutor who was unversed
in questions of Socialism, a comment which lacks credibility, given
Brunner's intelligent analysis. At any rate in his report Brunner came
to the conclusion that although Münzenberg and the other left wing
radicals bore the moral responsibility for the uprising of November
1917 it was inadvisable to prosecute the "unpopular foreigner" as it
could not be proved that he had planned the revolt. He concluded this
report with an urgent, and coming from the pen of a Swiss Public
Prosecutor, surprising appeal to the authorities to understand the signs
of the new age,

> not to close their eyes to the great idea that is determined to take shape:
> to create a new economic order without poverty and without dissipation.
> Fortunately there are other ways of realizing this ideal than the way of
> terror and dictatorship taken by Lenin. But one of these ways we must
> take if we want to move on at all.

The authorities of the canton of Zurich accepted Brunner's suggestion
and dropped the proceedings against Münzenberg on 28 December
1918. The factor which probably substantially influenced their decision
was the realization that British Secret Service agents had been behind
the strikes at the armaments factories which worked exclusively for
Germany. The authorities were relieved to leave these delicate matters
alone.

Events now precipitated themselves. Preparations for a twenty-four
hour strike to protest the troops sent to Zurich for the maintenance of
peace and order were interrupted by the news of the collapse of the
German Reich. Trade unionists and Social Democrats formed an action
committee in Olten and demanded, among other things, Münzenberg's
immediate liberation. The Swiss government was only too happy to
comply with this demand because with the changed political situation
in Germany there was nothing to prevent the extradition of this "unpopular foreigner". Münzenberg, now that Socialist revolution had apparently broken out in neighbouring Germany as in Russia, was more
than ever a dangerous element in Switzerland. Accompanied by two

---

[1]Report of the First Public Prosecutor, A. Brunner, to the authorities of the canton of
Zurich on the investigation into the unrest in Zurich in November 1917, Zurich 1919
(offprint from *Neue Zürcher Zeitung*).

policemen he was taken by car to Pfäffikon and handed over to two officers. From there the journey continued to the German frontier. Fritz Platten accompanied him as far as Schaffhausen. On the dark night of 10 November 1918 he was pushed across the frontier at Stein on the Rhine.

> I started off in the dark, saw in front of me as my goal the lights of Singen and suddenly fell up to the neck into a ditch filled with water. With difficulties I managed to extricate myself. Suddenly a German soldier with his gun at the ready shouted: "Who goes there?" When I did not know the password he shouted: "Halt, you are under arrest." I was back in Germany.[1]

[1] *Die Dritte Front*, p. 263.

III

The Communist Youth International

1. The Spartacist League

Münzenberg's first appearance on the stage of the German revolution had a certain irony. Whatever illusions he may have had, the "revolutionary" reality which he encountered at the frontier wore a soldier's uniform. The Swabian militia and its officers behaved as if nothing had changed in Germany. At the most they showed a certain helplessness. Although on 9 November the people's representatives in Stuttgart had proclaimed a general amnesty, returning deserters and the like continued to be arrested and locked up. Münzenberg had expected a sea of Red flags and enthusiastic crowds. Instead he found a sergeant who informed him that he could not be released because "everything must take its proper course". It was only on the intervention of a senior officer who had been Military Attaché in Berne and who knew Münzenberg's name from the Swiss press that he was released and allowed to proceed to Stuttgart.

Münzenberg had sent off two telegrams from Singen, one to *Rote Fahne* in Berlin and the other to the *Württembergische Staatsanzeiger* in Stuttgart. Hence several of his Spartacist friends were waiting for him at Stuttgart station, including Max Barthel and Edwin Hoernle.

Here everything looked different. Sharing a car with some sailors from Kiel with their uniform blouses decorated with red ribbons they drove to the Landtag where a session of the Soldiers' Council was in progress. But here a new disappointment was in store. All Münzenberg heard was "a call for calm, order, discipline and the barrack square".[1]

Initially developments in Württemberg took a course parallel to developments in other parts of the Reich. A Workers' and Soldiers' Council was formed on 4 November which on 5 November, even before the proclamation of the Republic, successfully demanded the publication of a new paper, *Die Rote Fahne*. The left wing group around Klara Zetkin, Jacob Walcher, Fritz Rück, August Thalheimer and Albert Schreiner, which during the war had joined the Independent Social Democratic Party (USP), and some of whose members had become Spartacists, had at the suggestion of the SPD sent Spartacists Thalheimer and Schreiner as ministers to the new Württemberg government. But as Münzenberg listened to the discussions of the Workers' and Soldiers' Council he realized rapidly that the majority of delegates was against all revolutionary experiments.

The person who played an important role in Stuttgart was Klara Zetkin into whose circle Münzenberg was accepted. He now began to concern himself with the reconstruction of the Youth Organization of Württemberg. There were also links, broken off during Münzenberg's detention, to be renewed with the youth organizations of other countries.

A few days after his arrival he published his first appeal to the "Young workers of Württemberg". He told them that the shackles of the anti-association law had been broken and that it was therefore up to the young generation to establish organizations everywhere, as they were the rock on which the future Germany must be built. A room was put at his disposal in the Landtag building for his new International Youth Bureau. On 30 November the first number of *Youth International* appeared on German soil. It earned Münzenberg strong criticism from the left. Johann Knief, the leader of the Bremen group of "International Communists of Germany", claimed that the journal still exuded the old spirit of education and reform. Knief said the appeal to the Socialist youth of all countries reminded him of the Second International and Klara Zetkin. He felt Münzenberg obviously did not appreciate the situation, was not sufficiently on the side of the Spartacists:

> It is not the spirit of the Communists. Dare we say: it is not *yet* their spirit?
> We are highly appreciative of Comrade Münzenberg's young, fresh force.

[1] *Die Dritte Front,* p. 269.

But we know that he must escape from the Degerloch[1] before he can reach us.[2]

Perhaps Münzenberg had struck too conventional a note in the *Youth International*. But at his meetings he voiced the demands of the Spartacist group clearly and distinctly. He convened a regional conference of youth representatives which agreed unreservedly to the Spartacist programme. On 1 December he and Fritz Rück held a meeting on "What does the Spartacist League want?" On 2 December he addressed five hundred delegates at the General Assembly of the USP. The other speaker was the moderate, Crispien, but Münzenberg's resolution which reflected the demands of the Berlin Spartacist group was adopted by an overwhelming majority.

Yet he did not lose sight of his own objectives. By telegram he invited youth delegates from various countries to a conference in Berlin on 7 December. He went to Berlin with a mandate from the Stuttgart Workers' and Soldiers' Council to attend the first Reich Conference of Workers' and Soldiers' Councils convened for 16 December.

The journey was trying. He went by open car to Munich and from there in crowded trains to Berlin. Münzenberg was convinced that it was there, in the capital, that the fate of the German revolution would be decided. Before leaving Stuttgart he had said to Max Barthel that "if revolutions were the locomotives of world history in Swabia they still travelled by puff-puff." Berlin was the place to go to if they wanted to build something great. At the same time he sent Barthel to Zurich to collect the archives of the International Youth Bureau which he urgently needed for his work. But in Switzerland, Barthel was promptly arrested and interned as a Spartacist. His detention was not unpleasant, as it was of short duration and he was fed all sorts of delicacies which as a soldier he had not enjoyed for years. But he returned to Stuttgart without the archives.

In comparison with Swabia, events in Berlin had taken a more violent turn. While Scheidemann on 9 November at a window of the Reichstag building proclaimed the Republic, Karl Liebknecht hoisted the red flag on the Berlin Schloss, proclaimed the "Free Socialist Republic of Germany" and demanded "all power to the Workers' and Soldiers' Councils." From the outset therefore there was disagreement between the majority Socialists under the powerful leadership of Otto Wels, the supporters of the USP whose left wing was controlled by revolutionary shop stewards from the Berlin factories, and a small but active Sparta-

[1]The Stuttgart district where Münzenberg lived with Max Barthel.
[2]Johann Knief in *Der Kommunist* (Bremen), 24 December 1918.

cist group. Leo Jogiches, the organizer of the Spartacist group, tried in vain to gain greater influence over the Soldiers' Councils because the returning army units constituted a substantial part of the Berlin population. On Jogiches' orders Peter Maslowski, a student, an ex-soldier and later a collaborator of Müzenberg's, founded a "Red Soldiers League" and edited its publication, *Der Rote Soldat*. But the other side was not idle. Otto Wels, appointed town commandant of Berlin, visited barracks after barracks to win the delegates of the Soldiers' Councils over to the moderate line of the majority Socialists and the people's representatives. Rosa Luxemburg took the "Kaiser Socialists" to task in *Rote Fahne*, and in Dresden, Munich, Stuttgart and Bremen the spokesmen of the USP began to turn against the Workers' and Soldiers' Councils, accusing them of deception and in the last resort of rejecting revolutionary measures. The situation in Berlin grew increasingly tense. The government of the people's representatives felt threatened by the growing discontent and called voluntary military units from areas near Berlin into the capital for protection. A clash between the two factions seemed inevitable.

Such was the atmosphere when Münzenberg arrived in Berlin. He immediately visited the officers of the Spartacist League, met Leo Jogiches and Rosa Luxemburg, and with Karl Liebknecht took part in various rallies. His invitation to the first post-war International Youth Conference had been accepted by only a few delegates. Travel conditions were still chaotic and some of those who wanted to come found no means of getting to Berlin. Swiss Emil Arnold, Italian Francesco Misiano, Russian Tobias Axelrod and his wife, a Bulgarian and Karl Liebknecht met and took the important decision to transfer the International Youth Secretariat to Berlin. The delegates to the conference took part in an international rally in the *Neuköllner Passage* halls on 18 December. Liebknecht's and Münzenberg's speeches were warmly received by the two thousand participants.

Meanwhile the first Reich Congress of Workers' and Soldiers' Councils had met on 16 December. From the beginning there was no doubt that the majority of delegates rejected the demands of the revolutionary left. Of the 489 delegates present, 288 were Social Democrats, 90 United Social Democrats, including ten Spartacists—and ten belonged to the Communist Bremen group. While the biggest demonstration that Berlin had so far seen—about 250,000 people had gathered—took place outside the Landtag building where the congress met, and while a succession of demonstrators' representatives pushed through into the conference room to state their demands, Rosa Luxemburg and Karl Liebknecht were refused entry to the Landtag on the pretext that they had no mandates. Karl Radek, who had illegally entered Germany as a

Russian delegate, refrained from attending when he saw the direction
the congress was taking. It ended with a clear victory for the majority
Socialists. The demand for a soviet republic was rejected by an overwhelming majority while the majority Socialists' proposal to hold elections on 19 January 1919 for a constituent national assembly was approved. "The Reich Congress of Workers' and Soldiers' Councils of
Germany representing the country's political power", the resolution
says, "Assembly transfers until the National Assembly decrees otherwise all legislative and executive power to the Council of People's
Representatives."[1] The Workers' and Soldiers' Councils had surrendered their power and declared their loyalty to parliamentary democracy.

When Münzenberg returned to the capital of Württemberg he carried with him the bitter realization that what had happened in the four
days at the Prussian Landtag was what his experiences with the Stuttgart Soldiers' Council had led him to expect. But he also realized that
the struggle for the new republic was by no means over. Among the
workers, particularly in the USP, there were strong revolutionary forces
ready to fight for the system of soviets, for a dictatorship of the proletariat—involving among other things the complete disbandment of the old
army, for a separation of church and state, for the election of judges by
the people, and for progressive social legislation. Many of these demands had been made by the spokesmen for the 250,000 demonstrators
in the assembly hall of the Reich Congress.

Originally it had been Münzenberg's plan to return to Berlin at the
end of December for a conference of the Spartacist group. But during
the journey from Berlin to Stuttgart he suffered a serious attack of
pneumonia, and was confined to bed for weeks.

The initiative for the Spartacist conference had come from Knief's
Bremen group which on 24 December had invited its followers in the
Reich to a Berlin meeting to discuss whether, with the left-wing radicals
from Hamburg and the Communists from Dresden, they should form
an independent party. There were marked political differences between the Bremen group and the Spartacists but Karl Radek, as the
envoy of the Bolsheviks, succeeded in reconciling the two groups and
in persuading them to found a joint party, the Communist Party of
Germany (Spartacist League).

Rosa Luxemburg and Leo Jogiches had tried to the last to delay the
foundation of this party which they regarded as premature. They were
convinced that it was better for the Spartacist group to remain part of

[1]General Congress of Workers' and Soldiers' Councils of Germany held 16–21 December
1918 in the *Abgeordnetenhaus* in Berlin. Stenographic Report, Berlin 1919, p. 88.

a mass party such as the USP. And indeed there were profound differences, for example on the issue of parliamentarism and of participation in the elections, that remained unsolved at the conference. By sixty-two votes against twenty-three (including those of Liebknecht, Rosa Luxemburg, Levi and Jogiches) those present opposed participation in the elections.

Shortly before the foundation of the KPD, on 29 December 1918, the deputies that were members of the USP left the government. Ebert and Scheidemann dismissed the police president, Eichhorn, a member of the USP, thus causing new clashes between divisions of the people's navy, headed by revolutionary shop stewards, and volunteer government forces. The campaign against the revolutionary workers grew and the fighting continued. The USP and the Spartacist League therefore called for a general strike. On 9 January *Rote Fahne* brought out a special edition with the headline: "Forward to the general strike. To arms, workers, comrades, soldiers". There was heavy fighting as early as 6 January and, under the direction of Georg Ledebour, the spokesman of the revolutionary leaders, Karl Liebknecht and Paul Scholze, a revolutionary committee was formed, demanding the overthrow of the Ebert-Scheidemann government. The Communist Party leaders, particularly Rosa Luxemburg, disassociated themselves from Liebknecht's high-handed decision to join this committee, and Karl Radek, in a letter of 9 January to the communist central committee, condemned the use of force and implored the KPD "to go slow with this unpromising struggle". But neither the USP nor the Spartacist League had sufficient influence to stop the revolutionary groups. There were repeated incidents, the newspaper district was invaded and the *Vorwärts* building singled out for occupation, and they evacuated three days later after a bitter struggle.

The news of the fighting in Berlin resulted in strikes and unrest in the provinces. In Bremen the Communists deposed the Senate and formed a council of People's representatives. On 9 January 1919 there was a demonstration in Stuttgart, organized by the USP, the Communists, the Red Soldiers League, the Social Democratic Association of War Victims and ex-soldiers and the Socialist youth, attended by about twenty thousand people.

It was on this 9 January that Münzenberg went out into the streets again for the first time after his illness. With Klara Zetkin, Schreiner, Hoernle and Rödel, he spoke in the Schlosshof to the demonstrators who then marched to the ministries of Labour and Foreign Affairs. From there they went on to the market square where the chief Burgomaster, Lautenschlager, tried to speak but was shouted down. The demonstrators were primarily concerned with economic demands and it was only during the course of the day that political demands were added. In Stuttgart and its surroundings there were concentrations of industrial workers whose means of livelihood were threatened because of the end of the war. Unemployment had risen considerably and the city authorities had failed to distribute food, raising discontent to an explosive point. In the name of the demonstrators, Münzenberg called for the dismissal of the civic administrators and invited the Workers' and Soldiers' Councils to take over.

In the afternoon the demonstrators reassembled and the negotiations continued at a meeting of the Workers' and Soldiers' Council. Meanwhile the provisional government took refuge at the central station and mobilized the loyal militia against the demonstrators. The meeting became increasingly turbulent after the demonstrators occupied all entrances to the meeting hall and insisted on immediate fulfillment of their demands. Then news arrived that a group of workers had occupied the building of the *Stuttgart Tagblatt*. It was decided at once to publish a "revolutionary organ" there, Hoernle and Münzenberg were elected editors and began work immediately. In search of a more impressive title than *Die Rote Fahne* (The Red Flag) they finally decided on *Die Rote Flut* (The Red Flood).

Münzenberg began preparing an appeal which went to the compositors page by page. Ten minutes later a member of the forty men workers' guard gave the warning signal. The first attack by the government troops seemed imminent, but the workers' representatives succeeded in persuading the soldiers to withdraw. Work on *Rote Flut* continued to the accompaniment of cheers for the Spartacists from the demonstrators outside. Suddenly a new group of officers and soldiers arrived, determined to liberate the *Tagblatt* from the 'Reds.' Now Münzenberg, Barthel and Hoernle argued with them until they too withdrew. Once more editor, compositors and printers continued their labours. But shortly before they had finished, a strong contingent of government troops surrounded the building. Meanwhile midnight had come and the revolutionaries decided to stay where they were, as *Rote Flut* was ready to go to press.

At that moment the convalescent Münzenberg, exhausted by the exertions of the day, collapsed with a high temperature. Two of his friends wanted to take him home, but they were stopped at the doorway by several officers. It was a dangerous moment but a sympathetic warrant officer intervened and pretended to arrest them. Münzenberg and one of his companions were allowed to get away at the next street corner. The adventure seemed over. One hour later government troops entered the building but allowed the workers to leave. Although *Rote Flut* was ready, only a few copies could be smuggled out. The next day the government was again in firm control of the city and on 11 January sent a telegram to the Council of People's Deputies in Berlin:

> We rejoice in the success of the Reich Government. With well trained
> security troops we in Stuttgart have nipped the Spartacist attack in the
> bud and have arrested the Spartacist leaders, Rück, Münzenberg, Max
> Barthel, Hoernle and Janus. We refused to negotiate.
> Provisional Government of Württemberg: Blos.[1]

Münzenberg and his friends did not expect the provisional government to take action against them; therefore they remained at home and
even held meetings. But they were mistaken. Two days later, at 5 A.M.,
four officers, revolvers in hand, came to arrest Münzenberg in the name
of the Blos Government. Together with Max Barthel and Albert
Schreiner he was at first taken to the government headquarters at the
Hauptbahnhof. From there they were taken to the Ulm military prison,
where Münzenberg immediately wrote a report on the circumstances
of the arrest and a manifesto entitled "The Revolution Continues".
Both documents were smuggled out of the prison by Karl Albrecht, the
officer who had been responsible for bringing the prisoners to Ulm and
who was secretly in sympathy with the Spartacists. In Stuttgart both
pieces were published by the USP paper *Der Sozialdemokrat*.[2]

Münzenberg was still weak from his recent illness and the excitement
of the events in Berlin; he was stunned when some days later the
terrible news of the assassination of Liebknecht and Luxemburg, and of
the cruel suppression of the uprising of the Berlin workers, reached Ulm.

Among other things the prisoners were charged with high treason
and revolt. But since they enjoyed the support of the Württemberg
workers and of the soldiers of the Ulm garrison it was feared that
attempts might be made to free them and they were therefore taken
to the prison of Rottenburg on the Neckar. The continued country wide
unrest, a ten day general strike and numerous demonstrations of sympathy for the prisoners persuaded the governor of Rottenburg Prison
to treat them as "political detainees" and grant them a special status
with considerable freedom.

While Socialist youth groups all over Germany exerted themselves on
behalf of their International Secretary, the Rottenburg detainees made

[1] Wilhelm Blos, *Von der Monarchie zum Volksstaat*, Vol.1, Stuttgart 1922, p. 96.
[2] Later, on the recommendation of Klara Zetkin and Münzenberg, Albrecht went to
Soviet Russia where he studied forestry. For a number of years he worked in north Russia
and Siberia and finally rose to the rank of Deputy People's Commissar for Forestry. In
1930 he wrote a book on Russian forestry that was published in Russia and to which Lazar
Katanovich wrote a preface. In the early thirties he fell from favour, was arrested and
subsequently expelled from the Soviet Union. He described his Russian experiences in
detail in *Der verratene Sozialismus* (Berlin 1938) which, with suitably pro-Nazi explana-
tions provided by Dr. Goebbels' staff, enjoyed a vast circulation in Germany.

themselves at home and began to write. Münzenberg's first long piece
was a pamphlet misleadingly but flamboyantly entitled "Down with
Spartacus." Its cover was decorated with a big black-white-red flag and
it was illegally distributed throughout the Reich. It was a masterpiece
of clever propaganda. In the chapter from which the pamphlet took its
name, Münzenberg listed all the bourgeois camp's accusations against
the Spartacists, presenting them of course as vicious slander. The rest
of the pamphlet was an account of the real aims of the Spartacist
League, as well as a short outline of his own activities. Münzenberg
claimed that it was the Social Democratic Party and not the KPD that
was destroying the unity of the Left. By the time the reader reached
the end of the pamphlet the Spartacists and Communists appeared as
pure innocents. It was true that they advocated soviets, the author
admitted, but only because the bourgeois parliaments were unable to
meet the demands of the new age. He firmly refuted any intention of
an uprising. Wisely, he refrained from quoting from the Spartacist programme, from mentioning the call to arm the proletariat, to set up a
workers' militia and to establish a revolutionary tribunal. There was
practically no mention of Russia or of the Russian revolution. Münzenberg's style in this piece was remarkably direct. He successfully avoided
all tedious party jargon, and the pamphlet had a widespread effect,
probably also on the outcome of the pending trial. At last, after the
prisoners had spent five months in detention, the case came before the
Stuttgart Assizes. The twelve jurymen listened sympathetically to the
statements of the accused. Meanwhile much had happened in the German Reich; the Munich Soviet Republic had collapsed, the Workers'
and Soldiers' Councils had been dissolved and army units were proceeding against striking workers everywhere. The Weimar National
Assembly had long since met. "The bourgeois Republic began to settle
down."[1] Therefore the jury was probably able to consider the case with
greater detachment. The prisoners moreover defended themselves
very cleverly. The witnesses for the prosecution could not refute the
fact—although one of them described Münzenberg as a notorious agitator—that there had been a peaceful demonstration and that armed
units had moved in on the demonstrators. Münzenberg declared that
the provisional Blos Government had itself overthrown the old constitutional government by revolt and high treason whereas they, the accused, had wanted nothing but to remind this provisional government
of the promises it had failed to keep and of the demands of the workers.
Not one of the demonstrators of 9 January had thought of overthrowing
the government.

The jury unanimously found the accused not guilty and awarded

---

[1] *Die Dritte Front*, p. 285.

them costs against the state. The foreman even said he regretted that it was not within his power to grant them compensation. The verdict was a triumph and the prisoners were welcomed by hundreds of workers at the prison gate.

2. *The Bolsheviks and the German Revolution*

Lenin received the news of the collapse of the German Empire during the sixth all-Russian Congress of Soviets. He commented triumphantly:

> We were right at the time to conclude the peace of Brest-Litovsk which we have now solemnly dissolved; the conditions imposed on the peoples of Germany and Austria by triumphant Anglo-American and Anglo-French imperialism are far worse than the German terms of Brest-Litovsk but they will be discredited in a similar way. In France, Italy, Britain and America revolution is on the march; the bacillus of bolshevism penetrates all walls. Never has world revolution, the victory of bolshevism been closer than now but never has our situation been as dangerous as at present.[1]

Two of Münzenberg's friends, the young Danish Socialist Christiansen and the Swede Carlsson, had been in Moscow in November 1918. When they visited Lenin in the Kremlin his first anxious question was about Münzenberg. How was he? Was he still imprisoned in Switzerland or was he in Germany and able to take part in the revolution? A little while later as the two Scandinavians were crossing Red Square a car carrying Karl Radek drew up. He told them excitedly that he had just sent a radio message to the German Government demanding to speak to Karl Liebknecht, and had been promised that Liebknecht would be called. This convinced him that revolution had really broken out in Germany.

But Radek's enthusiasm was very soon dampened. It was not Liebknecht who replied from Berlin but Hugo Haase, polite but cool. News of the revolution in Germany had led the Soviet Government to set aside 50,000 *pud* of grain from the Moscow food reserves for the starving German population. Haase expressed his gratitude but thought that as the Russian people were starving it would probably be better if the grain stayed in Russia. Moreover, President Wilson had assured the Germans that bread and fat would be imported in sufficient quantities to avoid a famine.

[1] Alfons Paquet, *Im kommunistischen Russland*, Jena 1919, p. 165 et seq.

Nor did the second item in this radio conversation bring any encouragement. On 5 November the Imperial Government, as one of its last official acts, had expelled the Russian Ambassador, Joffe. Radek asked Haase to rescind this order and to allow Joffe, still waiting at the Russian frontier town of Borisov, to return to Berlin. Haase replied that however desirable the restoration of diplomatic relations might be it would be better to mark time, to let Joffe return to Moscow and to recall the remaining German consular staff in Moscow to Berlin. Some agreement would no doubt be reached later.

Radek had not been prepared for this refusal. It occurred to him that, contrary to all rumours, what had taken place in Germany was a bourgeois revolution not a Socialist one. During the night following this radio conversation Radek wrote a pamphlet for distribution among German soldiers in Russia. It was entitled *Trau, schau, wem* (Look whom you trust). For some time the Soviet Government had been trying to influence German prisoners of war although without much success.

Initially the rumours that circulated in Moscow at the time were of a very different nature. It was said that the German Crown Prince had been shot, that hundreds of naval officers had been murdered in Kiel and Reval, that German soldiers had thrown their officers into the Dvina, and that the German army was fraternizing with the French, the British and the Americans at the western front. Germany was thought to be governed by a dictatorship of the proletariat and this Germany was referred to by *Izvestia* exclusively as the "German Socialist Federal Soviet Republic."[1]

The interest of the Russians in the German revolution was not, however, limited to enthusiastic observation of events from afar. They sought to make their influence felt at the very centre of things. A few weeks before his suicide in November 1927, Joffe told Louis Fischer that the Soviet Embassy in Berlin had been the headquarters of the German revolution. He said he had bought secret information from German officials and passed it on to the radical party leaders who had used it in their speeches and articles against the Imperial Government. He had spent one hundred thousand marks for arms for the revolutionaries. Tons of anti-monarchist and pacifist literature had been printed and distributed at the expense of his Embassy.[2]

After the break in diplomatic relations, leadership in revolutionary matters was at first assumed by Karl Radek who after a few weeks illegal sojourn in Berlin was arrested on 12 February 1919 and taken to the Lehrter Strasse prison. Radek transmitted to the leaders of the young

[1] Alfons Paquet, *op. cit.*, p. 166.
[2] Louis Fischer, *The Life of Lenin*, London 1965, p. 314.

KPD Lenin's wish to establish the Third International as quickly as possible. Rumours had reached Moscow of attempts to revive the Second International. A conference had been convened for this purpose at Berne by the British Labour Party. The Bolsheviks feared that the parties of the left wing might turn again to the Second International and sent an open letter to all left wing parties and groups inviting them to Moscow for the foundation of the Third International. Radek, who passed on this request, found that Rosa Luxemburg primarily but also Leo Jogiches, received the suggestion coldly. They sent Hugo Eberlein to Moscow with express instructions to vote against the foundation of a new International. But when it came to the vote Eberlein gave way to pressure from the Russians and other delegates and merely abstained.

The foundation, and simultaneously the first world congress, of the new International took place in March 1919 in Moscow. The Bolsheviks had invited thirty-nine organizations to attend. Last on the list was Willi Münzenberg as representative of the Socialist Youth International but he could not be present in Moscow on this historic day because he was in prison. Representatives of thirty-five of the groups invited appeared, in spite of considerable transport problems, but only the delegates of the Bolshevik Party and the KPD were accredited delegates of their parties, all the others represented small opposition groups. This fact did not prevent Lenin from making an enthusiastic speech welcoming the new International as the legitimate heir of the First and Second International and inviting all revolutionary parties to join. The Comintern was born; Grigori Zinoviev became its first President.

Radek was not inactive in his prison cell. He found plenty of opportunities to influence the fate of the KPD. Of all the Bolsheviks he was the one most familiar with German conditions and the one who had the closest links with bourgeois representatives of industry and the army. After the investigations pending his trial had come to an end he was taken into military detention. He was allowed to receive visitors in his cell and there he held what he later described as "a political salon." One of his first visitors was Karl Moor who had also visited Willi Münzenberg during his detention in Witzwil prison. Immediately after the October Revolution in 1917 Moor had gone to Russia and now looked after Lenin's interests in Berlin.[1] Moor not only helped to ease life for Radek

---

[1] Cf. Otto-Ernst Schüddekopf, *Deutschland zwischen Ost und West. Karl Moor und die deutsch-russischen Beziehungen in der ersten Hälfte des Jahres 1919*, Archive for Social History, Vol III, Year Book of the Friedrich-Ebert-Stiftung, Hanover 1963.

by using his many connections with the German Army and the Social Democratic Party he also established the contacts with the outside world that Radek needed. One of the most helpful was a telegram he sent in Radek's name to the writer and journalist, Alfons Paquet, who later became a good friend of Münzenberg's and a promoter of the International Workers' Aid. Paquet, whom Radek had met in Moscow in 1918, was ready to take up Radek's cause in the *Frankfurter Zeitung* to whose editorial board he belonged. Radek thanked him for his efforts in a long letter of 11 March 1919 in which he referred once more in detail to the situation in Germany. The letter reveals the same reserve and the same realism as the letters to the Communist Party Central Committee referred to earlier.[1]

Because of his connections Karl Moor, the link between Radek and Paquet, continued in later years to play the role of a *deus et machina*. In 1925 he visited Münzenberg in the *Unter den Linden* offices of the International Workers' Aid. This is where I saw him for the first time and thought him an impressive and attractive man in spite of his seventy-three years and in spite of the fact that he had come to Berlin for medical attention. He was accompanied by a resolute female whom he introduced as "his nurse." Later as we walked down the *Linden* with him and his companion he told Münzenberg that he had had enough of Moscow and intended to spend the rest of his life in Berlin. Digging Münzenberg in the ribs he pointed to his companion and observed that she had been sent with him because people in Moscow were afraid that he might say too much. Moor, apparently deeply disillusioned by developments in Soviet Russia, retired to a Berlin sanitorium, but the Comintern insisted on honouring him publicly. On his seventy-fourth birthday, 11 December 1926, the Executive Committee of the Communist International sent a telegram of congratulation signed among others by Stalin, to the "faithful, devoted friend of the Russian revolution." After his death in the sanitorium in 1932, the AIZ, the illustrated weekly of the Münzenberg concern, published an obituary of the "fighter Karl Moor."

3. Münzenberg and Parliamentary Democracy

Freedom's first gift to Münzenberg was the only party office which he was ever to hold: he was elected Chairman of the Württemberg Communist Party. His first act was to go to Berlin to establish contact

[1]Copy in the possession of the author.

between the Russian representatives and the illegal party headquarters. The differences of opinion on the attitude of the Communists towards democratic parliamentarianism had not been resolved. In a discussion between the representatives of the Hamburg Communist Party, Laufenberg and Wolffheim, opponents of parliamentarianism, and the party chairman, Paul Levi, who agreed with the Russians that the Communists must be represented in the bourgeois parliaments, Münzenberg sided with the Hamburg Communists.

The controversy on parliamentarianism went on unabated at the Reich Conference of the KPD which met illegally on 16 and 17 August in Frankfurt on Main. Münzenberg had obviously committed himself in advance so strongly on this issue that the party leadership in Frankfurt discussed a "Münzenberg case." Münzenberg defended himself by saying that the party's fields of activity were the revolutionary workers' councils not the parliaments which no longer represented an intellectual force.

> If we join these bankrupt institutions the workers will look upon them with new hope . . . Criticism of parliamentarianism is much more successful from without than from within. The masses which follow us today follow us because they are disappointed with the other parties, particularly with the USP which also claims that it is represented in the parliaments only as 'dynamite'.[1]

It was requested that a three man committee investigate the Münzenberg case." Among other things Münzenberg was said on his own authority to have sent a courier straight to Hungary, and to have been highly critical of the policy of his district party headquarters, all accusations which Münzenberg strongly refuted.[2]

The *Kommunistische Räte-Korrespondenz*, published illegally on 22 August, gave an account of an alleged struggle in Frankfurt between the delegates chosen by the local organizations and the members of the central party organization. The provincial representatives were said to have called for opposition to the "party bosses" and to have demanded that they should not be allowed to vote. There was also strong criticism at Frankfurt of the over-cautious attitude adopted by Hugo Eberlein at the behest of the former party leadership at the founding of the Comintern.

In spite of his election as District Chairman, Münzenberg still regarded himself primarily as a representative of the young generation.

[1]From the mimeographed report of the Reich Conference in the possession of Richard C. Chrisler, New York.
[2]From Paul Levi's personal notes, in the possession of Richard C. Chrisler.

After his release from prison he realized that other forces had not remained idle meanwhile and that he was in danger of losing control of the Socialist Youth International. In April 1919, Alfred Kurella had gone to Moscow as the representative of the Communist-orientated "Free Socialist Youth" to establish contacts with the newly-founded Russian Youth Association and the Comintern. On 29 May, Zinoviev appealed to the proletarian youth organizations of the world asking them to join the "Red Communist International with the Red Workers' Army" rather than the Second International resuscitated in February in Berne.[1] It was also decided in Moscow to convene a youth conference in Budapest which Kurella should attend, under the name of Bernhard Zeigler, as the representative of the Russian Youth Association. But the Hungarian Soviet Republic had in the meantime collapsed and he only got as far as Vienna. Münzenberg, as Secretary of the International Socialist Youth Bureau, also went to Vienna.

The Vienna meeting was organized by the Austrian youth organization, with a newly-founded Communist group of Austrian youth represented. The Social Democrats suggested that the proposed youth congress should be held in Vienna but the majority of delegates voted for Berlin. There was disagreement on who should be invited. The Socialists suggested that invitations should be issued to "all proletarian youth organizations rooted in the class struggle". The Communists opposed this, and their Austrian representatives even asked that the Socialist Youth Association of Austria not be invited. At this point Münzenberg intervened and insisted that the Austrian Youth Association which had always fulfilled its international obligations during the war be invited. The difference really arose from two basically different views of the tactics to be used. Whereas the Communists, headed by the Austrian group, refused to sit down at the same table with youth organizations which did not share their political credo, Münzenberg thought that invitations should particularly go to those who did not share his views so that he would have the opportunity to convert them—an attitude that was to typify his subsequent propaganda activity.

Meanwhile the police heard of the illegal meeting and arrested the foreigners in their hotels for having crossed the Austrian frontier without valid papers. Among them was an unusually high spirited young comrade, Elfriede Friedländer, née Eisler, who under the name of Ruth Fischer was to play an important role in the German Communist Party. She had made a strong impression on Münzenberg who had arrived

[1]Zinoviev's manifesto of 29 May 1919 was broadcast and published by the entire foreign Communist press.

ahead of his Stuttgart friends. He welcomed her at the station with a large bunch of red roses. "Fritzi" made a less favourable impression on Klara Zetkin who developed an immediate and strong dislike for this self-assured young woman. It was probably her influence that made her friend Paul Levi mildly reprimand Münzenberg at the Heidelberg Party Congress for insisting that Ruth Fischer be given political duties in the KPD.

The Second Party Congress, held from 20–24 October 1919, put the young party to its first serious test. This Party Congress also met illegally, first at the Wachenburg on the Bergstrasse, then in Heidelberg and Mannheim and finally in Dilsberg on the Neckar. Münzenberg attended as delegate of the Württemberg party district and spokesman of a "centre group," as he later called it. This group disagreed strongly with some of the views advanced by the party headquarters but also disagreed with the Hamburg group, which wanted a less centralized party and wished to concentrate the revolutionary struggle more on factory organization and the economy.

The Hamburg group had a substantial following in the Reich. They accused party headquarters of aspiring to a party dictatorship on the Bolshevik model and demanded an explanation of how party funds were used. Levi and the party headquarters were prepared for this attack and submitted a set of guiding principles which was about as uncompromising as possible and unacceptable to the opposition. After voting against these principles during a heated debate the opposition was expelled and prevented from further participation at the Party Congress. Levi consciously engineered this split because he regarded the opposition's syndicalist, anti-parliamentarian course as a threat. He later estimated that at that time only five to ten per cent of the members remained loyal to the party; the overwhelming majority formed a new organization, the Communist Workers Party (KAP). Karl Radek, still in prison, had tried to prevent the split. He gave Ruth Fischer a letter addressed to Levi urging caution. She did hand it over at the Party Congress but Levi was determined to act and ignored Radek's advice. The split also spread to the youth organization which broke up into the Communist "Free Socialist Youth" and the KAP "Proletarian Workers Youth."

At the Rump Party Congress Münzenberg took the left-wing opposition side. Although he was in favour of a strongly centralized party he demanded a greater share in decision-making for party members. But he was out-voted by the future right wing of the party, centred around Brandler and Thalheimer, to which Klara Zetkin, Walcher and Schreiner also belonged—the same group which in a second ballot also prevented his election to the Central Committee. Like the Hamburg rebels he was accused of "optimistic revolutionary romanticism."

On his way back to Stuttgart Münzenberg learned from the papers that the Public Prosecutor's Office had reopened treason proceedings against him and that a warrant had been issued for his arrest. He was determined to go to Berlin where the warrant was not then in force. For the first time he stepped on Berlin soil determined to remain there. He was thrilled by the hustle and bustle of this city. "The only city where one can work," he called it. Münzenberg valued many of the Berliners' qualities—intelligence, gaiety, and worldly manners. The "flight" to Berlin ended his brief period as a party leader and he was now once more able to devote himself whole-heartedly to youth work.

4. The Youth of the Revolution

Münzenberg's girl friend, Adele, arrived in Berlin from Zurich bringing with her the archives of the Youth Bureau. Two illegal rooms were hired, one of which housed the youth publishers, in a carpenter's shop in Schöneberg. The Bureau in charge of the preparations for the youth congress went to work. Young emissaries visited all countries of Europe, distributing invitations, resolutions and propaganda material. In the early days, the Scandinavian youth organizations provided most of the money, but even then Münzenberg was in contact with the Russian representatives in Berlin, with Karl Moor and later with James Reich, alias Thomas, who provided financial support for his Youth Bureau. At last everything was ready:

> After overcoming countless difficulties and technical problems, after se-
> cret frontier crossings and weeks of illegal existence by several delegates
> the first International Congress of the Communist Youth International
> was opened on 29 November 1919 in the dingy backroom of a public
> house in the outskirts of Berlin, protected by a handful of loyal comrades
> acting as guards against Noske informers and Noske soldiers.[1]

The Russian representatives had insisted that this Congress should be "Communist." On the pretext that insufficient attention had been paid to the international situation during the preliminary discussions in Vienna the Austrian Young Socialists were not invited to Berlin. Shatskin had stated that he could not "sit at the same table with an organization whose ideological basis is that of our main enemies, the Men-

---

[1] Willi Münzenberg, Omnibus Volume *Die Jugend der Revolution*, Berlin 1920. A list of affiliated associations with membership figures is given in *Die Dritte Front*, pp. 293 and 339 et seq.

sheviks."[1] *Rote Fahne* said at the time that the Austrians had not been
invited because of their passive or even counter-revolutionary attitude.
To make this trend apparent beyond doubt the "Association of Socialist
Youth Organizations" was renamed "Communist Youth International,"
over vigorous protests from some delegates who regarded this as a
serious technical error limiting the organization's range of action. The
new programme[2] said that the most important tasks of the Youth International were "the organization and execution of political campaigns,
the direct fight for Communism, participation in the overthrow of capitalist rule and the education of the young generation as the builders of
Communist society." War was declared on all non-affiliated proletarian
youth organizations, the right-wing Socialists and the "socialist centre,"
on the anarchists and the syndicalists.

A violent controversy arose between Münzenberg and Shatskin over
the Youth International's relationship with the Third International.
Münzenberg believed the youth organization must remain largely independent, Shatskin advocated unconditional submission. In the final
programme the disputed point was worded:

> Organizational relations with the Party are governed by two fundamental
> principles: 1. independence of the youth, 2. close contact and mutual
> help.[3]

The differences were thus glossed over, not resolved.

In the next twelve months the newly founded Youth International
succeeded—in spite of the markedly Communistic dictatorial conditions of entry—in winning over European Socialist youth organizations.
At the same time more and more left-wing workers' parties flocked to
the Third International. The revolutionary Socialists hoped that it
would accomplish a radical reorganization of the post-war world. The
Secretary of the Youth International travelled tirelessly from country
to country, "conquered" new associations and influenced "unreliable
elements" among affiliated organizations toying with the thought of
withdrawing and joining the Social Democrats.

Münzenberg still lived illegally in Berlin, without passport or valid
papers. In December 1919 he made a trip with some friends to Denmark in a hired fishing vessel to prevent a split in the Danish youth
organization. He went from Copenhagen to Stockholm to visit his
Swedish friends and the Bolshevik representatives. Having made no

[1] Karl Heinz, *Die Entwicklung der Kommunistichen Jugendinternationale*, Vienna 1922,
p. 7.
[2] *Die Dritte Front*, p. 375.
[3] *Ibid.*, p. 378.

effort to hide his movements, he was arrested. He denied being Münzenberg but the Swedish police did not believe him and he was put in
jail for three weeks. Later Münzenberg had little good to say about the
Stockholm prison. Although the building itself was modern the prisoners had to hand over their clothing at night, even their shirts. Münzenberg found this particularly mortifying. He was expelled from Sweden
and taken to Germany on the ferry. With the help of a sailor he hid in
a goods wagon, and with *sang froid* and good luck he avoided detection
and arrived back unmolested in Berlin.

But such incidents did nothing to dampen the enthusiasm of the
comrades of the Youth International Bureau. Although they were almost all without valid papers and on the black list of the police of every
country they did not hesitate to cross any frontier. One of their mottos
was: "Our field of activity is the world." This field of activity they were
not prepared to give up. Consequently they were continually being
arrested and imprisoned in some country or other, a prospect which
they regarded as one of the minor risks of being a revolutionary—a
nuisance which delayed their work.

Nor did Münzenberg become any more cautious after his Stockholm
experiences. He continued to illegally cross the German frontier although he usually used inaccessible mountain paths or lonely forest
tracks. Thus he appeared at Carlsbad where after a long heated discussion with the party secretary, who held forth against the "dangerous
union with the Communists," Münzenberg succeeded in bringing the
Social Democratic Youth Association of German Bohemia on to the side
of the Communist Youth International. At the same time his colleagues
were busy in France, Italy and the Balkans persuading the youth associations of these countries to join the Communist Youth International.
Their success was remarkable. Within a year forty-eight associations
with a total of over eight hundred thousand members joined the Youth
International. Only the Austrians defeated Münzenberg. He visited
Vienna on 15 and 16 May 1920 for a conference of the South-East
European Youth Associations and persuaded the organizations of
Czechoslovakia, Yugoslavia and Rumania to join his cause. But the important Austrian association would not capitulate although Münzenberg tried hard for months. The detailed exchange of letters between
his Bureau and the Young Socialists in Vienna had previously been
published in the pamphlet *Nicht wollen oder nicht können* (Unwilling
or Unable). Karl Heinz, then Secretary of the Austrian Young Socialists
later wrote to me:[1]

[1]Karl Heinz became the head of the *Schutzbund* and in 1934 emigrated via Brno and
Stockholm to the United States where he died in 1965.

Münzenberg came to Vienna in 1920 to persuade us to join. At the decisive conferences and meetings in May our view that we could not accept
the principles and statutes of the Communist Youth International decided
upon without us, won the day by a big majority. Because the Russians
insisted that we must accept the Communist resolutions unconditionally
we and several other Socialist associations founded the International
Workers' Community of Socialist Youth Organizations in Vienna in February 1921.

The Austrian Young Socialists objected particularly to the clause in the
statutes obliging them to fight not only the bourgeoisie but also "social
patriots and centre parties"—in this case their own socialist party.

During these months Münzenberg had paid little attention to party
life and political events in Germany. The struggle for the growth and
well-being of the Youth International occupied him completely. Thus
Kapp *putsch* in Berlin on 13 March 1920 caught him unawares.

When the Supreme Commander of the Reichswehr, General von
Seeckt, declared that he would not fire on *Freikorps* comrades, the
Reich Government evaded the ultimatum of General von Lüttwitz and
the *Freikorps* Ehrhardt who had appointed the nationalist East Prussian official Kapp as "head of government," by moving first to Dresden
and then to Stuttgart. The Republic was saved by the Social Democrats
and the trade unions whose leaders, Otto Wels and Karl Legien, had
stayed in Berlin and called upon the workers to come out on general
strike. Their appeal was immediately heeded everywhere in Germany.

Münzenberg shared a flat in a western suburb of Berlin with Leo
Flieg. When the general strike began they walked into the centre of the
city where the members of the illegal Youth Bureau were already
assembled in force. They had all brought the weapons which they had
hidden away after the war. Münzenberg who had never held a gun
before was given a quick instruction course. Everyone was convinced
that it would come to a clash between the workers and the army.

But the general strike quickly proved an effective weapon. After
three days the rebels put down their arms. The Communist Party had
played a dubious role during the Kapp *putsch*. At first the Berlin party
leadership had announced that the Ebert Government had collapsed
and that the workers must not "lift a finger to prevent the ignominious
end of the Republic—Liebknecht's and Luxemburg's murderers." Paul
Levi, with many other delegates to the Third Party Congress which had
met shortly before at Karlsruhe, had been arrested and was still in
prison. From his cell he managed to correct this absurd line and henceforth the Communists supported the strike. There was heavy fighting
only in the Ruhr where spontaneously formed "Red Workers Units,"

led by shop stewards and USP members, occupied many factories. Here the Kapp *putsch* showed that there was still revolutionary energy in the working masses. However, it was not the Communist Party but the USP that had known how to transform this energy into effective action. Hence the Bolsheviks' great interest in the left wing of this party.

For Münzenberg the decisive experience of this eventful year was his first visit to Soviet Russia. But the visit was preceded by some serious party problems. The bone of contention was the long arm of the Comintern in Berlin, the West European Bureau (WEB). At a session of the Youth International in June 1920, for which representatives of many affiliated associations had come to Berlin, there was a long discussion on the relationship of their group with the Comintern and the WEB. The Youth Executive was annoyed that Zinoviev, without informing the Berlin Youth Bureau, had addressed himself directly to the National Youth Associations via the WEB, inviting them to the Second Comintern congress in Moscow. Shatskin had also intrigued in this matter and had suggested that the next Youth Congress should be held in Moscow, a proposal which was categorically rejected by the Berlin Bureau. Nevertheless Shatskin continued to send telegram after telegram to Berlin.

Münzenberg was outspoken on the WEB matter at the June 1920 session of the Youth International:

> The executive committee work was severely impeded by the incredible indifference shown to the youth movement by the administrative office of the Communist International for Western Europe, the West European Secretariat. This office repeatedly refused to send on our letters and communications or to receive material for us and to transmit it to us.[1]

Criticism of the WEB was universal. Kurella and Schüller also joined in it. The Russian representative of the WEB, Comrade "Albrecht", who also spoke at the session made an effort to play down this criticism.[2]

But the WEB had also, weeks before, gone over to the attack, accusing the Youth Bureau of being ultra left wing with semi-anarchist tendencies; it claimed that the theory of a WEB offensive was the invention of the Youth Bureau's Vienna representatives. Münzenberg had answered these accusations with a public declaration in the Youth International's press service for May 1920 and had in turn accused the WEB of recommending to the Comintern the admission of the KAP and of

---

[1] Report of the First Session of the Bureau of the Communist Youth International, *Internationale Jugendbibliothek*, No. 11, Berlin 1920, p. 6.

[2] "Albrecht" was called Abramovich-Tsalevski and was an old Bolshevik who had returned to Russia in 1917 on the same train as Lenin. He had followed the fate of the Munich Soviet Republic on the spot as "Moscow's eye."

publishing an appeal to that effect without discussing the question with the Youth Executive.

Münzenberg was particularly displeased with the man in charge of the WEB, Comrade Thomas, who had arrived from Moscow in the autumn of 1919 with personal instructions from Lenin. James Reich, alias Thomas, was small, rotund and known in Party circles as "Fatty." He wore gold-rimmed spectacles and was always immaculately dressed. In his youth Thomas had been a member of the Socialist Party of Poland and in 1905 as a seventeen year old he had taken part in an attempt on the life of the Russian Governor in Warsaw. It was even alleged that he had thrown the bomb. Later he studied in Switzerland. After the October revolution he published the *Russian News* for the Russian Mission in Berne. Shortly afterwards, when the Russian Ambassador and his staff were expelled from Switzerland, Thomas was also forced to leave and went to Russia. His first task in Germany was to build up a publishing house, independent of the Communist Party, for the dissemination of Bolshevik Party books and journals. Thomas was in direct contact with Trotsky, whom he worshipped.

He lived illegally in Berlin and as a cover for his activities he founded a number of firms, such as the seemingly bourgeois bookshop in the Leibnizstrasse whose back rooms served as a meeting place for couriers and contact men. Thomas, a true master of conspiracy, was not arrested once during his year of activity for the WEB. He never received his visitors in the same place twice and no one knew all his offices and flats. He distributed money and false papers, provided illegal accommodations and served as a forwarding agent for secret mail. Lenin's sealed letters to Paul Levi passed through his hands. In 1924 when Trotsky lost his interest in the Comintern, and the financing of the Communist parties was centralized in Moscow, Thomas was removed from his post. Later, in Austria, he officially changed his name to Rubinstein and settled in Berlin to pursue his private research.

Münzenberg was reluctant to conduct his correspondence with Moscow through Thomas. Nor did he like the arrangement by which the Moscow funds destined for the Berlin Bureau were paid out by Thomas. It gave Thomas a curious satisfaction to keep the youth organization waiting. Leo Flieg, then Treasurer of the Youth Bureau, years later remembered Thomas' chicanery with bitterness. But it was not only the Communist youth that were dissatisfied with Thomas. Unification of the left resulted in the press of the United Communist Party of Germany (VKPD) being increased by thirty left-wing USP papers, many of which were in need of support because of the critical economic situation. Thomas frequently combined the provision of funds with political blackmail—anyone who did not strictly follow the correct line was given very inadequate support, or nothing.

Münzenberg hoped that he would be able to arrange a favourable settlement of these tiresome questions when he arrived in Moscow. At the last moment he almost did not go. Sitting with some foreign friends in a Berlin café he noticed several men at the door who were unmistakably police officers. He emptied his pockets of the papers which he habitually carried, gave them to his friends and tried to leave the café unnoticed—without success. He was arrested and taken to police headquarters. The following morning—it was a Sunday—he was interrogated by a policeman who told him that he had been arrested for desertion on a warrant issued in 1917. Münzenberg protested that this offence had been amnestied as long ago as 1918. The Prussian official regretted that because the warrant had not been withdrawn it was still valid. Moreover, there was also a warrant from the Stuttgart Public Prosecutor's office dating from 1919. The following morning, Münzenberg reported later,

> together with about forty petty thieves and pimps who had been arrested during Sunday I was brought before the prosecuting judge, an elderly gentleman with a jovial air . . . I was the last to be questioned. "Why are you here?" he asked. I referred to the commissioner's police charges and said that I failed to understand how I could have been arrested on the strength of a warrant of 1917 whereupon the examining judge had an apoplectic fit and declared that this was impossible. He opened my file, found on top the warrant of 1917, copied out by the officious police commissione, closed the folder again and said: "Those fellows up there must have been drunk again—of course this offence has long been amnestied and you must be released at once." Whereupon he gathered up his papers and disappeared.[1]

5. An Enthusiast in Soviet Russia

By the time the mistake was discovered Münzenberg, disguised as a Russian war prisoner, had escaped on a ship from Stettin that was repatriating several hundred Russian prisoners. Münzenberg was accompanied by the German Spartacist Ernst Meyer, the Swiss youth comrade Bamatter, and Goldenberg-Olivier, the representative of the Socialist students of France, whose journey from Germany to Russia had been organized by Münzenberg. This journey too had its share of incidents. During a police control the four "prisoners of war" were hidden in clothes lockers and almost suffocated. But nothing could dampen the

[1] *Die Dritte Front,* pp. 315 *et seq.*

travellers' high spirits because they were going to the country of the great socialist revolution. Goldenberg said years later that at the time Münzenberg was *gai et pétulant*. After their arrival in the Estonian port of Narva they travelled in a train with a wood-fired locomotive across the frontier to the first sizable locality in Russian territory, Jamburg. "We were thrilled after all the difficulties and dangers to stand at last on the soil of the Russian Soviet Union."[1] In Petrograd an enthusiastic welcome awaited them as guests of the Comintern and the Russian Youth Association. They were dragged from meeting to meeting, they were shown in days, even hours, all the achievements of the revolution. What made the strongest impression on Münzenberg were the children's homes installed in the palaces of the former imperial summer residence, Tzarskoye-Zelo, where thousands of children of Petrograd workers and soldiers were given a "model collectivist education". In a yacht which had once belonged to the Tzars the visitors sailed on the Neva and visited the stronghold of the Tzarists, the Peter and Paul fortress, where many Russian revolutionaries had been imprisoned.

As the Congress had not yet begun Münzenberg's party went on to Moscow. Immediately after his arrival Münzenberg called on Karl Radek, installed in the *palais* of the former German Embassy, and on other friends from his Zurich days. His most important visit was of course to the "old man" in the Kremlin. Lenin's first question was about the young generation. Then he asked for news of the Zurich comrades. But this was only a prelude. He quickly got down to the real issue, the differences between the Youth International and the Comintern.

Münzenberg and many representatives of the organizations affiliated to the Youth International continued to be vehement anti-parliamentarians. Later, at a commission meeting of the Congress, Lenin sent Trotsky as his emissary to convert Münzenberg to the view that participation in elections, parliamentary cooperation and work in the trade unions were necessary and useful. Münzenberg and other youth members showed equal determination in their opposition to the twenty-one conditions for union with the Comintern prepared by the Executive Committee of the Communist International (ECCI). The representatives of the youth organizations favoured a hard line, they wanted to preserve the "purity" of the Communist world movement. They demanded that every party that wanted to join the Third International should first prove by revolutionary deeds its right to membership. But their views met with bitter opposition from Lenin. Time and again he addressed them as "gauchistes and sectarians." In his speech to the Congress on 30 July he returned to this point:

[1] *Die Dritte Front*, p. 317.

What comrades Wijnkoop and Münzenberg have said, that they are dissatisfied because we have invited the USP and are in touch with its
representatives, is—in my view—wrong.[1]

In theory Lenin ought to have approved of the intransigent attitude
of the youth representatives but his main interest was to persuade as
many vacillating groups as possible away from the Second International. The Second World Congress clearly reflected Lenin's efforts.
Never again did such a motley crowd of socialists meet on Russian soil.
They ranged from Kautsky supporters to anarchists and syndicalists.
But however difficult as it was to achieve agreement on the disputed
issues, Lenin wholeheartedly approved of Münzenberg's work for the
development of the Youth International. "Never mind if you are called
a 'professional youth'. Without the young generation there can be no
Communist Party."[2]

The congress was opened by Zinoviev on 17 July 1920 in the Smolny
Institute in Petrograd. At the end of the first session the delegates,
accompanied by a large crowd, visited the Field of Mars where they laid
a wreath at the grave of the victims of the revolution. In the evening
the foundation stone was laid for a memorial to Karl Liebknecht and
Rosa Luxemburg. Then an international rally followed at which Lenin,
Jacques Sadoul, Paul Levi and Münzenberg honoured the memory of
the two dead martyrs. When Lenin appeared he was given a fifteen-
minute ovation. The youth delegates were somewhat taken aback by
this homage.

This was the time of the "white nights" at Petrograd. On one of these
nights, to celebrate the opening of the Congress a pageant was presented for which the scenario had been written by Maxim Gorki. A cast
of twenty thousand performed on the steps of the Petrograd Stock
Exchange in front of a backcloth of the Winter Palace on which flew
the red flags of the revolution. The subject matter was the revolutionary
struggles of the past years. When the armoured car with the red sailors,
who were coming to the aid of the workers, turned the corner "we
delegates rose from our seats, shouting, gesticulating, not knowing in
our enthusiasm what to do next."[3]

The congress continued in Moscow, in the throne room of the Kremlin. It was decided to hold the debates in German and interpret them
only into French. The British delegates were indignant but Germany
was the great hope of the Bolsheviks. Those were the days of the Red

[1] Protocol of the Second World Congress of the Communist International, Hamburg 1921,
p. 351.
[2] *Die Dritte Front*, p. 318.
[3] *Ibid.*, p. 321.

Army's advance in Poland; on 1 August Bialystok and Brest-Litovsk had been taken and Warsaw was now under attack and expected to fall any day. In Moscow the atmosphere was lighthearted in anticipation of the end of the victorious campaign.

But there were also critical voices. Toni Waibel was present when Lenin visited Sokolnikov in a sanitorium near Moscow. An argument developed about the aims of the Polish campaign. Sokolnikov was firmly opposed to the advance on Warsaw and particularly on East Prussia. He predicted failure because there was no revolutionary situation in East Prussia, while the Polish population was strongly anti-Russian. But Lenin was obsessed by the idea that Germany must become "Soviet" to give Russia a breathing space.

Even though German was the language used and the presidium of the Congress was composed of party leaders from many countries—and even though there was unrestrained discussion between the representatives of all countries and all party groups—the Russians had firm control of the Congress. They prepared the agenda and the resolutions, manipulated all the commissions and discussed all the issues privately before the official meetings. And, of course, in the Russian party Lenin was in absolute control. A woman collaborator of Münzenberg's from the Berlin Youth Bureau who attended the Congress as stenographer found herself constantly in the company of Zinoviev, Bukharin and Radek who discussed—politely, in German—the problems of the Congress. These conversations all revolved around what Lenin said, his word was always final, and even the smallest questions were submitted to him. Münzenberg recalled one of the nightly visits of the German youth delegation to Bukharin. One of the young men produced an autographed picture of Lenin, which Lenin himself had given him. "This is a sacred picture," Bukharin said.[1] The deification of "the old man" had begun even before his death.

Now and again the atmosphere at the Congress was quite free and easy; the strict, boring ceremonial that weighed down later congresses had not taken over. On one occasion, Emmeline Pankhurst, the English suffragette, delivered an especially emotional speech. The speaker's coiffure failed to stand up to her passion and Lenin, seated at the stenographer's table, could barely suppress his mirth.

Münzenberg did not succeed in having the problems of the youth movement discussed by the Congress. After his return to Berlin he published a report noting that Zinoviev had deleted this point from the agenda. "It was only in small commissions and in the narrow confines of the Executive that youth questions were discussed and reports on the

[1] Cf. Max Barthel, *Kein Bedarf an Weltgeschichte*, Wiesbaden 1950, p. 99.

subject accepted." In the course of those discussions it was noted that the youth organizations in Spain and Belgium had transformed themselves into "young Communist parties." In France, also, the Communist youth association constituted the firm nucleus of a Communist Party as yet to be formed. The same process could be observed in the Swiss and the Scandinavian youth groups.[1]

Lenin understood Münzenberg's importance to the revolutionary youth. But he saw the Youth International as a means to an end. It suited his plan that the Communist youth groups should play an active part in the softening-up process of the left wing of the Socialist parties, that they should encourage the split of these parties and contribute to the formation of Communist parties everywhere.

Münzenberg revealed in his report on the congress that the Comintern had recognized the need for an independent youth organization. He demanded political freedom of action for the youth organizations because most of the newly founded Communist parties were only beginning to become truly Communist: the youth organizations must speed them on their way, that was their noblest task. This was an optimistic interpretation of the Moscow decisions and Münzenberg's expectations were soon to be destroyed by the Comintern and the Russian Youth Association.

After the Congress, Münzenberg and forty other foreign delegates went on a propaganda trip from Moscow to Odessa. Captain Sadoul, a Frenchman, was in charge of the party and Angelica Balabanoff acted as interpreter. The railway carriages were decorated with symbolic representations of the Third International, and in the front and rear an armoured car with mounted machine guns was manned by Kronstadt sailors. The train stopped at each small station, and crowds gathered everywhere, often waiting patiently for twenty or thirty hours to have a glimpse of the workers' representatives from the West. At all hours of the day and night the delegation was asked to address meetings and attend party celebrations. The tour had been arranged not so much for the delegates as to show the Ukrainian population that the Soviet Union had international allies. Traces of the civil war were everywhere; the train passed through villages and small towns where entire populations had been butchered.

In Kiev, evacuated only eight weeks previously by the Poles, Münzenberg made an impassioned speech. On 2 January 1920 a pogrom had taken place in Fastov near Kiev in which thousands of people had been killed. The Kiev youth group, whose two thousand members were

[1]W. Münzenberg, *Der Zweite Kongress der Kommunistichen Internationale und die Kommunistiche Jugend-Internationale*, Berlin 1920.

mostly Jews, had founded a "Münzenberg Club." Münzenberg's address ended: "Christ was crucified only once but the Soviet Union has been crucified a hundred times."[1]

The next step of the journey proved exciting. A Ukrainian anarchist, Machno, who had the sympathy of the population, was still fighting with his band for an independent Ukraine. He had the support of the railway-men who informed him in advance of the train's arrival. Machno's men then lay in wait for the train and shots were exchanged. Odessa, where the delegates stayed for a few days, had shortly before been taken for the third time by the Bolsheviks. The approach to the harbour was mined and French cruisers blocked the entrance.

On his return to Moscow, Münzenberg prepared for his trip back to Berlin. This time he went as a German "prisoner of war." Before his departure the Kremlin supplied him with ample material for his revolutionary activities in Berlin. Because foreign currency was then in very short supply in Russia, the Russian Politbureau had asked the Cheka for several sacks of confiscated diamonds. They were handed to trusted Communists for their work abroad. Münzenberg successfully smuggled this small fortune—stitched in the cuffs of his jacket—through all controls. In Berlin he handed the stones over to Thomas who arranged for his middlemen to convert them into cash.

6. Münzenberg Loses the Fight for the Independence of the Communist Youth International

After the Second World Congress the Russians began to systematically intervene in the policy of the section of the Comintern that was most important in their schemes, the KPD. The plan was to forge this party into an instrument that would permit the German proletariat to rise to the top. An important role in the Russian plans was played by the USP whose dominant left wing had been steadily moving closer to the Comintern since 1919. The USP had sent four delegates to the Second Congress and the leaders of the party's left wing were in favour of affiliation with the Third International. This affiliation was to be voted on at a Party Congress called at Halle on 12 October 1920. The party's right wing was represented by Kautsky and Hilferding and also by Lenin's former friend, the Menshevik Martov. They warned against affiliation and against all revolutionary experiments. At the invitation of the Left the Comintern's president, Zinoviev, put in an appearance,

[1]Max Barthel, *Vom Roten Moskau bis zum Schwarzen Meer*, Berlin 1921.

having been given an entry visa by the German government. Otto Strasser, in Halle as a journalist, described the speech with which Zinoviev harangued the delegates for several hours trying to persuade them to join the Comintern as "an elemental event". He described Zinoviev as painting a "colossal picture" of the Russian revolution and a future "workers paradise."[1] Zinoviev succeeded in winning over the majority: 236 delegates voted for affiliation and 156 against. Shortly afterwards, on 4–7 December 1920, the left wing of the USP and the KPD joined forces. The independent Social Democrats brought with them 270,000 members (out of an original total of over 800,000). The new party was called the United Communist Party of Germany (VKPD). With this establishment of a mass party which, as Münzenberg noted at the Third World Congress, was not joined by "the trusted core of officials and active workers," the influence of the Spartacists declined noticeably, particularly as the Russians rejected Paul Levi's suggestion to allow the old KPD (Spartacist League) to continue to exist as a group within the new party.

The Russians had never broken off relations with the Communist Workers Party (KAP), which had been expelled in 1919. Although Paul Levi had threatened to leave the Second World Congress of the Comintern, the Russians allowed the KAP to attend with its own delegation. This Russian double dealing continued after the Congress. Unknown to the KPD leadership, the Comintern maintained its contacts with the expelled group, particularly through Borodin who for some months acted as a link with the KAP in Berlin, living in a boarding house on the Kurfürstendamm with false papers showing him to be a Russian émigré. Borodin demanded that Communist Party leadership re-establish closer links with the KAP because the party's behaviour, although correct and confident, lacked the revolutionary vigour which, in the opinion of the Russian comrades, was to be found among the KAP. Felix Wolf (Nikolai Rakov), a member of the WEB who had taken an anti-parliamentary line as early as 1919, was also in contact with the comrades of the KAP. These contacts culminated in preparations for a March rising when KAP representatives were elected to a secret bureau charged with preparing bomb attacks. There were other Comintern emissaries, Karl Radek for example, who went over the heads of the leadership and intervened in party politics or, like Rakosi, provoked open conflicts. In the course of a discussion on splitting tactics at a Party Central committee meeting, Paul Levi clashed with Rakosi who defended splitting provided it helped to create clarity. Levi, who was fundamentally opposed to this approach, was defeated in the voting and

[1]Otto Strasser, *Exil*, Munich 1958, p. 29.

thereupon withdrew from party leadership, together with Klara Zetkin and three former independents.

Paul Levi's period as party leader had ended because he could not be a willing tool of Moscow. Kurt Geyer, then a member of the Central Committee, commented in November 1948 in a letter to Ruth Fischer:

> In the Spartacist League and in the original Communist Party after Rosa's death, in this small group which in 1919 was politically loosely knit and weak, and which was full of intellectuals, he could just about occupy a leading position . . . given his marked individualism, his aestheticism, his south German tradition and his bourgeois Jewish culture, his appreciation of the good things of life and therefore his involvement in Western civilization he could not have been less suited to be the leader of the Communist Party.[1]

Given the tactical line of the Comintern it is not surprising that increased pressure was also brought to bear on Münzenberg for showing too much independence of thought and action. The successes of the Youth International failed to make him appreciate the realities that he was up against. In the autumn of 1920 the Youth International had reached its peak of expansion—forty-nine organizations with well over 800,000 members had joined. An impressive list of publications in many languages gave evidence of its propagandist activity. In his account, *Ein Jahr Kommunistische Jugend-Internationale* (One Year of Communist Youth International 1920), Münzenberg described the tasks as he saw them: the youth must be "schooled in revolution and Communism and . . . led as enthusiastic fighters to join the Comintern and its parties, and only if there are no such parties or if they fail in their duties shall it take independent action". He was even more explicit in the *Youth International* of February 1921: "Never, never can the young allow the Party to tell them what their political attitude should be."

But at the Third All Russian Congress of the Communist Youth Association on 4 October 1920 Lenin, in a speech on the basic tasks of Communist youth in a socialist republic, assigned to the young no political tasks whatsoever, giving them instead exclusively educational duties: let them acquire general knowledge, let them learn all about Communism, fight illiteracy, conduct cleanliness campaigns, plant vegetable plots in the suburbs and maintain Communist morale.[2]

Meanwhile the Russian Youth Association did everything it could to sabotage co-operation with the Berlin Bureau. In a letter of 10 Novem-

[1] Quoted with kind permission of Kurt Geyer.
[2] V.I. Lenin, *Die Aufgaben der Kommunistichen Jugendorganisation 1920*. No. 10 of the pamphlets of the Youth International.

ber 1920 the Russians said that the "independence" granted to the youth organizations at the Second Congress was to be understood in a tactical sense only. The Muscovites demanded that the next Youth Congress be held in Moscow. In two letters to Zinoviev—1 and 14 December 1920—Münzenberg said categorically that the Comintern had no right or cause to change the decision of the Youth Bureau to hold the Congress in Germany. That decision had been confirmed in Moscow. Both letters remained unanswered.[1]

Like Münzenberg the majority of the Communist youth associations was in favour of preserving limited autonomy. The Italian organization, which was most strongly opposed to any form of supervision and which had given its fullest support to the proposal that the next Congress should be held in a Western country, issued a pamphlet written by its Secretary, Luigi Polano, in which he criticized those of his comrades who wanted absolute political autonomy. The youth organizations must neither be above the Communist parties nor outside them; while being subject to Communist discipline they must exercise their functions as the *avant-garde*, as the driving force, and watch that the Communist parties did not deviate to the right, towards opportunism. But Polano rejected the Russian view that the youth organizations should no longer concern themselves with politics, that they should be completely under the control of the respective Communist parties and should not be entitled to discuss and to criticize.

On 18 February 1921 a meeting of the Bureau of the Youth Executive was held in Berlin attended by a few international youth delegates and Borodin as the Comintern's representative. Münzenberg addressed the meeting. He used the following arguments in support of holding the Congress in a Western country: the political situation demanded a demonstration in the West; if the youth organizations met in Moscow delegates would be away from the political struggle for months. Moreover, the youth leaders would learn nothing new in Soviet Russia about the problems of the economic struggle. He closed with an open challenge: any change in the character of the Youth International was out of the question.

This view was shared by all delegates with the exception of Alfred Kurella, who represented the otherwise unrepresented Russian Youth Association, and Borodin. Both voted against the resolution in which the Executive Bureau of the Youth International expressed its disapproval of the Russian association and its leader Shatskin "who has grossly offended against discipline by advocating Moscow as the venue of the

---

[1] Cf. also Alfred Kurella, *Gründung und Aufbau der Kommunistischen Jugendinternationale*, Berlin 1929, p. 155.

Congress."[1] It was decided to send Kurella, Mielenz and Köhler to Moscow to convince the Comintern and the Russian Youth Association that the line of the Berlin Bureau was right. But Mielenz and Köhler were unequal to the pressure brought to bear upon them by Zinoviev and Shatskin. Köhler changed his point of view, bowed to the arguments of the Russians and supported the proposal that the Youth Congress should be held in Moscow. The delegates returned at the end of February bearing a resolution by the Executive Committee of the Communist International to this effect and a letter from Bela Kun to the Berlin Youth Bureau. They were accompanied by the Hungarian Pogany, who had come to Berlin with the secret order to prepare a revolutionary campaign and thereby to force the KPD finally to take the offensive.

Münzenberg was deeply disappointed by Mielenz and Köhler whom he described as "Muscovites." They said that only the lingering crisis in Russia had caused their "change of heart." Rakosi and Bela Kun joined Pogany in trying to make it clear to the German Party Central Committee that the time had come to strike as Germany was in a revolutionary situation. As Münzenberg's Berlin Bureau was busy preparing for the Congress, the unrest became more marked, culminating in the rising in central Germany and the bitter fighting for the Leuna works near Merseburg. But however critical Germany's economic and political situation, the mass of the German workers was not prepared to man the barricades. They had no intention of taking up the Communist invitation to begin a general strike. After weeks of bitter street fighting, the revolt collapsed. On a Sunday in March 1931, the Communist District Office of Halle-Merseburg organized memorial meetings for the victims of the March unrest ten years before. I accompanied Münzenberg who had been invited to attend the celebrations. We drove in a lorry from village to village from workers' colony to workers' colony, accompanied by a group of the banned *Rote Frontkämpferbund*, to visit graves of victims. The true background had obviously been forgotten or it had never been known to the ordinary party members. The victims, it was now said, had died in the revolutionary struggle "against the Prussian police and the reactionary Social Democratic Government." It was not the irresponsible operators in Moscow and their German henchmen who were to blame for their death but the Social Democrat Severing and his security police.

In *Internationale Jugend-Korrespondenz* (No. 15, 1921) Münzenberg had expressed himself against the March action. He rejected the theory that the time had come for a show-down. In his opinion the counter-

[1]Alfred Kurella, *op. cit.*, p. 156.

revolution was still too powerful. In addition to the German Youth Association, the Scandinavians were on his side, while the Italians, Swiss and Austrians were in favor of offensive action. Münzenberg's criticism of the March events gave his opponents occasion at the next Youth Congress to accuse him of opportunism and of an anti-Moscow attitude.

But it was not only among the young that opinions differed on the March events. In the KPD the controversy developed into a fight against Paul Levi and his supporters. Levi had asked to be given an opportunity to speak but the Central Committee refused his request. The former party leader now chose to publicize his views and issued the pamphlet *Unser Weg. Wider den Putschismus* (Our Road Against Putsch Tactics), a devastating criticism of the March adventure and of the emissaries of the Comintern. This was interpreted as an unforgivable breach of discipline. Levi and his supporters, who included the majority of the Communist Reichstag members, were expelled from the party.[1] Münzenberg's friend, Valeriu Marcu[2] left the KPD with Levi. But Münzenberg was no longer as close to Marcu as in the past, nor was he prepared to join the Levi group.

Up to the last moment Münzenberg had hoped that the Russian Youth Organization would abandon its obstructive tactics and participate in the Second International Youth Congress planned for the end of March. The Berlin Bureau had postponed the start of the conference to 7 April solely for this reason. But when the Congress opened at Jena in the House of the People the Russians were absent as were representatives from Spain and Portugal. Otherwise the representatives of the twenty-five sections invited appeared, as well as many delegates of associations not affiliated to the Youth International.

The following telegram was received from the Comintern in Moscow:[3]

[1] Occasionally there was violent criticism also from party members. A Communist wrote in *Vorwärts* of 4 December 1921: "Those international confidence tricksters and adventurers who flock to Berlin from all over the world and who congregate around the 'West European Secretariat' which spends millions annually and works independently of the party must vanish immediately. Our elegant boarding houses and smart restaurants are crowded with those characters who live on Russian money and who know nothing of the German movement or of the workers' movement in general but who think that all that is necessary for a putsch is money."

[2] V. Marcu, the son of a director of AEG in Bucharest, was sent as a sixteen year old by the Rumanian revolutionary and later leading Bolshevik, Christian Rakovski, to Lenin in Switzerland, a country which Marcu hailed enthusiastically as a democracy. Lenin entrusted him with secret missions which took him via Paris to Moscow and Rumania where he was arrested by the German occupation authorities. After his break with the Communists he wrote historical biographies the best known of which, *Scharnhorst oder das grosse Kommando,* earned him the friendship of General von Seeckt. In 1933 he emigrated to Nice, contributed to émigré papers, including *Neuen Tagebuch* and in 1941 he went to New York where he died during the Second World War.

[3] V. Marcu, *Ein vereitelter Weltkongress der Jugend,* in *Sowwjet* (Berlin), May, 1921, p. 49.

Moscow, 2 April. Inform participants of Youth Congress that the Executive Committee of the Communist International supports the proposal of the Central Committee of the Russian Youth Organization which regards the meeting as a private conference and asks that the Congress be postponed and convened in Moscow.

The telegram aroused indignation among the participants. Although Kurella and the Lithuanian delegate, Kobetski, immediately submitted a motion in line with that of the Russian association, the vast majority voted against them. Pogany, who was still in Germany, defended the theory that the time had come to take the offensive. Kurella attacked Münzenberg for being friendly with Valeriu Marcu and for suggesting that Paul Levi might be invited to address the Congress.

Meanwhile the attention of the Jena police had been drawn to the Congress, which was meeting illegally, and the majority of the delegates could expect arrest. Therefore the Congress was transferred to Berlin where it was easier to "disappear." In Berlin, Münzenberg received a further communication from the Comintern:

Berlin, 10 April 1921. To the Executive Committee of the Communist Youth International.

Dear Comrades, The ECCI requests me to inform you of the following: at its meeting of 5 April it decided to regard the conference convened by the Executive Committee as an informal discussion and to hold the Congress of the Youth International in Moscow in conjunction with the Congress of the Communist International.

The representative of the Executive Committee the Communist International in Berlin, J.
[i.e. James Reich-Thomas][1]

This renewed, more emphatic intervention—amounting to an order to break off the Congress—filled the youth representatives with anxiety and confusion. At a meeting with Münzenberg, the Scandinavian delegates expressed their resentment of Moscow's actions. To the Danish delegates, Nielsen and Henriksen, this pressure seemed particularly intolerable. They had left the Social Democratic Party because it did not operate democratically, now the more severe discipline of the Comintern was to be imposed on the Youth International. They returned to Denmark and refused, like many other delegates, to accept the Moscow invitation.

This proved to be a typical Moscow manoeuvre, repeated countless times with other parties. First came a recommendation to act in accord-

[1] Alfred Kurella, *op. cit.*, p. 169.

ance with their suggestions. If this was of no avail, a threatening order followed. "Münzenberg . . . vainly explained half weeping half laughing that the youth organization had never yet sinned against the authority and infallibility of the little Bureau of the Executive—the order was there and no sophistry could do away with it," Valeriu Marcu wrote in Paul Levi's journal *Sowjet* (Vol. 12, 15 May 1921). The Comintern representative, Pogany, declared that the youth organization must obey. Anyone who was for holding the meeting in Germany must be a secret supporter of Hilferding and Scheidemann. Now above all when Paul Levi was rebelling obedience was imperative. In Moscow the Youth International would be "purged of opportunist elements."

In the meantime the meeting in Berlin, also held illegally, continued. If the participants wanted to meet for secret discussions they went to Neu-Ruppin, where a member of the youth organization had a sailing boat, or else they met in the evening in the foyer of the Unter den Linden opera house which Münzenberg had designated as the most suitable rendezvous for conspirators in Berlin.

Münzenberg had half decided to resign from the Youth International but could not bring himself to take the final step. Although he dismissed the delegates with the request that they appear in Moscow two months hence he still faintly hoped that he could push through his line. In an article in the May number of *Youth International* entitled "A Precedent?" he attacked the Moscow decision:

> We are still convinced that this is not a precedent nor a measure which signifies a new attitude of the Executive Committee of the Comintern to the Communist youth movement and its organizational independence. We see no reason or cause why the Communist International should do away with or even restrict the organizational independence of the Communist youth organizations and we would see this as doing serious damage not only to . . . the Communist youth movement.

Did he really still believe this? After all in 1919 and 1920 he had been among those who had most firmly supported the twenty-one points, the need for revolutionary discipline and for full power for the Comintern. For days he wandered alone in the Thüringer *Wald* trying to come to terms with himself. He was reluctant to give up the Youth International which he regarded as his own creation. But at the same time he felt that he could not carry his point in the face of opposition from Moscow, that the process of centralization, of domination of all Communist organizations by Moscow, had become inevitable.

In June 1921, Münzenberg visited Russia for the second time, as a delegate to the Third World Congress of the Comintern, and to continue the scheduled Youth Congress in July. The political climate had changed considerably since 1920. The government had been through months of crises. Peasant risings against compulsory requisitioning, the complete collapse of industry, continual strikes by hungry workers had caused Lenin to change course and to proclaim at the Tenth Party Congress of the Bolsheviks his new economic policy, NEP. This meant the end of war Communism. Opposition groups had grown up in the Bolshevik Party, including the "workers' opposition" and a more moderate left wing group around Trotsky. They wanted to restrict the powers of the political police and of the party bureaucracy, and to give independence to the trade unions. They also attacked the new class within the party which profiteered from the revolution. These differences were about to be discussed at the Tenth Party Congress when on 28 February 1921 the Kronstadt sailors mutinied and were joined by the Kronstadt Soviet. The Kronstadters, who in 1917 had been in the vanguard of the October Revolution, had earlier expressed support for the striking Petrograd workers and in pamphlets had made the economic demands which Lenin, almost simultaneously, conceded to the whole country by proclaiming NEP. Furthermore they had made political demands: secret elections to the soviets, freedom of speech and of assembly for all revolutionary groups, free trade unions and the liberation of political prisoners. The Bolshevik press of Petrograd embarked on a smear campaign against the Kronstadt insurgents, the like of which had not been seen in Soviet Russia. Military units, under the leadership of the future Marshal Tukhachevski, were assembled to storm the fortress. After several abortive attacks in which the regiments were forced to venture on to the brittle ice of the Neva, and after most of them had refused to fight their "little brothers" or had joined the rebels, Tukhachevski finally prepared an attack which three hundred of the delegates to the Tenth Party Congress joined as political commissars. For two nights and one day the bombardments continued, then Kronstadt was taken by the government troops. The surviving insurgents who did not escape to Finland were arrested and after secret trials lasting for months were usually sentenced to death by the Cheka and shot.

In Kronstadt comrades had fought against comrades. This fact caused profound shock among the Bolsheviks. During the fighting Lenin said to a friend of Victor Serge who witnessed the events in Petrograd: "This is the Thermidor. But we do not let ourselves be guillotined. We make our own Thermidor."[1] A merciless campaign was now waged not only against the Kronstadters and the rebellious peasants but also against the remaining Mensheviks, against scientists and writers who were ex-

[1]Victor Serge, "Kronstadt 1921," in *Politics* (New York), 1947.

pelled from the country, and against the opposition within the Party itself—and thus against any tendency towards independence among the Comintern parties.

Very little was heard of this struggle at the Third World Congress. The only speaker to ignore the group discipline of the Russian delegation and to appeal to foreign delegates to support her programme was Alexandra Kollontai who belonged to the Workers' Opposition. Other speeches did reflect the participants' anxiety about the situation in Russia. Münzenberg expressed the opinion of many disillusioned Communists who saw in the Bolshevik Party the only guarantee for the new Russia's existence: "The more the Communist Party of Russia must, because we remain passive, fight alone and with the most difficult means; the more fervently our heart beats for this party . . . There can be no reason for us to betray our comrades and to abandon them at a time when they are hardest pressed."[1]

In other contributions to the discussions Münzenberg appeared as a moderate left winger and cautiously opposed the concessions made to the right at the Congress. But the turn to the right was unmistakable. The March activities and all revolutionary adventures were condemned, Russia needed a breathing space.

Immediately after their arrival, the youth delegates were firmly taken in hand by the comrades of the Comintern and the Russian Youth Association to hold them to the Russian line and to isolate Münzenberg. During the early weeks he still had the majority behind him but the Russians brought their heavy artillery into play against him. At a conference of the Russian Youth Association, Bukharin and Bela Kun condemned Münzenberg's policy. The controversies within the delegations were bitter but in the end the resolution submitted by the Russian Youth Association was adopted unanimously. The Congress, which met from 14 to 24 July, merely approved formally what had previously been decided in the commissions. The Youth International was transferred to Moscow. Lasar Shatskin became Münzenberg's successor, although none of the foreign delegates wanted a Russian to head the organization. Bitterly disappointed, Münzenberg delivered a piece of self-criticism to the Congress that was in marked contrast to the previous extensive, confident report on his activities which he had submitted in Russian and German simultaneously. The result of the Congress was entirely in line with Lenin's wishes, even though he protected Münzenberg against personal attacks: "Münzenberg put a paper and a platform at my disposal during the war when we could not publish our ideas

[1] Protocol of the Third Congress of the Communist International, Hamburg 1921, p. 254.

anywhere."[1] But this did not alter the fact that those who had expressed themselves in favour of the independence of the youth organizations were henceforth given "bad conduct notes" by the Russians, whereas those who had toed the line almost all became dedicated Stalinists. As spokesman of the Russian youth group Voja Vujovic[2] reported on the Congress:

> Free from all contact with the rotten bourgeois world, without threat from the Noske bandits and under the loyal protection of the bayonets of the Red Army . . . the Second Youth Congress could quietly study the revolutionary experiences of the entire international proletariat and of the Russian proletariat in particular.[3]

---

[1]Based on private information from Emil Arnold.
[2]Goldenberg-Olivier recalls Vujovic as a very pleasant Serb whom he had come to know as a student in Paris where he had been a co-founder of the "Communist Youth of France." In 1928 Vujovic was expelled from the Party as a supporter of Trotsky and deported to Siberia where he disappeared, as did his brothers Gregor and Rada. Goldenberg-Olivier met Vujovic for the last time in 1927 in Moscow where Vujovic complained about "Fascist methods in the Comintern." He said that he had written a protest letter to the Russian Central Committee.
[3]*Communist International*, No. 18, 1921.

IV

The International Workers Aid—
Supply Column of the Proletariat

1. An Assignment from Lenin

As the Second World Congress of the Comintern was meeting in Moscow, the after-effects of the years of civil war were creating a crisis throughout Russia. In the spring and summer of 1921 not a drop of rain had fallen in the important corn growing regions of the Lower Volga and the Tartar Republic. On 26 June 1921 *Pravda* wrote that twenty-five million people were starving. Supply, administration and the transport of vital goods—and this was the most terrible consequence of the civil war years—had almost come to a complete standstill. People fled from the famine, leaving their homes and escaping to other parts of the country where the situation was said to be less hopeless. But the limited stocks of food were soon exhausted by the endless stream of refugees.

An appeal by the Russian Central Committee of July 1921 informed all party organizations in Russia of the seriousness of the situation and asked them to cope with this "tremendous natural disaster" with all the means at their disposal. Above all, the flood of refugees must be stemmed and redirected to parts of the country where there were some food supplies. This, however, could only be done with about a million people. The others were at the mercy of the famine.

The Bolsheviks turned to the world for help. On 13 July, Maxim Gorki addressed an appeal to "all honest Europeans and Americans" in which he said:

> Gloomy days have come for the country of Tolstoy, Dostoyevsky, Mendeleyev, Pavlov, Mussorgsky, Glinka and other world-famous men, and I venture to trust that the cultured European and American people will understand the tragedy of the Russian people, and immediately come to their aid with bread and medicines.[1]

The reply of the then chairman of the American Relief Administration (ARA) and future President of the United States, Herbert Hoover, arrived ten days later. Hoover said he was ready to give immediate help to the famine areas if the Soviet authorities agreed to the same conditions that had been granted to his organization in ten other European countries where it had been feeding about three and one-half million children since the end of the war. He promised to start feeding a million Russian children at once. An agreement was reached in Riga with the Russians and in August the ARA began work in the famine areas.

Chicherin, People's Commissar for External Affairs, meanwhile approached Fridtjof Nansen for help. Nansen's achievement in repatriating two hundred thousand prisoners of war from Siberia had aroused the admiration of the whole world. The Norwegian immediately visited the most distant corners of the famine areas. What he saw there moved him deeply. He was certain that the number of starving people was in reality far higher than the Soviet Government was prepared to admit in its official reports. He estimated it at approximately thirty million. An International Committee for Aid to Russia in which twenty-two charitable organizations from all parts of the world joined forces was set up with Nansen at its head. But Nansen's effort to enlist League of Nations aid failed. The Western governments were not prepared to give official assistance since they regarded this as tantamount to supporting the Bolshevik regime.

On 12 November 1921 Nansen gave an address to the International Labour Organization in Geneva "To the Conscience of the Nations." Münzenberg subsequently published this speech as a pamphlet. Nansen denounced the governments of the Western powers and called upon

---

[1] Quoted in X. Joukoff Eudin and Harold H. Fisher, *Soviet Russia and the West 1920–1927. A documentary survey*, Stanford 1957, p. 73.

the whole world to give immediate help as otherwise hundreds of thousands would be doomed.

Workers' organizations in all countries, regardless of their political affiliations, tried to help. The British trade unions sent a party to Russia, the International Federation of Trade Unions called for funds, and the Vienna International—the so-called 2½ International—published an appeal for aid on 25 July 1921, as did the German USP. All of this was done spontaneously without the Soviet Government asking them specifically for help.

The famine relief operation now became a political factor of considerable importance. Lenin was quick to realize that a joint campaign by foreign workers of all political affiliations effectively counteracted the activities of the bourgeois charitable organizations. At the same time the prevailing anxiety over the fate of the starving million created a common basis of interest and this allowed the Russians to ignore party differences and to appeal to those workers abroad who previously would not have been receptive to any word from Soviet Russia. Therefore, on 2 August 1921, Lenin addressed the following appeal to the workers of the world:

> Some provinces in Russia suffer from a famine which is hardly less serious than the deprivation of 1891. It is the unhappy consequence of Russia's backwardness and of the seven years of war, first the imperialist war and later the civil war in which the landowners and capitalists of all countries have embroiled the workers and peasants. Help is needed. The Soviet Republic of workers and peasants expects help from the workers, from those employed in industry. Both are everywhere oppressed by capitalism and imperialism. But we are convinced that they will respond to our call in spite of their own difficulties caused by unemployment and rising prices. Those who for the whole of their lives have had personal experience of the pressure of capitalism will understand the position of the workers and peasants in Russia. They will understand, or will sense with the instinct of the worker and the exploited, that it is necessary to help the Soviet Union as the first country to be given the thankful but difficult task of abolishing capitalism. The capitalists of all countries in turn seek to revenge themselves on the Soviet Republic. They are preparing new plans for intervention and counter-revolutionary conspiracies. We are convinced that the workers and the peasants will come to our assistance with all the more energy, with all the more self-sacrifice.[1]

An All-Russian Central Aid Committee was founded and granted the right to set up branches abroad. During these weeks a restless, gloomy Münzenberg sat in Moscow. As increasingly alarming reports came in

[1]Quoted in Willi Münzenberg, *Solidarität, 10 Jahre IAH, 1921–1931*, Berlin 1931, p. 188.

about the nation-wide catastrophe, he himself went through a difficult personal crisis. The Youth International, built with so much revolutionary energy, had been taken from him. After more than five years of close contact with the Bolsheviks, Münzenberg should have recognized this move as characteristic of their methods, but in his heart he regarded it as treason and human failure among friends. He saw through the double game which the Russian Comintern leaders had played with the German Communists. On the one hand the Third Congress had condemned "putsch tactics" and thereby the whole of the Left, on the other it had sanctioned the March rising—which Paul Levi had so passionately condemned as a Bakuninist putsch—as an example of a legitimate mass movement of the German workers.

Münzenberg now learned personally what the struggles behind the scenes were about. Moscow's claim to power must be satisfied at any price. Although this experience gave the healthy young man a nervous stomach ailment which he retained to the end of his life, it was in the last resort beneficial. From those summer days of 1921 onwards, Münzenberg saw the Moscow headquarters in a new light. He did not break with the "Turkestanis," as Paul Levi had called them. Their cause was too close to his heart, and he also was convinced that the Bolshevik revolution was essential to a victorious socialist revolution in other countries.

Even so he could not imagine that he would ever work for the cause of the revolution in Moscow. He had never learned to like the city. Everything there remained alien—the people, the language, the clumsy bureaucracy, the pressure. Even in later years, when he paid frequent visits to Moscow, this uneasy feeling did not change. He continued to admire the Bolsheviks, their daring experiment and the extent of their power but after more than two weeks in Moscow he became restless and irritable. He longed to return to the West.

No doubt one factor contributing to his stomach ailment was his strange diet. A barrel of herrings, which he had bought in Riga as an iron ration, had long been eaten up. The Comintern delegates received the usual minute rations of bread accompanied by hot water with a few tea leaves. From time to time caviar was distributed, of which Münzenberg grew so tired that he never touched it thereafter. Now and again he pulled himself together, visited Karl Radek and implored him to find him a sensible occupation. He also pestered Lenin who told him to display some self-discipline.

However, Lenin was probably the only person in those years who recognized the real genius of this restless young man. Although Münzenberg's political drive, his inclination towards independent thought and action conflicted with Comintern policy, they were qualities too valuable to waste. Lenin found him a job which made the best use of his qualities for the Communist cause while removing him from the internal German Communist Party quarrels and protecting him from attacks from the Moscow Comintern headquarters. For, although his future activity fell within the framework of the Comintern, he was to be given considerable freedom of action. Lenin proposed that Münzenberg build an international organization of the various proletarian famine relief programs, which were then fairly uncoordinated. Münzenberg accepted with pleasure. He understood at once that Lenin's assignment gave him a special position from which he could ward off all Party opposition.

Back in Berlin he immediately threw himself into his work. On 12 August, a few days after his return, he published the first appeal of his newly founded Foreign Committee for the Organization of Workers' Aid for the Famished in Russia (IAH). The appeal invited the Vienna International and the Third International as well as to the International Federation of Trade Unions and the Red Trade Union International to a joint conference. The organization of the committee Münzenberg solved in his own style: he was given a room in the building of the Berlin city administration which served primarily as an official and telegraphic address. It was not difficult to find helpers. There were a number of young men and women from the Youth International who very nearly equalled their ex-chairman in vitality and enthusiasm. With them he began to set up a provisional office in the flat of an old Communist, Luise Kahn, at the Moabit Wikinger-Ufer. Working day and night they prepared the first appeal and organized the founding Congress. Münzenberg turned first to all existing workers' aid committees, workers' parties and other organizations which had already initiated campaigns for the Russian workers and peasants. He urged their local offices to deal only with his committee at the international level as he was the official representative of the All Russian Central Aid Committee. At the same time he invited a number of personalities at home and abroad to put themselves at the disposal of the Workers' Aid. Acceptances came quickly, from artists, writers, scientists and politicians. His first appeal was signed among others by Käthe Kollwitz, Albert Einstein, Arthur Holitscher, Maximilian Harden, Heinrich Vogeler, Alexander Moissi, George Grosz, Leonhard Frank, Martin Andersen-Nexö, G.B. Shaw, Anatole France, Henri Barbusse, Auguste Forel and Henriette Roland-Holst. Münzenberg later wrote that the signatories to this first appeal could be described as "co-founders of the International Workers' Aid."[1]

The International Federation of Trade Unions in Amsterdam had

[1]Willi Münzenberg, *Solidarität*, op. cit., p. 196.

decided a few weeks previously to initiate a relief campaign. On 13 August one of its secretaries, Edo Fimmen, visited Berlin to discuss with the Russian Embassy the technical aspects of sending ships with food and other assistance to Russia. This was Münzenberg's first meeting with a man who was later to become a close friend. Münzenberg tried in vain to persuade the International Federation of Trade Unions to join his committee. Fimmen said that the trade union shipments must go straight to Soviet Russia without passing through any other organizations. After Münzenberg had told him how he saw the role of his committee Edo Fimmen, who was several heads taller than Münzenberg, slapped him cheerfully on the back and suggested that he should go home and leave the famine relief campaign to the trade unionists.

Fimmen came from the Dutch middle classes. He was a senior employee in a big oil concern when he met his first wife. She was an active member of the Salvation Army and through her Fimmen received his first insight into the social misery that existed behind the neat bourgeois façades of his home town of Amsterdam. After a short time he joined the Salvation Army and soon afterwards accepted a post as Secretary of the Dutch Employees' Trade Union. This was the beginning of a career that was to make him one of the best-known international trade union leaders between the two world wars. In 1919 he founded the International Federation of Transport Workers (ITF) which was joined by specialist associations from all over the world. From 1920 to 1922 he was Secretary of the International Federation of Trade Unions. In the winter of 1918 he had been in charge of a relief operation in Vienna which had lost its agricultural supply areas when Hungary and Czechoslovakia became independent states. Within a few days Fimmen raised millions and sent ten large goods trains with food to Vienna.

In a telegram of 16 August to the Second International, whose secretary at that time was Ramsay MacDonald, Münzenberg proposed that the campaigns of the Second International parties should be combined with that of his Aid Committee which received its instructions from the Third International. There was an exchange of letters which ended with MacDonald's statement that henceforth all donations in cash and kind collected by the Second International would be channelled through the Amsterdam International Federation of Trade Unions.

Münzenberg therefore did not succeed at first in bringing the representatives of the two big Socialist bodies under the Communist hat in spite of the fact that there was no lack of sympathy among the trade unions for Soviet Russia. "Workers, help Soviet Russia. A collapse of Soviet Russia would be a misfortune for Europe," an appeal of the International Federation of Trade Unions had said, a pronouncement which so profoundly shocked the German Social Democrats that they refused to publish the appeal in their press. Britain's trade union leader O'Grady raised a substantial sum of money by appeals and lectures and personally visited the stricken areas to distribute food.

The work of the first weeks was interrupted by the Jena Party Congress of the KPD which met from 22 to 26 August in the buildings of the Zeiss works and which Münzenberg attended together with a few foreign friends. In spite of the serious setbacks which the Party had suffered as a result of the unsuccessful March action and the rebellion of Paul Levi and his group, it had—according to *Inprecorr*—361,000 members, 33 daily papers with 230,000 subscribers and, divided into twenty-eight districts, covered the whole of Germany.[1]

One of the three chairmen of the Party Congress, Ernst Reuter-Friesland, spoke as representative of the Central Committee. He, who a few months later was to express the opposite view and for that reason was forced to leave the Party in January 1922, in Jena approved of Paul Levi's expulsion and defended the Russians' ruthless fight against the Right. Reuter called upon the whole Party to do everything in its power to help the Russian anti-famine campaign. Münzenberg was given valuable assistance in Jena—the promise that he could use the Communist Party machinery for his work and that the aid campaigns already in progress would be centralized in his committee. The official blessing of the German Party had now been given to the venture.

2. Hunger in Russia—The Whole World Helps

On 21 August Münzenberg's committee succeeded in sending the first aid ship from Stockholm to Petrograd. By October the most important aid committees had become affiliated to Münzenberg's organization. Within a few months the aid to Russia campaign of the workers' movement had become a world-wide venture. From Scandinavia to South Africa, from Argentina via Australia to the United States, ships set out under the auspices of the International Workers' Aid to bring food and other necessary provisions to Russia.

Germany suffered from inflation and the economic situation of the German workers became daily more hopeless. But substantial donations arrived even from Germany. A big proportion of the contributions, estimated in the final report at approximately five million dollars, came from the American Friends of Soviet Russia.

For the first time—and within a very short period—Münzenberg had

[1] *Inprecorr* of 6 October 1921.

proved that he was capable of extending his network across the whole world. He initiated a large-scale publicity campaign. Picture postcards and illustrated papers, films, pamphlets and prospectuses, every known and a few new advertising media were used. Münzenberg recognized what every advertising man is now told in his first week of training: the effectiveness of pictures. And he knew how to obtain the best artists of the day for his campaign. Münzenberg also quickly became aware of the great potentiality of aiming his advertising at particular groups. In America for instance special committees of trade unionists, women, children, gymnasts, artists and musicians were formed to advertise the cause. In Bulgaria, and at times also in Germany, committees were set up which collected food from farmers and peasants. So-called "flower days" were organized in Britain, Scandinavia and Holland on which bunches of flowers were sold in the streets, mainly by children, for the benefit of the workers aid campaign. Another effective and original method was used primarily in Germany: groups of children and young people would go from house to house, singing revolutionary and Russian songs and then take a collection. Several of the ideas used in this first campaign became guidelines for the subsequent propaganda methods of the KPD. On 1 November 1921 the IAH published the first number of an *Illustrierte Arbeiter-Zeitung,* under the motto "Soviet Russia in Word and Picture." This paper grew into the AIZ *(Arbeiter Illustrierte Zeitung)* which by the beginning of the thirties had a weekly circulation of 420,000 copies and which became one of the most important Communist propaganda organs.

Naturally there were sceptics and opponents. Workers' pointed out that because of the severity of the economic plight enough could not be given and that the little that was given never reached those for whom it was intended. Münzenberg sought to dispel these reservations in a lecture. Every worker's penny counted, it was not the size of the sums given that was important but the number of those who gave; the money was used abroad to buy goods which were sent direct to the famine areas. The Communist Workers Party (KAP) refused to join in the IAH's collections because it regarded such ventures as out and out "Social Democratic and opportunist," likely only to reawaken and to strengthen lower middle class ideas among the workers. The only way to give revolutionary aid was to organize a proletarian revolution in all capitalist countries. Münzenberg replied that the argument was attractive but that the KAP refused to divulge its recipe for overnight revolution. The KAP's tactics had so far had the contrary effect. The proletarian revolution was not a quick attack, it was a lengthy war. The aid campaign was part of the great historic happening that was called the proletarian revolution. Münzenberg also attacked the "alms and charity soup" methods—that is the ways in which the pacifist and humanitarian bourgeois organizations rendered assistance. But those who contributed their bit to IAH thereby joined the ranks of the revolutionaries. Every donation for Soviet Russia was a revolutionary gesture.

Meanwhile the famine was reaching its peak. The area affected stretched from the mouth of the Volga in the south to Kazan, the old Tartar capital in the north. The worst affected region was around Samara on the middle reaches of the Volga. Saratov, the birthplace of Chernishevski on the right bank of the Volga, was then the economic center of about half a million settlers of German origin whose villages stretched along the banks of the river. The German writer Franz Jung, who worked in the Comintern press department, was sent to this part of the famine area in the autumn of 1921. He came back with a staggering report. He had travelled down the Volga in a GPU launch. The banks of the river were crowded with refugees. They had fled from the Steppe in the desperate hope of finding a ship to take them away from the death zone. Patiently they waited, singing and dying because typhus had broken out and was claiming countless victims. The dead and the dying were handed on until they reached the edge of the crowd where bodies were piled up by the hundreds. Jung and his companions saw many houses in the German villages with their windows and doors boarded up. When they broke into the house they would find the family, starved to death, seated at the table with an open Bible on it.

How many people died of hunger was never announced; probably the figure was not known. Official sources later spoke of two million dead.

Meanwhile Münzenberg had succeeded in setting up his own organization in Soviet Russia for the distribution of food and other goods. German and Austrian prisoners of war who had put themselves at the disposal of the Bolsheviks in 1918 formed the nucleus of Münzenberg's staff in Moscow. The city Soviet put a big, dilapidated office building at the disposal of the IAH. A Latvian, Alexander Vladimir Eiduck, became the representative of the Russian Government to the foreign aid organizations. In 1918 he had been an officer of the Kremlin Guard and had later joined the Cheka. His duties were to see that all aid contributions were immediately passed on to the famine areas. He was also to make sure that the representatives of the various foreign organizations could come and go without red tape. The ease with which the representatives of these aid organizations moved about in Russia is almost unimaginable today. The authorities placed storage and free transport at their disposal. They gave them every conceivable support. At the time Soviet Russia was an "open country" in which hundreds of representatives of bourgeois, trade union and Communist aid committees worked smoothly with an equally large number of local authorities, with the army and the police authorities. The suspicion that later became so typical of the Soviet Union had, if it existed at all at the time, given way to gratitude for the generous aid of the world.

Whereas the big charitable organizations fed anyone, IAH aid was from the outset distributed according to political and propagandist considerations. Together with the Russian trade unions and the local Soviets food distributions were made first to skilled workers in order to get production started again. Propagandawise, the many reports from the different parts of the famine area ensured that the eyes of the world were focused on Russia. In Kazan it was primarily forest and cottage workers who were supplied with monthly food parcels, in Orenburg it was leather, metal, textile and transport workers, and in Chelyabinsk it was miners and agricultural workers. A food parcel generally contained flour, groats, sugar, meat, fat, tinned milk, beans and cocoa.

In Zaryzin, later Stalingrad and today Volgagrad, the IAH took over a big fishery where 18,000 fishermen were so undernourished they could not work. Near Kazan and Chelyabinsk the IAH ran several farms, in Moscow it organized a shoe factory and an out-clinic and in Petrograd it took over a workshop for the maintenance of buildings. Those were only a few of the ventures of the IAH during the famine relief days.

Much time was devoted to relief work among Russian children, for whom it was naturally easiest to find foreign contributions in cash and kind. In the summer of 1922 the IAH had over a hundred children's homes in Russia, from the Ukraine to the Urals, some of which it ran itself, some of which it merely supplied with food. From June 1922 to May 1923 the IAH sent over three and one half thousand tons of food to Russia under the children's aid scheme.

Max Barthel, who had worked with Münzenberg since 1918, was responsible for the propaganda among artists and intellectuals. "We succeeded," he wrote, "in persuading a number of well-known artists and scientists to put their names to our appeals." These were people who, without being Communists, sympathized with the Soviets. Barthel continues:

> It was those who believed in the future, who were open to new ideas, who felt for the workers and the oppressed who were, without being conscious of it, drawn into the maelstrom of Russian propaganda.[1]

[1]Max Barthel, *Kein Bedarf an Weltgeschichte*, Wiesbaden 1950, p. 159.

In the famine relief campaign Münzenberg for the first time used the method that later played such an important part in his activities, to interest bourgeois intellectuals in the cause of Soviet Russia and exploit their views for propaganda purposes. He sent "uncommitted" writers to the famine areas and used their reports in his campaign in the Western countries. He asked Arthur Holitscher, Franz Jung and Martin Andersen-Nexö to visit the Volga region and write reports which he published. The illustrations which Käthe Kollwitz provided for some of these reports are among her most important works. In her poster "Hunger" an emaciated child with big eyes stretches out his hand for a bowl of food with a gesture of such unforgettable urgency that the poster has become a symbol of the misery of the innocent. Gabriele d'Annunzio, who at that time was beginning to flirt with Fascism, raised his voice in a wordy appeal and accused governments the world over of the thousandfold murder of the peasants of Russia.

During the anti-hunger campaign it became obvious that it was not enough to supply Russia with food and clothing. The Russian economy was in a catastrophic state, and industry, trade and agriculture were urgently in need of help. There was a shortage of tools, materials, and cash, as well as of experienced organizers. NEP helped alleviate this shortage by granting concessions to foreign firms to bring the necessary people and materials into the country. IAH was also used for this purpose. It now extended its activities to include economic aid as well as famine relief. The result was a confusing mixture of political propaganda and varied economic interests.

Max Barthel, the worker poet and IAH propagandist, expressed the new programme in verse:

> Hin durch das endlose Russland, hin nach
> Europa,
> die Losung im Rhythmus von stampfenden
> Kolben:
> Maschinen, Maschinen, Motore, Traktoren! . . .
> Arbeiter, Brüder, Weltveränderer!
> Gebt, gebt und helft, aufzubauen
> die grosse, klassenlose proletarische
> Gemeinschaft,
> aller Proleten rings auf der Erde! . . .[1]

---

[1] "Across endless Russia to Europe, the pounding pistons spell out the slogan: Machines, machines, engines, tractors . . . Workers, brothers, men who change the world! Give, give and help to build the great classless proletarian community of all proles of the world." Published in *Sowjetrussland im Bild*, Autumn 1921.

Soon gifts of tools, machines, lorries, tractors and other goods poured into Russia. The American trade union leader Hillman arrived with $250,000 for the reconstruction of the economy. Soviet authorities gave the IAH one concession after another, paying no attention to the fact that the machinery of this organization was small and lacking in expertise. They clearly regarded the organizational enthusiasm of the IAH workers and of their chief as sufficient. The IAH now gave up the big Tsarytsin fishery which Münzenberg later described as the "birthplace of productive economic aid." But it took over a far bigger fishery which worked thirty miles of the river near Astrakhan near the Caspian Sea. New trawlers were built, foreign trawling equipment introduced and stores set up. The fishing collective was one of the biggest in Soviet Russia. In 1923, under IAH direction, it caught about three and one-half thousand tons of fish.

The IAH took over workshops and small and large enterprises all over the country. In many places it set up schools for craftsmen. IAH workmen repaired dilapidated buildings, erected new houses and adapted industrial works to the requirements of the new age.

This economic activity inevitably brought to the fore opponents who during the months of hunger relief had remained relatively silent. In 1924 the ADGB (Allgemeine Deutsche Gewerkschaftsbund), the German Trade Union Federation, published a polemical pamphlet aimed at Münzenberg and the IAH under the title "The Third Column of Communist Policy—IAH. Based on authentic material."[1] Among other things this pamphlet contained excerpts from the protocols of an international review commission which had accompanied Münzenberg to Moscow in May and June 1922 to investigate the finances of the local IAH and its economic enterprises. Münzenberg later denied the authenticity of the published material but it obviously came from IAH workers or members of the Commission. The Commission found much to criticize in the methods of the Moscow branch. The greatest scandal was caused by a so-called *Ural AG* which had been set up by Franz Jung, with a big flourish in the Russian press, and which, contrary to instructions from Berlin, had seized all the tractors donated by the American Aid Committee, instead of distributing them to farms run by the IAH. The Review Commission was particularly indignant about the total lack of accounts. According to the protocols published in the ADGB pamphlet Münzenberg had said to the Commission:

We can submit documentary evidence of how we all, and I in particular, fought Jung and all these elements, of how I was threatened at gunpoint

[1] *Die Dritte Saüle* . . . , Berlin 1924, Verlagsgesellschaft des ADGB.

when I wished to inspect the accounts of the IAH in Moscow, of how Jung
wanted to have me arrested because my question to one of his employees
about the entering of transports in the books meant that I suspected his
management.[1]

According to the same source Paul Scholze, one of the members of
the Commission, added: "The accounts are in a terrible state, there is
no suggestion of a system." And Olga Kameneva, Trotsky's sister and
for many years an IAH worker in Moscow, had said: "There is no
accounting system in the Russian branch of the IAH. This is not restricted to the IAH but applies to Russia in general, otherwise Trotsky
would not have said at the last conference: 'The time has come to draw
up a balance sheet which we still do not have.' "[2]

The Commission's criticism referred primarily to plans of Franz Jung
who had announced the establishment in the Urals of a vast agricultural
enterprise with four hundred tractors to be centered on a modern city
of concrete. According to the ADGB pamphlet Münzenberg commented as follows to the commission on this venture which quickly
came to nought:

These incredible, fantastic plans were published in all Moscow papers and
in the bourgeois press. A poster was published announcing for example
that the tractors would arrive in St. Petersburg on 15 March etc., that on
18 March the foundation stone of the city of concrete would be laid. You
think I am joking. But these things were announced, the plan was submitted to Lenin personally and to the Supreme Council of the Workers
Defence and it was only postponed because of our last minute intervention. The affair created a big stir and preoccupied the public for months.
The party was directly involved through distinguished members of its
organization and now faced a big scandal. The joint stock company was
set up. Later it was discovered that in spite of scrutiny by two Commissions the land was unsuitable for the use of tractors.[3]

These seemingly authentic protocols give a slight insight into the
conditions prevailing in those early years of NEP in Soviet Russia. The
confused situation in the Moscow Office of the IAH only mirrored the
large picture that could be seen everywhere in the country. Soviet
Russia had become a playground for amateurs and ruffians. In some
respects it was possible to draw a parallel between the noisy activity,
the economic improvisations, the tendency to look for short term solu-
tions and the brilliant ruthlessness in business life, with conditions in

[1] *Die Dritte Säule*, p. 17.
[2] *Ibid.*, p. 17.
[3] *Ibid.*, p. 18.

California or Alaska at the beginning of the century. If Jung, in the best Wild West manner, stuck a gun under Münzenberg's nose to prevent him from examining the accounts, the gesture was absolutely in keeping with the time and the place. Another, fairly tough, IAH member in Moscow, Rogalla, who as a German prisoner of war had stayed on in Russia, summarized the prevailing mood in the phrase: "Life dictates the conditions." It was quite possible for great achievements to take place in such a climate. But there were also many failures that had serious consequences.

Münzenberg, the perfectionist of the organization, certainly did not like these haphazard methods. It is surprising that he succeeded, in spite of all the turbulence and confusion, unfamiliar as he was with the Russian language and in the last resort also with Russian customs, to get his way, to bring some order into the chaos and run the IAH's economic enterprises on Russian soil for years on a reasonably productive basis.

In the spring of 1922 his old friend Christiansen met him in Moscow. The Danes had sent a big consignment of dried milk which had got lost somewhere en route. Christiansen was surprised at the assurance with which Münzenberg arranged everything with the Russian authorities within a short space of time. He noticed how much Münzenberg had changed within the course of one year. His boundless idealism had given way to matter of factness tempered with a good deal of cynicism. Christiansen had the impression that Münzenberg was above all happy that there had been no break with the Russians.

Among the Berlin IAH staff was the journalist Max Wagner. Münzenberg knew him from the days of the Youth International. Wagner was working for a transport firm when Münzenberg offered him a job because he urgently needed someone to see to the technical matters connected with shipments and rail consignments. Münzenberg had not the faintest idea what a bill of lading was or what papers were needed to send goods by ship or rail. But he had an infallible eye for the person who had the knowledge, energy, and enthusiasm for such work. Wagner was constantly on the move between Hamburg, Stettin and Revel to get shipments moving.

Even then he thought of Münzenberg as the embodiment of the type of American entrepreneur who handles goods worth millions. At the end of January 1923, together with Münzenberg and two other IAH members, Wagner attended the KPD Congress in Leipzig. Upon their arrival in Leipzig Münzenberg immediately went to the biggest hotel in the city to reserve rooms for himself and the delegation. The other Communists were somewhat taken aback by this unproletarian behaviour.

As the IAH began to make its mark in Soviet Russia, Münzenberg's name became increasingly known to the Russian public. Several children's homes were named after him. A motorized fishing vessel on the Volga was named "Willi Münzenberg." The IAH, as represented by Münzenberg and his staff, was given the honorary command of a militia battalion in Petrograd. Finally Münzenberg was made an honorary member of the Petrograd Soviet.

It was above all Lenin's personal interest in the reconstruction work that popularized the IAH in Russia. In a letter to the Workers Aid Committee in the United States Lenin praised the great success achieved on the state farm of Tolkino near Perm by the tractor group composed of Americans under the leadership of Harold Ware. He proposed that Tolkino should be designated a model *sovkhoz*. The letter ends: "In the name of our Republic I express to you our profound gratitude. No help is of such great importance to us now as that given by you."[1] After Münzenberg had addressed the Fourth Comintern Congress on hunger relief and economic aid Lenin wrote him a personal letter on 2 December 1922 in which he said among other things:

> In addition to strong and continuous political pressure on the governments of the bourgeois countries for recognition of the Soviet Government, a broadly based campaign of economic aid by the proletariat of the world is today the best and most practical form of assistance rendered to Soviet Russia in its great economic struggle against imperialist concerns; it is also the best way of supporting the socialist reconstruction of its economy.[2]

By the end of 1922 the Soviet authorities had brought the famine under control and supplied the regions concerned with the necessary food and seed grain for the next harvest. Thus the activities of the foreign charitable organizations on Russian soil came to an end. The main share of the aid had come from the ARA. In all, this organization provided sixty-three million dollars worth of clothing, medicine and food, twenty million of which had been made available by the U.S. Congress.

There was a big gap between these sums and the ten million dollars worth of aid rendered by all the charitable organizations that combined forces under Nansen. Smaller still was the IAH contribution which amounted to about five million. The Soviet Government was fully conscious of the magnitude of the ARA assistance. On 10 July 1923 the Council of People's Commissars adopted a resolution warmly thanking

[1] From the Protocol of the IHA Conference of 20 November 1927, published by Willi Münzenberg, IAH Publishing House.
[2] Full text in Willi Münzenberg, *Solidarität*, p. 192 et seq.

Herbert Hoover and his colleagues in the name of the Russian people:

> Now that the famine is over and the colossal work of the ARA comes to
> a close, the Soviet of People's Commissars, in the name of the millions of
> people saved and in the name of all the working people of Soviet Russia
> and the Federalized Republics, counts it a duty to express before the
> whole world deepest thanks to this organization, to its leader, Herbert
> Hoover, to its representative in Russia, Colonel Haskell, and to all its
> workers and to declare that the people inhabiting the Union of Soviet
> Socialist Republics will never forget the help given them by the American
> people, through ARA, seeing in it a pledge of the future friendship be-
> tween the two nations.[1]

The situation was different in the sphere of political propaganda.
There the achievements of the ARA were minimized from the start and
gradually relegated to limbo. As early as October 1921 Trotsky wrote
that the charitable organizations were only giving aid so that trade with
Russia could be resumed.[2] While Eiduck, in his report on hunger relief,
described the activities of all relief organizations the officials responsible for political propaganda sought to make the workers forget bourgeois aid contributions. Olga Kameneva, for instance, wrote in her
report "The International Proletariat and its Aid to Soviet Russia,"
published by the IAH publishing house in 1923:

> The aid of the bourgeoisie was limited, its efforts to save the starving
> millions were small, even minute compared with the assistance rendered
> by the international proletariat. The bourgeoisie saw in the hunger in
> Russia its ally.

And Münzenberg went so far as to claim some years later:

> The capitalist world did almost nothing to help. The only assistance which
> could come from abroad was the assistance of the world proletariat which
> admired the Soviet Republic.[3]

3. Münzenberg Enlists Support for Russia's Economic Reconstruction

To put the IAH's extensive transactions on a commercial basis Münzenberg in 1922 founded a company, *Aufbau, Industrie & Handels AG*,

---

[1] Full text in Eudin and Fisher, *Soviet Russia and the West*, p. 75.
[2] Russian Correspondence [published by the Comintern, with no place of publication], No.
7/9, 1921.
[3] *Fünf Jahre Internationale Arbeiterhilfe*, [IAH] Berlin 1926, p. 5.

in Berlin. The company began by buying up German film licences for Russia. Success was immediate. Almost all German films then on the market were brought to Russia. The company was set up by the Executive Committee of the IAH. It is worthy of note that on this occasion a ruling was adopted that later held good for all companies set up by Münzenberg or other Communists, namely that shareholders, directors and members of the board were not entitled to remuneration from the profits of the company.

Meanwhile Münzenberg had embarked upon a much more daring venture. Encouraged by Russian and American friends he had drawn up a plan for floating an international workers' loan. The scheme had been agreed to by the IAH Executive Committee on 22 August 1922 and approved by the Council of People's Commissars in Moscow on 13 September. The *Aufbau, Industrie & Handels AG* would issue abroad —and only in convertible currency, thereby in practice excluding workers in Germany which was in the middle of an inflation—bonds to a total of one million dollars at five per cent interest. The repayment date was fixed for 1 January 1933. The Soviet Government guaranteed interest and repayment. The Guarantee and Credit Bank for the East, just established in Berlin, would underwrite up to eighty per cent of the loan as representative of the Russian State Bank. About this new, unusual way of making propaganda and for giving help to Soviet Russia Münzenberg wrote:

> Who should subscribe to the workers' loan?
> The answer is clear: the workers of all countries and of all parties. Because it is in their interest that capitalism does not reappear unaided in Soviet Russia. They all will one day overthrow their own capitalists and then it will be of the greatest importance that Soviet Russia shall have a capable agricultural system that can supply them with bread. Those who subscribe to the workers' loan contribute to the liberation of the working class of all countries.
> How do you subscribe to the workers' loan?
> Payments are accepted in the currency of any country and can upon request be transferred into dollars. There are 1.5 and 10 dollar shares, 1,000, 5,000 and 10,000 mark shares, 10, 50 and 1000 franc shares etc.
> Above all trade unions, co-operatives, sickness funds etc. must subscribe to make the economic aid a real venture of the whole working class. It is the duty of every militant worker to propose at meetings of his organization that it should take up one or more shares of the workers' loan.[1]

With great enthusiasm and with the assistance of a bank official, Henry Meyer, an original member of the Spartacist group, the bonds

[1] *Bruder hilf! Aufruf an die Arbeiter und Werktätigen aller Länder zur Zeichnung der 1. Arbeiteranleihe für Sowjetrussland.* Berlin 1922, p. 20.

and dividend warrants were printed in units of what were then convertible currency, and handed over to the IAH sections for sale. Then suddenly the head of the State Bank of Russia, Scheinman, and his Swedish adviser, Olof Aschberg, panicked; they feared that a loan issued so obviously for purposes of political propaganda might put a great strain on the foreign branches which they were just then setting up, and on their commercial relations with the outside world in general. After long and heated negotiations in Moscow, and not without Lenin's occasional intervention, the State Bank went back on its original commitment to promote the loan, so that Münzenberg's assumption that co-operatives, Socialist city administrations and other public bodies would subscribe did not materialize. But neither did the gloomy predictions of the Social Democratic press—that the workers' loan would be a certain failure and that the Russians would never redeem it. In the winter of 1932/33 the Berlin Guarantee and Credit Bank for the East set up a department to deal with the settlement of the loan. This office continued to function even after Hitler came to power. It enjoyed extra-territorial status and carried out the redemption of the loan with interest in an orderly fashion.

Olof Aschberg wrote in 1947 in his reminiscences on the fate of the international workers' loan:[1]

> The plan could never be implemented because it proved impossible to achieve a collaboration between the Social Democrats and the Communists.

This was false. The plan did not fail, and the reason why it was not the success that Münzenberg had anticipated has already been given. Aschberg's share in the decision of the State Bank of Russia to back out of the loan venture did not, however, affect the friendly relationship between him and Münzenberg which continued up to the death of the latter.

In many ways the Swedish financier was an unusual person. He was born in Stockholm in 1877, the son of a Russian Jewish immigrant who had worked his way up to a position of shop-owner. Olof's extraordinary talent for finance revealed itself early. When Münzenberg came to Stockholm in 1917 for the International Youth Conference Aschberg, whom he then met for the first time, was already a successful banker and businessman who had founded the first Swedish bank for trade unions and co-operatives (NYA-Banken) in Stockholm in 1912. At the time he was in close touch with leading Social Democratic politicians.

[1] Olof Aschberg, *Aterkomst*, Vol. 2, Stockholm 1947, p. 48.

One of his most intimate friends was the Swedish Prime Minister, Hjalmar Branting.

In the summer of 1917 Aschberg paid his first visit to Petrograd to establish contacts with the provisional government. He suggested to the Russians that a "freedom loan" should be raised in the *Entente* states. The Swedish Government agreed and immediately subscribed two million roubles through NYA-Banken.

In Stockholm he was appointed Economic Adviser to the Second International Conference which never took place. A few days after the October Revolution he was again on his way to Petrograd to keep an eye on the Russian interests of his bank. He found the leading Bolsheviks as enthusiastic and confident about the future as he was himself. When the left wing Socialists held a mass meeting to dispel some of the wild rumours about the crimes of the Bolsheviks, Aschberg was among the speakers for the defence. He thereby incurred the displeasure of Stockholm society. He was called a traitor and accused of siding with the Bolsheviks merely for reasons of greed. The NYA-Banken were immediately put on the black list of the *Entente* countries and soon also on those of the central powers. Britain and the United States blocked the bank's assets. Hjalmar Branting tried to intervene but the foreign powers refused to lift the boycott unless Aschberg left the bank's board. He left the board, sold his shares and devoted himself exclusively to his business with Soviet Russia.

In 1918 he was once more in Petrograd, participated at the historic dissolution of the Constituent Assembly and held extensive discussions with the Bolsheviks' economic experts Bronski, Piatakov, Emenshinski, whom to his surprise he found to be less expert than very inexperienced economists. When Bronski told Aschberg that a decree had been promulgated cancelling all Russian debts abroad, Aschberg pointed out that with this irresponsible step the Bolsheviks would ruin their credit in the world. Bronski thanked him for the warning by bursting into laughter.

In 1919 Aschberg, together with the recently established Soviet Agency, began to sell Russian gold on the Stockholm market. The international boycott to which Russian gold was officially subject was avoided by melting down the ingots and giving them the markings of the respective purchasing countries.

Trade between Aschberg and the Soviet Government was greatly stimulated by Lenin's declaration of NEP. The People's Commissar for Finance, Sokolnikov, re-organized the State Bank, made Aschberg's friend Scheinman president and stabilized the Russian currency. New monetary units, *chervonets*, were put into circulation, twenty-five per cent of the new issue being covered by gold. The Commercial Bank of Russia was set up for foreign trade; it occupied luxurious offices in the centre of Moscow. Tarnovski, the former head of the Bank of Siberia in

Petrograd, was made its president and Olof Aschberg became chairman of the board. As early as 1920 Aschberg had opened offices in Berlin and Copenhagen which now also handled Russian financial transactions. The Berlin office was shortly afterwards transformed into the Guarantee and Credit Bank for the East.

Aschberg's villa in Dahlem soon became a political and social centre but he did not by any means confine himself to contact with Russians, or with Germans who were in close touch with the Russians. In spite of his involvement in the Soviet Russian economy he continued to have close links with Social Democrats, particularly in Sweden. His German friends included Karl Legien and other trade union leaders.

The workers' loan had not been going long when I, purely by accident, first called at the Berlin offices of the IAH in the late autumn of 1922. Henry Meyer, who was desperately looking for an assistant to bring a little order into the general chaos, immediately put me to work writing letters to foreign IAH sections and sorting loan certificates by currencies. Little did I know at the time that the kindness that I was rendering the long-suffering Henry Meyer would end up in a collaboration lasting many years.

Münzenberg was absent at the time; it was said that he was in Moscow. The IAH offices were situated in an old building in Unter den Linden, in a flat which had once belonged to the Russian Red Cross and later to the Soviet embassy. Meanwhile the old Tzarist Embassy had been given back to the Russians who handed over their office to Münzenberg. The place was a beehive. A constant stream of foreign visitors passed through the offices. One office housed the editorial staff of the illustrated paper *Hammer and Sickle*, in another a young girl from Leipzig was in charge of the section for aid to Russian children. In the old conservatory, a draughty glass box, the wife of the expressionist dramatist Reinhart Göring was bashing away at a typewriter; she was Russian and translated into German all incoming letters and telegrams, as well as captions on pictures and articles for various publications. A few rooms further along there were the unclassified archives with thousands of photographs of the hunger regions, of revolution and civil war in Russia and of the manifold activities of the IAH. Mountains of postcards were sent from there to all over the world.

Soon after the start of my temporary employment Münzenberg returned from his trip. His impending arrival created an air of nervousness and the staff worked even harder than before. Münzenberg passed through the offices, occasionally saying a word of welcome and casting a quick glance at the staff. Seeing a strange face, he stopped at my table. Henry Meyer introduced me but Münzenberg remained absent-minded and worried because the workers' loan seemed to produce ever more complicated problems.

We were paid in dollars, between two and three dollars a week, which we changed in the Friedrichstrasse at the rate of the day. In those days we were in close touch with the neighbouring Russian Embassy. All IAH employees were allowed to use the Embassy canteen which was in one of the splendid rooms in a wing of the building.

The Russian staff at that time still lived in a style reminiscent of the early days of the revolution. The Ambassador, Krestinski, and the Consul, Brodovski, and their families, secretaries and typists, messengers and porters, and we "outsiders" from the IAH all met for our midday meal in the same dining-room, and ate the same food, simple but substantial traditional Russian fare which seemed princely indeed to us Germans who for years had subsisted on what we got from the U.S. food kitchens. Outside the office, differences of rank were kept to a minimum. All were comrades.

Krestinski was a quiet, thoughtful man, a "revolutionary idealist" as Alexander Barmine called him, "to whom power and prestige made no difference either in manner or in loyalty. He served the party and the revolution with a pure devotion up to his death."[1] Münzenberg was very friendly with him and was admitted at any hour if an urgent problem was involved.

The top floor of one of the wings was occupied by a man who was very important to the smooth running of Münzenberg's varied activities, Mirov-Abramov, the representative of the Russian *apparat,* officially then Third Secretary at the Embassy. Through his hands passed all the threads of the conspiratorial activities of both the Narkomindel and the Comintern. In the days of the Weimar Republic the extraterritorial rights of foreign representatives, including those of Soviet Russia, were sacred and Mirov could therefore pursue his activities from the Embassy for many years. A stocky bespectacled man, always polite and with excellent manners, Mirov was the right man if Münzenberg needed to consult Moscow by telegram, if he required a visa, or if he had other urgent technical or organizational problems. Before the First World War, Mirov had studied in Germany and then lived for a time in Brandenburg on the Havel. Since that period he had been sympathetic towards all things German and he had tremendous respect for the organizational genius of the Germans. He was married to a young Russian Jewess, Lola, whose parents had been driven to Berlin by the revolution.

Ruth Fischer has said in *Stalin und der deutsche Kommunismus* that after 1921 Münzenberg withdrew from Party activity, that he no longer took part in the various forms of in-fighting, and that he already had one foot outside the Party camp.[2] The facts were somewhat different. After

[1]Alexander Barmine, *One Who Survived,* New York 1946, p. 156.
[2]Ruth Fischer, *Stalin und der deutsche Kommunismus,* Frankfurt am Main, 1948, p. 744.

the expulsion of Paul Levi and his group the KPD remained until 1923 in the hands of the so-called "Right." The Party leader, Ernst Meyer, and his successor, Heinrich Brandler, allowed Münzenberg to go his own way because, in spite of past differences of opinion, they regarded him as one of their group.

As early as 1920, Paul Levi, in a speech to the Reichstag, had advocated closer links between the Weimar Republic and Soviet Russia. These efforts were intensified in 1922 when the Soviet Government began to abandon its isolationist foreign policy. At that time Radek was negotiating with Seeckt about more intensive co-operation between the Reichswehr and the Red Army. The Moscow Comintern leadership therefore insisted that efforts should be made within the national parties to establish a united front "from above," i.e. to seek contacts and collaboration between the leaders of the Communist and the Socialist Parties as well as the trade unions. As part of this united front policy the Comintern suggested a joint meeting with representatives of the Second International and of Friedrich Adler's International, a meeting which was in fact held from 2 to 6 April 1922 in Berlin. This was the eve of the conference of Genoa and it was important to the Soviet Government that the Socialist and Communist Internationals should exert joint pressure in the Soviet interest during their negotiations with the Western powers. The Russian delegation under Karl Radek proposed that a proletarian world congress should be convened but the proposal met with no response because the Socialists were not prepared to render as much political assistance as that. On the contrary, both Emil Vandervelde and Ramsay MacDonald demanded that before there could be any joint action the Soviet Government must withdraw its military forces from Georgia. (In February 1921 the Menshevik Government in Georgia had forcibly been deposed by the Bolsheviks.)

The Committee of Nine, established at the Berlin Conference, gave up the ghost in the summer when a trial of social revolutionaries was staged in Moscow ending with death sentences for fourteen of the forty-seven accused. In his eagerness to achieve united action, Radek went so far as to give way to the protests of the reformists and promise that the Socialist lawyers, Vandervelde, Kurt Rosenfeld and Theodor Liebknecht, would be officially allowed to defend the accused. But he had not consulted Lenin who promptly disowned his overzealous emissary, Radek. Without having even seen the accused, the Socialist lawyers were sent home again. In his article "We have Paid too Much,"[1] Lenin crossed his t's and dotted his i's in rebuking Radek. However, the accused were not executed.

[1] *Pravda*, 11 April 1922.

But more important than the ultimate failure of the Berlin Conference is the fact that the Socialists were sufficiently bent on collaborating to join in an appeal on behalf of Soviet Russia: "For the Russian revolution and for the establishment of political and economic contacts of all states with Soviet Russia" and "for the establishment of a united proletarian front in every country and in the International."[1] This pro-Russian mood among the Socialists greatly helped Münzenberg's activities. In April 1922 the two "war cripples," Russia and Germany, met in Rapallo and sealed their rapprochement with a treaty. It was this rapprochement that carried Münzenberg along. With his ability as an organizer, with his talent as a propagandist, he promoted the cause of Soviet Russia among the German middle class.

He developed the required technique to a fine art and gave as much proof of this in the intimate circle of Communist IAH officials as of his passionate commitment to the Communist cause. The ADGB pamphlet for 1924, already quoted several times, reproduced lengthy statements which Münzenberg had made to the IAH Committee in connection with the international conference which he was preparing for July 1923 in Berlin. They give an excellent picture, even if perhaps not accurate in every detail, of the resources and ingenuity of Münzenberg the propagandist:

Nansen and British and German Quaker representatives are expected for the conference. It is also possible that several Red Cross organizations will be represented, from Germany, Czechoslovakia and possibly also from France. It is interesting that the Red Cross from Fascist Italy has sent a letter of good wishes to the congress. In addition there will be about 80 representatives from German industry, engineers, industrialists, scientists, artists, writers and journalists, people connected with the 'Friends of the New Russia' club. Representatives of various trade union groups and two members of the Italian Socialist Party who at their last Party Congress were critical of the Soviet Union will also be there. As you can see it will be a motley gathering. Only speakers previously agreed upon will be allowed to take the floor; all political discussion must be avoided. The affair must end with the adoption of a resolution expressing willingness to collaborate in the rebuilding of Russia. The objective at the World Congress must be to encourage the businessmen who attend to return to their firms eager to advocate the cause of Soviet Russia. But we must do everything to see that the Conference finishes on the same day because otherwise it would break up on Monday. We have further decided that Comrade Aussem, the Ukrainian representative for Berlin, shall organize a five o'clock tea on Monday afternoon for the IAH people and those congress members who belong to workers' organizations. . . . If *we* invite

[1]Julius Braunthal, *Geschichte der Internationale*, Vol. 2, Hanover 1963, p. 268.

them this immediately becomes a party issue but if the invitation comes from someone else the matter takes on a different complexion. It will be easier to arrange a united front at the Kronprinzen-Ufer in the old Embassy building over a cosy cup of tea than yesterday in Friedrich-shain.[1] The whole affair must end with a bluff.[2]

According the the same source Münzenberg said to IAH officials some time after the conference:

We exist basically to make large-scale propaganda for Soviet Russia. In countries where the revolutionary political struggle is of less importance, [as] in America, our IAH committees will temporarily have to take charge of establishing the Communist Party. When I was in Holland I saw rallies being held in cities where there have been no Communist meetings for years. It has become possible for us to set up propaganda centres for the IAH almost everywhere in the world. I know of no other international workers' organization whose complicated, many-sided tasks range from political propaganda, parliamentary intervention, the winning over of bourgeois circles, the establishment of committees, the organization of children's aid, cinematic work, business transactions down to the sale of herrings, matches and paraffin, propaganda for the workers' loan, and the establishment of an organization that has laid the foundation stone for systematic work in the future. . . .

You know that since it has become convinced that the revolution is slowing down, the Communist International is in search of a broader basis in form of a united front. Here the IAH can take steps which the political parties cannot take.

Recent events in America have shown that the police will take action against us. Therefore we must avoid being a purely Communist organiza-tion. Now especially we must bring in other names, other groups, to make persecution more difficult. The question of the New Russia Clubs is par-ticularly important in this context. To me personally they are of no great interest; indeed it is not very exciting to set up "Clubs of Harmless Peo-ple." Let us have no illusions about the importance of these clubs. But it is a question of penetrating the broadest sections of the population, of gaining the support of artists and professors, of using the theatre and the cinema and of stressing everywhere that Russia abandons everything, that Russia humbles herself, that Russia is doing everything to preserve world peace. We ourselves must join these clubs. We know, of course, that we cannot persuade some comrades of the Berlin organization to join. One can hardly expect Ruth Fischer and Maslow to set up such clubs. I personally also prefer the Red Hundreds. It is important to penetrate the other press, the trade union press, the bourgeois press. It is obvious that the IAH which is not only mixed up with these clubs but actually founded

[1] Reference to disputes between Communist and non-Communist workers.
[2] *Die Dritte Säule*, p. 13.

them seeks to use them to establish contacts between a wide range of bourgeois elements and Russia. This is of more use to us than constantly reading in the Communist press how well off Russia is.

If we look at the world conference which was convened by us we note with satisfaction that it ended with the adoption of a resolution. It was a conference in which the greatest successes were achieved in the very field where we must henceforth intensify our efforts and we must capture the intellectuals who sympathize with Russia. A commission has been set up which includes among others *Fimmen, Peus, Aussem, Frey* and *Paquet*. It must continue to promote cultural activities . . .[1]

Münzenberg attended the Fourth World Congress of the Comintern, which met in Petrograd and Moscow from 5 November to 5 December, 1923 as an advisory delegate of the IAH. Lenin's illness overshadowed the congress. In May of the same year, suffering from severe arterial sclerosis, he had had his first stroke. By October he had recovered sufficiently to begin work again. But it was a weary, aged Lenin who addressed the delegates of the Fourth World Congress to prove to them the need for the introduction of NEP. His speech ended with the statement that the most important task in the period that lay ahead was to learn, because only through knowledge could the revolutionary work be really understood.

The other speakers dealt with a very concrete topic: the Rapallo treaty needed theoretical justification so that left-wing Communists especially could accept this pact with a bourgeois government. The members of the KPD had voiced their disapproval in unmistakable terms. Bukharin defended the treaty. He argued that there was no difference between a loan and a military alliance with bourgeois states:

> And I maintain that we have grown up sufficiently to conclude a military alliance with a bourgeois country so as to crush another middle class with the help of this bourgeois state.

He added that it was always possible to exploit any alliance, that this was merely a strategic or tactical expediency. It was the duty of the Communists of that country to ensure the victory of that bloc.[2]

Münzenberg's speech was an account of what had been achieved and a survey of what the IAH hoped to achieve in the future. Now that the famine was practically over the need for hunger relief was coming to an end and it was being replaced by aid for the reconstruction of Soviet Russia's economy. He said that IAH, through its work in Japan and the

[1] *Die Dritte Säule*, pp. 12 and 24.
[2] Protocol of the Fourth Congress of the Communist International, Hamburg 1923, p. 420.

United States, had succeeded in advancing the cause of Communism.
He disagreed with his critics. The chairman of the KPD, Ernst Meyer,
had demanded the immediate termination of famine relief because it
focussed world attention on the famine thereby bringing "the revolution into discredit." Zinoviev too had noted that the Second International had tried, not without success, to make the famine the starting
point of an anti-Comintern campaign. There was something in what
those critics said. Bourgeois and Socialists of all shades, most persistently
the Mensheviks, pointed a warning finger at the millions of victims and
said: "There you see the result of the revolution: Want, death and
destruction."

4. 1923—A Fateful Year for the Weimar Republic

It began with the occupation of the Ruhr. Germany had fallen into
arrears with reparation payments imposed upon it under the Versailles
Treaty, above all with deliveries of coal and wood to France and Belgium. Therefore, on 13 January French and Belgium troops occupied
the Ruhr. The Cuno Government recommended passive resistance, a
proposal which only the KPD initially opposed in the Reichstag. All
production on the Rhine and in the Ruhr came to a stop and the
German currency finally collapsed completely so that by the late summer of 1923 one dollar was worth between two and three hundred
million marks.

At the KPD Party Congress which met in Leipzig from 20 January
to 1 February, there was little mention of the occupation of the Ruhr
and its political significance. The Russian press on the other hand was
quick to react. On 8 February, Bukharin wrote in *Izvestia* that "a
worsening of the situation is of advantage to the proletariat because the
restoration and consolidation of the capitalist order in Western Europe
presents a threat to us." Thereupon Losovski, the Secretary of the
Communist Trade Union International, commented in *Pravda* that
what neither the Comintern nor the Red Trade Union International
had accomplished was being achieved by Poincaré and Lord Curzon.
Each fresh conflict opened the eyes of new hundreds of thousands of
proletarians.

Before long there were strikes and clashes in the Ruhr because food
was getting short. Now it was the Russians' turn to participate in relief
work by sending supplies to the Ruhr. *Rote Fahne* of 20 March 1923
announced under the heading "Solidarity" that the All Russian Trade
Union Association was sending flour for 375 thousand tons of bread to

the struggling Ruhr workers in return for the assistance which they had rendered during the great Russian famine. The distribution of the first Russian consignment of flour was carried out by the IAH and a Reich Committee of Works Councils and Consumer Co-operatives.

Max Wagner went to Hamburg and Bremen to take charge of the Russian shipments. Customs and shipping firm officials watched as the Ukrainian wheat, whose quality they admired unreservedly, was transferred from the ships to the goods trains. At the time there were some among the otherwise very bourgeois citizens of the Hanseatic cities who flirted with Russia which they regarded less as the "Soviet" state than as the "great empire in the East." At any rate the Hanseatic senates, police and customs officials welcomed the Russian initiative out of genuine, if not openly expressed, sympathy for Russia.

The Reich authorities and the local authorities in the Ruhr were less happy. Soviet trade union representatives accompanied the grain transports and made propaganda speeches. The authorities vigorously protested these "Bolshevization attempts." There was an exchange of letters between the Foreign Office and the German Ambassador in Moscow to whom Radek had complained that German authorities were obstructing the Russian relief campaign. Finally the Foreign Office, in spite of protests from the Prussian police, agreed to the continued distribution of aid in the Ruhr on the grounds that the Russians had so unequivocally taken a stand against Poincaré.

At the Leipzig Party Congress, Münzenberg was elected for the first time to the Central Executive of the KPD, the future Central Committee. On 17 March an international "Conference for the United Front and Against Fascism", took place at Frankfurt am Main, which Münzenberg attended. The foreign parties were invited to express themselves against the occupation of the Ruhr. This put the French Communists in a difficult position— Moscow was demanding they oppose the anti-German sentiment of their own people. For example, Albert Vassart, a young French Communist and one of Münzenberg's friends, was asked to put up posters in the Ardennes—in places which had been completely destroyed by German troops during the war—proclaiming: "Oppose the war-monger Poincaré, help the German revolution." The angry population nearly lynched the Communists.

In spite of the rapidly growing crisis the leaders of the Bolshevik Party displayed considerable restraint. In an interview[1] with *The Manchester Guardian* correspondent, Arthur Ransome, Trotsky admitted that although the Soviet Government was interested in a victory of the working classes in Germany it was not in its interest that revolution

[1] *Die Rote Fahne*, 10 March 1923.

should break out in an already weakened Europe. The bourgeoisie could then bequeathe the proletariat nothing but ruins, as had been the inheritance of the Bolsheviks when they took power.

After his election to the Central Executive, Münzenberg took more part than before in the political work of the KPD. He made a number of public speeches on topical political questions, for example on 31 May in Berlin on: "The Struggle in the Ruhr. Who are the Traitors?" The question shows that the KPD was no longer exclusively concerned with the struggle against the growing misery and with the radicalization of the proletarian masses, but that it obviously thought it necessary to join issue with the nationalistic propaganda as practised by the Right. Why not a common front with the nationalists against France? Radek had no scruples and seemed to see advantages in this idea. He expounded his views to the enlarged Comintern Executive on 21 June and on 10 July wrote his famous Schlageter article in *Rote Fahne.*

On 6 September, Jules Humbert-Droz wrote a confidential letter to Zinoviev complaining that the nationalistic line of the German party made the work of the French Communist Party considerably more difficult and lessened the sympathies of the French workers for the German revolution. A state of confusion would result if the impression was created that the German revolution accepted nationalist and revanchist elements. Humbert-Droz demanded that Karl Radek explain this problematic new line in the French Communist press.[1]

The German party members viewed Radek's *volte-face* with suspicion or open hostility while the party intellectuals winked knowingly at each other and saw the whole thing as one of Radek's tactical manoeuvres to promote Communism among the German nationalists. Radek had recognized quickly that the majority of the nationalist minded masses was drawn less towards the capitalist camp than towards the Socialist camp—a realization shared by a then insignificant man named Hitler. Years later Gregor Strasser described National Socialism as "the great anti-capitalist longing of the masses."

Indeed at no time before or after was there more sympathy and concern for Communism among the German lower middle classes. In Berlin and in other big cities there was a curious feeling, as though the population expected the Communists to radically change an untenable situation. But even then it was doubtful whether German lower middle class sympathy for Communism went so far as to include its real goal, revolutionary upheaval. In contrast to the radicals among the party leaders, the group around Ruth Fischer and Arkadi Maslow, Münzenberg was by no means one of those who believed that the most favoura-

---

[1] J. Humbert-Droz, *L'Oeil de Moscou à Paris,* Paris 1964, p. 193 *et seq.*

ble moment for revolutionary action had come. He took a very sceptical view of the situation in the summer of 1923 and was convinced that even if there was a military coup the SPD would side with Seeckt and the Minister of Defence, Gessler, rather than with the KPD.

On 24 June 1922, the day after the murder of the architect of the Rapallo Treaty, Walther Rathenau, the party began to set up an *Ordnerdienst* originally designed to protect Communist meetings and demonstrations. In case the party was prohibited this system would continue and maintain the link between the members and the leadership. After Rathenau's murder, young Communist members of the IAH kept their guns in the IAH Berlin office. During 1923 young party comrades everywhere were ranged in groups of five. The strictest laws of conspiracy applied: each member of the group knew only one trusted comrade, the man who had set up the group, and one member of the neighbouring group of five.

As the wave of strikes and hunger demonstrations grew party members became very anxious. They all thought that the moment for action had come. The Communist youth of Berlin went to the Märkische Schweiz for rifle practice. But there was no organized preparation for the struggle. The general mood was one of revolutionary romanticism combined with the fervent hope that a general strike would suffice to bring the party to power. After all the general strike had proved most effective during the Kapp putsch.

In June the party organ *Die Rote Fahne* began to publish articles on civil war, and guerilla fighting tactics, and eye-witness accounts of the revolution and civil war in Russia. But the Russian party leaders advised caution. They remembered only too well the fiasco of March 1921 and warned against individual action. But when the Cuno Government resigned on 12 August the attitude of the Russians changed overnight. The SPD had withdrawn its support from the Cuno Government because of its attitude towards the worker governments in Saxony and Thuringia. Cuno was replaced by Stresemann who succeeded in forming a strong coalition. The Russians feared that Stresemann would come to terms with the Western powers. This must markedly diminish Russian influence in Germany and might lead to an improvement of the seemingly hopeless economic situation. On 26 September Stresemann put an end to the passive resistance in the Ruhr. At the same time an emergency law was adopted transferring the executive power in the Reich to the Minister of Defence, Gessler. Gessler in turn transferred the Executive power to the Reichswehr generals of the Army Corps District Commands who were told to use these powers if circumstances demanded.

The government's main concern was to break up the so-called Red

Hundreds, the proletarian defence organization which had been set up in Thuringia and Saxony, for the KPD had started planning some time before for the possibility of an uprising and thus an armed conflict with the *Freikorps* and also with the police and the Reichswehr. The party had appointed military leaders in rural districts. For example, an IAH worker was one of the three military leaders in the Berlin-Mitte district. The comrades there had some small arms and one machine gun which they carried about well concealed from one hideout to another so that it would not fall into the hands of the police. One of the military leaders of this district, a former artillery officer, had prepared a map showing all police stations and other important buildings. When the police eventually found this map they thought that it was the work of a Russian expert.

As early as March 1923 the Russians had in fact sent military experts to Germany so that their experience could be put at the disposal of those who might be preparing an armed uprising. Walter G. Krivitsky, a high ranking officer in the Soviet Intelligence Service, says in his memoirs that he and five or six other Russian officers were ordered to Germany where they began to train Communist fighting units in the vicinity of the Ruhr. The Russian experts prepared lists of all Communists who had fought in the war and gave them assignments for which their training qualified them. The existing *Ordnerdienst* was used, under the direction of Section IV of the Red Army, to establish military units which would form the nucleus of a future army.[1]

Meanwhile the members of the Comintern could not agree on whether the time had really come "to make a move" in Germany. The arguments went on during July and August. In September the Comintern decided to send its most experienced men to Berlin—Bukharin, Radek and Piatakov.

But the bourgeois parties and the Stresemann government acted quicker than the Communists. When a general strike was proclaimed in the Ruhr on 27 September, one day after the end of passive resistance, Stresemann managed to contain the big movement of strikes and revolts by setting up a *Rentenbank* and announcing that a new currency, the so-called *Rentenmark*, would be issued shortly and that this would end inflation. The general strike was stopped on 1 October. The situation in the Ruhr began to stabilize itself although serious clashes and looting continued to occur because unemployment had increased rapidly, rising from four per cent in January 1923 to about forty per cent by December.

In September, Münzenberg visited Russia. In the Kremlin he met

[1] Walter G. Krivitsky, *I Was Stalin's Agent*, New York and London 1939, p. 55 *et seq.*

leading representatives of the Soviet trade unions. A tragic earthquake had occurred in Japan on 1 September 1923 and the Japanese trade unions had approached the IAH for help. Jointly with the Russians Münzenberg raised a considerable sum of money and sent relief ships to Japan. But the Japanese refused to allow the ships to enter their ports, being convinced that they would bring not only flour but Communist propaganda material as well. Only the understanding attitude of Prefect Aumuro finally made it possible for part of the gifts to be unloaded on Japan's northernmost island, Hokkaido.

But more important than the Japanese earthquake was the "revolutionary situation" in Germany. The Russians, who were convinced that the clashes which had started in Saxony and Thuringia would spread, feared that the struggling workers would be cut off from the outside world and that their fighting efficiency would be impaired by a lack of food. They therefore arranged with Münzenberg to send food to Saxony and Thuringia through the IAH. During October several shiploads arrived, were transferred onto trains and sent to Saxony. The police, claiming that while searching the goods trains they had found hidden weapons, arrested the transport leaders and searched the Berlin office of the IAH. But nothing serious came of the incident.

The Chairman of the KPD, Heinrich Brandler, who had spent some weeks in Moscow in September, had been present at the heated discussions on the character of the "workers government" and on the desirability of the Communists joining it. Finally, in spite of Brandler's opposition, it was decided that the Communists should join the governments of Saxony and Thuringia. On 10 October Heinrich Brandler, Fritz Heckert and Paul Böttcher became members of the government of Saxony and on 16 October Karl Korsch, Theo Neubauer and Albin Tenner joined the Thuringian government. The fact that there were Communists in the government and that the training of the proletarian Red Hundreds now took place openly was a welcome excuse for the district commander, General Müller, to threaten to depose the government of Saxony.

Münzenberg meanwhile had also gone to Dresden to supervise the distribution of Russian grain and to discuss with the Saxon government the question of supplying machinery to Soviet Russia. At the suggestion of the ECCI the leaders of the Communist Party had also made their way to Saxony. Although the Russian military leader for Germany, General Skoblevsky-Gorev, had warned against any uprising because of shortage of arms, and although a responsible member of the Comintern delegation sent to Berlin had advised against it, the Party leadership decided to risk the attempt. On 20 October, Brandler's call for a revolt was published in *Rote Fahne*. A councils conference was called for 21

October at Chemnitz, ostensibly to popularize Russian grain transports in Saxony, but in reality to submit a draft resolution to this body demanding a general strike and armed resistance against the Reichswehr. The draft resolution was rejected by the overwhelming majority of delegates. Thereupon the KPD leadership decided to drop its plans for an uprising—not only in Saxony but also in other parts of Germany. On 22 October the Reichswehr marched into Dresden, declared the government deposed and banned the Communist Party in Saxony. A banner headline in *Berliner Nachtausgabe* announced: "General Müller Establishes Order in Saxony." But in spite of the Chemnitz decision there was an abortive rising in Hamburg immediately afterwards.

On 21 October 1923 the political head of the Hamburg KPD, Hugo Urbahns, together with two shop stewards, went to Chemnitz to attend the conference of the works councils. When they arrived in Chemnitz in the evening, the conference had already finished. Urbahns sent one of the shop stewards straight back to Hamburg and travelled himself via Berlin to Hamburg where he arrived on the evening of 22 October. He made straight for his home and went to bed, behavior which makes it seem unlikely that he returned with an order for an uprising. On 23 October at about 5 A.M. an attack began, under the military leadership of Hans Kippenberger, on the police barracks in the districts of Barmbeck, Winterhude and Uhlenhorst. A few hours later Urbahns informed the illegal Hamburg party leadership of the central committee's decision not to attempt a rising. But it was 5 o'clock in the afternoon before the signal to withdraw reached the Barmbeck contingent. In a superbly planned retreat Kippenberger led his men out of the area surrounded by the police with practically no losses.[1]

After these set-backs the disaster was not long in coming. On 23 November the Communist Party was banned, together with all its organizations.

[1]This description is based mainly on oral information provided by Heinrich Brandler. He disputes above all that the so-called Hamburg rising was started because the courier from Chemnitz did not arrive in time and refuses to accept the accusation often made against Hermann Remmele that as courier he had failed to inform the Hamburg party leadership in time of the Chemnitz decision. Brandler says that Remmele had nothing to do with the Hamburg affair, that he had been sent by the central committee to Kiel to buy arms offered to the KPD. If one accepts this account, the Hamburg uprising was clearly started by the military and their Russian advisers without consultation with the political party leadership.

V

Propagandist for Soviet Russia

1. The New Era

"I ban the Communist Party of Germany and all its organs" announced the poster put up on the orders of General von Seekt. But the IAH was not among the organizations listed. While the Ministries of the Interior and police hunted down leading Communists, the IAH escaped prosecution. There were many reasons for this. The organization's activity in Germany was still comparatively insignificant. Moreover, Münzenberg had just begun to set up soup kitchens and bread distribution centres everywhere and to reshape the IAH into an organization providing aid for the unemployed German workers.

On 9 December 1923 an international IAH congress met in Berlin at which prominent Social Democrats like Edo Fimmen enthusiastically welcomed the help given by the IAH to German workers. Indirectly addressing his critics of the Second International he said:

> The workers are suspicious, they say that the IAH is Moscow's secret instrument. If there were other organizations ready to help all would be well. But there are none . . .[1]

[1]"The Trade Unions and the IAH." Speech by E. Fimmen at the IAH World Congress on 9 December 1923, Berlin.

Many of the intellectual elite of Berlin belonged to the Committee for German Hunger Relief.[1] In two hundred and forty-six large and small cities, feeding centres were set up for the unemployed and in Berlin alone there were fifty-eight kitchens which provided seven thousand meals a day. Voluntary Communist and Social Democratic helpers vied with each other in the distribution of food. Welfare and youth offices wrote letters expressing their gratitude for the assistance rendered. In exempting the IAH from the ban on the Communist Party the Reich Government was probably motivated partly by political considerations: a memorandum on the IAH, asked for by the Prussian Ministry of the Interior, had given a favourable account of the organization's relief work. Also Münzenberg was in the confidence of the Russians, and the German Government was more than ever interested in economic and military contacts with Soviet Russia. For the proscribed KPD it was of great advantage that the ban did not extend to the IAH. Literature, information and other material was distributed to communist officials in the Reich through the IAH groups and some of the hardships of the ban were thus avoided.

After the failure of the KPD's dilettantist attempts to grab power in 1923 and after equally unsuccessful but more ominous coups by the Right—the Küstrin putsch of the Black Reichswehr and the Hitler putsch in Munich—the consolidation of the currency brought about a stabilization of the political situation. Münzenberg said to his chief collaborators early in 1924 that for the time being he regarded Germany's revolutionary period over. He felt they should resign themselves to this and concentrate on patient ground work in an effort to gain influence over the non-Communist working masses. The basis of their activities must be enlarged through the united front and in that field the IAH was freer than the political parties to take the initiative. In countries where the Communists were persecuted the IAH would operate in liaison with other groups.

At the same time Münzenberg began to cut down on the increasingly

---

[1]The appeal which the IAH issued for German hunger relief was signed among others by Count Arco, Hermann Bahr, Adolf Behne, Adolf Busch, Franz Theodor Csokor, Wilhelm Dieterle, Albert Einstein, R. Eickhoff, A. Eloesser, Franz Karl Endres, Ottomar Enking, Olga Essig, Otto Falkenberg, S. Fischer, Leonhard Frank, Eduard Fuchs, George Grosz, Stud.-Rat Gutmann, Dr. Hallbauer, Dr. Fannina Halle, Hans von Hentig, Wilhelm Herzog, Wieland Herzfelde, Max Hodann, Baurat Alfons Horten, Herbert Ihering, Siegfried Jacobsohn, Leopold Jessner, Karsten-Nielsen, Bernhard Kellermann, Leo Kestenberg, Lehmann-Russbüldt, Dr. Liebmann, Paul Löbe, Dr. Luserke, Moritz Melzer, A. Mendelsohn-Bartholdy, Franz Oppenheimer, Max Osborn, Bruno W. Reimann, Ernst Rowohlt, Hermann Sandkuhl, Dr. Simmel, Dr. Simons, Dr. Schairer, Max von Schillings, Dr. Helene Stöcker, Ernst Toller, Prof. Emil Preetorius, Heinrich Waentig, Prof. A. Weissmann, Franz Werfel, Justizrat Dr. Werthauer, Paul Westheim, Ines Wetzel, Dr. G. Wolf, Berta Lask, A. Segal, Otto Nagel (W. Münzenberg, *Fünf Jahre IAH*, p. 71 et seq.).

complex commitments of his organization in Soviet Russia. Trading links abroad which had involved the sale of a variety of items all the way to pig's bristles and cow's tails were simply broken off. Many enterprises in Russian cities and in the countryside were handed back to the local authorities. But he kept control of and strengthened those concerns that could be of use for propagandist activity abroad, particularly the production and distribution of Soviet films.

Münzenberg's sober estimate of the German situation differed from that of the new KPD leadership, which after weeks of argument had been entrusted to Ruth Fischer, Arkadi Maslow and Ernst Thälmann. Ruth Fischer had hoped that Münzenberg would put himself at the disposal of the new "leftist" leadership but he had little sympathy for their radicalism. In the past the Berlin Left had ridiculed the IAH as the "red Salvation Army." Ruth Fischer's complaint that Münzenberg's actions were high-handed and taken without Party approval failed to move Münzenberg. In its two years of existence the IAH had proved its usefulness. A German section with its own statutes was set up and others quickly followed in Belgium, France, Austria, Great Britain and elsewhere.

As the IAH consolidated, the Social Democrats launched a campaign against it. Friedrich Adler, who had attended the first IAH congress in 1921 as representative of the Austrian workers council, on 6 May 1924 sent to all affiliated parties a trilingual circular from London from the Secretariat of the Second International which said:

At its session in Luxemburg the Executive noted that the IAH is a Communist institution designed to work politically for the Communists under the cloak of the 'united front'.[1]

In the pamphlet published in 1924 by the ADGB, already referred to, the IAH was described as the "third column of Communist policy," the two others being the Communist Trade Union International and the Comintern. The IAH was described as Moscow's "diplomatic instrument . . . which stirs up the waters and confuses the spirits, which collects cash under the cloak of charity and which recruits blindly trusting supporters particularly among the middle classes in an effort to smooth the path for the wild plans for world revolution harboured by the rulers in Moscow."[2] The real objective of the IAH, which presented the image of a proletarian relief organization without party allegiances, must not "be judged by its official rallies arranged occasionally with the support of as many bourgeois organizations as possible and

[1] Circular in the Archives of the International Institute for Social History, Amsterdam.
[2] *Die Dritte Säule*, p. 4.

in collaboration with prominent personalities from the bourgeois camp". This and also "the many-sidedness of the IAH's activities," its "fusion of business and politics" were "horse-dealers' tricks" which followed the "Leninist recipe of using cunning and ruses and of concealing the truth." The circular went on to say that, in fact the internal leadership of the IAH (the Committee of Twenty-One and the five members of the Executive Bureau) consisted exclusively of Communists and that the whole organization had "been founded expressly for Communist Party purposes."[1]

In the years 1925/26 other parties, the Belgian Workers' Party for instance, also published documentation of Communist activity by the IAH. But at the same time the British Labour Party and the British Trade Union Congress adopted a resolution confirming that the IAH pursued its relief activities without indulging in political propaganda; the Australian Labour Party even joined the IAH corporately. It was therefore easy for Münzenberg to refute Adler's attacks and claim that the IAH was not committed to any party programme and had no links with any party.

Even at that time it was questionable as to who was really responsible for Münzenberg's activities. From the start his orders had come from various quarters. It all began with Lenin's mandate and the orders of the Russian Government. Then the Comintern had intervened. Later the Russian trade unions became the IAH's most important promoter giving it a large sphere of activity in Soviet Russia. Münzenberg made the most of this obscure situation. He steered a middle course. When he was attacked by the Communist country parties he took refuge behind the Comintern which left the responsibility for IAH matters in Russia to the Russian party. His Berlin bureau became the meeting place for visiting Communist officials from every country and political refugees from Hungary and Italy also called on him as soon as they arrived in Berlin. Even Elena Stasova, a member of the Secretariat of the Russian Party who was in Berlin in 1924 as representative of the Russian Politburo and who had the confidence of the Comintern's Wilhelm Pieck and Hugo Eberlein, frequently appeared in Münzenberg's office. The younger staff members had great respect for this woman who, in her plain clothing, hair drawn back into a thin bun, a pince-nez on her nose, looked the archetype of a Russian intellectual of the old revolutionary school. By and by even Stasova tried to adapt to the metropolitan style of Berlin. She was interested less in our adherence to the party line than in our clothes and our hats. One day she proudly

[1] *Ibid.*, p. 4 *et seq.*

showed us a new, smart, green velvet hat—which went somewhat oddly with her austere face.

With his new duties Münzenberg developed his own way of life. In spite of intensive work for which there were no fixed office hours he found time for surprise excursions, for visits to the theatre and the cinema and for parties. He threw himself enthusiastically into the hectic life of Berlin. Whereas most Communist officials adapted their customs to the "proletarian" way of life, Münzenberg nonchalantly went his own way. He was the first to buy an automobile for his office; at first it was a Chevrolet coupé, later an enormous Lincoln limousine. He also regarded it as quite normal to use taxis and horse-drawn cabs because it seemed more important to him to be mobile than to bow to arbitrary prejudice.

The ECCI met in Moscow in January 1924. Delegates discussed the defeat of the KPD and the causes for the failure of the uprising in the autumn of 1923. In his report on "The Situation of the KPD" Zinoviev disassociated himself from Radek whom he held responsible for the debacle in Germany. The argument over whether a revolutionary situation had or had not existed in Germany in the autumn of 1923 was merely a prelude to the bitter struggle that was taking shape between Stalin, who had been joined by Zinoviev and Kamenev of the "old guard", and Trotsky's supporters—a struggle which had begun even before Lenin died on 21 January 1924. Radek was a Trotsky supporter but he clung to the view that there had been a revolutionary situation in Germany and that the Comintern and the German party leadership had let the opportune moment slip past. *De facto*, however, Zinoviev as President of the Comintern had been responsible for the guidelines given to the German Communist Party. His report was characterized by vitriolic attacks on the German Social Democrats whom he described as "the fascist wing of the workers movement" and as "a component of fascism." He made the same attacks on the Italian Socialists calling their leader, Turati, a "fascist Social Democrat."[1] It was therefore at an early stage that attempts to link the Socialists and the Fascists began to be made. In the summer of 1923 Münzenberg issued a bulletin with Valeriu Marcu in which Marcu attempted an analysis of the new phenomenon, Fascism. He expressed the view that Fascism was the result of the mistakes of the workers parties in Germany and Italy, that the Fascists had filled the void created by the revolutions which had not occurred. He saw this not as an accident "but as the gloomy prospect of a terrible age to come which we may perhaps regret but which we did not create and which is the manifestation of the last epoch of capitalism".[2] But the Comintern did not approve of such criticism of the

[1] G.Zinoviev, *Die Lage der KPD*, in *Die Internationale*, (Berlin), January 1924, p. 40.
[2] *Sichel und Hammer*, No. 7, Berlin 1923.

workers parties, which included the Communists, and Münzenberg had to give up his collaboration with Marcu.

Münzenberg returned to Berlin in low spirits from this ECCI session, and from Lenin's funeral. Not that the death of Lenin, who had been seriously ill since March 1923 and unable to work, had come unexpectedly. But with Lenin, Münzenberg's most important support in Moscow had gone. After four years of dealings with the Bolshevik party leadership he knew enough to look anxiously to the future. To everyone's surprise Trotsky had taken no part in the struggle for the succession. For years people had named him in the same breath as Lenin and the Russians had regarded him as Lenin's predestined successor. Now it appeared that new men were coming to the fore.

At the ninth KPD Party Congress, which met illegally from 7 to 10 April 1924 in Frankfurt, Münzenberg was put up as a candidate for the impending Reichstag elections in the electoral district 19 (Hesse-Nassau). He was elected and until the end of the Weimar Republic remained Communist Deputy for this constituency. The elections of 4 May 1924 brought the Communists an unexpected gain; they now held sixty two seats. Münzenberg entered the Reichstag with the new ultraleft group. Most of the Communist deputies had the same objections to the "bourgeois" parliament as Münzenberg had voiced in 1918 and 1919. They expressed this contempt by attending the opening session in black shirts and red ties. They also armed themselves with toy trumpets which they blew whenever they disapproved of what President Paul Löbe or other deputies said. Although Münzenberg continued to think little of parliamentary procedure he disapproved of these silly demonstrations and felt ashamed of his colleagues.

Münzenberg paid another visit to Moscow in the summer, this time to attend the fifth World Congress of the Comintern as a non-voting delegate. In the corridors off the Kremlin throne room the IAH had prepared an exhibition of its numerous activities. Otherwise Münzenberg did not take part in the deliberations of the Congress which revolved once more around the defeat in Germany; the aim was to discredit Trotsky and Radek and place the anti-Trotsky campaign on an international plane. The congress decided on the so-called "bolshevization" of the affiliated parties. The grouping of members by the districts in which they lived which had been taken over from the Social Democrats was now replaced by so-called works cells. Party members were grouped according to their places of work and members who lived close by were assigned to those particular works cells. This procedure resulted in an atomization of membership but was never completely carried out by the German Communist Party so that the two forms of organization, street cells and work cells, existed side by side. The Comintern Congress proposed the training of "professional revolutionaries." Party schools were set up where talented young Communists were instructed in dialectical materialism and other subjects so that they could later become officials.

A new era had dawned in the Communist parties.

2. A Trust is Born

When the KPD was banned Münzenberg began looking for a publishing house which could be used for propaganda purposes beyond the IAH framework but which would not at once be branded as Communist. Felix Halle, a lawyer, offered him a publishing imprint in his possession from the pre-1914 days: *Neue Deutsche Verlag*. Münzenberg gratefully accepted the gift and the firm was registered in his name.[1] One of his first publications was a popular illustrated pamphlet, *Lenin*, which appeared in a mass edition at the beginning of 1924, two weeks after Lenin's death. After his return from Moscow, Münzenberg gave us the photographs which he had brought back and demanded that the pamphlet be out within a week. This was how the *Neue Deutsche Verlag* was begun, without experts, without capital, without a distribution service, without connections with the book trade, but full of enthusiasm and determination, aided by the banned but active party organizations that gave their whole hearted support to anything connected with Soviet Russia. The IAH's illustrated paper, at first entitled *Sowjetrussland im Bild* (Soviet Russia in Pictures), and later rechristened *Sichel und Hammer* (Sickle and Hammer) was handed over to the new publishing firm, to the great satisfaction of the responsible IAH officials who regarded the foundation of the publishing house as one of their chief's whims. With the introduction of a stable currency there was less money available than before, yet bills had to be paid and expenses covered. In the first years of its existence the publishing house was in financial difficulties, living from one cheque to the next. When all sources dried up I went for help to the Party Treasurer of the Fischer-Maslow Central Office, Arthur König. In 1919/20, during the fighting in the Ruhr, König —with Peters, Hammer and Maslowski—had been among the leading Spartacist agitators in the Ruhr. He always helped us even if the party

[1] Felix Halle was known to all Communists. He had published a popular book *Wie verteidigt sich der Proletarier vor Gericht?* (How does the Proletarian Defend Himself in Court?) and he acted as Communist Defence Counsel in political trials. In 1933 he and his wife emigrated to Russia. In 1937 the aged Halle was arrested and taken to a mass cell in the Burtirki prison in Moscow where he met other Communists who suggested sarcastically that he ought write a book on how a German proletarian should defend himself in a Soviet court. Halle vanished forever. At his arrest his wife, Fannina, committed suicide by throwing herself down the stair shaft of their hotel.

leadership was not exactly delighted at having competition. Ruth Fischer at this time described her old friend Münzenberg as a robber knight because he was setting up his own organization without asking her permission. He had realized that this was the only way in which his publications could reach a new, non-political section of the working public class market.

We travelled from district to district, negotiated with the party's district officials, sat in smoky party offices with street vendors and gradually established our own distribution network which delivered the paper direct to subscribers. Branch offices of the publishing house of the *Arbeiter-Illustrierte Zeitung* (AIZ), the renamed *Sichel und Hammer*, which appeared weekly from 1925 onwards, were set up in all German-speaking regions, in Switzerland, Austria and Czechoslovakia. The publishing house had successfully broken into the market.

To begin with the AIZ was edited by Franz Höllering, an Austrian journalist who had formerly edited the sports paper *Arena* in Berlin with Bert Brecht and John Heartfield. Münzenberg had met Höllering through Kisch. Höllering left the AIZ after a short time and Lilly Corpus, Ruth Fischer's former secretary at the Berlin party headquarters, took over as editor. She came from an upper middle class Nuremberg family. Her grandfather was Albert Ballin, a friend of Wilhelm II and the founder of the German merchant navy. She had come in contact with the Communist movement through Alexander Abusch, who also came from Nuremberg.[1] During Höllering's tenure as editor he introduced a modern, effective style of photographic journalism. Münzenberg observed:

> The AIZ differs fundamentally from all other illustrated papers. It is devoted wholly to the life and fight of the workers and of all working sections of the population. It brings pictures of factories, strikes, of unemployment cards being stamped, of demonstrations, meetings, famine . . .[2]

The AIZ's political line took account of the desire of many people to see the unity of the political workers movement restored. The paper tried

---

[1] After 1933 Lilly Corpus emigrated to Paris where she collaborated with Münzenberg on a book on the persecution of Jews in Germany, *Der Gelbe Fleck* (The Yellow Patch), published by the *Editions du Carrefour*. She lived with J. R. Becher, and fled with him from Paris after the discovery in 1935 of a Soviet spy organization with Lydia Stahl at its centre. This led to numerous arrests and a trial. The Russian organization had kept secret documents in Lilly Corpus's and J. R. Becher's flat and after their escape these papers were discovered in the cistern of the W.C. In 1945 Lilly Corpus-Becher returned to East Berlin where as Becher's widow she was eventually decorated by Ulbricht.

[2] Willi Münzenberg, *Solidarität*, p. 84.

to meet this aspiration while not deviating too far from the current party line.

The AIZ's most important duty was to keep its readers informed on Soviet Russia. The reporting was wholly uncritical and used the most questionable means. Many workers wanted to read about a dream world, not reality. Neither the critical reports in *Vorwärts* nor any of Karl Kautsky's articles could change their attitude. They preferred the picture offered by the AIZ; in 1931 this culminated in a successful serial on the daily life of a Russian family, "The Filipovs." The photographs of the Filipovs were made available by the "League of Friends of Soviet Russia." The family with five children, some of them grown-up, was shown in their simple but attractively furnished flat at the breakfast table with eggs and milk for all. Later, in the tram on their way to work, they each had a comfortable seat. Life on the job was orderly and harmonious. The Filipovs' leisure time was a continuous idyll, spent playing on spacious sports grounds or casually purchasing a suit costing twenty-seven roubles for one of the sons. Seen against the background of the reality of 1930, 1931 and 1932 this serial becomes positively macabre. Compulsory collectivization had resulted in terrible food shortages everywhere. Patient queues waited day and night outside shops for something edible. The housing conditions of the average wage-earner in Moscow were terrible. Each family was entitled to one room, no more. As for public transport, anyone who had lived in Moscow could not but laugh at the sight of the Filipovs in their tram. Trams were always overcrowded, with people hanging from every door. Senior Russian officials were sarcastic among themselves about the Filipov serial. Such blatant propaganda annoyed them and the saying "as at the Filipovs" became their synonym for Potemkin villages.

The AIZ devoted considerable space to reports on the Red Army. Münzenberg and his Moscow representatives were in close touch with its propaganda sections. During one of our visits we were guests at the autumn manoeuvres and witnessed an impressive spectacle. Masses of soldiers assembled in the forest. The sight did not arouse the distaste in Münzenberg that one might have expected. He approved of the Red Army as an expression of the strength of the state, and he was impressed by this strength. Münzenberg celebrated the tenth anniversary of the Red Army's foundation, 28 February 1928, by bringing out a special number of the AIZ; its motto was an appeal to the German workers: "Defend the Soviet Union."

In 1932 he sent two groups of AIZ contributors and persons interested in the paper to Soviet Russia. The backbone of the firm's distribution service was about two thousand unemployed militant Communist officials. Every week they covered hundreds of miles on their bicycles taking our journals to every corner of the country. A group of them went to Leningrad and marched in the May Day demonstration under a big banner "AIZ Shock Brigade." At about the same time an invitation to visit Moscow was extended to the advertising managers of large German firms. Many availed themselves of the offer. In Moscow they were received ceremoniously by Soviet trade officials and royally entertained.

The unexpected success of the AIZ gave the French Communist Party the idea of producing a similar popular illustrated paper in collaboration with the local IAH. Münzenberg sent Lilly Corpus and me to Paris to assist our French comrades with the preparatory work. This was my first visit to Paris—with a forged passport because like Münzenberg's other close collaborators I was not given a French visa—and I was overwhelmed by the city, especially the leisurely way of life which to us, after the tempo of Berlin, seemed extremely old fashioned but not at all disagreeable.

Although I knew nothing about the special conditions of the French newspaper market I negotiated with great sang-froid in bad school French with the *Messageries Hachette* and the printers. With the help of the French comrades and the Communist *Banque Ouvrière et Paysanne*, which raised the money, the first number of *Nos Regards, Illustré Mondial du Travail* was—with great effort—brought out in time on 1 May 1928.[1]

At first it depended on chance, or Moscow's wishes, or the current Comintern campaign, what books the *Neue Deutsche Verlag* published. Moreover in 1924 there were already several Communist publishing houses in existence which did not welcome further competition. But as the result of its political connections Münzenberg's firm gradually collected some authors. In the autumn of 1924 we received a visit from Karl Radek who introduced his friend Larissa Reissner to Münzenberg. In 1923 she had accompanied Radek to Berlin and a few weeks after the collapse of the Hamburg rising she had gone to Hamburg to interview the revolutionaries. She brought Münzenberg the manuscript of her book *Hamburg auf den Barrikaden,* a vivid description of the Communist participants, their spirit of sacrifice, their enthusiasm and the great expectations they held for improving their circumstances.

Larissa Reissner was born in St. Petersburg in 1895, the daughter of a noted jurist. As a student she quickly became caught up in revolutionary circles and married Fyodor Raskolnikov, a member of the Bolshevik military organization of Petrograd who played an active part in the

[1]Shortly afterwards, when the Tardieu Government took action against the Communists, *Nos Regards* ceased publication. Later it appeared as an information sheet of the French IAH, and after Hitler came to power in 1933 as an illustrated weekly supplement of *Humanité.*

October Revolution. She was with him in the civil war when he commanded a Red flotilla on the Volga and afterwards when he was sent as Russian Ambassador to Afghanistan. While Fyodor incited the mountain tribes on the Afghan-Indian border against the British the high-spirited Larissa was the subject of much gossip in Kabul. She was a striking woman—tall, of generous proportions, with fair hair parted in the centre. She did not at all resemble the Russian women whom we had met hitherto and it was difficult to imagine a greater contrast than that between this *grande dame* and Radek, who was slight, cared nothing about dress, wore side whiskers and always had a pipe in the corner of his mouth. Münzenberg published *Hamburg auf dem Barrikaden*. Soon after it came out the book was confiscated and banned as an "incitement to civil war."

Münzenberg was approached for help in connection with another important matter relating to Communist underground work during the autumn and winter of 1923. This concerned the so-called Cheka trial which took place from 10 February to 22 April 1925 in Leipzig at the first senate of the state tribunal for the protection of the republic. On trial were several German Communists and the Soviet General Skoblevsky who with other Russian officers had set up an illegal military organization for the Communist Party. This organization had murdered one of its members, a hairdresser named Johann Rausch, who had given away Communist plans to the police. Felix Neumann, a party member whom Heinrich Brandler had appointed to the military leadership and who had also been caught, made sensational statements about the activities of his group which called itself the "German Cheka." His evidence led the Communist Party to disown him, to call him mad and to say that he was a police spy. Among other things Felix Neumann revealed the activities of Skoblevsky, also known as Gorev or Helmut, who had occasionally received him at the Russian Embassy in Berlin. There was evidence that Skoblevsky had provided substantial amounts in dollars for the illegal acquisition of explosives, for the establishment of an office for the production of false passports and for the pay of all members of the organization.

The main accused, Skoblevsky, Neumann and Poege, were sentenced to death for high treason, conspiracy, political murder, and contravention of the explosives law and regulations governing the carrying of arms. During the trial Münzenberg published a memorandum by Dr. Arthur Brandt, one of the twelve counsel for the accused, listing errors of form on the part of the court, transgressions by the police and complaints against police spies. When the death sentences were announced Münzenberg wrote a pamphlet, "Prevent a Three-fold Judicial Murder," in which he cited the numerous manifestations of sympathy for the accused which his campaign had produced. Fimmen and other well known personalities protested against the "shameful Leipzig sentences" and hoped that a powerful protest by the workers would lead to a reversal of the verdict and bring freedom to all victims of class justice. In his pamphlet Münzenberg claimed that Skoblevsky was a Russian refugee and that the court had failed to prove that he was a Soviet commissar. He then quoted *Izvestia* as saying that the Soviet Union had never claimed the right to interfere in German affairs.

By 1925 the worst period of the inflation was over and many people readily believed the Communist claims that everything that was being said in Leipzig and reported day by day in the papers was reactionary propaganda. The German Government, and above all the Reichswehr, had no interest in throwing too much light on the activities of the Russian army in the Ruhr, in Stettin, Weimar or Berlin in 1923.

The death sentences were not carried out. Skoblevsky was later exchanged for several students arrested and sentenced in Soviet Russia. The other accused were amnestied a few years later.

Friedrich Ebert's death led to a presidential election, the first ballot of which was held on 29 March 1925. The Communist Party put up Ernst Thälmann; the Social Democratic candidate was Otto Braun. In the first ballot the Social Democrats gained 7.8 million votes and the Communists 1.8 million. The Centre collected 3.9 million and the bourgeois parties as a whole 13 million. As no candidate had obtained an absolute majority there was a second ballot. Under pressure from its ultra-left wing the Communist Party leadership put up Thälmann again while the SPD asked its supporters to give their votes to the Centre candidate, Marx. On the night after the second ballot Münzenberg was on his way back from the Rhineland to Berlin. Special editions with the election result were on sale at Magdeburg station. Hindenburg had been elected President, having gained 14.6 million votes. Marx had received 13.7 million votes and Thälmann 1.9 million.

Münzenberg was annoyed that his party had helped the forces of reaction, that a monarchist had become President. He suspected all those groups who were the declared enemies of the working class—the Junkers, the Freikorps, the Black Reichswehr and the *völkisch* elements—those behind the new President. He realized that the election result would give new stimulus to the enemies of the republic. His anger was directed against the party leaders, Fischer and Maslow. He forgot that it would have been easy for the Comintern leaders to withdraw Thälmann's candidacy in the weeks between the two ballots. But all that came from Moscow was belated criticism. When the new President took office in May he announced in no uncertain terms that no one could expect him to change his political convictions.

3. Heading to the Right

To the great displeasure of the continental reformist trade unions relations between the British and the Russian trade unions became increasingly friendly during 1924. The powerful left wing of the TUC was interested in closer collaboration with the Russians. Edo Fimmen's mediation did much to establish these contacts. His International Federation of Trade Unions represented the left wing of the reformist Trade Union International and had for some time pleaded for links with the Russians. The Left believed that the Russian trade unions could thereby be brought back into the great family of European unions. The Russians on the other hand hoped that by collaborating with the TUC they might gain a foothold in the workers movement which they both hated and feared.

At the end of 1924 a British trade union delegation visited Soviet Russia. This visit was a propaganda coup for the Russians and they received the British accordingly. The visitors were given an enthusiastic welcome everywhere. The Soviet authorities spared no effort in fulfilling the wishes of their guests. Fimmen gave Münzenberg the chance to publish the German edition of the account of this first visit to Russia by a non-Communist trade union delegation. *Russia. Official Report of the British Trade Union Delegation to Russia and the Caucasus* was published in 1925 under the copyright of the General Council of the TUC. The book was carefully prepared, and included maps and an index. However much the reformist associations disapproved of the publication, compared with later "reports" the British observations were objective and by no means always favourable to Soviet Russia. The delegation was given an amazing amount of freedom. It visited countless factories and in Moscow it also inspected prisons and was allowed to talk to social revolutionary prisoners.

The delegation had been particularly anxious to visit Georgia. Anti-Bolshevik revolts which had broken out there in 1924 had been brutally suppressed by the authorities. In their report the British noted that Georgia was terrorized by the Cheka, that they had not been permitted to establish contact with the representatives of the opposition and that the authorities and the police consistently lied about the situation. Their conclusions were summed up in a claim which remains one of the most popular arguments of the apologists for Soviet methods. It combines factual statement with a bow to the dictatorial regime:

In the present system there is no room for political freedom and 'democracy'; everything is controlled, but the population willingly abandons the right of opposition.

The first German trade union delegation visited Russia in the summer of 1925. Its report was published under the title "What did 58 German workers see in Russia?" by the *Neue Deutsche Verlag* in an edition of one hundred thousand copies which was immediately sold out. The report contained a letter of encouragement which Edo Fimmen had sent to the delegation before its departure:

> You must proclaim the truth, that the working class of Soviet Russia is in power—that it has freed itself from its oppressors and has taken charge of its own fate.

Another Menshevik attempt to get the visitors to see conditions as they really were came from Theodor Dan. In a *Manual for Delegates Visiting Russia* (Prague, 1926) he wrote that the Russian wage level of 1913 had still not been regained, that there was no eight-hour day, that there was child labour and inadequate workers' protection. Instead of proletarian dictatorship, he continued, there was one party dictatorship —the worst type of Bonapartism.

During his frequent visits to Berlin, Fimmen was in the habit of going with Münzenberg to a small tavern in the Dorotheenstrasse, frequented otherwise almost exclusively by East Elbian Junkers, but Fimmen liked the food and atmosphere. The two men talked endlessly about the "Russians." Münzenberg was the cooler, the more realistic of the two. He was glad to have found a good friend in Fimmen whose influence was sufficiently great to give him an entrée to many trade union circles. Fimmen on the other hand was still under the illusion that after some initial excesses Bolshevism would move into democratic channels. During his visits to Moscow he had become friendly with Tomsky, the head of the all-Russian trade union organization, and he was prepared to believe that the Russians sincerely wished to establish contacts with Western trade unions. He thought that such a move could be the beginning of a turn to the right of overall Russian policy.

Friendly relations between the British and the Russian trade unions reached their climax in May 1925 when Tomsky led a Russian delegation to the annual Trade Union Congress at Hull. Shortly before the Russian trade unions had adopted a resolution demanding the establishment of an Anglo-Russian unity committee. The agreement to set up this "Anglo-Russian Trade Union Unity Committee" was signed on 14

May 1925 by Tomsky and Melnichansky for the Russians and by Purcell and Swales for the British.

This development gave the IAH a chance to become more active in Britain. Famine relief for Ireland was the first large campaign undertaken in 1925 by the British section of the IAH with the active support of Louis Gibarti and Ellen Wilkinson. Although Ellen Wilkinson had resigned from the British Communist Party in 1924 she was ready to assist Münzenberg with all his ventures. The IAH was called upon again during the labour troubles which occurred in Britain in May 1926 and which led to a general strike followed by a strike of miners lasting six months.

But the attempt of the Russians, with the help of the Anglo-Russian committee, to transform the general strike into a political campaign misfired. The "brotherly gift" of £72,000 which they had offered to the British trade unions was rejected by the TUC. By using the army and the police the Conservative government suppressed the strike in two weeks. At Tomsky's suggestion Münzenberg founded a branch office in Paris to bring politics into the beginning miners' strike. Everywhere, even in Germany, rallies were held in support of the striking miners. They were addressed by the popular secretary of the British union, A. G. Cook, and by Münzenberg. Through the IAH and the British Communist Party substantial sums of money originating from Russia were channeled into the strike areas. As the Communist influence became noticeable the right wing of the Labour Party became more critical of the Anglo-Russian committee which was unable in the long run to withstand this onslaught. In September 1926 the collaboration came to an end "because of intervention in internal British affairs."

From the start the policy of international trade union unity at the highest level had been the target of strong criticism from the left of the Russian party and the Comintern. Ruth Fischer, whose domination of the KPD was nearing its end, had attacked the Anglo-Russian committee at an ECCI meeting in 1925, describing it as "a move of Russian foreign policy, as an attempt at a rapprochement with the Socialist MacDonald Government." At the dramatic session of the German Commission of the ECCI on 12/13 August 1925 this statement—together with many other true and invented misdemeanours—was cited as evidence of her "anti-Bolshevik, Social Democratic mentality."[1] The clash between the Comintern and the Fischer–Maslow Central Office,

[1] From a circular of the KPD central office, containing: the report of the meetings of the ECCI of 12/13 August 1925, the text of the "open letter" criticizing the party leaders, Fischer and Maslow, the introductory letter of the KPD central committee of the end of August to the 'open letter' and a statement of approval by the political party workers of 1 September 1925.

with the help of an "open letter" from the ECCI to the KPD, led in September 1925, to the fall of the German party leaders. It was not, as the text of the letter might have led one to suppose, the result of a disagreement on principles. The new party leadership which had taken over only eighteen months previously had proved unsuitable to the Russians for pushing through the bolshevization of the German party, that is to say the party's unconditional subordination to whatever the Moscow line of the moment might be. Fischer and Maslow were leftists who had no intention of imitating Moscow's turn to the right. Moreover, they thought that they could still communicate with their Russian comrades. But Stalin had put an end to this.

Of the wordy accusations against Fischer and Maslow, those not without foundation were: they had in fact protested against Moscow's constant intervention; Maslow had dared to doubt the wisdom of the decisions of the Third World Congress; they had tried to make their own policy. The KPD leadership now went to a group dominated by the so-called "conciliators," former rightists like Arthur Ewert and Wilhelm Pieck who, while disassociating themselves from the Brandler group, spoke of a reconciliation with the right; but Thälmann and other leftists continued to belong to the leadership.

The changed party line was helpful to Münzenberg in his work. The KPD had grown steadily and quietly from 1924 onwards in spite of the ultra leftishness of the Fischer–Maslow group. There was a firm core of members, and the fact that the membership of "supra-party" organizations like the *Rote Frontkämpfer-Bund* increased showed that it was quite possible to gain adherents among workers who had no party allegiance. The campaign for the "expropriation of the princes" demonstrated that even in this period of constant development large scale propaganda activity could unite the most varied elements of the political left under Communist leadership.

The problem of compensation for the Hohenzollerns after the abdication of Wilhelm II had long preoccupied both the Prussian and the Reich governments. To start with the entire Hohenzollern fortune had been confiscated and put under state administration. A proposal by Otto Braun to make the fortune state property and to compensate the former ruling house with a suitable pension had been rejected in 1919.[1] Later there had been repeated settlement proposals and the lawyers of the imperial house had successfully begun to sue in the regular courts for one object of Hohenzollern family property after another. The problem demanded an early solution. At the end of 1925 the Social Democrats began to debate whether there should be a referendum on an

[1]Otto Braun, *Von Weimar zu Hitler*, Zurich, 1940, p. 212.

expropriation bill. These discussions came to the attention of the League for Human Rights, and René Kuczynski, a well known statistician and a supporter of the League, informed Münzenberg. Kuczynski had been in close contact with the IAH since 1923 when Münzenberg had sent him to France to collect money for starving Germans.

Münzenberg was grateful for Kuczynski's information because he immediately recognized the propagandist value of this development. At his suggestion the League formed an "anti-settlement committee." Within a few days this *ad hoc* committee was joined by the KPD— whose leaders had at first opposed the plan—the IAH, the *Rote Frontkämpfer-Bund*, the International Federation of Free Thinkers, all republican pacifist organizations, the Nelson Federation, the syndicalists and numerous sporting and cultural associations. When the SPD saw that the Communists had deprived it of the initiative, it also joined the committee and the campaign for a referendum, and the ADGB and the *Reichsbanner* followed suit. On 14 December the League for Human Rights invited the above named organizations to a preliminary meeting. The KPD and the SPD jointly prepared, printed and distributed propaganda. The text of the draft law was also drawn up in joint consultation. Meanwhile about twelve and one half million people had registered, thereby providing the required support for a referendum. But the Reichstag rejected the draft law when it was submitted. Meanwhile the affair had grown into a prolonged and massive campaign for the expropriation of the princes and against compensation for them. It was now discovered for the first time what vast sums many of them had already received.

Münzenberg participated in this campaign by publishing a pamphlet, "Not a Penny for the Princes," and a special edition of the AIZ. To win the referendum the parties of the left would have needed twenty million votes. Fifteen and a half million electors voted yes and some tens of thousands voted no. Although the plebiscite had failed and the law was finally rejected the result was more than satisfactory. It showed what great support the KPD could mobilize if it joined forces with the SPD.

For internal party purposes the KPD tried to exploit this successful attempt at collaboration with the SPD leadership and the managers of the AGDB. "Only by taking a new course was it possible to achieve the recent successes as regards the SPD . . . only the new central office could adopt such tactics towards the SPD and the ADGB . . . ," Münzenberg said in the pamphlet referred to above. Both parties interpreted the campaign after their own fashion. While the Communists claimed that the attitude of the masses towards the plebiscite showed that the working classes were moving to the left, the Social Democrats noted that on this occasion the Communists had taken the Social Democratic line.

As Reichstag Deputy Münzenberg in 1926 was a member of the *Feme* committee which was charged with investigating some particularly brutal murders by right-wing radicals. He acted as KPD *rapporteur* to this committee which, hopelessly hampered as it was by obstructionist tactics on the part of the Reichswehr and the Bavarian Government, failed to clear up the murder of Bauer, a student member of the *Blücherbund* to which the murderer had also belonged. Bauer's murderer, Zwengauer, had been given a life sentence by a regular court, but was a few weeks later transferred to a hospital from which he had escaped. Since then he had vanished. Proceedings against the members of the *Blücherbund* who had helped the murderer escape had been quashed. In his report Münzenberg appealed to the public. He accused the Right of preparing a monarchist restoration in Germany.[1]

There were also other occasions on which Münzenberg, as Reichstag Deputy, was used for Comintern and party duties. In 1926 he visited Budapest to attend the trial of Mátyás Rakosi, whom the Comintern had illegally sent to Hungary from Moscow to rebuild the banned Communist party. He and other Communists were arrested. The trial was scheduled to start on 12 July. The Comintern feared—not without reason—that the accused would be sentenced to death. It found good defence counsels for them and approached internationally known personalities to take up Rakosi's case and to put pressure on the Hungarian authorities. I accompanied Münzenberg to the German-Czech frontier. His mood was anxious. He disliked the thought of visiting a country where the Communists were persecuted without mercy. But the Hungarians, apparently intimidated by the international protest action, not only gave him an entry visa but allowed him to meet the accused and their lawyers.

Finally Rakosi was sentenced to eight and one half years imprisonment for "incitement to class hatred and seeking to rebuild the banned CPH." On completion of this sentence he was retried in 1934 and sentenced to life imprisonment as a former People's Commissar in the Hungarian Soviet Government. In 1940 he was deported to the Soviet Union in exchange for the Hungarian flags captured by Russian troops, as Austrian allies, in 1849 during the defeat of Kossuth's rising.

4. Münzenberg the Founder

After the defeat of 1923 the Russians had turned their attention in Berlin to a newly formed political group with left wing inclinations. At the Reichstag elections of May 1924 the "Republican Party", founded by Carl von Ossietzky and the journalist Karl Vetter, wanted to appeal

[1] *Inprecorr*, 27 July 1926.

to electors with left wing sympathies who would vote neither for the Social Democrats nor for the Communists. Whereas Ossietzky was a confirmed anti-Communist his partner was not averse to secret collaboration with the Russians. The new party had also founded a paper, *Die Republik*, which was forever in need of funds. On one occasion Münzenberg returned from the Russian embassy and showed me a substantial sum of dollars which he was supposed to hand over to Karl Vetter for the *Republik*. This was one of the rare instances when Münzenberg did not discreetly carry out such orders. The "Republican Party" suffered a devastating electoral defeat, it dissolved and shortly afterwards *Die Republik* ceased publication.

There was yet another left wing Berlin paper, *Die Welt am Abend*, owned by a group of editors who had belonged to the former United Social Democratic Party. When the paper's circulation fell to three thousand copies in 1926 one of its owners, Emil Rabold, asked his editor-in-chief, Walter Oehme, to approach Münzenberg and to offer him the paper at a price of ten thousand marks. Emil Rabold was a first class journalist and a popular one, a man without roots, a supporter of the left and an old follower of Ledebour. He died in the mid-fifties penniless and embittered in exile in London. Münzenberg did not accept the offer at once, he vacillated and wanted to know whether Oehme, whose abilities he respected, was willing to stay on as editor-in-chief. When Oehme agreed Münzenberg asked how much would be needed to promote the paper. Oehme thought that about forty thousand marks was required to which Münzenberg nonchalantly replied that such resources were available. Later, when *Die Welt am Abend* was a flourishing paper, he admitted to the surprised Oehme that he had never possessed these forty thousand marks. While Münzenberg was still negotiating with the editors, the business manager of *Die Welt am Abend* sold the copyright of the paper to another group because he did not want it to fall into Communist hands. Münzenberg was therefore compelled to institute legal proceedings to obtain the name. The case ended with a compromise and Münzenberg finally acquired *Die Welt am Abend* for seven thousand marks.

An important prerequisite for the success of an evening paper was a good distribution service. For this department of the newly-founded *Kosmosverlag* Münzenberg engaged Hans Schüler who had formerly distributed the Independent Social Democratic (USP) paper *Die Freiheit* in Berlin. Work began with modest means; altogether about twenty thousand marks was available, advanced by an advertisement firm. The new moderate party line favoured Münzenberg's latest venture. The editorial board of the paper consisted of Communists and men without party allegiance, the latter mostly with a USP past. They spoke a language which Berliners understood. Party politics were avoided as far as possible. The Comintern and the Communist Party approved of the Communist cause having a popular evening paper at its disposal in Berlin. When, in a short period of time, the paper's circulation reached over one hundred thousand the party leadership demanded the appointment of a political editor whom they could trust.

The first of these was Otto Heller, a capable journalist and a pleasant colleague, who quickly found himself at loggerheads with the party central office for "right-wing deviations." Ernst Thälmann demanded his dismissal. Münzenberg, who personally had a high regard for the quite popular Heller, did not stand up for his editor but, as Heller told his colleagues, dropped him. As always when Münzenberg had acted under pressure from the party and against his convictions he sought to make amends as far as possible: he arranged for his ex-editor to visit Russia and Siberia. Heller wrote an interesting book about his travels in Siberia which was published by the *Neue Deutsche Verlag*.

After 1930 Münzenberg found himself increasingly on the defensive as the party line was rarely in harmony with his guidelines for *Die Welt am Abend*. The trusted party man was now Paul Friedländer who frequently found himself facing a united editorial front.[1] The party called for stronger attacks on the SPD. But the editorial board considered it more important to stress the growing Nazi threat. Altogether it held the view that the paper was a left wing mass publication and not an organ of the KPD. If it was impossible to reach agreement—on what should be given prominence in the front page headlines, for example —Münzenberg was asked to arbitrate.

At the beginning the paper was printed by the Friedrichstadt printing works—the party printers—but as its circulation grew the party printer could no longer cope and it was produced by a non-Communist firm which offered long term credits; the management and the editorial board welcomed this less close contact with the Communist Party. Within a short time *Die Welt am Abend* became the most widely read working class paper in Berlin. Münzenberg had a special affection for the vendors who did much to popularize the paper. These Berliners, whom Münzenberg described as the "party's treasure," were not so much concerned with politics as they were with the fact that Münzen-

[1] In 1933 Paul Friedländer emigrated to Paris where he worked for the KPD. At the outbreak of the war, like most Communists, he was interned in the camp at Le Vernet. When he produced a written protest against the Stalin-Hitler pact he was expelled from the Communist cell of the camp and ostracized. Whereas after the collapse of France all the other Communist officials escaped overseas with Mexican or American visas the Communist apparatus prevented Paul Friedländer from obtaining such an emergency visa. He remained in the camp and was later taken by the Nazis to Auschwitz where he was murdered.

berg was very useful to them in getting wage increases out of the management.

The growing popularity of the paper was reflected in the matinées and mass meetings held every month under the auspices of *Welt am Abend*. The matinées at the Scala and the Wintergarten were always sold out and almost every well known cabaret artist and actor of the day appeared—from Rosa Valetti, Blandine Ebinger and Kate Kühl to the unforgettable Berlin comedian Paule Graetz. The popularity of the shows at the Lunapark, with music and dancing, was such that the Berlin transport authorities regularly laid on extra transport. The *Welt am Abend* also took part in "international solidarity days" organized by the IAH on every 14 June from 1929 onwards. Vast numbers of people with bands and banners marched to some big open air restaurant near Berlin and the occasions were always emotional. With an unfailing sense for grand effects the organizers in 1929, during the controversy over the building of the armoured cruiser "A", erected a dummy ship which at the end of the show disappeared into the waters of the Karlshof to the accompaniment of muffled explosions. A photograph from the year 1930 shows Münzenberg at one of these festivities, proudly leading a large crowd into the Rehbergen stadium. Although party members made fun of these shows of the "Münzenberg shop" the participants found them most impressive.

A morning paper produced on the same popular lines as the successful evening paper was the obvious next step. The management of *Die Welt am Abend* pressed for the idea, and Münzenberg was attracted by the plan, but wondered what the party leadership would say about even more direct competition to *Rote Fahne*. And what about the economic situation which was rapidly deteriorating in the winter of 1930–31? The party had fewer objections than Münzenberg had feared, as it realized this paper might be useful if *Rote Fahne* was banned for any length of time.

A decision was reached to found a new firm, *Wilhelmstadt GmbH.*, and Münzenberg handed over ten thousand marks to the paper's management for preparatory advertising. This capital was almost lost because that very night the safe of the *Welt am Abend* was forced open. But the thieves went away empty handed: in his haste the manager had locked up the notes in a bookcase. The preparatory advertising campaign for the proposed *Welt am Morgen* was in full swing when a temporary injunction was served on its publishers by the *Welt am Montag*, stopping them from using the suggested title because of the danger of confusion. Advertising space had been rented, posters were about to be printed and the publication date had been fixed. The simplest way out was to change the name of the paper and it therefore appeared early in 1931 as *Berlin am Morgen*. As editor-in-chief Mün-zenberg had found a Viennese journalist, Bruno Frei (Freistadt), who presented himself as "a leftist without party allegiances" and who quickly found the right tone for the Berlin reader. In spite of the terrible unemployment which particularly affected readers of workers' papers, *Berlin am Morgen* quickly acquired sixty thousand subscribers and eighteen months later needed no further subsidies. The paper created a sensation in 1932 with a series of revelations about the fraudu-lent activities of the clairvoyant Erik Hanussen. It also exposed the existence of close links between him and the National Socialist leader-ship. Shortly after Hitler came to power Hanussen was murdered in mysterious circumstances.

Meanwhile Münzenberg's trust continued to expand. Otto Nagel, the great proletarian artist whose gaunt figure and sad gaze personified all the proletarians whom he had ever painted, suggested to Münzenberg the publication of a satirical paper. *Der Eulenspiegel*, whose co-found-ers included Heinrich Zille, was published by the *Neue Deutsche Verlag* and reached a circulation of fifty thousand by 1931. Many artists who years ago had contributed to the artists relief scheme of the IAH worked for *Eulenspiegel*. The journal was ambitious. It wanted to over-take the left wing bourgeois satirical journals without at any point ever equalling the caustic wit and sure aim of the political jokes of *Simplizis-simus* for example. Nagel was much too serious and too slow and his colleague, Fritz Erpenbeck, did not dare make fun of party officials, so their satire remained primitive and ineffectual. *Eulenspiegel* still ap-pears in East Berlin today without any improvement in quality.

One of Münzenberg's favourite organization was the "Association of Workers Photographers" with its organ *Der Arbeiterphotograph*. Mün-zenberg had financed its foundation and supported it whenever he could. He believed this association helped the ideological and technical education of working class photographers. The worker photographer was "the eye of the working class" because he alone, in Münzenberg's, opinion could see the world around him objectively, being closer to reality that the bourgeois photographer. The journal's losses were made up by the *Neue Deutsche Verlag*. In 1931 the AIZ sent a worker photog-rapher around the world but his photographs were poor; indeed the workers' photographs were only rarely usable and on the whole of a much lower quality than those of press photographers.

A late project of Münzenberg's, the illustrated women's paper *Der Weg der Frau*, was very successful. The first number appeared in July 1931 in the middle of an economic crisis, when unemployment figures approached six million. But it was cleverly produced and its circulation soon rose to one hundred thousand copies. Marianne Gundermann, a Communist who had been reprimanded by the party in Halle for "conciliatory deviation," became the paper's editor.[1] She received her guidelines from Münzenberg who, remembering his Swiss experiences, demanded a minimum of politics and a maximum of articles on fashion, domestic questions, sports and hygiene.

The last paper which Münzenberg founded in Germany was much less successful. As there were no daily papers in Berlin on Mondays two bourgeois weeklies appeared on that day. To provide a Communist counterblast Münzenberg brought out the *Neue Montagszeitung* in 1932. The paper, which was not edited as well as the others, had no chance to improve. Hitler's rise to power put a stop to all such efforts.

The succession of friends, party comrades and sometimes even strangers who sought to interest Münzenberg in this or that project was never-ending. If the prospects were reasonably favourable and the venture could be used for propaganda purposes he was rarely able to resist. As early as 1924 and 1925 he provided the IAH with funds to set up a "red" co-operative in Freiberg and a co-operative stocking factory in Apolda. He helped a comrade in Braunschweig who wanted to produce a new type of adding machine. In Ruhla in Thuringia the IAH and the local Communist group began to build a children's home. Because of the economic crisis and the fact that almost the whole local group left the party with Heinrich Brandler, the building remained unfinished; the *Neue Deutsche Verlag* battled with mortgages and loans and provided the funds for its completion.

One of Münzenberg's last involvements in 1932 was in a Berlin cigarette factory whose owner had pro-Communist leanings. The National Socialists had persuaded a Dresden firm to enclose in its brand, The Drummer, pictures of Nazi celebrities. Thereupon the manufacturers of Solidarity cigarettes, in which the *Neue Deutsche Verlag* had a share, enclosed pictures of workers' leaders in their packets. Within a few months the sales of Solidarity rose considerably and the factory received numerous letters from smoking workers who enthused over Red Selection at two and one half pfennig a cigarette, or Collective at three and one half pfennig and who congratulated Münzenberg on his enterprise.

If he sensed profits for his firms Münzenberg was quite ready to engage in the extremely bourgeois business of speculation. When for example one of the partners of the Berlin banking firm of Von der Heydt made a proposal which from the Communist point of view was

[1] After 1933 Marianne Gundermann suffered the fate of so many German Communists. She emigrated to Moscow, was arrested in 1937 and vanished without a trace.

somewhat suspect Münzenberg was quick to agree to it. In the period of the first Five Year Plan the industrialisation of Soviet Russia was proceeding rapidly and Germany became one of Russia's chief suppliers of machinery and industrial installations. To help the Russians pay for these deliveries a German banking consortium had agreed to accept Russian bills of exchange maturing in twelve to eighteen months. At the time there was considerable speculation in Berlin in these "Russian bills" which changed hands at a discount of up to thirty per cent. This showed how doubtful the continued existence of Soviet Russia seemed at the time. Münzenberg laughed at the "bourgeois cowards" and invested his available cash resources in Russian bills.

Yet the Russian economy was in a very critical state. The Soviet trade delegation office in Berlin was run by Lyubimov and Weitzer[1] who controlled all business operations abroad. If, in spite of all their efforts, there was not enough money to pay maturing bills Rosengolz, the People's Commissar for Foreign Trade in Moscow, had to ask the Politburo to authorize the dispatch of gold to Berlin by air.

The rapidly growing number of firms in Münzenberg's "trust" required more and more staff, and it is revealing to see what his assistants thought of him. All who came into contact with him in those years are agreed that without insisting too much on his authority he demanded a maximum of initiative, speed and hard work from his staff. He was not interested in technical details, interfered rarely in the day to day work and knew how to delegate authority: but he expected results. He detested laziness and hated aimless talk. "At staff meetings we outlined the plans for the coming weeks. Anyone who wandered off the point was interrupted at once. On those occasions Münzenberg's tone of voice quickly became ironical."[2]

Whereas most of the younger staff members worshipped him as the "great leader," the older ones were more critical. A colleague of many years standing later said that Münzenberg had suffered from a strong sense of inferiority and had felt a constant need to prove himself. This he saw as the driving power behind Münzenberg's remarkable achievements. Failure filled him with pessimism and despair. This colleague even speaks of a psychological malformation. At the same time he notes that Münzenberg was a highly talented man who was his own severest critic. His tragedy was that he could never relax.

[1]Weitzer, whom Münzenberg had known since 1922, worked in the Paris branch of the Russian trade representation office after 1933. During the Spanish Civil War he was sent to Madrid where he was in charge of Russian deliveries of arms and goods to Spain. In 1938 he was recalled to Moscow and disappeared at the same time as his chief Rosengolz who was shot on 15 March 1938 as "an enemy of the people."
[2]According to Curt Brauns, a one-time member of Münzenberg's staff.

Was he vain? Certainly he did not lack this very human quality. In a posthumous work[1] Brupbacher sketches a portrait which is undoubtedly that of Münzenberg. In a very critical description of his old friend Brupbacher says that vanity was one of the driving forces in Münzenberg's political career:

> In the fight for socialism he reserved the big role for himself. A noble objective, an immense ambition, an urge to mount the highest rostrum in the world . . .

But Brupbacher admitted that Münzenberg's main concern was not to gain power for himself but to rally the proletariat to socialism. Or as another colleague of his put it: Münzenberg had something of the reformist zeal of the old Thuringians and in spite of all his experience retained an unshakable faith in the power of the workers.

The magnetic force of Münzenberg's personality counteracted such contradictions as may have been in his nature. Therefore he could weld into a unified team the differing temperaments that helped to run his firms. Whatever criticisms his colleagues may have had they were agreed that he was a great man in the true sense of this misused word. Münzenberg always kept his distance. Although he used the familiar *du* in talking to old party members, and to colleagues if they came from the proletariat, there was no familiarity. The many bourgeois intellectuals who worked with him and for him were only rarely invited to use *du*. This was his subtle way of reminding them that among the Socialist fraternity they were only tolerated—if benevolently tolerated—guests. They all felt his magnetism, from the firm's manager to the most junior newspaper seller, and this probably explains why the few surviving members of the old "Münzenberg shop" thirty years later still retain a feeling of kinship, why they see themselves as the last members of a family scattered all over the globe.

5. *Münzenberg Breaks into the Film Industry*

It is not surprising that, as a dedicated propagandist, Münzenberg quickly realized the potentialities of what was then still a new mass medium. In *Film und Volk,* (Film and People), a journal affiliated with one of his enterprises, he wrote that it was "demagogic" to describe the film as "neutral art".

[1]Fritz Brupbacher, *Der Sinn des Lebens,* Zurich 1946, p. 44 *et seq.*

The bourgeois and the Socialist parties and the churches have film organizations and production units ... We must devote the same energy to this
medium as to newspapers and publishing houses. The film is the most
modern means of propaganda.

These words were written in 1929, the year that the talking film was
born. *Aufbau, Industrie & Handelsgesellschaft,* a company founded by
the IAH, had been buying up German film licenses and distributing
films in Soviet Russia since 1922. In these early years, immediately after
the end of the civil war, artists in Russia also had turned their attention
to the film. They set up collectives to make films, without state subsidies
and with the most primitive technical aids, but they were carried along
by genuine artistic enthusiasm. One such collective was the *Russ* group;
when it approached the IAH for help it had already produced an excellent film, *Polikushka,* based on Tolstoi's novel and featuring the well-
known actor Moskvin. At Münzenberg's suggestion a joint film
company named *Meshrabpom-Russ* was set up in Moscow on 1 August
1924. Thanks to his political connections Münzenberg was able to raise
the necessary capital and the production of feature and propaganda
films went ahead. This organization formed the nucleus of a film company which later, after the collectivization of the Russian film industry,
remained outside the *Soyuskino* state trust, as an "organization of the
international proletariat." It employed hundreds of workers and owned
two big studios, cinemas and a sound film factory.

By then the *Russ* group no longer formed part of the organization
which was owned exclusively by the IAH. But the *Russ* team had left
its mark on the firm's productions. Its members were young, uncommitted directors and actors who were seriously concerned with finding a
new artistic style in keeping with changed Russian conditions. Creative
activity in Russia had not yet been standardized. The avant-garde was
allowed to experiment to its heart's content, unrestrained by ideologies.
Meshrabpom-Russ therefore made films that impressed not only Russia
but the rest of the world, such as Protozanov's *Aelita,* Feodor Otsep's
The Tobacconist from Mosselprom or the propaganda film *His Call,*
another of Protozanov's works which glorified the life and work of
Lenin. This film, with its new camera technique, was shown for years
at Communist gatherings throughout the world.

The history of *Meshrabpom-Film* shows how the pressure of the
Soviet regime increased until the avant-garde artists' collectives were
finally dissolved. *The Postmaster,* with Moskvin in the main part, made
after the *Russ* group had broken away, is a last reminder of the artistic
work of this group. *The Mother,* the first of the world-famous films of
Meshrabpom's greatest director, Pudovkin, made in 1926 and based on

Gorki's novel, already has a Socialist realist flavour, although this art form could then still produce creative work. In his *Last Days of St. Petersburg*, made for the tenth anniversary celebrations of the Russian revolution, Pudovkin moved even further in the same direction and his last and best known work, *Storm over Asia*, conforms completely to the official anti-colonialist line. Films had become an instrument of political propaganda.

Meshrabpom-Film supported the experiments of a young Russian engineer, Tager, who invented a process of making sound films. The first Russian sound film, *Road to Life*, was one of the most successful films ever produced by *Meshrabpom-Film*. It described life in an institution where *desprisorny*, the waifs and strays who had become a public nuisance in Russia, were re-educated into useful members of Soviet society. A few days after its German première the film, directed by Ekk, was sold to twelve countries.

Meshrabpom-Film soon became the main support of the IAH in Soviet Russia. Numerous foreign experts were invited to assist in film making. With their help "film cells of proletarian art" were later to be set up in the capitalist world. Contracts were signed with German, mostly Communist, writers. Among the German producers engaged, not all of whom were Communists, were Erwin Piscator, Karl Junghanns, Hans Richter, and the Dutchman Joris Ivens. The German actors who were attracted by *Meshrabpom-Film* included Lotte Lenya, Paul Wegener, Alexander Granach and Fritz Genschow.

In 1928 *Meshrabpom-Film* became a limited company. Its turnover had meanwhile reached millions; between 1924 and 1931 it produced a total of 241 films mainly for the Russian market, including numerous cultural films and propaganda films. Before Münzenberg founded his own film distribution and production firm in Berlin, Soviet films were shown by the national organizations of the IAH. The secretary of the American IAH, William Kruse, for instance was responsible for the distribution of Russian films in the United States, Canada, Mexico and Argentina.

The IAH's distribution of Russian films, particularly in Germany, could not really compete with the activities of the commercial distributors until it was put on a business footing. The opportunity came in 1925 when an old friend and comrade from the Swabian Spartacist days, Emil Unfried, informed Münzenberg that the KPD wished to dispose of a firm as yet unknown to the public. This firm, called *Prometheus*, had just produced a propaganda film, *Nameless Heroes*, for the party. Münzenberg seized the opportunity, took over the firm and appointed Unfried and Richard Pfeiffer as managers. Initially however the Soviet representatives in Berlin were not over-anxious to distribute their films through the newly established firm. They preferred to find commercial distributors who seemed to offer greater security. But in the end the first joint German-Russian film, *Superfluous People,* was distributed by *Prometheus.* The film was directed by the Russian, Rasumny, and almost all the well known Berlin actors of the period, including Werner Krauss, Eugen Klöpfer, Albert Steinrück, Fritz Rasp and Heinrich George, took part. But in spite of this talent the film was a failure. Success came soon afterwards, however.

On 21 January 1926 the film specialist of the Soviet trade delegation telephoned the *Prometheus* office and invited the management to the preview of a new Russian film that was being shown to a select audience at the Russian Embassy on the occasion of the second anniversary of Lenin's death. Pfeiffer recalled later that the film had already started when he entered the darkened cinema. A young Russian student was playing the accompaniment on a theatre organ. The happenings on the screen were so thrilling that Pfeiffer's party forgot to take their seats and remained standing for the whole performance.

This film, *Battleship Potemkin,* the story of a sailors' mutiny in 1905, was a masterpiece of crowd direction, without revolutionary clichés. In a letter to Eisenstein, Ernst Toller later called it "the first successful great collective performance." Unfried and Pfeiffer acquired the distribution rights immediately after the performance, although the Russians did not really believe that they would get it past the German censor. The silent film was given German sub-titles and edited superbly by Piel Jutzi. It was then submitted to the censor and promptly banned throughout Germany. *Prometheus'* lawyer, Paul Levi, appealed to the chief film censor. Shortly before the appeal was due to be heard it was learned that one of the assessors, Alfred Kerr, was just about to go abroad. At Pfeiffer's insistence Erwin Piscator telephoned Kerr (Berlin's most influential theatre critic) and implored him to see the film before he left.

The small projection room at the chief censor's office was full of military and government officials invited by the chairman, Oberregierungsrat Seeger. After the showing Paul Levi was given the floor. With his characteristically direct approach he attacked the arguments of the censor who had asked for the film to be banned on the grounds that it was revolutionary propaganda. Levi gave a lecture on the nature of revolution. He quoted Rosa Luxemburg who had written that revolutions were not "made" but erupted spontaneously when conditions were right. The masses remained the mainstay of revolutionary movements. But this was not the subject matter of the film. A few sailors refused to eat bad meat. When their superiors tried to force them to do so the sailors resisted from a sense of self-preservation. That was really the whole story. Everything arose spontaneously out of this situation. Where was there any preparation for revolution?

The experts conferred. Levi later recalled that Alfred Kerr had used his passport to jot down notes. It was Kerr's spontaneous comments that persuaded the censor to release the film. Some cuts were demanded and with Levi's and Kerr's assistance *Potemkin* was steered through the censorship. Münzenberg, who had anxiously followed the negotiations on the telephone, triumphantly rushed to the Communist Party head-quarters to announce the victory.

Because of a casual reference by Kerr in a theatre review to a superb Russian film which he had seen recently the Berlin film world was in a state of unusual excitement. The film was shown to theatre proprie-tors; although greatly impressed they all refused to show the film on the grounds that it would lead to demonstrations in their cinemas. Finally the tenant of the *Apollotheater* in the Friedrichstrasse said he was willing to take the risk. The first showing was scheduled for 29 April. *Prometheus* commissioned a young talented composer, Edmund Mei-sel, to compose a suitable musical accompaniment.

The right wing press, particularly Hugenberg's *Lokalanzeiger,* heard of the film and sounded the alarm, calling it revolutionary propaganda and the bolshevization of the screen. They insisted terrible conse-quences would ensue if this inflammatory film was shown in German cinemas. Seeckt asked the Prussian Government to ban the film. Five hours before the première a party from the Prussian Government ap-peared in the *Apollotheater* and demanded to be shown the film. The party included Otto Braun, the Minister for Culture, Schmidt, Ober-reichsanwalt Ebermayer, the Berlin police president, Grzesinski, and other notables. After the fourth act Otto Braun got up and told Paul Levi that he had no intention of pulling the chestnuts out of the fire for the Right. The film would not be banned. The police president an-nounced officially that the première could go ahead.

Meanwhile long queues had formed outside the theatre. Many well known stage and film personalities, including Emil Jannings and Asta Nielsen, were among the patient crowd. The expected riots failed to materialize. Instead the film was enthusiastically received by the first night audience. The success of the film was due not only to Eisenstein's masterly direction[1] but also to the new photo-

[1]In 1928/29 Eisenstein, accompanied by Alexandrov and Tissé, visited Europe, the USA and Mexico. There they produced the excellent unfinished *Que viva Mexico.* On the tenth anniversary of the October Revolution Eisenstein made *October* which was followed by the propaganda film *The General Line.* This film was set in a Russian village and was coldly received by the party critics. With the hardening of the Stalinist line towards artists Eisenstein was among those who came to grief. He was regarded as politically unreliable and made almost no more films. His last work *Ivan the Terrible* remained unfinished. In the end, together with Pudovkin, he directed the State Film Institute in Moscow where he died on 11 February, 1948, at the age of fifty.

graphic techniques of cameraman Eduard Tissé.

Eisenstein was twenty-eight when he and Tissé made the film at Odessa. For days they sat by the harbour waiting for the sun to appear until Tissé finally suggested that they should film in the fog. They hired a boat and Eisenstein later described the occasion as the cheapest day's shooting of the whole film. "The hire of the boat cost only 3 roubles and 50 copecks for the entire day."[1]

As no commercial distributor had wanted to take on the film *Prometheus* had shouldered the political risk and now earned a well deserved success. Every cinema in Germany wanted to show the film. Douglas Fairbanks and Mary Pickford came to Berlin and saw it at a special showing; they were so impressed by Meisel's music that they immediately invited him to Hollywood. Under pressure from the Right and the Reichswehr the Ministries of the Interior of Württemberg, Bavaria, Hesse, Thuringia and Mecklenburg-Schwerin again appealed to the censor's office and the film was banned. Münzenberg staged a protest rally against this ban at the Charlottenburg *Piccadilly-Palast* which was attended by everyone of note in the Berlin art world. The main speaker was the writer Hans Jo Rehfisch. In spite of all protests and in spite of assurances by the Prussian representative at the censor's office that the film had not endangered law and order anywhere in Prussia, new cuts were demanded. Only then was the film finally allowed to be shown. Immediately after they took over, the National Socialists banned *Battleship Potemkin*. But they continued to show the film for educational purposes at Goebbels' film academy.

In Berlin, the most international of all the cultural centres of the twenties, there was then a continual coming and going of Russian actors, theatre companies and directors. Most of these artists were not party members but they did much to popularize the Soviet Union with Berlin audiences. The most attractive of these Russians was Pudovkin. He came to Berlin with a Russian company to play the lead in *The Living Corpse*, a joint German-Russian film based on Tolstoi's play, directed by Feodor Otsep and sponsored by *Prometheus*. Koval Samborski, who had played Lenin in *His Call*, was invited to Berlin and later made a film with Henry Porten. Anna Sten, an attractive Russian actress who had played the main part in the *Meshrabpom* film *Yellow Passport*, came to Berlin before going on to achieve fame in Hollywood.

Over the years *Prometheus* produced a considerable number of films, among them the comedy *1 times 1 equals 3*, based on a scenario by Bela Balasz and Hans Kosterlitz, with Claire Rommer, Margarete Kupfer, Georg Alexander, Siegried Arno and Veit Harlan; *Schinderhannes,*

[1]S. Eisenstein, *Die zwölf Apostel*, Berlin 1960, p. 375.

based on Zuckmayer's play, and directed by Kurt Bernard, and the sensational documentary *Hunger in Waldenburg* by Piel Jutzi.

Piel Jutzi also directed the *Prometheus* film *Mother Krause's Journey to Happiness*. This film was originally intended to honour the popular Berlin artist Heinrich Zille who had died shortly before. Otto Nagel, a friend of Zille's, was invited to write a "class-conscious" scenario. When he failed in his task Richard Pfeiffer invented a melodramatic story:

> Mutter Krause, a non-political working class wife, has two sons. One joins the workers' movement, the other falls into the clutches of the under-world. During a robbery at a pawnbroker's shop he guards the sleeping owner while the others clean out the shop. When he sees that the sleeping woman wears an amulet that he knows to have been pawned by his mother he plunges his knife into her. He has become a murderer. His mother learns this while attending a Communist Party garden fête with her other son. Unnoticed she creeps out, returns home, opens the gas tap and escapes to 'happiness'. The other son and the bride whom he has introduced to the proletarian movement, take to the road with his com-rades and set out for a hopeful future.

This story made a good film script but as always *Prometheus* had no cash. The film could not be expensive. Frau Schmidt, a member of the *Staatstheater am Gendarmenmarkt,* was engaged to play Mutter Krause. She liked the part and was willing to accept a fee of two hun-dred marks provided the others did not get more. Everyone who worked on the set, actors and technicians, was less concerned with money than with making a Zille film. Altogether the film cost thirty-five thousand—a remarkably small sum even for those days, when films usually cost about ten times as much. The film was a great success.

Unlike Münzenberg's other firms *Prometheus* was forever in financial difficulties. The sums needed were always large and the desperate prob-lem was where to find them. Münzenberg held countless agitated con-ferences; one hectic telephone conversation followed another. Sometimes proceeds received from hiring out Russian films were used. On those occasions Münzenberg went to Moscow to persuade Arkadi Rosengolz, the powerful head of the Commissariat for Foreign Trade, to allow the distribution charges to be paid in roubles. Using the Mos-cow Meshrabpom funds meant that urgently needed foreign currency was lost to the Russians. It was not surprising that the head of the Russian film industry, Shvechikov, hated *Prometheus.* His films were meant to earn money abroad and he totally failed to appreciate that although Münzenberg did not bring in much foreign currency he used the Russian films successfully for political propaganda. The Comintern and the leaders of the German Communist Party took little interest in Münzenberg's film activities. Of all his firms *Prometheus* was the one least subjected to party control or criticism.

Münzenberg had set up another company, *Weltfilm*, in 1928 which distributed films to workers' organizations. Its first director, Erich Heintze, a tubercular young worker from Berlin-Moabit, quickly succeeded in acquiring a monopoly in the distribution of films to all workers' organizations, cultural associations and sports groups. By an arrangement with film producers in Moscow, Münzenberg procured for *Weltfilm* the exclusive right to a recent technical innovation which transferred normal sized films onto small reels. This made it possible to show films in even the smallest village. Later Emil Unfried[1] took over *Weltfilm*. On Münzenberg's orders he set up branches in most European countries with IAH organizations.

6. The Struggle for Power in the Soviet Union

From 1925 onwards I frequently accompanied Münzenberg on his trips to Moscow. We generally stayed in the old fashioned but very comfortable Hotel Metropole. After 1921 Münzenberg avoided the Hotel Lux where prominent Comintern members and foreign Comintern officials were put up; it was a place of constant intrigue where everyone spied on everyone else.

My main impression of Moscow was one of strangeness. There was no European city like it. From the top floor of the trade union building one saw the whole city. The gilded domes of countless churches and chapels gleamed in the sunlight. There was a church in the middle of the Arbat, a busy main street, and the famous chapel of the miraculous Iberian madonna, always surrounded by crowds of believers, then stood at the entrance to Red Square. Opposite, on a red-brick building which later housed the revolutionary museum, the icons had been replaced by a plaque with Marx's words: "Religion is the opiate of the people." Lenin's tomb in Red Square was not yet a splendid mausoleum but a simple wooden structure, painted dark red. Next to it, by the Kremlin wall, were the graves of victims of the October Revolution and of

---

[1] After 1933 Emil Unfried and a Swiss film man founded their own company and produced popular films, including military films which found Goebbels' approval and which made considerable sums for Unfried. He bought a big property near *Königswusterhausen* where he awaited the advance of the Russians in 1945. For a time he travelled between the Russian and Western zones. He arranged meetings in the Russian zone and identified himself with the land reform. But one day he was arrested by the Russians and taken to Oranienburg concentration camp where he died on 16 June 1949 after a long illness.

many prominent Russian and non-Russian Communists.

These were the peaceful years of NEP. Living conditions were crowded but there was plenty of food. It was possible to have a good midday meal for one rouble and a cream slice cost five copecks. Party members had not yet cut themselves off completely from the rest of the population. The maximum party income which varied from 225 to 300 roubles was meant to be in line with the income of a skilled metal-worker. In spite of the fact that food was plentiful, people lived simply —not only the Russians but also the foreigners who had come to help to rebuild the Soviet Union or to work in the scientific institutes.

Münzenberg's colleagues in *Meshrabpom*—the Russian section of the IAH—organized our stay. They informed the Russian frontier officials of our arrival, they reserved hotel rooms, they placed a car at our disposal and saw to all other formalities. We were invited to visit clubs and factories, to make excursions from Moscow and to attend theatre and opera performances; I was overwhelmed by the spontaneous hospitality of the Russians.

The *Meshrabpom* house had its own atmosphere. One felt as though one was in the West, not in Russia. The fact that most of the foreign employees lived in the building intensified the impression of a world apart. The first floor was occupied by the temperamental director of *Meshrabpom,* the Italian Communist Francesco Misiano,[1] a friend of Münzenberg from the Swiss days who faithfully informed Münzenberg of all happenings in the Comintern and the Russian party. A South American born Jew of Russian descent by the name of Shalito issued an IAH bulletin for the Russian press, the administration of the building was managed by an Austrian and the treasurer was a Russian.

Münzenberg obtained the rights to a travel guide to the Soviet Union which was being prepared by the "Society for Cultural Relations with Foreign Countries." Alexander Rado,[2] a Hungarian émigré and a talented geographer who had worked for the Soviets as early as 1920/21 in the Vienna telegraph agency *Rosta*, supervised the editorial prepara-

[1]Misiano had been a Communist deputy in southern Italy before escaping abroad from a fascist persecution. He was in charge of the Moscow IAH office until its liquidation in 1936. In 1934 he was denounced in the party cell of the Comintern as a conciliator and reprimanded although he humbly admitted his errors. Misiano could not take the malicious intrigues and accusations. He realized that the revolution was ruined. In 1935 he fell ill with a serious stomach complaint of which he died in August 1936.
[2]Alexander Rado became known to the world in general by running a Soviet spy network in Switzerland during the Second World War. He had connections with the German General Staff and after the start of the German-Russian war he passed valuable information to the Soviets. When the network was discovered by the Swiss authorities Rado succeeded in hiding for a year in Geneva with a pro-Communist professor at the University. In the autumn of 1944 he flew from Paris to Moscow where he was arrested and not heard of again for years. Since 1958 Rado has lived in Budapest.

tions. The book was full of information and maps, above all it contained detailed plans of all major cities in the Soviet Union—Moscow, Leningrad, Kharkov, Kiev and Odessa. It was the only guide which the Soviet authorities allowed to be published. As the war psychosis and the fear of espionage grew the Russians bought up all available copies of this *Guide to the Soviet Union*, which had appeared in German, French and English, and withdrew it from circulation. (In Berlin, where Rado edited the mimeographed *Geopress*, a curious collaboration later developed between the *Neue Deutsche Verlag* and the press department of Lufthansa. In 1928 the Soviet Government concluded an agreement with Lufthansa for a joint Moscow-Berlin transport service and founded a company, *Deruluft*, for that purpose. Rado prepared route maps for the companies which were produced by the *Neue Deutsche Verlag* and distributed free to passengers. This association was most useful while it lasted. For a fraction of the regular air fare we could travel in single-engined Junkers planes everywhere in Germany and in fifteen hours we could be in Moscow.)

During my first stay in Moscow, Münzenberg and I visited his many friends and acquaintances. We called on Klara Zetkin, who then lived in a wing of the Kremlin, in austere white-washed rooms reminiscent of monastery cells. It was amusing to see how shy the otherwise self-assured Münzenberg became when he introduced me to the old lady. He greatly respected Klara Zetkin and knew her strict views on marriage and the family, and how he breathed a sigh of relief when she obviously approved of me.

Another person living in the Kremlin was Karl Radek who worked at the University for the Peoples of the East. He had been deprived of his position as adviser to the German section of the Comintern but his interest in Germany continued and he gave us much interesting news. We also visited Trotsky who sat like a reigning monarch in his office in the Electrosavod. Dressed in a light grey lounge suit he looked distinguished and very un-Russian. He was extremely polite, very reserved and slightly arrogant. Münzenberg later gave me an account of their private conversation. Trotsky had tried to make him an ally in the struggle among the Soviet leaders. But, however much Münzenberg admired Trotsky as the creator of the Red Army and—beside Lenin—as the brain behind the October Revolution and the co-founder of the Soviet state, he was too cautious to commit himself to any one side in the fight for power. During the discussion Trotsky tried to convince Münzenberg that the Comintern's policy towards the British trade unions, and therefore also Münzenberg's activity in this sphere, was irreconcilable with a truly Bolshevik policy. But Münzenberg believed that the Comintern would forfeit any chance for effective action if it followed Trotsky's implacable line—which bore a marked resemblance to the attitude of the German extreme left.

These differences did not prevent Münzenberg from publishing Trotsky's writings in Berlin, or making propaganda use of his name which was extremely popular abroad. In 1926 Trotsky spent several weeks in a Berlin sanatorium. Münzenberg visited him and acquired the German rights to *The United States of Europe*. In this work Trotsky attacked Münzenberg's friend Edo Fimmen who under the same title had portrayed a united Europe which in many respects resembled the scheme still awaiting realization in the Common Market. Trotsky criticized Fimmen's "reformist illusions." In his view a united Europe was possible only after a world revolution.

At about the same time Münzenberg came to an agreement with Thomas, a former Comintern man and an admirer of Trotsky, on the publication of ambitious books, the *Illustrated History of the Russian Revolution* and the *Illustrated History of the Russian Civil War*. Thomas, who now called himself Rubenstein, lived in a quiet Berlin suburb to which he had brought his vast library and important private archives. We worked on these volumes for two years and I searched for missing photographic and documentary material in the revolutionary museums in Leningrad and Moscow. At that time museums and archives were still relatively accessible. Most of the staff were not members of the party; they were helpful and provided vast amounts of material, largely uncatalogued. Documents and photographs were available for both sides.. Pictures and books by people who had fallen out of favour were not yet banished to "poison cupboards." When the Comintern heard of our venture Bukharin despatched two "red professors," V. Astrov and A. Slepkov, to Berlin to help and to supervise Thomas. He was afraid that Thomas might include too much subtle propaganda for Trotsky. The red professors were very happy in Berlin, they enjoyed the bourgeois life and Thomas got on well with them; consequently a full account was given of the role of Trotsky and of other opposition leaders.

But the struggle within the party became more acrimonious in 1926. At the Fourteenth Russian Party Congress in December 1925 the temporary alliance between Stalin, Zinoviev and Kamenev had come to an end. While Trotsky remained cautiously in the background, Zinoviev and Kamenev, on behalf of the Leningrad delegation, strongly attacked Stalin, Bukharin and Rykov for their opportunist policy, their un-Marxist thesis of "the building of Socialism in one country," and their view that the peasants would never peacefully integrate into Socialism. The seriousness of the party crisis was underlined by a unique occurrence: Zinoviev came out with a supplementary report to the report of the

Secretary General, Stalin. Mobilizing all the forces he could, Stalin succeeded in removing Zinoviev from the Politburo in July 1926. Zinoviev and Trotsky now combined forces in an opposition bloc. When this bloc registered a number of successes at Moscow factory cell meetings the Politburo issued a warning. Although Trotsky and Zinoviev submitted to the Central Committee's decisions on 17 October both were expelled from the Politburo. Zinoviev also lost his mandate as Russian delegate to the Comintern. One month later Bukharin addressed the seventh session of the expanded Comintern Executive in place of Zinoviev, and Stalin reported on the Russian party. The struggle within the Russian party had spread to the Comintern sections.

When it came to the next plenary session of the Comintern in May 1927 Stalin had done such a thorough job of "cleaning up" the Comintern organization that the two Russian representatives of the opposition, Trotsky and Vujovic were expelled in spite of the Italian delegation's protests. Zinoviev was refused entry to the assembly hall by the armed guard on duty. Only after energetic protests by the German delegate, Arthur Ewert, was Zinoviev allowed into the hall.

The security precautions at this Comintern session assumed dimensions hitherto unknown. Anyone who wished to enter the Lenin hall on the first floor of the Comintern building where the executive met had to pass at least six check-points. A permanent guard at the entrance inspected every visitor's credentials. At the bottom of the stairs leading to the meeting hall a second guard checked the special pass required for the meeting, at the top of the stairs stood the third, in the middle of the corridor the fourth, the fifth at the entrance to the hall and immediately behind the door, inside the hall, was the sixth. The guards were therefore only a few feet apart, nevertheless each one of them studied the pass with intense seriousness. But the situation was not humorous to the participants who patiently showed their papers as though this was a matter of life and death.

No protocol of this session has ever been published. The main topics were the situation in China and the alleged threat of war which was made much of because Great Britain had broken off diplomatic relations. The Russian opposition had prepared its documentation which had been distributed to the delegates. It included a letter to the Central Committee of the Russian party signed by five hundred old Bolsheviks, fighters from the pre-1917 years. Although Münzenberg had attended the December meeting of the Executive Committee of the Communist International (ECCI), it seems that he was not fully aware that the conflicts among the Russian leaders were reaching a climax. He was concerned with developing his organizations, he was preparing the Brussels Congress, and apparently failed to realize the seriousness of the situation in Russia. In his opinion the ideological differences between the protagonists did not concern any issues that vitally affected the Soviet Union's future; as for a struggle for power between individuals, this was not the first one. Then, in November 1927, he witnessed a series of dramatic events.

For the tenth anniversary celebrations of the October Revolution the "Society for Cultural Relations with Foreign Countries," whose chairman continued to be Olga Kamenev, had asked Münzenberg to invite friends of the Soviet Union from all over the world to a congress in Moscow. The visitors were the guests of the Russian Government which paid all their expenses, including travel. Münzenberg went to Moscow with a large group of German and foreign friends of the IAH. We were put up at the Hotel Paris, a small, old fashioned, pale pink building at the corner of Tverskaya and Mokhovaya. On 7 November, the day of the traditional big parade and demonstration in Red Square, several oppositionists gathered on a first floor balcony of the hotel facing the crossroads. They displayed large photographs of Lenin, Trotsky and Zinoviev, put up a banner and began to shout opposition slogans to the crowds below. Others tried to address the multitude. The mounted militia quickly intervened; there was a scuffle outside the hotel in which the police indiscriminately attacked bystanders. Several people were arrested. Soon afterwards GPU officials charged into the hotel where, apart from Russian officials, several foreigners from Münzenberg's delegation were staying. The GPU men tore down the pictures and banners and searched the hotel from top to bottom. This caused great excitement in the hotel, but among the crowds, outside the incident produced no response whatsoever. The masses had become indifferent to conflicts among the party leaders. I remember that the comments of party members on similar incidents in other parts of the city were always critical of the opposition for appealing to the public. They felt the party should resolve its problems in private not in front of the entire nation. A pamphlet published in German, English and French and distributed to foreign delegates attacked the Trotskyist opposition as traitors, "whites" and counter-revolutionaries. The delegates, at a loss to understand what was behind all this, were somewhat confused by these outbursts.

The incidents on the occasion of the anniversary of the October Revolution gave Stalin a welcome pretext: the Central Committee, the Central Control Commission and the Fifteenth Party Congress of the CPSU expelled hundreds of oppositionists from the party, including all the leaders. Kamenev and Zinoviev tried in vain to save themselves by recanting. Most of the oppositionists, including Trotsky and Radek, were exiled; the less prominent were arrested and imprisoned. The banishments caused a greater stir in the bourgeois world than in the Soviet Union where even in Lenin's day it had been common practice to send unpopular party members to distant parts of the country. Most foreign Communists at first regarded such banishments as a mild party punishment, all the more so as the particular circumstances and the brutal behaviour of the GPU remained unknown.

Karl Radek was banished to the Siberian town of Tomsk. His wife was allowed to accompany him. They found a flat and he informed us of his new address: Gogolevskaya 33. His first card in which he asked us for newspapers and journals was signed "Red Front". We remained in correspondence with him for the duration of his banishment. In spite of his initial refusal to recant and in spite of his prophetic words that "strong nerves" would be needed as banishment "was a trifle compared with what is still in front of us,[1] he capitulated and was allowed to return to Moscow in 1929. We visited him shortly after his return. He had not yet been allowed to rejoin the party, and lived in primitive quarters in the basement of an old block of flats. His kidney complaint troubled him and he looked old and dejected. But a year or so later he was back in favor with the great *Voshd*—the "leader"—and lived in the Dom Pravitelstvo, a large grey cement skyscraper inhabited only by senior party officials. His spacious flat provided a splendid view of the Kremlin and the Moskva. Radek reclined on an enormous square divan, surrounded by books, papers and manuscripts in many languages. At the time he wrote leaders for *Izvestia*. Although he no longer had any political influence in the party or the Comintern he had become a foreign political expert and a contact man for many embassies in Moscow. He boasted to Münzenberg of his excellent relations with the German Embassy. After 1931 he was allowed to travel abroad again. He visited us in Berlin where as an important official he stayed in the Soviet Embassy.

When Münzenberg attended the Seventh World Congress in Moscow in 1935 Radek still lived in the Dom Pravitelstvo. Meanwhile he had risen to the position of unofficial adviser to the dictator. He was inordinately proud of this fact. He was in direct telephone communication with the Kremlin, and Stalin called up at every hour of the day and night to inform himself on questions of foreign policy, on foreign newspaper commentaries or similar matters. At this last meeting between Radek and Münzenberg, Radek made no mention of domestic policy, of the murder of Kirov and the new wave of arrests of oppositionists. On the other hand he held forth at length about the progress of the Russian economy and the improvement in living conditions.

[1] *Opposition Bulletin (Russian)*, No. 6, October 1929, Berlin.

How could Münzenberg have accepted the fall of the idols of the October Revolution, the disappearance of Zinoviev and Trotsky, without becoming alarmed? He had certainly taken Trotsky seriously even though he had never liked Zinoviev, who was too hysterical, too highly strung, too far removed from the political realities of post-war Europe for Münzenberg. Stalin and the men around him, Rykov, Bukharin, and Tomsky seemed more sensible, more sober, more realistic to Münzenberg. He felt the fortunes of the Comintern might improve under the new man, who although no great orator, seemed to be a man of action. Moreover, the old battle-tried Comintern team, Piatnitsky, Bukharin, Manuilsky, Kuusinen and Knorin, remained. For Münzenberg, as for many other party officials, the Comintern was his political "home." He felt that he belonged to the big international family of leading officials. He was taken seriously in the Comintern, an interest was taken in all his political problems and he was advised down to the last detail. And the Comintern was the link with the Russian party, with the victorious representative of the revolution, the embodiment of the power of a great state. The Comintern's protection guaranteed the satisfaction of great ambitions, it ensured an outlet for a restless urge for activity. The common jargon, the intimacy with Communist officials the world over —from Australia to Iceland—created a feeling of solidarity which needed to be subjected to far greater strain before it would be destroyed.

All the rumours, the savage sentences on the followers of Trotsky and Zinoviev—which convinced men like Max Levin, who was then employed by the Comintern, that Stalin would not shy away from any murder—were pushed aside as ridiculous exaggerations. Münzenberg was not the only one to do this. He spoke no Russian, so he had to talk with Stalin through an interpreter. Therefore the two men met face to face only two or three times over the years. Nor was Münzenberg, according to his own statements, particularly interested in closer contacts. It was impossible to see Stalin when one wanted to. Münzenberg loathed bureaucratic formalities and hated having to make an appointment days in advance.

Münzenberg began to have real doubts only when Stalin, having eliminated all his rivals, became the object of great hero worship. But even then it was easy to find excuses for the never ending stream of articles of homage on the occasion of Stalin's fiftieth birthday: the primitive *mushik* wanted a leader; Stalin himself did not wish for this adulation; he tolerated it for tactical reasons. By 1930 cinema audiences stood up and applauded when Stalin's picture appeared on the screen.

Münzenberg's Moscow friends who had been privately amused at the situation found nothing to joke about in these latest developments.

7. The Call of the Oppressed Peoples

From 1924/25 onwards the Comintern had concentrated increasingly on uncommitted pro-Communists. This becomes clear from Comintern directives published by *Inprecorr:*

> For certain specific purposes mass organizations which are uncommitted but potentially pro-Communist represent an important means of organizing Communist influence on the masses. They can be autonomous or independent organizations. Their organizational form must be as elastic as possible. Apart from individual membership there is also the possibility of collective association. In every country there must be an agreement with the party leadership on which of these organizations are entitled to invite the trade unions to collective association.
> Among existing uncommitted but potentially pro-Communist mass organizations it is above all the work of Red Aid that must be assisted by the Communists. Also important is participation in bodies like the International Workers Aid which have developed as independent non-party organizations and which today have a substantial following.
> Anti-war leagues and organizations against colonial terror and against the oppression of Asian peoples in several countries must be considered as potentially new pro-Communist mass organizations. In countries where the liberated masses of workers and peasants express enthusiastic sympathy for Soviet Russia (particularly in connection with a workers delegation campaign), associations of worker friends of the new Russia may be considered . . .
> We must so to speak create a whole solar system of organizations and small committees around the Communist Party, of small committees that are in practice under the influence of our party (but not under its mechanical direction).[1]

Through its world-wide connections the IAH in particular had very early come into contact with a number of movements that had joined forces against imperialism and colonialism. In 1924 the improvement in the economic situation began to make IAH aid in Germany unnecessary. Münzenberg now concentrated increasingly on other countries where the social and economic situation was still sufficiently bad to make aid worthwhile from a practical and therefore also from a propaganda point of view.

In May 1925 a wages strike in a Japanese textile factory in Shanghai grew, after the intervention of British troops, into a general strike which spread to the major Chinese cities and led to a national revolt against foreign capitalism and to a month long trade boycott of the

[1] *Inprecorr*, Vol. 6, no. 68, p. 1065 and no. 52, p. 725.

British crown colony of Hong Kong. The brutal methods which General
Chang Tso-lin in Peking and the representative of British interests in
Nanking, General Wu Pei-fu, used to suppress this movement incensed
the West and produced a strong feeling of solidarity for the Chinese
nation. Many people followed with interest the activities of a young
officer, the former commandant of the military academy of Whampoo,
Chiang Kai-shek. With Moscow's assistance Chiang Kai-shek was setting
up a new state based on the teachings of the founder of the Chinese
Republic, Dr. Sun Yat-sen, who had died recently. With IAH support
a "League against Colonialism" was established in Berlin. It was directed by Louis Gibarti and Lucie Peters and had contacts with University of Berlin students from China, India, Indonesia, Indo-China and the
Arab countries, and later also with students in Paris and London. The
German authorities were very suspicious of the venture which
preached: "Germany must have no colonies." The Reichswehr ministry
tried repeatedly to smuggle its spies into the League.

Münzenberg hoped to persuade the International Federation of
Trade Unions to take joint action on China; however, he received a
rebuff when the International Federation declared that it would first
consult the Chinese trade unions with whom it was in touch. The British
behaved differently. The TUC demanded concerted international aid
for China. The appeal was signed by well known workers and trade
union leaders—Lansbury, Cook, Gossip, Hicks, Tom Man, Maxton, Ellen Wilkinson and MacLean. Münzenberg noted with satisfaction that
a number of influential Labour Party members welcomed his activities.
Evidently it did not worry them that the initiative had come from a
Communist.

The Weimar Republic was generous in giving asylum to members of
colonial freedom movements. There were more than a hundred Chinese students at Berlin University. The Kuomintang had an office in
Berlin and Münzenberg was on friendly terms with its secretary, Liau.
Ho Chi-minh who then lived in Paris paid repeated visits to Berlin on
his way to and from Moscow. The Indian Communist Manabendranath
Roy first published his journal, *Vanguard*, in Berlin in 1922. There was
another leading Indian journalist, V. Chattopadhyaya, in Berlin and he
too was on friendly terms with Münzenberg. Chatto, as we called him,
came from a wealthy Indian family. He had studied in London from
1911 to 1914. At the start of the First World War he went to Berlin
because the German Government gave active assistance to the Indians
in their fight for independence. At that time Chatto was an anarchist.
His first wife was the American author Agnes Smedley. Having for years
been an honorary member of the Berlin "League Against Imperialism"
he went to Leningrad in 1933 as a language teacher. He coached se-

lected young Russians of both sexes in the most important Indian dialects of the regions where his pupils would be used by the Russian espionage service. During the mass arrests in 1937 he met Margarete Buber-Neumann in Moscow and told her that he was very afraid of being arrested. Above all he was worried about his German wife and his three children. His premonitions came true for he soon disappeared. In 1947 the Indian Government made enquiries about Chatto's whereabouts through its ambassador in Moscow, Mrs. Pandit. The Russian authorities merely told her that Chatto had died of pneumonia.

Münzenberg persuaded several Norwegian and Austrian professional associations to join the China campaign. Because of the generous contributions of the Russian trade unions the newly founded IAH section in Peking was able to supply $250,000 for food and clothing. But "in spite of these reasonably good results the real importance of this campaign lies in the moral and cultural assistance which the IAH was able to give the Chinese people in its struggle for national and social freedom."[1] This kind of assistance took the form of an appeal which was signed by many German artists and writers. Copies of the appeal were put up in Peking in poster form and it was published by the Chinese press. On 16 August 1925 Münzenberg organized a "Hands off China" congress in the Berlin *Herrenhaus,* the purpose of which was to "link the Western proletariat with the proletariat of the East."[2] He struck up a lasting friendship with Sun Yat-sen's widow, Madame Sun Ching-ling, with the result that from then on Madame Sun's name always appeared in connection with Münzenberg's ventures. The British Government reacted very nervously to the campaign which Borodin, Chiang Kai-shek's Russian advisor, conducted in China and which Münzenberg publicized in Europe.

To many Western liberals, colonies were the most flagrant example of the ruthless exploitation of man by man. This sympathy for the colonial peoples was fully justified if one bears in mind the social state of the colonies at that time, the dreadful working conditions, the starvation wages, the child labour and the inferior legal status of the indigenous population. It was therefore natural that Münzenberg should think of bringing together the representatives of the colonial freedom movements and the friends of the anti-colonial movements and parties of the West.

The Comintern and the Russians had tried in 1920 in Baku and in 1921/22 in Irkutsk and Moscow to bring together the representatives of several Asian freedom movements. The attempt had failed because

[1] W. Münzenberg, *Fünf Jahre* IAH, p. 116.
[2] *Ibid.,* p. 120.

the national revolutionaries of Turkey, Persia and other Asian countries had refused to toe the Comintern line. In his address to the Second Comintern Congress, Lenin had spoken of fairly far reaching assistance for colonial freedom movements. He wanted the Communists to be free to establish temporary links with national freedom movements in the colonies and in backward countries and even to enter into short-term alliances with them, a point of view fiercely rejected by the Indian Communist, M. Roy. Roy wanted from the start to organize a mass struggle of peasants and workers to free themselves from all forms of exploitation and he wanted to found Communist Parties in the colonies. His objective was the establishment of soviet republics through revolution. National revolutionary liberation must not be left to bourgeois freedom movements.

This discussion continued at the Third and Fourth Comintern Congresses. The newly established Chinese Communist Party went further than Lenin and demanded a "four class alliance" between the bourgeoisie, the lower middle classes, the peasants and the workers. The Chinese Communists did not feel that Roy's call to fight the national bourgeoisie was applicable to China.[1] In contrast to the Second International the Comintern stressed its determination to support colonial liberation wars. The Communist Parties in the mother countries were exhorted to agitate against their own governments for the liberation of the colonies and to support independence movements physically as well.

In an article on 3 August 1926 Münzenberg proposed for the first time "a colonial conference." In doing so he emphasized the Communist point of view that in the interest of the proletarian revolution the Communists must assist the oppressed nations in their fight for freedom. He distinguished between his own ideas and the vague phrases of bourgeois pacifists like Hellmuth von Gerlach who had prayed for French victory over the wild hordes of the Riff Kabyle. At the same time he announced the formation in Germany of a league against colonial terror and oppression which proposed to invite the representatives of colonial and semi-colonial countries to an international conference. Many declarations of support had already come from China, India, Egypt, The Sudan, South Africa and other African countries.[2]

The Paris agents of the league who were seeking to establish contacts in the French colonial empire soon came up against the French authorities. Therefore it seemed advisable to hold the planned congress in Brussels. Emile Vandervelde had just become foreign minister of Belgium and it would have been difficult for him as a Socialist and as

[1] *Ostprobleme*, Vol. 14, no. 2, 26 January 1962, p. 34.
[2] *Inprecorr*, 3 August 1926, p. 301 *et seq.*,

Secretary of the Second International to say no to a congress against colonialism. Münzenberg sent Gibarti to Brussels to negotiate. Vandervelde stated his conditions: there must be no mention of the situation in the Belgian Congo, and the Belgian Sûreté demanded a list of delegates to the preparatory committee. When these conditions were met the Belgian Government would make available the mediaeval Palais Egmont near Brussels. Münzenberg was very excited when Gibarti reported to him and he accepted the conditions at once. The list of delegates would be shortened if need be, and as yet there was no freedom movement in the Belgian Congo whose representatives could be invited to the congress. For months afterwards the Paris press reproached the Belgian Government for admitting these revolutionaries.

When Münzenberg discussed the plan in Moscow, the Comintern's first reaction was sceptical. Münzenberg was warned of the ideological confusion that such a congress would cause. Roy and Codovilla in particular opposed the idea. At first Münzenberg was discouraged and he sent a telegram to Berlin asking Gibarti to go slow. But then Gibarti wired news of a coup: the two Nehrus, Jawaharlal and his father Motilal, the influential leader of the Indian National Congress, supported the idea of a congress. Suddenly Moscow was also in favour of the idea, and Marcel Rosenberg, an official of the Russian Foreign Office, was sent to Berlin to act as an advisor.

The reasons for Moscow's diplomatic interest in such a congress were manifold. The Russians were heavily committed in the struggles in China and they feared British intervention. They felt that pressure could be exerted on the British Government at a congress where British Labour representatives were present. Any anti-British stirrings, such as Nehru's statement in India or the support given to the Brussels congress by the former Egyptian Prime Minister, Khediv Mohammed Hafiz Ramadan, helped the Russian cause and were reason enough for the Kremlin to give political support to the proposed congress.

A "League for the Struggle Against Imperialism" had been organized as early as 1924 by Chinese Communists in Moscow. Münzenberg picked up the name and used the National Communist Parties to form branches of the league in as many Western countries as possible. The idea was that these branches would send delegates to the congress to provide a Communist influence, as no official invitations had been issued to representatives of the Third International or the Communist Parties. Gibarti was sent to Paris to ask Henri Barbusse to take charge of the secretariat of the congress bureau. Other famous writers joined the preparatory committee, among them the Spanish novelist Ramón del Valle Inclán, and Manuel Ugarte, a former Argentinian senator and one of Latin America's most important writers. The French Communist

Party did not want Barbusse to be in charge as it was planning to make a strong attack on him for his "rightist and conciliatory" attitude. Münzenberg asked Gibarti to plead with the French party leaders to postpone this controversy for six months. Barbusse was essential to him for the proposed congress. After that the French party could do what it thought best.

A few weeks before the congress a quarrel broke out between Münzenberg and Gibarti, who had made some indiscreet remarks about the IAH to one of Münzenberg's opponents. Münzenberg showed Gibarti the door. Shortly afterwards he ran into Gibarti at the Russian Embassy and, as though nothing had happened, asked how he was, what he was living on, and suggested that Gibarti come and see him. Münzenberg needed him more than ever because an assistant who knew every name and every organization the world over and who could correspond in five languages was invaluable; Gibarti returned and continued to work for Münzenberg.

During this period Münzenberg, now 37 years of age, began to change his mode of life. Since his return to Germany in 1918 he had lived the life of a "professional revolutionary," in offices, travelling, escaping from the police, in hotels and coffee houses. From time to time he had retired to a furnished room with a Pankow worker's family whose address nobody knew. These habits he now abandoned. He rented a few rooms in Zelten 9a, one of the old houses at the Berlin *Tiergarten*, mostly occupied by retired Wilhelminian officers and officials. But even this was not a home in the bourgeois sense; the house belonged to Professor Magnus Hirschfeld[1] whose Institute for Sexual Sciences occupied a building close by. Hirschfeld, although himself a Socialist, was kindly disposed towards the Communists and offered the flat to Münzenberg. The many corridors and a room which gave access to others were plastered with the sexual symbols of primitive peoples and other relevant photographic material, and visitors to the institute wandered through our corridors also.

This flat soon enjoyed a considerable reputation in the Comintern. Not only were there curious things to be seen, the rooms were also suitable for meeting illegal visitors from abroad. Emissaries arrived

[1]With Havelock Ellis, Auguste Forel, Max Hodann, Helene Stoecker, Alexandra Kollontai, the Brupbachers and the Russian Pashe-Osserski, Magnus Hirschfeld founded in 1928 a World League for Sexual Reform. After the sensational electoral success of the National Socialists in the autumn of 1930 he told us that he would leave Germany forever. He was quick to appreciate what was happening, went on a trip around the world and returned in 1934 to Europe where we met him for the last time in Paris in a flat near the Eiffel Tower. In a mauve dressing gown the dying man sat in an armchair and talked of his travels. Shortly afterwards he died in Nice.

from Moscow, Dimitrov met his Balkan representatives there, in fact the place was a hive of activity.

In the weeks before the Brussels congress Marcel Rosenberg visited Münzenberg every evening. They sat together on the Biedermeier sofa surrounded by papers, registration forms from prominent visitors, and galley proofs of bulletins. Münzenberg was very enthusiastic and somewhat impatient at Rosenberg's dampening pedantry. He knew how precarious his plans were, how much they depended on Moscow's support. In the weeks before the congress he occasionally was awed at his own courage, wandered about in an absent-minded way and mumbled melodramatically to himself that he was gambling for high stakes. His staff of young, enthusiastic assistants had no such doubts, they pushed him ahead and contributed substantially to the success of the meeting.

Münzenberg felt this campaign would assist Russian policy, but he also thought it was of greater importance. As with all his activities he was working for a Socialist future for the world. The "damned of this earth" for him included all colours and races. Rosenberg, who had an intimate knowledge of the Near East and the Middle East and who saw the Russian Foreign Office dispatches, tried to temper Münzenberg's enthusiasm. He analyzed the personalities of the various parties, advised caution in issuing invitations and warned against delegates who might be too reactionary or pro-British. Above all he held forth on the various political groupings in the mandate territories and colonies and on their attitude towards Soviet Russia.

Since 1925 there had been unrest, revolts and wars against the colonial powers in many areas. In Spanish and French Morocco the Riff Kabyle rising led successfully for years by Abd el-Krim was put down when France brought in two hundred thousand well equipped soldiers. Abd el-Krim surrendered and was exiled to Réunion Island, but his demand for an independent North Africa had unleashed powerful impulses. The "North African Star" was the first big Freedom movement of the Mohammedans and their leader, Messali Hadj-Ahmed,[1] attended the Brussels congress as delegate.

A rising in Java in 1926 was avenged by the Dutch colonial administration with punitive expeditions and death sentences. The leader of the Indonesian freedom movement *Sarikat Islam,* Mohammed Hatta, was one of the prominent participants at the Brussels congress. Later he was kept in prison for years by the Dutch in Indonesia; when Indonesia became independent Sukarno successfully kept him in the background.

[1] Expelled from Algeria, Messali Hadj-Ahmed today (1966) lives as a political refugee near Paris.

In Latin America, United States troops occupied Nicaragua in February 1927, while in Mexico a national people's government under President Calles set about pushing Standard Oil out of the country, abolishing foreign concessions and effecting an agrarian revolution with the expropriation of church latifundia and large estates. Münzenberg's old friend, Professor Alfons Goldschmidt, was at that time a visiting professor in Mexico City and had established contacts with Calles. The Mexican Government was very interested in the proposed congress and contributed large sums to support it. The Mexican Ambassador in Berlin, Ramón de Negri, was one of the League's most active promoters. During a dinner which he gave for Alexandra Kollontai, who was on her way to Mexico as Russian Ambassador, and to which Münzenberg and other members of the League had been invited, Kollontai promised to do her best in Latin America to make the congress a success.

The Indian National Congress sent its young Secretary-General, Jawaharlal Nehru, and other Indian representatives to Brussels. Nehru's friend, the journalist Nambiar, who later became Indian Ambassador to Bonn, was a member of the delegation. How strongly the Brussels meeting influenced Nambiar became clear when thirty years later, after the Indo-Chinese frontier war, he stressed to the present author the basic difference between that first encounter of representatives of the colonial peoples with members of the Western world and the unsatisfactory consequences of the Bandung Conference. In his view the "spirit of Bandung" was not comparable to the optimistic enthusiasm that had inspired the delegates to the Brussels anti-colonial congress. The delegates had all come to Brussels to voice their wishes and demands, they had all been filled by one great hope, and most of the voices had not been those of Communists. Those who had assembled in Bandung had been the representatives of former colonies. But there had no longer been any talk of a joint struggle. On the contrary, clear imperialist differences had emerged. There was no Afro-Asian solidarity. China, ambitious to become a great power, wanted to transform the small states of Asia into satellites, and the new African black republics tried to throw out all Asians.

Nehru too was aware of the difference between the high hopes of Brussels and the brutal reality of Bandung on which he commented sadly in a private conversation with Gibarti. It was Nehru who, in his opening speech at Bandung, paid tribute to Münzenberg, the initiator of Brussels.

The Brussels Congress was attended by delegates and visitors from all over the world. Hindu princes, Kuomintang generals, leaders of Asian freedom movements and trade union officials from Asia, Africa, South America and Oceania met politicians from the liberal, Socialist and Communist camps of Europe and America for the first time. Romain Rolland, George Lansbury, Upton Sinclair, Albert Einstein, Henri Barbusse, Madame Sun Yat-sen, J. D. Nehru and Maxim Gorki were elected honorary members of the presidium. Gandhi sent a telegram regretting that he could not be present in person; Victor Margueritte telegraphed:

> . . . Colonial oppression is one of the most reprehensible forms of imperialism. This terror of force is the more reprehensible as it directed against the weakest; it degrades not only the nation which uses it, it destroys civilization itself . . .[1]

Albert Einstein in a message of greetings condemned the fact that a few white nations ruled the world and, addressing himself to Münzenberg, said: "I . . . am convinced that the successful accomplishment of the task which you have undertaken is in the interest of all to whom the dignity of man is dear." Numerous Socialists from Belgium, Switzerland and above all Britain came as delegates or guests. The Secretary of the British Miners' Union, Cook, sent his representative, S. O. Davies, and demanded "firm action against the reactionary forces which are in evidence also in some workers' parties."

Communist delegates and guests had strict instructions to keep in the background. On the evening of 10 February 1927 the Congress was opened in the fine old hall of the Palais Egmont by Henri Barbusse who made an impassioned speech and thanked the hosts, the Belgian Government. Apart from Münzenberg the only Communists to address the conference were Harry Pollitt and the Japanese Comintern representative Katayama. Manuel Gomez who spoke for Latin America had, it is true, for years been used by the Russians, but he was not internationally known as a Communist. The Communists worked behind the scenes, in the commissions in which solid Communist blocs played an important role. The Russian delegation consisted of a trade union group under G. N. Melnichansky, and Comintern and Bolshevik Party observers. The Komsomol was represented by Besso Lominadse, who was then still one of Stalin's intimate friends.

Altogether one hundred and seventy-four delegates attended, representing one hundred and thirty-four organizations from thirty-seven countries. One hundred and four came from the colonies or from territories "oppressed by imperialism," seventy from Europe and the United States. The Chinese, who had twenty-five representatives from

---

[1]This and the following quotations, unless stated otherwise, are taken from the "Official Protocol of the Congress against Colonial Oppression and Imperialism. The Signal Flame at the Palais Egmont." Berlin 1927.

China and numerous visitors from European Kuomintang groups, were the most influential group. The fraternization that took place between the Chinese delegates and the British and Indian delegates greatly impressed those attending the Congress.

Münzenberg was in his element. He moved easily among the crowd, one of his staff always by his side to interpret for him. He personally met all delegates and gave a particularly warm welcome to the British Labour Party guests. He sent his agents to the commissions, listened to advice and demands from the Comintern representatives and, just like all the others, was full of the infectious enthusiasm which this first big meeting of representatives of all races generated. In his final speech he said:

> We . . . believe that today we can discern the outlines of the development of the next decades which in our opinion . . . will bring the liberation of the colonial and semi-colonial peoples. By organizing man's will we shall try to hasten this development and to achieve freedom more quickly for these peoples.

Edo Fimmen deserved special credit for the success of the congress and the foundation of the League. Big and powerful, with a great shock of hair, Fimmen was very good at running the meetings. He translated proposals, interventions and speeches, smoothed troubled waters, conferred with Russian and other trade union representatives and always remained the proud, combative Socialist who, in spite of his sympathy for the Russian revolution, rejected Russia's excessive political demands and insisted on the political and intellectual independence of the trade union movement. As Secretary of the International Federation of Trade Unions he had travelled widely and had the confidence of the Indonesian and Japanese associations, as well as of the Latin American unions. Like Münzenberg his utmost desire was for world-wide collaboration among all progressive Socialist forces but he was realistic enough to know exactly what could be accomplished at any given moment.

Probably the greatest success of the Brussels Congress was George Lansbury's attendance. The Grand Old Man of the Labour Party had spent his youth in the colonies and had seen the exploitation of the colonial peoples in Asia. As far back as 1896, at the London Congress of the Second International, he had made a passionate attack on colonialism at a time when the Socialist parties had only just begun to be concerned with this matter. Now he appeared in Brussels, expressed his agreement with the organizers' aims and made a moving speech. He urged that the freedom movements in Asia and Africa unfurl the red flag of Socialism, rather than dissipate their strength in nationalism. He thought that something had occurred at the congress which had so far happened only rarely in the history of mankind: its members had proclaimed the indissoluble unity of the black, yellow and white races. In his report in *Labour Weekly* he indignantly denied that this anti-colonial movement was directed by Moscow and said that the predominant characteristic of the Brussels Congress had been its spontaneity. He praised Münzenberg's most active assistants, "comrades" Bach and Gibarti, who had made the congress a success and he closed with the observation that God and nature had made all peoples of the earth of the same blood.

The Comintern too was satisfied with the course of the Congress. There had been a few awkward moments. For example, the Korean representatives put to the vote a resolution condemning Japan's predatory imperialism—a move which the Russians tried to stop because they did not want to strain their relations with Japan. But by and large the result was politically satisfactory. Even the aged Piatnitsky to whom Münzenberg accounted for the sums received from the Comintern—he even returned some spare dollars—observed that the affair had after all cost less than he had feared.

As the newly formed "League Against Imperialism" proceeded to establish contacts all over the globe, the colonial powers felt threatened and took counter-measures. *The Times*, which had initially ignored the Congress, published a leader on it and on its background. The British authorities arrested delegates of the League who wanted to enter India and they exerted enough pressure on the Belgian Government to prevent further League meetings from taking place there. Hatta was kept under lock and key for months in Holland. In Paris the French arrested a Senegalese, Lamine Senghor, who died of tuberculosis in prison. The Mexican trade unionist and League representative, Julio A. Mella, was murdered in Cuba. From the start one of the declared enemies of the League was the Secretariat of the Second International, although at the pre-war congresses member parties had always opposed capitalist colonial policy and demanded independence for the colonies. There were also those, like Eduard Bernstein in Germany and some Socialists in Britain, who argued that there ought to be colonies provided they were used to develop natural resources, and that it was not wrong for civilized countries to settle underdeveloped territories provided there was no oppression of the indigenous inhabitants.[1] This ambivalent attitude prevailed until many Socialist politicians openly supported the Communist initiative.

What damned the League once and for all with the Secretariat of the

[1]Julius Braunthal, *Geschichte der Internationale*, Vol. 1, Hanover 1961, p. 312.

Second International was that Münzenberg's name was linked with it. Friedrich Adler spoke of a new Communist united front manoeuvre and observed that the Communist initiators had learnt from bitter experience to operate more cautiously. Lansbury had unanimously been elected Chairman of the Executive Committee at the Congress. A few months later, when he was elected Chairman of the Labour Party, he resigned. He was succeeded by Fenner Brockway, an executive member of the Second International and Chairman of the Independent Labour Party. Brockway regarded the warnings of his International as exaggerated and unjustified, and he criticized their attitude in letters and articles. In a letter to Friedrich Adler on 8 April 1927 he said that the role the Communists had played in bringing about the Brussels Congress had been exaggerated. The Kuomintang, the Indian National Congress, the Egyptian nationalists and the Latin American parties were not Communists—a further reason for active Socialist participation in the League. In conclusion Brockway, who belonged to the League only as a private individual, asked whether there was anything in the statutes of the Second International to prevent his party, the ILP, from joining the League.[1] Adler's reply was clear: without question the parties of the Second International could not join other international political bodies. Adler wanted the next session of the Executive to take a unanimous decision on the question of the League. He was certain that the Communists were the real founders of the League. From the start they had wanted to keep the Second International out; for tactical reasons they had therefore not invited the Third International either. In conclusion Adler expressed surprise that Brockway should have accepted the chairmanship of the newly founded British section of the League.

Meanwhile in August 1927 Brockway attended a meeting of the League and a mass meeting in Cologne at which the audience's enthusiasm made a lasting impression on him. He told Friedrich Adler that he had attended the Cologne gathering as a private citizen. There he had carefully investigated Adler's allegations of Communist intervention and Communist financial assistance to the League and he was now absolutely certain that there was no truth in the accusation that the League was financed out of Russian funds. The payments from Moscow were insignificant compared with the contributions from other parties and national groups. He finished by saying that the Socialists would make a big mistake if they stayed outside. In his paper, *The New Leader*, Fenner Brockway continued the attack on 26 August 1927:

[1] See Friedrich Adler's correspondence in the Archives of the International Institute for Social History, Amsterdam.

Personally, I think it would be suicidal if Socialists refrained from association with this movement even if it had been initiated by the Communists.
It has done what the Socialist International has failed to do—seriously
begun the task of uniting the proletarian movements among the coloured
races . . . The suspicions which have been aroused are absolutely unjustified . . . The Brussels Conference cost £1,700. Of that amount only £30
came from an organization with Communist connections. Since the conference there has been no contribution remotely connected with Moscow
. . . The League Against Imperialism may be an important bridge across
the existing gulf.

But the Executive of the Second International did not give way. At
a meeting on 12 September 1927 it adopted a resolution demanding
that neither the Second International nor its affiliated parties should
have anything to do with the League. The strongest, and most effective,
attack on Brockway for collaborating with the Communists came from
Otto Wels. Only the Jewish-Socialist *Bund*, the Polish independent
Socialists and the Italian Nenni Socialists voted for Brockway. The
majority forced him to resign his League offices. He was replaced by
another ILP leader, James Maxton; indeed in general the British section
of the League was run mostly by Labour members.

Events in China were to have a profound effect on the further development of the League. On 20 March 1927 the Chinese strike movement had led to the occupation of Shanghai by the strikers. An
executive committee of Peoples' Delegates was set up as Chiang Kai-
shek moved his troops into the city. *Pravda* compared the situation with
the Russian October days and described it as a victory for the advancing
world revolution. Borodin increased Russian pressure on the Communists active in the Kuomintang and on the left-wing of the Kuomintang.
In Shanghai these groups elected a provisional government and used
the workers militia to expropriate the middle classes. Chiang Kai-shek
realized that he would lose the fruits of his victory if he continued to
give the Russians a free hand. Added to this there was the opposition
of powerful bourgeois elements within the Kuomintang and threatening ultimata from Britain, Japan and the United States. At the end of
March rumours circulated about an impending split in the Kuomintang.
In the Moscow party the opposition headed by Trotsky demanded the
withdrawal of the Communists from the Kuomintang. They were out-
voted by Stalin's supporters.

At the beginning of April, Chiang Kai-shek appealed to the Shanghai
workers to lay down their arms while denying any intention of wanting
to liquidate the Communist Party. But in the night of 12 April he struck
a decisive blow against the Communists. In a terrible blood bath all
known party officials in Shanghai and Nanking were arrested and ex-

ecuted together with thousands of workers. At the same time he broke off relations with Soviet Russia. The Communist trade unions were rendered powerless and the Communist-controlled University of Shanghai was closed. Stalin's China policy had ended in a defeat.

As early as 1926 the Russian opposition had warned the Soviet Union against becoming too closely involved with the Kuomintang. Now the Russian Politburo reversed gears. At the end of July 1927 it sent Besso Lominadse to China to depose at a party conference of the Chinese Communist Party its recently elected secretary, Chen. Lominadse criticized the "right-wing deviations" and the "opportunism" of the Chinese Communist Party which had done nothing but faithfully follow Moscow's line. At the same time the Russian press called for the formation of soviets in China. Münzenberg realized that in these circumstances the League would soon find it impossible to continue to cooperate with bourgeois national-revolutionary parties. Looking back on the League's work Münzenberg observed that the temporary defeat of the Chinese revolution had been a momentous loss to the League Against Imperialism.[1] For the moment however the impetus of Brussels continued to be effective. The League spread to every colony where it had a nucleus of supporters. The British section published a quarterly, *The Anti-Imperialist Review*, which came out also in German and French editions. But the League did not remain unaffected by the Comintern's sharp turn to the left. This became very clear at the League's second and last congress which took place on 21 July 1929 in Frankfurt am Main.

The Russians appeared with an official delegation led by the trade union secretary Melnichansky. He strongly attacked the British Labour Government and its failure in India, he welcomed the Indian revolutionary movement which for him was confined to Communists and reminded his audience that Soviet Russia was not on principle against all wars.

Münzenberg spoke in a similar vein, directing his fiercest attacks against the Socialists and particularly against Friedrich Adler. Meanwhile a bitter struggle was going on behind the scenes. Mohammed Hatta and James Maxton tried to persuade the congress to adopt a moderate resolution. Their attempts were rebuffed by the Comintern delegate, Manuilsky. He attacked the Socialists present and the delegates from the colonies and finally with the help of a solid Communist majority pushed through an uncompromising resolution. Friedrich Adler's predictions had come true. His friend Bjarne Braatoy who at-

[1] *Inprecorr*, 20 December 1927.

tended the Frankfurt Congress sent him an interesting report on the differences between the Russians and the other delegates.[1] Chattopadyaya, a member of the Berlin League office, poured out his heart to Braatoy, saying that he was above all an Indian nationalist and would always join forces with whatever power was most consistently anti-British. Nevertheless he regretted the attitude of the Russians, as he regretted that of the Socialist International towards the League and Münzenberg. He stressed in particular Münzenberg's ability to raise money, saying there was no need for him to turn to Moscow, he took what he required for the League from his publishing houses.

Manuilsky's most violent attacks were aimed at the League's Secretary, James Maxton, who was the only prominent British Socialist still active in the League. Shortly before the end of the Frankfurt congress the League's loyal supporters took the logical step: Maxton, Fimmen, Nehru and Hatta resigned. In a conversation with Nambiar, Nehru later said that he was convinced that the Russians had deliberately destroyed the Anti-Imperialist League because it did not fit in with Stalin's new line. The Russians no longer wanted anything to do with independent political forces, they tolerated only pro-Communists who submitted to Russia's political line of the moment.[2]

The Frankfurt Congress was very like the congresses which Münzenberg organized later. The enthusiastic spontaneity of Brussels was replaced by masterly staging. A General Sandino from Nicaragua handed over a blood-stained flag; large works delegations from Münzenberg's constituency welcomed the congress; the local League organization had everything perfectly organized.

But in the years to come the League only seemed to function independently. In reality it was subject to Comintern discipline and was used for Comintern campaigns. James Maxton was attacked because his party, the ILP, in 1929 joined forces with the German opposition Communists under Heinrich Brandler, with the Norwegian Workers' Party and with the Dutch International Socialists. The League representatives in Mexico were expelled because they had supported the right-wing opposition Communists in the United States. Finally, at one of the last plenary meetings of the League on German soil, in 1931, Nehru was described as "traitor to the cause of the liberation of the Indian people from the British imperialist yoke."

[1]Braatoy's letters to Adler of 6, 8, and 13 August 1929, Archives of the International Institute for Social History, Amsterdam.
[2]Information given by Nambiar to the present author.

8. The "Red Millionaire"

Hugo Eberlein, who looked after the finances of the Communist Party press in Germany, disapproved of Münzenberg's feverish efforts to branch out in new directions, particularly as the latter's dailies had quickly become accepted in Berlin. The Comintern on the other hand noted with satisfaction that Münzenberg's firms were self-supporting whereas the Communist Party press was always in need of financial assistance. But the very fact that Münzenberg's many enterprises were financially independent soon gave rise to curious rumours. The ideas of friend and foe were however vastly exaggerated. From the start his activity had annoyed the Social Democrats and, as he had more than once successfully persuaded influential men and women from among their ranks to support this or that venture of his, they attacked him in their press as a scheming seducer. Following up various rumours the Social Democratic journalist Eugen Prager early in 1929 launched a new type of attack on him. Prager's article on the Münzenberg trust, which was published by various papers including *Vorwärts*, "revealed" Münzenberg as a calculating businessman and an unprincipled master of a financial empire.[1]

Shortly before, *Vorwärts* had also made itself the mouthpiece of proletarian Young Communist attacks on Münzenberg. On 21 February 1929 it reported that some time previously Münzenberg had organized a "Red ball" with an admission fee of ten marks. The paper continued:

> The Central Committee of the Communist Youth has passed a protest resolution against Münzenberg and his supporters, containing the following sentence:
> 'We hope that proletarian fists will be found to beat up this collection of parlour Communists."

Münzenberg was most irritated by Prager's series of articles and replied at length in *Der Rote Aufbau* of May 1929. Prager had compiled a long list, containing a number of errors, of Münzenberg-controlled enterprises and organizations. Münzenberg countered by giving the German, Austrian and Belgian Social Democrats a list of their numerous business ventures and of their links with the capitalist economy. Münzenberg fiercely rejected the accusation that the Münzenberg trust was

[1] *Der Abend* (late edition of *Vorwärts*), 30 March 1929.

financed by innocent workers' pennies and that it was inadequately supervised. He outlined his basic attitude as follows:[1]

It is not the existence of economic concerns that determines whether the workers organization which controls them is socialist or not socialist but the manner in which the concerns are organized and the purpose which they serve. Proletarian organizations have not merely the right but the outright duty to own economic enterprises. Only political fools, philosophical speculators in coffee houses or tired folk who have made their peace with capitalist society and who in return have been given a civic position or an editorship can do without economic enterprises in support of broadly based revolutionary mass propaganda and agitation. As we do not belong to any of these categories we shall continue in spite of all attacks to strengthen the campaigning power of our organization with proletarian economic concerns. We are not Utopians, we lack the illusions of an Owen or of the Social Democrats who hold leading positions in their trade union and economic enterprises and who believe that capitalism can be conquered peacefully by giving the working classes more economic concerns. As Marxists we know that capitalist society can only be conquered by the proletarian revolution, that the day will come 'when the arms of criticism will become the criticism of arms'. For us all economic enterprises belonging to workers organizations are therefore only means to the end of increasing revolutionary agitation. This is the only purpose which we recognize and to this end we directly devoted the few economic concerns connected with our organization which we established in recent years, using our own resources and our own means.

In building up his trust Münzenberg used unusual means to appeal to those masses who had no understanding for party political demands but who were instinctively attracted by Socialism or Communism. Peter Maslowski who worked with him for a number of years thinks that Münzenberg was far ahead of his time in the use of mass media such as newspapers, films, large fêtes or artistic events—which attracted a much wider public than the usual party entertainment ever could—mass media which later, particularly in America, became a normal part of party propaganda.

The rapid and successful development of Münzenberg's enterprises was due in part to the Comintern's swing to the right between 1926 and 1928 which permitted its parties to woo the broad mass of the working classes, and in part to the economic recovery of the Weimar Republic during this period. Münzenberg's enemies as well as some envious comrades circulated the rumour that the "trust master" had at his

[1]Offprint *Münzenberg-Konzern?* (from *Der Rote Aufbau*), p. 22.

disposal fantastic resources which he used to give generous support to the KPD. It was said that the Russians engaged in large scale economic transactions in Germany through him. Those stories, in which the right-wing press delighted, may have improved the credit of his firms with banks and suppliers but they were far from the truth. The assertion that he had "the Russians behind him" lived on. As late as 1937 the film actor George Alexander said in conversation with Leo Slezak and the former head of *Prometheus* Films: *"Prometheus* was run by the Bolsheviks. When they did not want to pay my salary I told them to sell a few diamonds from the Tsar's Crown."[1]

Münzenberg never regarded the earning of money as an end in itself, he was always concerned with propaganda for the workers movement or the Communist Party. None of his enterprises had substantial cash resources and Münzenberg could never have thought of diverting money to the KPD. Only his senior colleagues who were reliable and discreet knew the truth; they knew that the sums with which the various firms were founded and operated were modest in the extreme.

The "red millionaire" had no private fortune. It is true that he was extremely clever when it came to raising substantial funds for congresses, campaigns and aid. But personally he was subject to the Bolshevik order on the "party maximum" under which party members working in Communist organizations were paid on the lines laid down by the party. Whereas the non-party editors of his papers received salaries comparable to those paid by similar bourgeois firms, Münzenberg as Secretary of the IAH was paid about five hundred marks a month. His allowances as Reichstag deputy went to the party which gave him back one hundred marks a month to cover his expenses. His only financially worthwhile perquisite was a free first-class ticket on all German railways.

Münzenberg never possessed a personal bank account. He had no shares in the firms founded by him. As Reichstag deputy his income was exempt from taxation so that he never made an income tax return under the Weimar Republic; in short, although the firms which he ran were subject to all "bourgeois formalities," these did not exist for him.

There was nothing in Münzenberg's private life to lend credence to the legend of the "Red millionaire." If anything he was a man of modest demands. He liked to visit the theatre or the opera but his main love was books and he was not merely a passionate but a thorough reader. He had a low view of "proletarian poets" as representatives of contemporary literature if their artistic achievement was less significant than their proletarian origins or their choice of themes. He ridiculed the

[1]Reported to the author by Richard Pfeiffer.

frantic efforts of the Russian Association of Proletarian Writers and its German echo to counter bourgeois literature with "proletarian literature."

He liked to relax out of doors. Whenever time permitted he spent one or two days in Thuringia. This was the countryside of his youth where every hilltop and every castle evoked memories, and one needed to be a good walker to keep up with him. He had a youthful, naive way of communicating to others everything that intrigued him and he kept his companions in suspense with ever new surprises. On his visits to Erfurt he called on his sister Emmi, a widow who lived with her children in the old part of the town and who was totally unlike her brother.

Münzenberg had never felt any wish to spend a holiday in Soviet Russia. Therefore in the autumn of 1929 I persuaded him to get his Moscow office to organize a lecture tour which would take us and other IAH members to the south of the country. We travelled as VIP's in comfortable, upholstered train carriages. On the morning of our second day some curious figures suddenly appeared at a biggish station: teenagers, dressed in rags, their faces hardly visible under a coating of soot and dust. Begging for money and cigarettes they told us in unprintable language that they were also travelling south. These were *besprisorny* who travelled under the carriages on the wide axles. The railway police and staff pretended not to see them.

Our arrival times and the dates of meetings had been agreed upon in advance with the party and trade union authorities of the places concerned. But it was always necessary to approach the local GPU for assistance in finding accommodations in the overcrowded hotels. The first meeting took place in Kharkov; all the others were similar. The audiences looked tired and overworked, and apparently had come only under pressure. They were not interested in what these foreigners had to say. It was only occasionally after a meeting that a German-speaking Jew, an older official who knew Münzenberg's name from earlier days or a former Menshevik, came up and showed an interest in the world outside Russia. The enthusiasm which had characterized life in the early post-revolutionary years was gone.

We spent two days as guests of the Abkhazian Government in Sukhumi on the Black Sea. Our host was Nestor Lacoba. We met him through Heinz Neumann who was holidaying in Sukhumi at the time. Lacoba and his brother were then among Stalin's closest friends.[1] He

[1]Nestor Lacoba died a natural death in 1936 before he could become involved in any of the big trials to which his whole family and almost all his political friends fell victim. The Abkhazian leaders were alleged to have plotted the murder of Stalin. See Walter Kolarz, *La Russie et ses Colonies,* Paris 1954, p. 320.

received us in his villa set in a large park. The former owner, a distinguished elderly nobleman, now occupied the gardener's cottage and looked after the park. The villa was a rest home for senior officials of the autonomous Abkhazian republic which like the Mingrelian and the South Ossetian republic had recently been carved out of the territory of rebellious Georgia so as to weaken its political influence.

The Abkhazian comrades celebrated our arrival with a feast. As the festivities approached their climax the guests drew the revolvers which they all carried and proceeded to play the popular game of "Cuckoo": three sides of the room were cleared of furniture and the light was turned off. A player went into one of the empty corners and called out "cuckoo," the signal for his opponent to aim at the caller's feet and to fire. Only a quick leap to one side could save the player. At this point things became too much for us West Europeans and we retired.

The next morning two GPU officials accompanied us by car to Batum. We drove on bumpy roads southwards along the shores of the Black Sea and crossed fast running rivers on fragile wooden ferries. Our companions told us of frequent ambushes of party officials sent to collectivize the Caucasus.

From Batum we continued to Baku, the oil city on the Caspian Sea, from there to Tiflis, the capital of Georgia, then still a sleepy provincial town. The air was sub-tropically mild and the way of life of the people sitting in cafés on shady boulevards had nothing Russian about it. Towards evening our Georgian host took us by cable railway to a local vantage point. At first we could still see the city and the plain surrounded by big bare mountains. Then night fell and the entire countryside was enveloped in darkness. Only the small speck of the town itself was visible because Tiflis alone had electricity.

The climax of the trip was an excursion which took us from Tiflis across the Caucasus to Vladikavkaz. We travelled by automobile along the old Gruzian highway which bisects the central Caucasus from north to south. The road took us close to Gori, Stalin's birthplace, which was not yet an official place of pilgrimage. We stopped high above the little town and Heinz Neumann sang all the Georgian songs he knew in honour of the party's secretary general. In the heart of the mountains, close to the snow-covered 16,500 foot Kazbek peak, the road was deserted. There were no tourists, no vehicles. Now and again dark shapes stood silently on the mountain slopes, wrapped in black cloaks with cartridge belts around their waists—Georgian shepherds or peasants who stared at us in hostile silence.

The countryside was austerely beautiful. The Terek, whose praises were sung by Pushkin, pushed its foamy way through weird gorges.

Whenever we went downhill the Georgian driver turned off his engine to save petrol and we proceeded at breakneck speed into the valley. We stopped at an old inn and roasted our shashliks over a wood fire. Münzenberg was at ease and happy. For the duration of this journey Moscow, Berlin and the rest of the world with its conflicts and complications had ceased to exist for us.

9. Moscow Tightens the Reins

Compared with what came afterwards, the KPD's development between 1925 and 1928 was peaceful. It was true that there was fighting between various groups, that there was the warning signal of the open letter against the Fischer-Maslow group, that there were sharp clashes with the Left which after its exclusion from the running of the party had collected some support in Berlin, the Ruhr and Hamburg. But by and large the party's membership remained stable, particularly in the provinces. This period of prosperity was reflected also in the Reichstag elections of 20 May 1928 which brought the Communists 3.2 million votes as compared with 2.7 million in 1924.

At the Sixth World Congress held in July and August 1928, the Comintern outlined its programme. On the subject of mass organizations without party allegiance the statutes said:

> Communist groups must be established, even if there are no more than two party members, in all uncommitted mass organizations of workers and peasants (trade unions, co-operatives, sports associations, ex-soldiers associations etc.), in their governing committees and their conferences and congresses, and also in civic and parliamentary bodies. Such action will strengthen the party and ensure that its policy is pursued in these organizations and groups . . . Note: Communist groups in international organizations (Red Trade Union International, International of Red Aid, International Workers Aid etc.) are controlled by the Executive Committee of the Comintern.[1]

In the debate that followed Bukharin's report, Münzenberg spoke on this topic which was of considerable concern to him personally. He criticized the lack of attention given to work among non-party organizations and regretted the fear some party leaders held that this activity would lead to opportunism and to "semi-Menshevik deviations". In fact party circles were curiously averse to the type of work that Münzenberg considered a necessity:

[1]Protocol of the Sixth World Congress of the Communist International, Hamburg-Berlin 1928, Vol. 1, p. 103.

We want to arouse an interest in those millions of apathetic and indifferent workers who never take part in political events, who are not interested in the economic and cultural struggle of the proletariat and who simply have as yet no ear to hear the propaganda of the Communist Party.[1]

Many leading communists regarded these attempts as something inferior to regular party work.

At this world congress, Münzenberg's friend Leo Flieg, together with Hugo Eberlein, was elected to the International Control Commission —a sign of great trust. The congress was apparently still dominated by the Russian Right. The Soviet delegation included Stalin, Bukharin, Rykov, Molotov, Manuilsky and Skrypnik. But behind the scenes it was rumoured that Stalin was preparing a blow against his rightist collaborators—Bukharin, Rykov, Tomsky and others. The KPD leadership was not immediately affected by these developments although the congress had rejected a proposal by Arthur Ewert[2] to bring the German Right back into the party leadership. This now consisted of a Politburo in which there were conciliators and leftists, officially under the leadership of Ernst Thälmann but *de facto* controlled by Ewert and others. Then an affair, unimportant within itself, caused a serious crisis in the KPD.

The political leader in Hamburg, Wittorf, Thälmann's brother-in-law, had taken one thousand eight hundred and fifty marks from party funds without accounting for it or without making a repayment. In the interest of the party's good name in Hamburg, Thälmann tried to hush up the affair. Meanwhile Hugo Urbahns, the expelled ex-leader of the Hamburg Communists, got wind of the embezzlement and informed a secretary of the Communist group in the Reichstag who was in touch with the conciliators. This was an opportunity not to be missed by Thälmann's opponents. Hugo Eberlein visited Hamburg, found that the money had been embezzled and reported to the Politburo. The Central Committee was convened at once on 26 September to review Thälmann's behaviour.

---

[1] *Inprecorr* of 20 July 1928.

[2] Arthur Ewert who was born in East Prussia had been a member of the SPD and the trade unions since 1908. After his removal from German party work he was used by the Comintern as its emissary to other countries. Münzenberg met him in 1934 in New York where he had been seconded to the American Communist Party as an adviser. In 1935 together with other international emissaries he was sent to Brazil where Prestes was involved in a military coup. The revolt failed, Ewert was arrested and sentenced to thirty years imprisonment. During his imprisonment he became mentally deranged and in 1950 Brazil returned him to East Berlin where he died a few years ago in an institution.

When the happenings in the Hamburg KPD leadership became known in Moscow and the Russian Politburo immediately sent the Comintern emissary, Petrovski-Bennett, to Berlin. He telephoned our flat from the airport saying that he must speak to Münzenberg. But Münzenberg was already at the Central Committee meeting from which no one could be summoned. Petrovski brought Stalin's express instructions that the German central office was not to take action against Thälmann but to submit the whole matter to the ECCI. But the harm had been done. That night the Central Committee had decided unanimously to suspend Thälmann and its decision was published the next day in *Rote Fahne:*

> The Central Committee strongly disapproves of the concealment of the Hamburg events by Comrade Thälmann as an error which has seriously damaged the party ... Until the matter has been settled Comrade Thälmann is relieved of his functions.

Walter Ulbricht had avoided casting his vote by retiring to the lavatory at the crucial moment. The same evening he went to Moscow followed by a triumphant Hugo Eberlein and a despondent Ernst Thälmann.

But Eberlein had rejoiced too soon. On 6 October Stalin called together the members of the Comintern presidium present in Moscow. Bukharin, Manuilsky, Bela Kun and Humbert-Droz were on holiday in the Caucasus. The rump presidium decided to reinstate Thälmann. Although he had committed a serious mistake his political opponents in the Central Committee had exploited the incident in the interest of their group. There must be no groups within the party and changes must be made in the Central Committee, the Politburo and the editorial board of *Rote Fahne*.

Humbert-Droz immediately wrote a letter to Piatnitsky protesting this decision. Such an intervention on the part of the presidium would destroy the authority of the German party leadership which had decided unanimously—Thälmann included—to relieve Thälmann of his functions. Piatnitsky was too afraid of Stalin, whose strongest ally in the KPD was Thälmann, even to forward the letter to the presidium. When the Comintern presidium re-assembled Bela Kun who had been on holiday with Humbert-Droz and who, like the Swiss, had disapproved of Thälmann's reinstatement whispered anxiously to Humbert-Droz: "There's nothing we can do. We must keep our mouths shut. The struggle against Bukharin in the Russian party has begun."[1]

[1] Letter of 7 November 1962 from Jules Humbert-Droz to the present author and J. Humbert-Droz, *L'Oeil de Moscou à Paris*, p. 295.

One week later the German Central Committee reinstated Thälmann by a majority of votes. This was the beginning of the drive against "rightists" and "conciliators". Even Münzenberg was now forced to declare himself. The time was past when he could steer clear of internal party quarrels. To start with he participated at a Reich party workers conference on 3–4 November 1928. At this meeting Thälmann spoke on the international situation and Heinz Neumann, newly appointed to the German party leadership, on the situation in Soviet Russia. The Right concentrated its attacks on Neumann whom it later, in a circular of 18 November, described as the real "big man" in the party. Münzenberg defended Neumann and called him a good revolutionary. Gerhard Eisler, one of the prime movers against Thälmann in the Hamburg affair, tried to save himself by attacking the Right, and Wilhelm Pieck cloaked his defection with a kind of farewell speech to his "old comrades." The only person to preserve his dignity and stand by his political views was Arthur Ewert. The Right had lost before making its case.

As whip for the new party leadership Münzenberg faced the difficult task of eradicating the rightists in his electoral district. This attempt assumed dramatic dimensions in Offenbach near Frankfurt, the centre of the German leather industry where the rightist Communist Heinrich Galm, a good friend of Münzenberg's, was in control. Münzenberg and the Frankfurt officials tried vainly to convert the Offenbach Communists to the new party line. The local group left the KPD *en bloc* and set itself up as an opposition KPD. In Frankfurt too there were stormy meetings. Willy Strzelewicz, then a young student and a member of the KPD, listened with growing dismay as Münzenberg defended the revision of the Thälmann decision. He felt that secretly the speaker held very different views. When the young man dared to criticize the *volteface* of the Central Committee the party secretary, Oskar Müller, demanded his party card. In the German party, as in the CPSU(B) discussion, the attempt to convince by argument had been replaced by the threat of expulsion from the party unless the line laid down from above was accepted unquestioningly. The young student had been right in his instinct. Münzenberg must have hated the new line because it threatened his whole work.

After heated arguments in the Comintern between Stalin and Humbert-Droz, whose only supporter was Klara Zetkin, the KPD was handed a new open letter in December 1928. It described the right wing as the enemy of the party and said that Brandler and Thalheimer could no longer be allowed to be in the Comintern. Yet all that the right wingers had done was to give voice to their reservations about the hardened line against Social Democracy, about the new intransigent trade union policy, and about the ending of the united front tactics. They had described the new line as an inferior version of the Fischer-Maslow policy, which indeed it was.

Münzenberg arranged for Heinz Neumann, who had come to Berlin with his Georgian girl-friend Zinaida, to have a room on our floor in the Zelten. A friendship quickly developed between him and Münzenberg, two very different people. Political interest in Neumann and a fair amount of opportunism had probably motivated Münzenberg at first. Neumann not only had close connections with the men around Stalin and with Stalin himself, he was also a member of the German party leadership and therefore a very valuable ally. But Münzenberg's liking for the young man was not based solely on cold calculation. Neumann's quick intelligence, accompanied as it was by unusual knowledge, impressed the older man. Neumann was an amusing person, a good talker whose store of witticisms seemed inexhaustible, but who also ridiculed with complete lack of respect the weaknesses of his friends and opponents in the party and thereby made many enemies. After becoming a Communist in 1920 at the age of eighteen he had worked in Moscow for a while for the Comintern. His unquestioning subordination to Stalin and the new line, the speed with which he joined the Thälmann and Remmele group earned him the hatred of the rightists and the conciliators who circulated countless malicious stories about him. They also held him personally responsible for the cruelly suppressed uprising in December 1927 in Canton which had been sparked off by the Russian party leadership; as Stalin's emissary Neumann had been in charge of the preparations. After that they called him the "butcher of Canton".

In June 1929, the last legal KPD party congress was held in Berlin-Wedding. It now conformed to the Soviet model in all respects. The "leader of the German proletariat", Ernst Thälmann, was received with "tumultuous ovations" and welcomed with a thundering triple "long live Moscow." In a short but pompous speech Münzenberg proclaimed the party's complete solidarity with Soviet Russia and concluded with an address of loyalty to Stalin:

We feel at one with the French Communists, with the British Communists, with the Russian revolution, with the world Communist Party under the leadership of comrade Stalin.[1]

The new hardened Comintern line was a direct consequence of developments in the USSR where industrialization was proceeding at the

[1]Report of the Proceedings of the XII Party Congress of the KPD, Berlin 1929.

expense of the independent peasantry. This was the so-called First Five-Year Plan. The rural population in Russia was the victim of a tragedy of almost unimaginable dimensions. Enforced collectivisation met with stubborn peasant resistance. They refused to let their property become part of the collectives and when the state used force they killed their livestock, reduced the acreage under cultivation and destroyed their harvests. Soon there was neither fat nor meat to be had. Bread was already rationed in the cities in 1928. In November 1929 Stalin proclaimed the "liquidation of the *kulaks* as a class." Originally *kulaks* had been peasants who owned enough land to permit the employment of one or two farmhands. As the opposition of the rural population grew anyone who resisted the authorities was dubbed a *kulak*. The destructive brutality grew, the peasants resisted, hundreds of Communist officials were murdered and the struggle against "the *kulaks* as a class" culminated in the most massive expulsion the world had seen hitherto. By 1931 five million Russian peasants had been sent into exile or to concentration camps. After his rejection of the Russian brand of Communism the Rumanian poet Panait Istrati wrote about this period of terror:

> Even if with their next 'five-year-plan' they [the Bolshevik rulers] succeed in bringing happiness to the whole of mankind I would ask them to account for the bones which their happiness-machine has crushed.[1]

To force the starving townspeople to make a supreme work effort and also to stifle from the outset all criticism of the over-ambitious five-year plan, Stalin staged several "trials of noxious elements." The police were on the look-out everywhere for alleged acts of sabotage. Several trials achieved notoriety, such as the Ramsin trial, the Shakhty trial of mining engineers and the "trial of the 48" at which leading officials in charge of food supplies were held personally responsible for the growing food shortage and sentenced to death.

The "amalgamation" principle which came to be universally applied at the political trials of the later period was already in evidence at these early trials. The police brought into court as a group employees from various branches of industry, professors who had criticized the plan, and small time crooks. Public trials were held only after many dress rehearsals had convinced the GPU that the accused would play the roles allotted to them.

While the "Menshevik trial" was in process all Communist parties

---

[1] Panait Istrati, *Auf falscher Bahn,* Munich 1930, p. 123.

and all prominent Communist officials were forced to condemn the accused. In court the accused, who included Nicolai Sukhanov whose books on the Russian revolution are among the best on the subject, admitted to fantastic crimes. They said that they had plotted with the Second International against the Soviet state, although there was no doubt that for eleven years they had had no links with Mensheviks abroad. Their alleged misdeeds were a welcome pretext to intensify the propaganda against Socialists abroad.

Early in February 1929 Stalin disposed of an enemy who had exerted a strong influence on the party even from banishment, and of whom he was most afraid. He expelled "citizen" Lev Davidovich Trotsky from Russia for "organizing an illegal anti-Soviet party". Trotsky was deported to Istanbul and with the consent of the Turkish authorities finally settled on the small island of Prinkipo (Büyük Ada) on the Sea of Marmara. Almost at the same time Münzenberg's publishing house produced the second volume of the illustrated history of the Russian revolution which dealt with the civil war years and which still paid full tribute to Trotsky's outstanding historic role.

10. Where Is the Enemy?

As a result of the KPD slander campaign against the SPD, begun at Moscow's behest, Münzenberg's opportunities for influencing non-Communists and Social Democratic workers in particular diminished. But while in Germany the obstacles became more formidable, the IAH was able to achieve notable successes in other countries such as the United States during the depression years. Its programme fitted in with the American urge for international solidarity and self-help. In the past America's contribution had been limited to financial assistance—albeit of some magnitude—to Russia, Germany and China. But in the twenties dramatic strikes occurred in the United States in which the "Workers International Relief" assisted workers struggling for their rights. These strikes occurred mostly in industries not yet affiliated to trade unions, where wages were low and working conditions poor. The factory owners hired a private police force—called "Pinkertons" after the famous detective—which set about breaking the strikes with brutality and frequently with bloodshed.

The active New York Secretary of the IAH, Ludwig Landy, who like many IAH workers came from an East European Jewish immigrant family, set up special aid committees; in 1926 for example, in conjunction with the textile workers he created the "Joint Defense Relief Committee" and in 1927 during the miners' strike in Pennsylvania and Ohio he founded the "Pennsylvania and Ohio Miners Relief Committee." There were armed clashes in 1929 in the town of Gastonia in North Carolina during a strike of textile workers. In a night raid on the tents provided by the IAH for evicted workers' families, the woman secretary of an aid committee was shot dead. Rapidly increasing unemployment —before long there were ten million unemployed in the United States —gave the IAH an excellent opportunity to popularize Communist ideas in "God's own country." The first congress of the "Workers International Relief" in Pittsburgh was attended by as many as three hundred and sixty-four delegates.

The more the Bolsheviks became involved in their domestic problems the more they pressed the foreign parties and their aid organizations to give them propaganda backing. An important part of this campaign was the Russian claim that war against the Soviet Union was imminent. Countless non-Communists were gained for the Russian cause with this bugbear, by playing above all on the latent pacifism of the intellectuals. Between 1930 and 1936 the campaign against such a war never stopped to influence the Comintern—and thus Münzenberg's activity. At first the instrument used for this purpose was a "Federation of Friends of Soviet Russia." In March 1930 this organization convened an international conference at Essen, which Münzenberg helped arrange. The federation published a journal entitled *Der Drohende Krieg* (The Threatening War). In December of the same year Münzenberg used the "trials of noxious elements" in Russia as an occasion to set up in Berlin an International Committee for the Defence of the Soviet Union—Against Imperial Warmongers. The appeal which was sent out when this body was founded said that the Moscow trials proved "what had been clear to every politically conscious person, that influencial imperialist trusts, groups and general staffs are in league with the Russian counter-revolution preparing a well planned war of intervention against the Soviet Union."[1] The appeal culminated in the claim that these circles saw war against Soviet Russia as the only way out of the world economic crisis. The document was signed by such intelligent men as Alfred Kerr, Kurt Hiller and Kurt Tucholsky. A questionnaire distributed at the same time by the Communists among leading intellectuals on "How I shall behave if the imperialists attack the Soviet Union" was filled in seriously and at length by the majority of these people.[2] The campaign was accompanied by a glorification of

[1] *Inprecorr* of 7 December 1930.
[2] *Ibid.* of 5 December 1930.

the Red Army. In an article entitled "Twelve Years of Red Army" Münzenberg used the method which became characteristic for the writing of history in the Stalin era. Any person in ill-favor was ignored; the creator of the Red Army, Trotsky, was not mentioned. On the other hand Münzenberg appealed to German Communists: "Let us prepare ourselves and do everything to ensure that we do that part of the duties which is our lot."[1] This guarded call for civil war was enough for the authorities to confiscate the relevant *Inprecorr* number and imprison the editor, Heinrich Kurella, for one year in the fortress of Gollnow.

With the fall of the Müller Government in March 1930 the SPD went into opposition. The new Chancellor, Heinrich Brüning, unable to obtain a majority in the Reichstag for his economic programme, asked Hindenburg for emergency powers on the basis of Article 48 of the Constitution. Germany too was now in the full throes of the world-wide economic crisis, with the number of unemployed increasing rapidly, and the hitherto fairly insignificant National Socialist Party offering itself as the saviour. For the first time its propaganda succeeded in penetrating the National Socialist factories and working class areas. The KPD leadership was fully aware of the dangers which threatened workers from this quarter. In its proclamations it demanded massive political and physical opposition to Fascism. But while calling for resistance and for counter-measures against Fascist terror in factories and at employment exchanges, it continued to attack the SPD, urging that the struggle against "social fascism" and "social fascist trade union bureaucracy" should not be neglected.

As these official pronouncements described the Brüning Government as Fascist, the workers—to the extent that they listened to the Communists—tended to underestimate the real threat which Hitler presented. Communist reaction to the September elections of 1930 which gave the National Socialists an overwhelming victory was characteristic of this attitude. The number of votes cast for the National Socialists rose from 800,000 to 6.4 million and instead of twelve deputies they now had one hundred and seven in the Reichstag, thereby becoming the second strongest group.

Münzenberg listened to the radio announcement of the election results with some Communist friends. I sensed that he was surprised, even shocked, by the extent of the National Socialists' success. But he controlled himself because his friends were content that the KPD had also considerably increased its support—from 3.25 million votes to 4.5 million—an achievement which they celebrated as a great victory. During

[1] *Inprecorr* of 9 December 1930.

the election campaign Heinz Neumann had tried to cut into the National Socialists' appeal by "proclaiming a programme for the national social liberation of the German people", a line suggested by Moscow and drawn up by himself. The programme was designed to win over the undecided lower middle classes to the Communist cause. The election results showed the futility of his efforts. In spite of adopting phraseology the Communists could not compete with the National Socialists.

After the elections, *Weltbühne* published an interview with Münzenberg in which he was asked whether he did not regard the tremendous Nazi success as a "disavowal" of the KPD's policy, whether a tactical change in the KPD's hostile attitude to the SPD and to the possibility of joint defence measures was on the cards, and what foreign policy he regarded as desirable. Münzenberg's replies were curiously schizophrenic. On the one hand he sought refuge behind loyal party phrases, completely rejecting the possibility of collaboration between the SPD leadership and the KPD, on the other he showed himself aware of the terrible threat to the KPD and the republic:

> We Communists know all too well that the fascists want to start their 'national liberation struggle' at home with the least dangerous part, with hitting workers over the head.[1]

All his papers and journals called for a united front against the Nazi threat. This unity became more than ever the hope of the simple "party soldier." A front page picture in the AIZ of this period shows a *Reichsbanner* man and a Communist united in the struggle against the Fascists. But Münzenberg could not completely desert the party line which continued to be relentless opposition to the Social Democratic leaders with whom it would have been necessary to discuss joint action.

The National Socialists were quick to capitalize on their victory at the polls. The NSDAP had built up a modern party machinery, well organized and autocratically directed. It had about fifteen hundred employees, all of them male, who earned between one hundred fifty and two hundred marks—which in those days of unemployment provided some degree of security. Immediately after the election the party held 70,000 meetings in the whole of the Reich and its Berlin Gauleiter, Joseph Goebbels, drove in an open car through Neukölln and Wedding, the traditional strongholds of the Berlin workers, and addressed meetings there. Because the National Socialists regarded the Communists as their most dangerous enemies they employed terror methods, shooting and murdering Communists without scruple.

[1] *Die Weltbühne*, 23 August 1930.

The Communists did not avoid the confrontation, they resisted. In place of the banned *Rote Frontkämpferbund*, they founded the *Kampfbund gegen den Faschismus* to protect themselves against attacks from the SA. At the first congress of this *Kampfbund* in December 1930 at Düsseldorf, Münzenberg made the main speech to one thousand delegates. The illegal KPD organization concentrated its persuasive force on the SA whose members consisted largely of unemployed young workers. The quarrels in the NSDAP between the Strasser opposition and the leadership which was loyal to Hitler were exploited to the full to create suspicion and uncertainty among young SA recruits. Quantities of material were published for their benefit, among them a pamphlet, "Who has betrayed us?" and a so-called journal of the opposition Nazis, *Das Sprachrohr* ("The Mouth-Piece"), subtitled: "Of the Upright Soldiers of the German Revolution in the NSDAP." Lieutenant Scheringer, a young National Socialist who at the Ulm trial had been sentenced to imprisonment for Nazi activities in the Reichswehr and at Gollnow had been converted to Communism by Communists imprisoned there, demanded in a public declaration that the people must be ready to take up arms against the National Socialists. Leaflets were distributed in which he called upon the SA to join the Communists. Occasionally this propaganda successfully persuaded the odd SA man to leave "the party of princes, counts, barons and Junkers," as it was called in a declaration by the Breslau SA man Artur Kurek who had "joined the ranks of the red class-front, the party of Karl Liebknecht and Rosa Luxemburg."[1]

The most obvious and most important step, the only one which might have brought success, could not be taken: the formation from above of a united front with the SPD. In a long speech to the Ninth Plenum of the ECCI in April 1931, Thälmann even claimed:

We shall see the Social Democrats succeed in Germany, if they have not already succeeded, in using their supporters to set up terrorist formations designed for civil war. These will certainly one day fight side by side with the National Socialists facing us across the barricades.[2]

As far as his foundations and rallies went, the years 1930–32 were very successful ones for Münzenberg personally. In the autumn of 1931 he organized a world congress in Berlin to celebrate the tenth anniversary of the IAH. Hundreds of delegates from at home and abroad attended and messages of congratulations were received from all over the world. It was for this occasion that he produced the detailed account of

[1]AIZ of 13 November 1932.
[2]*Inprecorr* of 5 June 1931, p. 1207.

his activities entitled *Solidarität* which in 527 pages lists all the achievements of the IAH. Münzenberg's publishing activities had also continued to expand. The list of publications included numerous novels by Russian authors and works of non-fiction by Eugene Lyons, Henri Barbusse, Michael Gold, Louis Fischer and Anna Louise Strong on the Soviet Union or on the world political and economic situation. Among the many German authors whom Münzenberg published were Kurt Kersten, Gustav Regler and Egon Erwin Kisch. A rediscovery was the Portuguese writer Eca de Queiroz, then almost unknown in Germany, from whose many works the *Neue Deutsche Verlag* chose for publication the novel *Das Verbrechen des Pater Amaro*. A monograph appeared on the life and work of the artist Diego Rivera who at that time represented the Mexican Communists in the executive committee of the workers and peasants bloc.

In 1929 the publishers had persuaded Kurt Tucholsky to write texts for selected photographs and photomontages by John Heartfield. Tucholsky set about this task with considerable reservations. He distrusted the militant and orthodox world of the Communist Party. But John Heartfield and I went on calling on him until we finally persuaded him to change his mind. The Communist press praised *Deutschland, Deutschland über alles* as a courageous book. The publishers said in a sales promotion letter "that although this is not a Communist book it contains much material that will help to unbend these sections whom we wish to bring into closer contact with our movement." However the financial paper of the German book trade refused to advertise the book because of Heartfield's photomontage on the cover.[1]

Münzenberg had founded a book society, *Universum-Bücherei für Alle*, in 1926 which made relatively expensive books available to workers. In 1931, after five years of existence, it had forty thousand members —a considerable number considering the economic crisis and unemployment. For a monthly contribution of one mark members received four times a year a book of their choice and an illustrated monthly, *Das Magazin für Alle*. In July 1931 there appeared as the hundredth volume Boris Pilniak's novel *The Volga Flows into the Caspian Sea*. But by then artists no longer enjoyed the relative freedom which they had once had in Soviet Russia and Pilniak's novel was strongly attacked by the Communist press. It was said that the publishers had wrongly described the book as a novel about the five-year plan, but that in fact the main characters were dreamers and counter-revolutionaries. The influ-

---

[1] In 1964 Rowohlt Verlag reissued *Deutschland, Deutschland über alles* using a photographic process which reproduced the imprint of the Neue Deutsche Verlag.

ence of Tolstoi and Dostoyevsky on Pilniak was severely condemned. There was no more room in the Soviet Union for the individuality of an intellectually independent and creative human being.

While his ventures prospered, Münzenberg was increasingly depressed about the political situation. It was only to his closest friends that he dared to express his fears about the future. Outwardly he gave many of his colleagues the impression, not without justification, of being a calculating cynic intent on satisfying his ambition. But today's critics who puzzle over the unrealistic course which the KPD took in those years often forget to consider the atmosphere in which these things happened. The party leadership, like all Communist officials, whether they belonged to the party or to the opposition, greatly overestimated the fighting strength of the workers. They still thought in terms of the pre-war days and of the revolutionary period that followed. Münzenberg argued occasionally with Heinz Neumann about the latter's "calf-like optimism" and warned him against over-estimating the strength of the KPD: Neumann replied by calling Münzenberg a "rotten opportunist" and a "bureaucrat." Many workers and employees no longer thought in terms of the revolutionary class struggle. The old vocabulary was out of date. Long unemployment and the meagre welfare service assistance had cut off millions from the desired rise into the middle classes. What the NSDAP had to offer them was tempting and it was simple: a people's community in which all would be equal, the work they so urgently needed, and national dignity. But above all, these things would come immediately and not some time in the future.

Since the autumn of 1930 the National Socialists and the *Stahlhelm* had been calling for a plebiscite against the Prussian Government, the last stronghold of Social Democracy. This plebiscite was finally staged in February 1931, the objective of the National Socialists being to dissolve the Prussian Landtag and to obtain a majority in Prussia. At first the Communists had seen the plan for what it was:

> The demand of the National Socialists for a plebiscite has only one aim, to prepare the way for the rule of fascist dictatorship. We Communists refuse to take part in this deception of the people,

the Communist Landtag Deputy Schwenk had said on 15 October 1930.[1] After the campaign for the plebiscite had begun in earnest in February 1931, the KPD Central Committee on 17 February published an appeal in *Rote Fahne* opposing the "plebiscite of the forces of reac-

[1] Stenographic protocol of the Prussian Landtag proceedings of 15 October 1930.

tion." At the same time, however, it indulged in the usual insults to the Social Democrats whom it accused of preparing the way for the fascists: "No class-conscious worker", the appeal said, "shall lift a finger to preserve the administration of bosses like Braun, Grzesinski and Severing."

July 1931 was a time of economic crises. Because of the withdrawal of foreign money, because of assistance payments being made to the unemployed and because of the enormous fall in production, the major German banks collapsed. On 11 July share prices fell sharply, 13 July brought the great bank crash, the Danat bank collapsed and other banks were also in difficulties. The stock exchange closed and the Reich Government took over the Danat bank. On 14 July all banks were closed and the export of capital was prohibited. On 16 July only wages and salaries were paid, all other transactions were blocked. Bank rate rose from three to ten per cent and later fifteen per cent. Brüning visited Paris to seek a moratorium on reparations payments.

On Monday 20 July, Münzenberg had a meeting at the Café Bauer in the Potsdamer Platz with Neumann who urgently wished to see him. Neumann showed him a telegram from the Comintern ordering the German party leadership to participate in the National Socialist plebiscite against the Prussian Government. The reason given by Moscow was that the KPD must participate in extra-parliamentary mass campaigns. Neumann reported that both Thälmann and Remmele had at first opposed the decision and that Thälmann had avoided taking action by departing from Hamburg. Münzenberg regarded the decision as madness and categorically refused Neumann's demand that he should popularize it in his papers. Comrades who daily expected to be killed by the National Socialists would never understand why such a collaboration was necessary. It was one thing to fight the SPD leadership, it was a very different thing to make a common front against it with the mortal enemy of the working class.

Neumann tried to puzzle out the meaning of the Soviet decision. Stalin had criticized him in April because in Thuringia the KPD and the SPD had jointly moved a vote of no confidence in the National Socialist Minister of the Interior, Frick, an action which had led to Frick's fall. With the serious crisis the Soviet Union faced, Stalin was anxious to avoid a civil war between the Communists and the National Socialists. He wanted a stable Germany even if ruled dictatorially by the right, and the German right could only come to power after the elimination of the SPD.

In an attempt to justify its sensational volte-face the KPD leadership on 21 July addressed an ultimatum to the Prussian Government. It demanded the lifting of the ban on the *Rote Frontkämpferbund* and the end of the confiscation of publications as well as the lifting of the emergency regulations. That Severing should reject this demand on 22 July was predictable. On the same day the KPD Central Committee "decided" to take part in the National Socialist plebiscite which it re-christened the "red plebiscite"—as though this would change the situation. Because *Rote Fahne* was banned, *The Manchester Guardian* and *The Times* were the first papers to carry this piece of news. On 27 July there followed an account in *Inprecorr* of a long-winded explanation given to party officials by Thälmann, who had meanwhile returned obediently from Hamburg. He claimed that by taking part in the plebiscite the Communist Party would make a deep breach in the Hitler front and divide the bourgeois camp. The same line was also followed in the background material provided for party speakers in which it was said that "any weapon suits us if by aiming a blow at this Prussian Government we strike at the entire bankrupt, accursed capitalist system."

With *Rote Fahne* banned, it was now the daily duty of Münzenberg's *Berlin am Morgen* to defend the "red plebiscite." The decision caused indignation and incomprehension among party members and even more among the non-party editors of the Münzenberg press. "You have behaved as though you had Nazi agents in your Central Committee," said the revolutionary pacifist Kurt Hiller in an open letter to Münzenberg whom he described as the KPD's "most brilliant organizer", as its "richest, and in spite of all his enthusiasm, most realistic and unconstrained intellect," and even as "by far the greatest personality since Rosa Luxemburg and Karl Liebknecht were murdered."[1] Hiller concluded his letter with the words:

> And if you personally, Willi Münzenberg, (whom I continue to admire as one of the cleverest men among the German left) swallow this decision without injury to your health then . . . I admire your stomach.

In his conversations with the editorial staff Münzenberg himself had nothing good to say about the decision. The staff urged him to publish nothing. But party orders were party orders and he was a leading official. On 6 August a leader appeared in *Berlin am Morgen* entitled "Why vote for the red plebiscite?", in which Münzenberg attacked the Social Democrats, the "right wing renegades" and "scribblers and intellectuals who believe themselves to be radicals." Hiller's comment was that Münzenberg "replied in eight full length columns, with numerous quotations from Marx, Engels, Liebknecht, Bebel, Mehring and Lenin, none of which came near to the heart of the matter."[2]

[1] Kurt Hiller, *Köpfe und Tröpfe*, Hamburg 1950, p. 39 et seq. The open letter is reprinted there.
[2] *Ibid.*

The plebiscite, which was held on 9 August and which ended in failure, led to a far-reaching loss of confidence in the KPD. The party order to vote was ignored in many cases.

On this 9th day of August Berlin was in a mood of tension rarely seen before. From dawn to dusk I visited all the workers districts and I probably spoke to several thousands who were indignant that the Communist Party should aid and abet the right wing radicals,

wrote Hubertus, Prince of Löwenstein, who was was then working for the *Reichsbanner*.[1]

At a time when the Weimar Republic was shaken to its very foundations, when united action was vital for the German workers, the KPD leadership blindly obeyed orders from Moscow. That the instructions had come from Moscow and had not, as was claimed for years afterwards, been invented by Heinz Neumann was confirmed in the autumn of 1932 at the twelfth plenary session of the ECCI when in his report Piatnitsky praised the German party for the disciplined manner in which it had followed the Executive Committee's decision on the red plebiscite.[2] In an article entitled "Must fascism really be victorious?"[3] Trotsky claimed that Stalin had defended Communist participation in the fascist plebiscite in a speech to Moscow party workers but that this part of his explanation was not published in *Pravda*. Trotsky further said that Stalin's policy of cautious silence, of burying his head in the sand and of giving way was a betrayal comparable to that of the Social Democrats on 4 August 1914. Such thoughts must have occurred to every politically conscious Communist, Münzenberg included. Behind his apparent indifference there was growing nervousness. What did the Russians want? Münzenberg too must have seen that if things continued like this the Russians would destroy the KPD.

11. Patron Saint of the Fellow Travellers

Münzenberg has been called the inventor of the "fellow travellers," those auxiliary troops of Communism which remain invaluable to the present day and which are recruited largely from the ranks of the intellectuals. Without being party members, they display active sympathy for Communism and give it moral support in public. Münzenberg did not invent them, they existed from the start. His achievement was to mobilize them on a scale hitherto unknown and to put them in the service of the Communists.

[1]Prinz Hubertus Löwenstein, *Die Tragödie eines Volkes*, Amsterdam 1934, p. 54.
[2]Information given by Kurt Müller who attended the session.
[3]Bulletin of the Opposition (Russian) of 8 December 1931.

Among those who even before Münzenberg, immediately after the first world war, successfully devoted themselves to collecting signatures for proclamations and appeals on behalf of the Communist cause was Alfons Paquet. In this period it became evident that—after the collapse of the old values and hopes—the Utopia and the ethos of Communism appealed, at least temporarily, even to persons and circles who normally had little in common with left wing intellectuals. For example an "appeal to the proletariat," prepared by Paquet early in 1919—a passionate avowal by the "intellectuals" of the fellowship linking them with their "brothers in the proletariat"—was signed not only by the Jewish religious philosopher Martin Buber and the Neo-Kantian Paul Natorp but also by Martin Dibelius, then a theologian at Heidelberg, and by Wilhelm Schäfer, author of the *Dreizehn Bücher der Deutschen Seele* (Thirteen Books of the German Soul). A letter from the publisher Kurt Wolff to Paquet, dated 10 August 1919, shows that when it came to the great, if abstract, ideas of classlessness and solidarity many intellectuals were sincerely if, given the political background of such appeals, uncritically ready to declare themselves. Wolff had been asked to sign an appeal which Paquet had prepared for a meeting of the Frankfurt KPD in the name of intellectuals attracted by Communism. He replied:

> I am genuinely delighted by your request and ask you of course to count me among those who support the spirit and content of this declaration.[1]

In the first post-war years many of those interested in Communism had thus reached the periphery of the KPD. They believed in grandiose Utopias and rigorous theories, and were pushed on by bad social consciences, and hope for a successful revolution. This had happened before Münzenberg made the first systematic effort to woo this group when he founded the IAH. His magic word was solidarity—at the beginning solidarity with the starving Russians, then with the proletariat of the whole world. By substituting solidarity for charity Münzenberg found the key to the heart of many intellectuals: they reacted spontaneously.

It was only rarely that they had intimate knowledge of the political and economic issues involved. Almost all of them lacked even an elementary knowledge of Marxist theory. But it was after all not concrete political arguments but general moral sentiments that made them support Münzenberg's campaigns. When he spoke of the "sacred enthusi-

---

[1] As the Communist Party line hardened and the terror in Soviet Russia increased Paquet disassociated himself from all Münzenberg's initiatives. The author wishes to express her deep gratitude to Paquet's heirs for being allowed to examine Paquet's posthumous papers which include the letter of Kurt Wolff quoted above.

asm for the proletarian duty to help and to assist"[1] he touched on that
almost exalted readiness for sacrifice that is found wherever there is
faith. In January 1926, Alfons Paquet said:

> My party is the IAH. I helped to set it up and its spread throughout the
> world is linked with everything that I expect from the ultimate victory
> of the workers' cause, mutual assistance and greater mutual understand-
> ing;

and in a telegram of congratulations on the occasion of the fifth anniversary of the IAH he said:

> Within the space of a few years the IAH has transformed some human
> rights into a reality, it has done a tremendous amount to instil fire and life
> into the word internationalism for the workers of all countries.[2]

Even after the first wave of emotion and enthusiasm had passed the
attraction of Münzenberg and his organizations for the intellectuals did
not diminish. New motives were added to the old ones. In the years
after 1923 people were disappointed with Social Democracy, they felt
that it shared in the responsibility for the failings of the Weimar Republic. Later, at the beginning of the thirties, they were afraid of a crisis,
of fascism, and anxious about the growing inability of governments and
administrations to take action. On 11 September 1931 the *Manchester
Guardian* reported:

> A terrible apathy is descending on the German public—neither at home
> nor abroad does anything seem to be of any use. Nazis and the Commu-
> nists fight murderously in the streets and neutralize one another in poli-
> tics. The Socialists are paralyzed . . . The number of German intellectuals
> —lawyers, doctors, authors, painters, actors and musicians—who say
> 'Communism must come' is enormous.

Although the last remark was exaggerated, the readiness of the intellectuals to make themselves available for Communist campaigns had
not diminished. Their lack of political insight tempted them in spite of
all evidence to the contrary to regard Communism as the only effective
counterweight to the Hitler movement. When finally in 1933 the concept of anti-Fascism came to overshadow the concept of Communism
it was even easier for the honest opponents of Fascism to cast aside all
reservations and to identify themselves with those who claimed to be

[1] W. Münzenberg, *Fünf Jahre IAH*, p. 10.
[2] *Ibid*., p. 179.

the most determined opponents of the common enemy.

The reasons for which men and women in intellectual occupations readily put themselves at Münzenberg's disposal were varied and sometimes complex. Many of them were convinced that only the Communist movement was ready to fight with every available means for the realization of a better world, for social progress and emancipation. With *every available means*: because even the most honorable of these intellectuals felt compelled occasionally to stretch a point for these great aims. Did not the disappointment of these people with the liberal bourgeois parties or the Social Democrats stem from the fact that they were reputed to be weak, ready to compromise, opportunist and therefore incapable of great accomplishments? What was characteristic of their intellectual approach was that they were usually not prepared to consider the pros and cons of the controversies between the bourgeois parties and the Communists but were always ready to agree with the latter because they were convinced that the bourgeois form of society had had its day and that "historic right" was on the side of the young Communist movement. But apart from such idealist motives considerable intellectual vanity and even corruption were involved. People were tempted by honours and substantial monetary rewards, they enjoyed visiting Russia where they were fêted in a way they would never be at home. Vain men had their price, they were easy to attract and could be manipulated without difficulty. Most of these intellectuals were not conscious of the significance of their actions. Some were unwittingly misled, unsuspecting victims of blind credulity. Communism and also National Socialism revealed a paradoxical shortcoming of many intellectuals: their critical intellectuality did not extend to politics, they were intellectuals but they were non-political.

Münzenberg was quick to recognize and to exploit this weakness. Arthur Koestler recalls that he displayed a kind of amused, friendly contempt for intellectuals, that he respected them without taking them quite seriously.

Münzenberg himself, however, was anything but an intellectual. He was a self-made man, without much education, not even always entirely sure of his spelling; and yet he always found the right note with which to open the ears and hearts of men and women of far greater learning. A great deal of his influence was undoubtedly attributable to his personal charm. He listened patiently to the intellectuals' problems, he gave them a long rein and avoided playing the party man. He seemed the reverse of a narrow doctrinaire, and certainly was, after his fashion, however strictly he was forced to follow the party line. The élan with which he swept the intellectuals along with him in the desired direction was not simulated by a talented actor, it always was the result of a mixture of honest conviction and tactical consideration.

Münzenberg's ability to organize contributed greatly to his success. If possible he left nothing to chance, particularly not the manipulation of fellow travellers. He knew exactly whose collaboration or signature was of particular value in a given matter and he made systematic efforts to obtain these names. With this end in view he had created a network of contact men. Otto Nagel maintained the links with the creative artists, Otto Katz was responsible for relations with actors and the film world, Kurt Kersten and Egon Erwin Kisch for contacts with writers and journalists. It has been claimed that Münzenberg had few scruples about using his friends' names for campaigns without their approval. This may have happened now and again but it was not the rule.

But as the Comintern asked him to run more and more campaigns and to set up more and more committees the original spontaneity seemed increasingly to be replaced by cold routine and flashy staging. Willy Strzelewicz, who in 1931 worked on a commission organized by Münzenberg within the IAH framework to investigate the brown terror, has described an incident which to him seemed characteristic of Münzenberg's methods. When signatures were being collected for an appeal Münzenberg told his secretary to ring up Einstein and to ask him for his signature. He added that he himself would contact Kerr; this he did and was at once told that he could use Kerr's name.

A tragi-comedy serves as proof of the lack of scruple with which the Soviets not only took advantage of the uncritical preparedness of the intellectuals to let Münzenberg use their names but also exploited Münzenberg himself for their own purposes. On 21 August 1931 Inprecorr carried an article by Münzenberg entitled "Stop the Hangman." He told his readers that some months earlier the Secretary of the Pan-Pacific Trade Union Federation and his wife, both Swiss-born, had been arrested in Shanghai.[1] The man's name was not mentioned and Münzenberg gave no details of what had happened in Shanghai. A few days later his second article appeared under the impressive sub-title: "World protest against the proposed murder of the trade union secretary in Shanghai." In a few days Münzenberg had mobilized all his organizations and many friends and ensured that Sun Yat-sen's widow was bombarded with telegrams asking her to intervene on behalf of the prisoner. These telegrams were signed—in addition to many known Communist intellectuals—by Alfred Kerr, Carl von Ossietzky, Ernst Rowohlt, Bernard von Brentano, Lion Feuchtwanger, Paul Westheim and almost the entire teaching staff of the Berlin Academy of Arts, Karl Hofer, Leo von König, Hans Baluschek, Hugo Gropius, Mies van der

[1]The following account is based on Inprecorr reports of 21 August to 30 October 1931.

Rohe, Willie Jaeckel, Bruno Taut, Otto Dix and also by Leopold Jessner and Paul Wegener. Up to this point the names of the victims still had not been announced. These personalities trusted blindly in Münzenberg.

Three months after the arrest of the nameless trade union secretary, on 7 September 1931, an announcement came from Shanghai. The Nanking Government proposed to publish Communist plans for a revolt and important secret materials found during the trade unionist's arrest. They demanded the heads of the prisoners who were said to be conspirators and criminals for whom there must be no pity. But on 11 September it was announced from Shanghai that Nanking was prepared to be merciful because the prisoners were foreigners. The protest seemed to have been effective. Meanwhile, Paul Klee, Alphonse Mucha, Max Pechstein and Theodore Dreiser had joined the signatories. On 21 October the prisoners' names were mentioned for the first time. It was said they were a married couple named Ruegg; the man had been sentenced to death at the beginning of October and his wife to life imprisonment. On 30 October Münzenberg founded a "Central Defence Committee to Save Ruegg" in Berlin. Efforts on behalf of "the Rueggs" were made everywhere abroad. The American Senator Borah even asked the State Department to exert pressure in Nanking.

But who was the mysterious Ruegg and why had the Russians not announced his name at the start? Ruegg's real name was Luft, he was born in the Ukraine, a Communist and member of the Soviet spy network of many years standing. He owned several false passports and at first it was not known which he had carried when he was arrested. He had been active in the illegal *apparat* in China since 1929. It finally came out that the passports he and his wife had when arrested belonged to a Swiss Communist couple resident in Moscow. The élite of the intelligentsia had thus, without hesitation, exerted itself on behalf of a personality whose real name and actual functions it never came to know.[1]

12. The Parade of the Freedom Fighters

In November 1931, at the time of the Japanese invasion of Manchuria and of the Chinese Communists' proclamation of a soviet government in the territories occupied by them, Münzenberg established an "Inter-

[1] After a campaign lasting many years Luft-Ruegg was released from Chinese imprisonment. He refused to return to the Soviet Union and commented that Trotsky had been right in his criticism of Stalin.

WILLI MÜNZENBERG:

national China Aid Committee" which Romain Rolland warmly welcomed in a letter:

> I wholeheartedly support every energetic solidarity compaign that is fought together with the heroic proletarian élite which sacrifices itself for the liberation of China; every campaign that assists the population of China, hit by misfortune and persecuted by various imperialist states.[1]

A war of aggression had now really broken out—even if it was not directed against the Soviet Union—and the Japanese attack gave the Communists an opportunity to mobilize famous anti-militarists from all countries. For some time now Henri Barbusse had given his name and his time to Communist campaigns of all kinds. He had recently written a biography of Stalin in which he glorified the dictator and praised the enthusiasm of the Russian peasants driven into joining *kolkhosi*. The German edition, *Stalin—eine Welt, gesehen durch einen Mann* (Stalin —a World seen by one Man), had been published by Münzenberg.

In 1927 Romain Rolland, vainly courted for years, had also gone over to the Communists. In *Libertaire*, a Paris anarchist paper, he had defended the Soviet Government and the "threatened" country during an investigation into oppression in Russia. He had written:

> Russia is in danger. A mighty coalition of imperialist powers all over the world, urged on by the British Empire, prepares to attacks the Soviet Union.

After that he too was a willing collaborator, particularly when it came to anti-war protest campaigns.[2]

Münzenberg welcomed the co-operation of these two writers because he wanted to give the anti-war campaign as broad a basis as possible and involve as many non-Communist organizations as possible. A wave of manifestations was begun which swept across all the countries in which the Communists had any influence. The manifestations were generally organized by the Anti-Imperialist League jointly with other Communist organizations. On 17 February 1932, a crowded meeting was held in the Pharussäle in Berlin under the motto: "Against the threatening world war. War on imperialist war." Rallies were held in New York, in Holland, Korea, Bulgaria and once more in Berlin on 3 March where Münzenberg was able to gather together numerous foreigner speakers at the sports palace. The next event was an "Interna-

---

[1] *Raubkrieg in China*, Berlin 1932.
[2] *Est et Ouest*, Paris, 2 April 1966 number. This also contains information on Romain Rolland's subsequent political development.

tional Week Against the Imperialist War" in Britain, Norway, Holland, Switzerland and France. On 20 March, Münzenberg invited all revolutionary workers organizations to a conference. In the course of this campaign a concept was invented which achieved considerable importance in the years to come. The term "freedom fighters" was used for the first time.

In April, Münzenberg founded a "German Committee for the Preparation of the Geneva Congress Against War," because the conference was originally planned to take place in Geneva. Romain Rolland, informed of the plans by Barbusse, issued a proclamation "To All" in which he appealed to anti-imperialist parties and associations to attend a world congress. The opening date was fixed for 20 July. The Communists used Rolland's appeal to set up preparatory national committees everywhere. Münzenberg also established a kind of "initiative committee" consisting of his trusted collaborator, Louis Gibarti, and Henri Barbusse who were supposed to coordinate with Romain Rolland. This was more easily said than done and quarrels developed behind the scenes between the two prima donnas and Münzenberg.

Barbusse, who took his role very seriously, had stopped in Zurich on his way to Rolland, who was then living at the Hotel Carlton in Lucerne, to call on Friedrich Adler at the Bureau of the Second International. Gibarti who was with Barbusse had vainly tried to dissuade him from this visit and, while he paced up and down outside, Barbusse inside sought to persuade Friedrich Adler to take part in the proposed congress. Adler left Barbusse in no doubt that he had not the slightest intention of supporting this new Communist manoeuvre. Armed with all the information that Barbusse had given him, he immediately wrote to Vandervelde and the Socialist Parties urging them not to take part in the proposed congress. The Comintern in turn severely criticized Münzenberg because it was assumed that this high-handed initiative had been his suggestion. Gibarti was summoned to Moscow as a whipping boy and made to give the Comintern details of the proposed congress and also of the Zurich incident. His explanation that he had been unable to restrain Barbusse was not believed and he was reprimanded.

Rolland on the other hand was indignant because without informing him Münzenberg had summarily postponed the congress to August and suggested another meeting place. The problems created by Münzenberg's dictatorial manner and the temperamental sensitivity of the intellectuals whom he courted are well illustrated by Rolland's letter of complaint to Barbusse:[1]

[1]In the possession of the author.

Lucerne, Hotel Carlton
jeudi 14 juillet 1932

Mon cher ami,

J'ai reçu hier votre télégramme de protestation contre la lettre de Adler à Vandervelde. Je m'y attendais. Je n'ai pas encore reçu la lettre explicative que vous m'annoncez.

J'ai bien eu l'impression que Adler avait complètement déformé votre pensée, et que la méfiance dont il était armé par avance lui a fait chercher et trouver dans cette entrevue de Zurich des motifs définitifs de boycotter le Congrès.

Mais je dois dire que toute la façon d'agir du Comité d'initiative - (en fait vous seul et Gibarti) - a tout fait pour semer ces défiances ce qu'aujourd'hui est pis que jamais.

Voici huit jours que j'ai vu, avec vous, à Lucerne, Gibarti. Je l'ai prié (oralement et depuis par lettre) de me tenir au courant de ce qu'il faisait. Il n'a pas daigné m'écrire un seul mot, pas plus que répondre aux démarches réitérées de Challaye. Et c'est par ce dernier que je reçois, aujourd'hui, communication d'une lettre, à en-tête imprimé de *Comité international pour la préparation du Congrès international anti-guerrier du 28 juillet 1932 à Genève*, avec mon nom imprimé à côté de ceux des autres membres du Comité d'initiative. Cette lettre, adressée: "*A tous les Comités (sic) nationaux du Congrès contre la guerre*" m'informe que "la date du Congrès a été fixée définitivement sûr (sic) le *20 et 21 août*" (par qui?) et que le Bureau International du Comité d'initiative (qui?) s'est mis en rapport avec le gouvernment français. (Donc, Bruxelles est abandonée?) Cette lettre circulaire, qui est adressée de Berlin aux Comités francais (et en quel style!) est signée de timbre imprimé: *Kampf-Kongress gegen den imperialistischen Krieg*. Il est visible que c'est la *Ligue contre l'Imperialisme* de Münzenberg que mène la danse et qu'elle s'est annexée notre Congrès. Ce n'est pas seulement un abus de pouvoir éhonté, c'est la plus insigne de maladresses et telle qu'un agent provocateur n'en commettrait pas de pire: car cela suffit à donner raison à toutes les accusations des Adler, Vandervelde etc. Je proteste avec une extrême énergie. Et d'autant plus que j'ait toujours refusé de faire partie de la Ligue de Münzenberg, sachant avec quel sans gêne inoui il abuse des adhésions occasionelles ou conditionelles qu'on lui consent, pour les employer à des campagnes différentes de celles pour lesquelles il les a sollicitées.

Je suis profondément dégouté de ces agissements. Ils compromettent les meilleures causes et ils écartent les meilleur volontés. Vous exprimez, à la fin de votre lettre du 11 juillet, des idées tout à fait justes à l'égard de "nos amis communistes", qui constamment "abusent de la situation privilégiée que leur esprit d'organisation et d'action leur a donné." Je regrette que ces idées vous ne les mettrez pas en pratique. Je vous le demande. Agissez énergiquement! Et dans le Congrès dont vous êtes l'initiateur et l'organisateur responsable, mettez fin à ces procédés.

Bien cordialement à vous
[sgnd.] Romain Rolland

My dear friend,

I received yesterday your telegram of protest against the letter of Adler to Vandervelde. I was expecting it. I have not yet received the clarifying letter which you say is coming.

I had, indeed, the impression that Adler had completely distorted your thoughts and that the suspicion with which he was armed in advance made him look for and find in that conference of Zurich concrete motives for boycotting the Congress.

But I must say that the manner in which the initiative committee (in effect you and Gibarti) has acted has contributed to sowing seeds of a suspicion which today is worse than ever.

It has been a week now since I saw Gibarti, with you, in Lucerne. I asked him (orally and since then in writing) to keep me informed concerning his activities. He has not deigned to write me a single word nor has he responded to the repeated inquiries of Challaye. The latter has sent me today a copy of a letter which contains a letterhead and the name of the *International Committee for the Preparation of the International Anti-War Congress of July 28, 1932 in Geneva* with my name printed next to those of the other members of the Committee of initiative. This letter, addressed: *To all the National Committees (sic) of the Congress against war* informs me that the date of the Congress has been definitely fixed upon (sic) the *20 and 21 of August* (by whom?) and that the International Bureau of the Committee of Initiative (who?) has contacted the French government (Therefore, has Brussells been abandoned?) This circular letter mailed from Berlin to the French Committees (and in what style!) carries the imprint: *Kampf- Kongress gegen den imperialistischen Krieg.* It is clear that this is the *League against Imperialism* of Münzenberg which is leading the dance and which has annexed our Congress. This is not merely a shameless abuse of power, it is the most glaring of fumblings and of such magnitude that our agent provocateur could not commit a worse one: because it is all that is needed to justify all the accusations of the Adlers, Vanderveldes etc. I protest with the utmost energy. And all the more so in that I have always refused to belong to the League of Münzenberg, knowing with what unheard of shamelessness it exploits circumstantial or conditional group endorsements, which other groups consent to, in order to exploit them towards ends that are different from those for which these associations were solicited in the first place.

I am profoundly disgusted by these actions. They compromise the best causes and drive away many of the most dedicated men of good will. You express, at the end of your letter of 11 july , thoughts which are absolutely correct regarding "our Communist friends," who constantly "exploit the privileged situation which their sense of of organization and action has given them." I deplore that you are not putting into practice these ideas yourself. I urge you to do so. Act with energy! And in the Congress in which you are the prime mover and the organizer put an end to these tactics.

Cordially yours.

Barbusse, who was better informed about the background, sought to pacify Rolland and apparently succeeded. For when the congress finally met in Amsterdam on 27/28 August, Rolland sent an impressive message and was duly honoured as patron of the congress. When Münzenberg called on him some years later in Vézelay, Rolland gave him a large signed photograph of himself, a gesture which greatly pleased Münzenberg who admired Rolland.

Organizational preparations for the congress were worked out to the last detail. Weekly lists were issued in the form of a printed document entitled "Who is attending the congress against the imperialist war?" giving the names of those who had accepted invitations. List three, for example, contained forty-six pages with details of every organization, individual and trade union group in every country. Only the Soviet Union was not represented. Not a single Russian name appeared, except that of Maxim Gorki, head of the convening committee. But among the doctors, lawyers, engineers, artists and scientists, who were grouped together by professions there was always at least one reliable Communist, such as Hilde Benjamin among the jurists.

When the preparatory work was completed Münzenberg paid one more visit to Moscow to receive last minute instructions and to discuss the financing of the congress. He took with him two colleagues who were visiting Russia for the first time. Münzenberg had not prepared them for what they might expect. He had merely observed that they should keep their eyes open and tell him what they thought. Both were horrified by the poverty, the hunger and the muddle although they enjoyed a relatively high standard of comfort at the Grand Hotel, were provided with tickets to the theatre and the opera and were above all well fed while Soviet Russia faced a terrible winter of starvation. After a week Münzenberg rushed back to Berlin and then raced on by car to Amsterdam.

The congress was well attended. Seventy-nine pacifist organizations, 151 other associations from the federation of ex-soldiers to the League against Anti-Semitism, 190 trade union organizations and 41 factory groups had sent representatives. Albert Einstein, Sigmund Freud and numerous other personalities telegraphed messages of support. In all 2,195 delegates from 29 countries attended, including Madame Sun Yat-sen. The Communists used the opportunity to hold international conferences of their numerous relief organizations in the shadow of the congress.

In his address Münzenberg left no doubt that he regarded the congress as a means of strengthening the Communist movement; he welcomed approximately three hundred Social Democrats who had come in spite of Friedrich Adler's warnings, and amid public enthusiasm claimed that these visitors were ready to join the Communists in the struggle against the Second International; he attacked the Trotskyists and extolled Lenin and Liebknecht.

The Dutch press was indignant that this congress had been allowed to meet, that "this Trojan horse [has been] let into our courtyard. Geneva, London and even Paris would not have the congress. It is merely a preparation for world revolution. Why should we be the victim?" *De Tijd* asked on 12 August 1932.

Of the participants only the anarcho-syndicalists criticized the congress which they claimed was being discreetly managed by Moscow. They said the slogan "War on Imperialist War" did not mean war on war in general but was merely a means of justifying a defensive war waged by the Soviet Union. The Russian state had the biggest military budget of all countries and it had entered into alliances with capitalist and fascist states. The anarcho-syndicalists were for the overthrow of the Russian dictatorship, for free Communism.

The British Labour Party on the other hand gave wholehearted support to the programme and the decisions of the congress. Its report "United Front Against War" was sent out "With the compliments of William Gilles, Secretary of International Department, Transport House." The report noted that the Amsterdam peace movement had begun as the result of the appeal by Rolland and Barbusse. It was not even suggested that Moscow might have been involved. The report described Münzenberg not as the initiator of the conference but merely as its organizer, although his speech was said to have been the most electrifying.

Such financing of the congress as was done by Münzenberg's organization was in the hands of his secretary, Hans Schulz. Presumably all the other Communist Parties present had their own budgets. Münzenberg's organization handled about thirty-eight thousand dollars of the costs of the congress. The account was sent by courier to Piatnitsky in Moscow. A copy which Schulz kept at his brother's was seized by the Gestapo after Hitler's takeover.

13. Collapse

There had been increasingly bitter clashes between the KPD leaders during 1931. Heinz Neumann, young and easy-going, was promoting the slogan: "Hit the fascists wherever you can". This the workers did anyway to keep the SA hordes at arm's length. But Moscow rejected

Neumann's slogan as amounting to an invitation to individual brutality. Altogether Stalin discouraged any offensive behaviour on the part of the KPD towards the National Socialists. In addition Neumann, who was intellectually far superior to Thälmann, intrigued against the party leader and collected supporters with the aim of pushing Thälmann out. Neumann's group included Hermann Remmele, Kurt Müller, who was in charge of the Youth Association, and a number of other leading officials. In the end the Comintern intervened, relieved Neumann of his Politburo functions "for anti-party group activity" and called him to Moscow. Stalin was probably helped in coming to this decision by the knowledge that Neumann had maintained close links with a group of young Russian Communists around Syrsov, Lominadse and Shatskin who had fallen from grace. These loyal Stalin supporters had occupied official key positions in Transcaucasia, Georgia and Armenia where they had been in charge of the enforced collectivization. The GPU's brutal extermination methods and the chaos in the countryside led them to be severely critical of Stalin's economic policy. In November and December 1930 they were publicly denounced as "Rightists and supporters of Rykov and Tomsky" and relieved of all party offices. Because Neumann continued to meet some members of this group during his visits to Moscow, Stalin was profoundly suspicious and regarded Neumann as insufficiently reliable for responsible work in Germany.

When it became clear that the breakup of the Weimar Republic was not far off, the KPD was no longer a factor in politics. The differences at the top did not even penetrate to the rank and file. Most members were unemployed and the industrial workers, to the extent that they still belonged to the party, lacked the determination to fight. For years now the party leadership had not been elected but appointed by the Comintern. The eleventh ECCI Plenum in the spring of 1932 witnessed a reprimand of two writers in the German propaganda department, Emel and Kraus, for having described Social Democracy as the "main support of fascism." In the opinion of the ECCI, however, it was merely the "main support of the bourgeoisie."[1]

The KPD's obstructionist policy in the parliaments prevented any possibility of the republican parties resisting the National Socialists. At the Prussian Landtag elections in April 1932 the National Socialists increased their vote from half a million to eight million. Instead of tolerating the Weimar coalition the KPD brought in a vote of no confidence in Otto Braun's government which had resigned and continued in office only because no absolute majority could be found for a new

[1] *Kommunistiche Internationale*, Vol. 4, 1932.

prime minister. These were the tactics of political madness. The electors who voted for the KPD in hopes of a firm, united opposition to National Socialism were disappointed. The presidential elections in the spring of 1932 completed the demoralization of the Left: the KPD did not even attempt to discuss with the republican parties the possibility of a joint candidate but put up Thälmann in the first and second ballots, whereas the SPD in the second ballot voted for Hindenburg to prevent Hitler from being elected President. The paralyzed Social Democrats were confronted by an active National Socialist Party which knew how to exploit its opponent's weaknesses and how to win over with great rapidity large sections of the lower middle classes and the rural population.

We spent Whitsun 1932 with friends in the Fichtelgebirge and then travelled down the Main towards Würzburg. From the Franconian villages young men in white shirts and top boots flocked to the rallying points of the proscribed SA. The sight made a strong impression on Münzenberg who commented that this was a popular movement against which his party was powerless, that it was impossible to stop Hitler and that a unification of the working class, if it could be achieved, would no longer save the day. He did not know that this would be his last holiday in Germany.

Meanwhile the 20th of July approached. The Prussian Government knew that the new reactionary Papen Government planned to appoint a Reich Commissioner in Prussia and to overthrow the Land government. On the morning of 20 July as Papen announced the dismissal of the Prussian Government Rudolf Olden,[1] several Social Democratic deputies, some editors of *Welt am Abend* and Münzenberg and I waited anxiously at the corner of Wilhelmstrasse and Unter den Linden to see if the old government would mobilize the police and if the trade unions would call a general strike. The unanimous opinion was that unless there was immediate action everything was lost. Olden took Münzenberg to Höltermann, the head of the Reichsbanner, to discuss joint action by the Reichsbanner and the Communist Kampfbund. Höltermann refused to play. He was not anxious to compromise himself by joining forces with the Communists.

Toni Waible, then *Reichinstrukteur* of the Central Committee of the KPD, pressed Wilhelm Pieck as to why nothing was happening, why no general strike was being called. Pieck was completely lethargic. The

[1]Olden was at that time an editor on the *Berliner Tageblatt*. He emigrated in 1933 via Prague and Paris to London. At the beginning of the war he was interned and in 1940 he was invited to the United States. During the voyage the vessel, the *City of Benares*, was torpedoed by a German submarine and Rudolf Olden lost his life.

Politburo could not act because Thälmann had not been seen for three days. Nevertheless on 21 July the KPD and the reformist trade unions called for a general strike, thus performing a 180 degree turn. Now that it was too late they called for action on behalf of the deposed Prussian Government whose fall they had helped to bring about.

But nothing happened. The trade unions were afraid of civil war. While the Social Democrats argued about whether the Prussian police would fight for the dying republic or not[1] the Prussian Government retired quietly.

Events now moved rapidly towards the collapse. The National Socialist terror against the Communists and Socialists became daily more brutal. On 12 May 1932 in the Reichstag dining-room National Socialist deputies beat up the editor of the *Reichsbanner Zeitung*, Helmut Klotz, because his paper had published letters by the homosexual chief of staff of the SA, Ernst Röhm.[2] The Reichstag elections of 31 July 1932 made the National Socialists the strongest party. A wave of indignation—but also of impotent horror—swept the country when a Communist agricultural labourer was literally trampled to death by five SA men in the Upper Silesian village of Potempa. Hitler sent a telegram of sympathy to the murderers after sentence had been passed on them and he amnestied them immediately after his takeover.

Münzenberg was restless and irritable during these weeks as he sensed what was in store for Germany. He suffered from insomnia and paced up and down at night as though he was literally waiting for the Nazis to carry out their threat of staging a "night of the long knives." The Papen Government took ever more ruthless action against Communist organizations and also against Münzenberg's enterprises. On 1 September the IAH office was occupied by a large police contingent. The material of the Amsterdam anti-war congress was seized and the police showed particular interest in correspondence and declarations of support. Several editions of the AIZ were confiscated. On the fifteenth anniversary of the October Revolution a special edition of the AIZ was

---

[1]Even decades later two of the leading SPD officials at the time, Kurt Geyer and Kurt Hirschfeld, still disagree. Hirschfeld thinks that the *Schutzpolizei* would have taken the side of the striking workers against the Nazis, that Bavaria and Hesse had assured Prussia of assistance and that Wilhelm Leuschner had promised to send Hessian police units. Hirschfeld told the author that he was later asked by Schleicher why the SPD had done nothing on 20 July. The Reichswehr had waited for a lead. Kurt Geyer on the other hand thinks that the majority of the Prussian police officers were pro-Nazi and would never have gone to the defense of the republic.

[2]Klotz, a former lieutenant commander of the German Navy and a member of the NSDAP, became a Social Democrat, emigrated to Paris in 1933 and took French citizenship. When the Germans entered Paris in 1940 he was arrested by the Gestapo and executed for high treason.

published carrying on its title page a photograph of Stalin with the caption: "We shall not desert our socialist fatherland in the hour of danger." To the immediate, far greater danger which threatened Germany reference was made only in Münzenberg's leading article:

> In these difficult days in the history of Germany when the life and death of the German workers movement is at stake, the working masses in Germany, if they want to live and be victorious, must break once and for all with the socialist-chauvinist policy of compromise . . .

A UFA newsreel of the opening of the Reichstag on 30 August 1932 shows Münzenberg hastening into the building followed by Göring and Goebbels for whom the cameramen had positioned themselves at the entrance of the building. The National Socialists enjoyed their party's triumph to the full. Hermann Göring took over from Paul Löbe as President of the Reichstag. Seventy-five year old Klara Zetkin[1] had travelled from Moscow to Berlin to open the Reichstag as its oldest member. We welcomed her in the lobby where, breathing with difficulty and seriously ill, she waited surrounded by her friends for the start of the session. In spite of her bad health she made a courageous speech and implored the left to collect its forces because of the fascist threat. But her words fell on deaf ears; the KPD preferred to pursue its suicidal policy of obstruction.

In September Münzenberg was once more in Moscow as the twelfth ECCI Plenum met to discuss the deviations of Neumann and Remmele. Neither Neumann nor Remmele were allowed to reply to the accusations, they were not even allowed to speak; thereupon Remmele decided to stay away from the meetings. It was only in whispering campaigns, not in public, that Münzenberg was named as a follower of Neumann. He listened to Piatnitsky's speech and commented to Heinz Neumann and Kurt Müller who were sitting beside him that things were more difficult for them than for him because he was still needed by the Russians. He no longer had any illusions about Moscow's attitude towards the opposition who were not even given a hearing and whose

---

[1]In 1925 Klara Zetkin ceased to work in the KPD and devoted herself exclusively to working for women in the international sphere. She had clashed strongly with Stalin over the Wittorf affair. Since then he detested her and referred to her in obscene language. Bukharin's fall had been a heavy blow to her. She remained in touch with her friends from the Spartacist days although most of them belonged to the expelled KPD opposition. In her articles and speeches she paid the obligatory lip service demanded by the Comintern of its officials. Although she was aware of the decline of the Communist movement and of the totalitarian development of Russia she wanted to continue to be identified with the Russian revolution, or as Münzenberg sarcastically put it, she "wished to be buried in the Kremlin wall."

deviations or mistakes were a few years later held against them as crimes.

In spite of the drop in the number of votes cast for the NSDAP at the Reichstag election of 6 November 1932 and the resulting optimistic commentaries which spoke of the collapse of the NSDAP, Münzenberg remained pessimistic. He had reason enough. On 23 January 1933 the SA, protected by the Prussian police, demonstrated outside the Karl Liebknecht house, the KPD's headquarters on the Bülowplatz, and the Communists did not lift a finger. On 20 January the party leadership had received a telegram from Moscow ordering the German Politburo to see that there were no clashes between National Socialists and Communists during this demonstration.

On 30 January 1933, as Hitler's followers celebrated his appointment by Hindenburg as Reich Chancellor with a tremendous torchlight procession past the Chancellery, Münzenberg left his flat never to return. He lived clandestinely in the west of the city in a room in a new building which we had found for him. At the last editorial meeting of his dailies, attended by Hans Gathmann, Kurt Kersten and Paul Friedländer as well as by Hermann Remmele, Münzenberg gave an analysis of the situation: Fascism was coming in any case and would probably remain in power for some time. His organization would try to issue its papers for as long as possible, although *Rote Fahne* had already been banned, as had *Vorwärts*. Münzenberg commented to Kersten that the party officials reminded him of dancers who had failed to notice that the curtain had come down. Two or three more weeks and everything would be over.

On 19 February 1933 everyone of note in left wing democratic Berlin gathered for the last time in the Kroll halls for the rally *Das Freie Wort* (Free Word). The committee *Das Freie Wort* had been founded in August 1932 at the suggestion of Georg Bernard, under the chairmanship of Heinrich Mann and Rudolf Olden. When Göring's officials banned a meeting of the "League for Human Rights" at which Carl von Ossietzky was to have spoken, Rudolf Olden, Kurt Grossmann and Münzenberg had within a few days organized a meeting in the Kroll halls. Several hundred invited guests attended and Georg Bernard and Harry Graf Kessler presided, as well as Professor Tönnies and Professor Heine. In spite of constant gibes from the colonel of police who supervised the proceedings the meeting went on for several hours. In the course of the morning a group of Social Democrats, including Friedrich Stampfer and Toni Sender, came across from another meeting which had just ended at the Volksbühne and asked for permission to read a message from Thomas Mann. Everyone spoke up courageously against the National Socialist dictatorship. When Professor Dr. Wolfgang Heine accused the National Socialist Minister of Culture, Rust, of knowing nothing about culture the meeting was stopped by the police. The assembled company realized that such a belated manifestation of unity could not prevent the death of the Weimar Republic. Everything was too late. Free speech in Germany had been silenced.

VI

An Anti-Fascist Breaks with Moscow

1. Escape to Safety

On the evening of 27 February 1933 Münzenberg was to address an election meeting in the little town of Langenselbold to the east of Frankfurt am Main. Because of attacks on Communist gatherings and daily clashes with the National Socialists, because of the semi-legal state of the party since 30 January 1933 he took certain precautions. Contrary to his usual custom he did not stay at a hotel and telegraphed to his chauffeur, Emil, to drive his car over to Frankfurt on Sunday, 26 February. On Sunday evening he met Emil at a Frankfurt café which he frequented. However serious the situation he never forgot the pleasurable side of life. They therefore decided to start the following day by watching the carnival celebrations in Mainz because Emil had never seen a carnival procession. Towards evening they arrived in Langenselbold. The meeting was crowded. Münzenberg made a passionate speech and made some telling points against the Nazis. He was enthusiastically applauded and even the country constable who was there to preserve order approvingly shook his hand. Ten minutes after Münzenberg and Emil had left the meeting an SA commando arrived to arrest him.

Meanwhile events had taken a dramatic turn in Berlin. The Reichstag had gone up in flames and warrants of arrest had been issued for almost all leading Communists. Münzenberg knew nothing of what had happened in Berlin. He visited the flat of the IAH secretary, Paul Schöfer, and played Skat until Schöfer's wife returned home around midnight and reported that apparently something was happening in Berlin. There was much excitement and people were talking of a fire in the Reichstag building. She knew nothing precise.

This news was sufficiently serious to make the Skat players abandon their game. Around 1.30 A.M. Münzenberg left and went to bed. Emil stayed up because he was supposed to collect me from Frankfurt station upon my return from Switzerland. But he failed to find me and returned to his hotel. No sooner had he fallen asleep than I awakened him unceremoniously. As I left the train still half asleep I heard the news vendors' cries and saw huge banner headlines everywhere: "The Reichstag on fire. The Communists have set it alight. Warrants of arrest issued against all Communist officials." I rushed to the first open café and put through a call to Münzenberg's Berlin flat where his secretary, Hans Schulz, and his wife were staying so that there would always be someone to answer the telephone. The police had called at the crack of dawn and presented a warrant of arrest bearing an ancient photograph of Münzenberg. But the Nazis were not yet in full control. One of the police officers recognized Hans Schulz's wife, the daughter of the prominent Social Democrat and former police president, Karl Zörgiebel. The policeman took Sonia aside and whispered to her that she and her husband should flee at once and warn us. The same day the flat was put under police observation. The authorities expected important Communist officials whose names were on their wanted lists to appear there, a somewhat naive expectation because in the circumstances nobody dared to visit Münzenberg's flat.

Emil and I now discussed how we could prevent Münzenberg from going to the café at the station where the two had arranged to meet. We positioned ourselves one at each side of the station square. Emil saw him first, ran towards him and took him to the car. We left Frankfurt in the direction of Darmstadt. What should we do next? It seemed pointless to return to Berlin where it would be almost impossible to go underground. Münzenberg's organizations and concerns were even less prepared for illegality than the party itself. In a small roadside inn we considered the pros and cons. Meanwhile the afternoon papers had appeared. They gave the names of several wanted Communists including that of Münzenberg. It was imperative to get him out of reach of the Nazis. The best idea seemed to be to take him to the Saar.

Suddenly I remembered that the father-in-law of my sister Margarete, the Jewish religious philosopher Martin Buber, lived not far from Darmstadt. Perhaps he or his wife could advise us. Although I did not know them well we decided to drive to Heppenheim. I left the two men in the car some way from the Bubers' home. Buber and his wife were aghast when they saw me, they did not know what to suggest. But after some thought Buber made a practical proposal. He gave me a letter to a friend of his, a university professor who lived in Saarbrücken, and suggested that Münzenberg go to ground there for a while and await events.

Now he needed a passport. This could only be got with the help of the Frankfurt comrades. We drove to Mainz where the carnival celebrations were in full swing, regardless of events in Berlin. We left Münzenberg on the Rheinpromenade among the carnival crowds and rushed off to Frankfurt. The police had not yet visited the offices of the *Neue Deutsche Verlag* and the AIZ. The place was deserted except for a young comrade who helped to sell the papers. Without hesitation he dashed home, got his own passport and gave it to me. Although the young man did not in the least resemble Münzenberg and was fourteen years his junior we had to take the risk. Our rescuer's name was Studzinski. Today he is SED burgomaster of the Thuringian toy manufacturing town of Sonneberg. Frankfurt was also in the throes of carnival celebrations. In the crush of the procession I had lost sight of Emil and the car. Perhaps he was at the café *Hauptwache* waiting for me. But at the door the waiter stopped me and told me that the police had been to look for Münzenberg. Finally we found each other, drove back to Mainz, picked up Münzenberg who was wandering up and down the banks of the Rhine in a snow shower and drove into the night along a deserted country road. Although all the frontier posts had that morning been issued by the Berlin authorities with descriptions of wanted persons the customs official merely briefly and superficially shone his torch into the car without paying attention to our passports. He probably thought that we were returning from the carnival festivities. The same night we arrived in Saarbrücken.

We took rooms for the rest of the night in a small inn. There was no thought of sleep. Münzenberg tried to appreciate the significance of what had happened. Not that he was very surprised by the turn of events. Since 30 January, with Hitler's appointment as Chancellor, he had daily expected an all out Nazi attack on the republic and the workers parties. Only a few days previously he had had a discussion in Frankfurt with former members of the *Rote Frontkämpferbund*. They had gone over to the SA and had told him frankly that, although there was nothing wrong with the Communists and although at heart they were on his side, Hitler made things happen more quickly, and they just could not bear to wait any longer. Many of them had been unemployed for over three years. They had no proper shoes, no warm coats. They were starving and they had reached the limits of endurance. Desperation had driven them into Hitler's arms.

That night in Saarbrücken Münzenberg expressed the view that Hitler was firmly in the saddle. His régime would last years, perhaps eight or ten years. It was doubtful whether he could be overthrown without a war, a far sighted view which distinguished Münzenberg from the majority of Communist officials. He concluded that although he had escaped with his life it was doubtful whether he would ever see Germany again. The following morning he introduced himself as Herr Studzinski to Martin Buber's friend who was somewhat taken aback but kindly offered him hospitality in his house on the Winterberg. The same evening I returned to Berlin with instructions for those of his colleagues who could still be contacted.

On the morning of 2 March 1933 the Berlin edition of *Völkischer Beobachter* carried an item under the heading "Münzenberg as an intellectual leader":

> Official sources state that among the many tons of material found in the Karl Liebknecht house there were forged orders from police officers and SA and SS leaders. The forged orders relate to security police commandos, to the use of motorized transport and similar matters. The documents discovered are even said to mention the poisoning of food and water supplies. The brain behind these doings is said to be the well-known Communist newspaper editor Münzenberg. So far Münzenberg has evaded arrest.

This news item was clearly meant to make the police intensify their efforts to arrest Münzenberg. The same issue of the paper also carried the notorious "Emergency Decree for the Protection of People and State" of 28 February 1933 which gave Hitler the green light for the relentless persecution of his political enemies and which signified the end of constitutional government in Germany.

During the night of the Reichstag fire several hundred Communist officials were arrested. Reports of arrest came in from all sides. It appeared that the KPD's preparations for survival in illegality were much less far advanced than had generally been assumed. The Nazis' sudden attack had caused chaos. Every Communist official who had managed, accidentally or by foresight, to avoid the first wave of arrests had to fend for himself.

On the morning of 28 February the police moved into the offices of the IAH, of the publishing house and of the dailies that formed part of

Münzenberg's enterprises. No further printed material was allowed to be published and all accounts were blocked. At this moment we benefited from a precaution which Münzenberg had taken two years previously. With the connivance of the then Russian consul in Berlin, Alexandrovsky, he had arranged for a certain sum to be deducted monthly from the earnings of the publishing house and deposited in a briefcase in Alexandrovsky's safe. Although the Moscow Foreign Office had forbidden its embassy employees to render such help Alexandrovsky was an old Bolshevik, he knew Münzenberg well and approved of this precaution. Having established contact with several colleagues I hurried to the embassy to collect from our reserve enough money to pay out the monthly salaries. But Alexandrovsky feared that I might be arrested on leaving the embassy and did not want me to go off with a large sum. We therefore arranged to meet at three o'clock in the afternoon outside the Café Wien at the Kurfürstendamm. Alexandrovsky would meet me in his green Ford, he would bring the money and I would join him in his car. Out of sheer nervousness I almost climbed into the car of a complete stranger. As we were slowly driving through the Tiergarten I embraced Alexandrovsky and unobtrusively pulled the packet of notes out of his pocket. A few hours earlier the papers had come out with the sensational announcement of Thälmann's arrest. We discussed the event. How could the leader of the party be so badly protected that he could fall into the hands of the police? In spite of years of preparation the party organization seemed to have neglected the most elementary precautions.

Münzenberg and Emil had meanwhile discovered that there was an easy way of obtaining a French visa. A travel agency sent their passports to the French consulate in Mainz. But before they could enter France as "tourists", one morning Emil found the professor's wife in a state of great excitement; she announced that the gentleman had departed after receiving a telegram, but that he had left behind a note. This she produced from under the tablecloth. In his note Münzenberg asked Emil if possible to wait for him at the station at Vorbach. But how had Münzenberg got to Vorbach which was the other side of the French frontier without a passport?

When Emil, with the help of a taxi driver who knew the countryside, got to Vorbach and found Münzenberg he discovered what had happened. That morning the professor had received an unsigned telegram which he showed to Münzenberg; it read "Depart immediately, Münz recognized". This had apparently so upset the professor that he had offered at once to drive Münzenberg to Vorbach. Later it emerged that the professor was well in with the National Socialists. Presumably he had seen Münzenberg's photograph in one of their papers and had realized that he was harbouring a "criminal". Therefore he had thought of this ruse and had sent the telegram to himself to get rid of his awkward guest. Münzenberg now needed to find accommodation in Vorbach where he could wait without papers until the arrival of his passport. People in the street whom he and Emil asked for the trade union house pointed to an inn at the top of the hill which they said was frequented by Communists. The two men went in, sat down and invited the innkeeper to their table. Münzenberg revealed his identity, was warmly welcomed and immediately given accommodation. The following morning Emil collected the visas and the two drove via Metz, Châlons sur Marne and Meaux to Paris. A little while later, I joined them after an adventurous escape.

2. Paris, a New World

Münzenberg was by no means persona grata in France. Since his collaboration with the Bolsheviks in the first world war and his activities as founder of the Anti-Imperialist League, the French authorities regarded him as an enemy of France and as a dangerous red agent. Nevertheless in 1932, after the Amsterdam congress, he had been granted an entry visa for the first time. At that time the French section of the *Comité contre la Guerre et le Fascisme*, founded at Amsterdam, had called for a big rally with international speakers. This took place on 3 September 1932 in Paris in the crowded Salle Bullier. Barbusse presided, Rolland and Gorki had sent messages and according to the Communist press Münzenberg's address was received with loud prolonged ovations. After the meeting many participants gathered in the street to voice their enthusiasm. There were clashes with the police whom we watched proceed brutally and ruthlessly against what was basically a peaceful crowd.

On this occasion Münzenberg had received his first, fleeting impression of Paris and its surroundings. The city delighted him. We had stayed at an old fashioned hotel on the Quai Voltaire, opposite the Louvre. Münzenberg was shown the city by friends belonging to the French Communist Party. Paul Vaillant-Couturier, then editor-in-chief of *Humanité*, invited us to an opulent breakfast in one of the small restaurants near the Halles where he was an habitué. The day before the rally we drove to Senlis where Henri Barbusse had a country house. This happened to be the first day of the shooting season. Crowds of hunters flocked to the woods and the fields, well fed, self-assured men. We were most surprised to learn from Vaillant-Couturier that these were not well-off bourgeois but mostly workers following their Sunday pursuits. The natural way in which the French workers enjoyed life was then still unknown to the German workers.

In December 1932 Münzenberg was once more in Paris for a working session of the anti-war committee at which he urged that the Amsterdam peace movement should be legalized in all countries. That meeting was attended also by Russian delegates. Elena Stasova and Nikolai Shvernik represented the Russian party, Georgi Dimitroff the Comintern. Soon afterwards, in January 1933, Münzenberg paid a visit to Moscow during which he discussed with the Comintern how to continue the work of the the mass organizations if the situation in Germany should deteriorate any further. Piatnitsky had suggested that if at all possible these activities should be continued from France where at the time conditions for the spread of Communist influence seemed as favourable as anywhere.

This moment had now come. Although Münzenberg had arrived in Paris illegally, as an emigrant he did not share the fate of countless politically and racially persecuted refugees who were frequently forced to fight bitter battles with the French authorities. Even as a persona non grata Communist he at least was no stranger to Paris and had many friends among the French Left.

Immediately after his arrival he visited the editorial offices of the illustrated journal, *VU*, where he met Marie-Claude Vogel, the publisher's daughter, a Communist whom he had known for some years. She at once put him in touch with Alfred Kurella who worked for the Comintern on Barbusse's journal *Le Monde*. Kurella in turn mobilized Barbusse and through him Münzenberg quickly gained access to influential sympathizers. In France the anti-war movement had brought many bourgeois intellectuals close to the Communists. Although they rejected the ultra left course of the Communists they participated in Communist initiatives and this participation accelerated as world peace seemed to them increasingly threatened by political developments. They were shocked by the collapse of everything that they had hitherto admired as German intellect and German culture. This collapse they were frequently much more aware of than many German intellectuals. Having rightly feared from the start that fascism would spread beyond the frontiers of Germany they regarded the anti-fascist battle as an urgent necessity and were ready to give their confidence and thus their support to a man like Münzenberg who not only had unusual propagandistic abilities but who had gained experience on the spot.

To begin with Marie-Claude's father, Lucien Vogel, put Münzenberg up at his country house in the forest of Maisons-Laffitte. The publisher of *VU* and co-owner of the popular fashion journal *Jardin des Modes* was a friend of the Soviet Union. Münzenberg had met him some years previously in Berlin while Vogel and his editors were preparing a special number on the political parties of the Weimar Republic. His daughter later married Paul Vaillant-Couturier and to this day remains one of France's most active Communists. She was remarkable for always faithfully following the party line. Vogel's country house and his Paris salon were meeting places for politicians and journalists, French civil servants, Russian émigrés and members of the Soviet embassy.

Münzenberg needed a resident's permit. Vogel and Barbusse, on whom Münzenberg had called briefly at his villa on the Côte d'Azur, put him in touch with the man most likely to help. Gaston Bergery was legal adviser to General Motors in France and a Radical Socialist deputy. It was during this period that he left the Radical Socialists and founded his own political group, the *Front Commun*, which was aimed against Fascism. For Bergery Fascism was a dangerous variety of Capitalism. It was in this sense that he opposed it, first in his organ *Mantes-Républicain* and later in the journal of his new group, *La Flèche*. Although well disposed towards Münzenberg's activities he thought it necessary to stress that he was in no way connected with the Amsterdam peace movement because he felt that an anti-Fascist front must consist not only of the two great left-wing parties but must include as wide as possible a variety of lower middle class and middle class groups. He regarded the influence of the Communists in the Amsterdam movement as so apparent that he saw it as a danger. Later his group was absorbed by the popular front movement.

Bergery declared himself willing to approach the Prime Minister, Camille Chautemps, on Münzenberg's behalf. The result was unexpectedly favourable. The cabinet decided to lift the ban on his entry and Münzenberg—and later also some of his closest collaborators—were given political asylum. I too profited from this generosity. To the great displeasure of the reactionary Paris police prefecture, we were given the much coveted *carte d'identité* as *réfugiés provenant de l'Allemagne*. We had thus negotiated the most difficult hurdle. Although Bergery had been asked to promise that his client would not intervene in internal French affairs, that he would not take part in the work of French Communist organizations, Münzenberg was in no way restricted in fighting the Hitler régime from Paris.

3. *The Struggle Continues*

Münzenberg threw himself into his work. He and a number of French friends founded a "Committee for the Victims of German Fascism." Count Karolyi, an Hungarian émigré who had lived in Paris for many years, agreed to head the French section. Lord Marley became the international president and with other British Labour politicians and intellectuals assumed responsibility for the Committee. One of its first members was Albert Einstein. This supra-party, international, political platform gave Münzenberg considerable scope in the fight against National Socialism. Within a short period he became the focal point of anti-Fascist propaganda in Western Europe.

Accompanied by Lord Marley and Henri Barbusse, Louis Gibarti visited Spain and founded a committee against Hitler Fascism. It was at this time that Münzenberg first began to take note of Spain with its special political problems. Gibarti's visit began a fruitful exchange which continued for years. The manifesto establishing the committee was signed by a number of prominent Spanish politicians and intellectuals, including the philosopher Miguel de Unamuno. The new committee assembled six thousand people in the Toros Monumental Arena at Madrid for a great, impressive rally. After the rally Gibarti ran into Heinz Neumann who had been sent out by the Comintern to reorganize the Spanish Communist Party. Neumann congratulated Münzenberg's representative on the success of the meeting and expressed his appreciation for the assistance the committee had given him in solving his own tasks in Spain.

On 10 May 1933 the book burning began in Germany in the square outside the Berlin Opera, and continued in Munich, Dresden, Breslau and Frankfurt. At the same time the National Socialists published lists of forbidden books, of books which they wanted to destroy. This cultural barbarism had an even more electric effect abroad than the news about the Nazis' treatment of their political enemies. Heinrich Mann and other German writers in Paris joined Münzenberg in calling for the establishment of a "German Freedom Library." A studio on the Boulevard Arago was put at the writers' disposal. There Münzenberg established a documentation centre where every National Socialist newspaper and pamphlet as well as material for his own publications was collected. This centre became the meeting point of many emigré writers, particularly Communists. At irregular intervals a printed news sheet was produced. French well-wishers donated a substantial number of German books so that the library soon became a credit to its name. Talks and lectures were given there and at times the centre also housed an illegal bureau in which an official of the "Red Sports International" and Richard Gyptner worked as the representatives of Dimitroff and the Comintern. We had settled in the Hotel Jacob in the street of that name which runs parallel with the Boulevard St. Germain. There was no lack of support for Münzenberg; friends offered help from all sides. The French poet Paul Nizan brought us together with the pleasant

French Swiss, Pierre Levi, a publisher of poetry anthologies and monographs on modern artists. Levi immediately placed at our disposal two rooms in his publishing house on the Boulevard St. Germain, and his firm's imprint, *Editions du Carrefour*, which was later formally transferred under a pseudonym to its new owners. His elegant blonde secretary, Violette, introduced us to the secrets of the French publishing world. We were ready to start producing books. In spite of a number of publications with large circulations the firm was in need of subsidies from the outset. At first the deficit was made good from the funds which Münzenberg had managed to transfer to Paris. Then the Comintern made up the losses. It owned *Carrefour* just as it owned the other organizations controlled by Münzenberg.

An increasing number of refugees from Germany flocked to the hotels around St. Germain des Prés and the two literary cafés, Le Flore and Les Deux Magots: writers, scholars, politicians, journalists and party officials who had escaped the terror or who by chance or good fortune had been released after a brief arrest. On 15 May 1933 Münzenberg wrote to his friend Fritz Brupbacher: "Ruth Fischer and Arkadi Maslow enthused about you." These two had just arrived in Paris after an adventurous escape by motor bicycle through Czechoslovakia, Austria and Switzerland. Münzenberg continued:

> Paris is becoming the city of émigrés. They arrive daily in their hundreds. This is the universal meeting point. So far about four thousand have arrived. As you know we are preparing a book on the Hitler Government and the Reichstag fire . . .[1]

Münzenberg had asked the Moscow office of the IAH to let him have Otto Katz as an assistant; from among the Berlin colleagues came Hans Schulz and a translator, Else Lange. These—with the two men's wives —at first constituted the entire *apparat* which Goebbels and his like described as the centre of Communist "atrocity propaganda" and which even today is described as the Paris "witches kitchen" of the "Communist agitprop specialists."[2] Around this nucleus gathered Communist officials who had escaped to the West and some more members of Münzenberg's Berlin firms who managed to emigrate to France unaided. From Berlin came Kurt Sauerland, the editor of the journal *Der Rote Aufbau*, and his friend Rudi Feistmann. They started immediately with the continued production of this journal which after January 1933 was called *Unsere Zeit*. The first number appeared in May 1933.

[1] Archives of the International Institute for Social History, Amsterdam.
[2] Fritz Tobias, *Der Reichstagsbrand. Legende und Wirklichkeit*, Rastatt/Baden 1962, p. 167.

It was printed in Strasbourg and published from Switzerland by the Universum-Bücherei. Bruno Frei had escaped to Paris when *Berlin am Morgen* was banned. At the same time Alexander Abusch also appeared. Abusch, alias Reinhard, who had been editor of the Communist *Ruhrecho* in Essen, was regarded as a member of the Neumann group. He had avoided arrest by escaping. With Abusch and Frei as editors Münzenberg founded *Gegen-Angriff* (Counter-Attack), a deliberate allusion to Goebbels' *Angriff* (Attack).

The journalist Berthold Jacob was then working in Strasbourg. He put us in touch with Mink, the owner of a printing firm, who was prepared to print *Gegen-Angriff* at his Imprimerie Française on the Rabenplatz. Mink himself published a daily, *La République*, written half in German and half in French.

Münzenberg arranged for Mink to print other journals and many books. The first number of *Gegen-Angriff* appeared on 1 May 1933. At first the paper appeared fortnightly, later weekly, and in 1936 it ceased publication.

In March the Marley Committee moved into an office in the Rue Mondétour in the Halles quarter, not far from the offices of the French section of the IAH. At times this office was Münzenberg's headquarters. From there he conducted his campaigns against the Leipzig Reichstag fire trial. In the autumn and winter of 1933/34 the office became a sort of transit camp for politically active emigrants of all shades who identified themselves with the struggle against Fascism. Gustav Regler, Arthur Koestler, Hans Siemsen and many others worked there for a time and then went their way. The office in the Rue Mondétour immediately became a scene of intense activity. Often we did not leave the building until the early hours of morning to eat an onion soup in one of the small bistros nearby. By that time the square in front of the office building was piled high with pyramids of fruit and vegetables.

The Marley Committee also set up a home in Maisons-Laffitte near Paris for refugee children from Germany. It was inaugurated by the French President himself. In his book, *The Invisible Writing*, Arthur Koestler gives a short but accurate account of the turbulent life at this children's home.

Noteworthy in this context is a secret report of the German political police, compiled from accurate and inaccurate information, on the first stages of Münzenberg's activities in the spring of 1933. On the basis of agents' reports a confidential account of the German Communist Party in exile[1] was prepared on 22 April 1933 by the political department of the German police presidium (the future Gestapo) to whom Münzen-

---

[1]Microfilm, *Institut für Zeitgeschichte*, MA 644, p. 867127 *et seq.*

berg had been known since the Weimar days. The report referred to
the "opening of a Communist publishing house in Strasbourg" and
mentioned the "feverish" preparation of anti-Fascist propaganda,
made "as ever by the centre at Paris with Münzenberg, Barbusse,
Romain Rolland at its head." Münzenberg was trying again to keep this
activity "as far as possible above party politics." Therefore he worked
"independently of the political party leadership, or rather the Comintern." An item of police information of 2 May 1933 not preserved on
the files deals specifically with "Münzenberg's efforts to establish a press
abroad." The account is supplemented by a further report of 10 May
1933 which says among other things:

> Through a contact Münzenberg has gained entry to the editorial offices
> of the workers paper at Saarbrücken from where he operates. The pur-
> pose of the Münzenberg circle is to organize from Saarbrücken a German
> language paper which is seemingly above party politics and it is likely that
> two new workers' papers will shortly appear in Saarbrücken and in Stras-
> bourg, on the lines of *Berlin am Morgen* and *Welt am Abend* . . .
>
> The new papers in German will certainly be propaganda sheets dealing
> almost exclusively with conditions in the Reich . . .
>
> Recently Münzenberg through his contacts approached all papers
> abroad which at some time or other have taken part in atrocity propa-
> ganda against Germany and conditions in the Reich. As is his custom
> Münzenberg again relies for preference on contributions from journalists,
> scientists etc. with famous names, that is on people who are known not
> only to him personally but who have some sort of contact with the central
> committee of the IAH. To be mentioned in this context are Einstein,
> Tucholsky and others . . . If this information is correct and if Münzen-
> berg's plans succeed it is likely that there will be a new flare-up of atrocity
> propaganda, particularly in connection with the Lubbe trial . . .[1]

The fears of the German police spies were not unfounded. The
régime was not yet sufficiently firmly established to accept calmly a
close and critical investigation of its methods by world opinion. In these
early months the foreign press joined forces in a general protest; there
was a united front of hostility and suspicion such as was never to exist
again in the future. Habit had not yet blunted people's minds or closed
their ears to the terrible tales which hordes of German refugees
brought across the frontiers. The Reichstag fire and its immediate
consequences had shocked the world. From 28 February onwards the
world press reported daily on the terror in Germany; it published contradictory statements by the Reich Government on which it passed acid
comment. Even undocumented news such as that of *Deutschnationale*

[1]Microfilm, *Institut für Zeitgeschichte*, p. 867150 *et seq.*

protests against the brown terror, information that was later collected in the disputed Oberfohren document, was taken note of. Münzenberg's share in this protest campaign was considerable. That he was a Communist seemed to be an accident rather than a decisive factor. It seemed as though political allegiances had been pushed into the background by universal indignation. The world was united in determined opposition to the German régime.

4. The Brown Books

In an attempt to justify the Reichstag fire decree and the wave of arrests of Communists that followed the fire the National Socialist rulers tried to produce new variants of their story of Communist instigators behind van der Lubbe. Münzenberg too was mentioned in that connection. In the Sunday edition of the *Völkischer Beobachter* (Berlin edition) of 5 March 1933, the day of the Reichstag election, there appeared under a banner headline which ran across the whole page and read "Cankerous Core of Communist Sub-men", on the left-hand side a large photograph of van der Lubbe (with the heading: "That is what he looks like, the red fire-raiser of the Reichstag") and on the right-hand side a photograph of Münzenberg (with the heading "The ringleaders flee to safety while the members are misused for the world revolution"). The article named Münzenberg as the leader of the Communist agitators who "shunned the light" and who had packed their bags in time. It concluded with:

Today this scoundrel is sitting somewhere abroad and from a safe distance watches what goes on in Germany. Let us give an answer to those traitors on 5 March. Every honest German worker will vote for Hitler, list 1.

The editor of the *Völkischer Beobachter* whose idea it had been to couple the names of Münzenberg and van der Lubbe did not suspect that this piece of imaginative journalism would soon come true in another sense.

With world attention focused on the Reichstag fire and its consequences, Münzenberg made the fire and the ensuing trial the focal points of his propaganda against Hitler. This propaganda culminated in two politically most effective—if highly controversial—publications, the "Brown Books,"[1] and in the London counter-trial. Of the two

[1] *Brown Book of the Reichstag Fire and the Hitler Terror.* With a preface by Lord Marley, Editions du Carrefour, Paris: August, 1933; *Brown Book II. Dimitroff contra Goering. Revelations about the real fire raiser. With a Foreword* by D. N. Pritt, Editions du Carrefour, Paris: April, 1934.

Brown Books it was the first that, by being politically highly topical, had a particularly strong and lasting influence on opinions about Nazi Germany. The Brown Book was an instrument of well-aimed propaganda and was consciously assembled from that viewpoint. The critics who present the book as a "Communist effort" and as a complete "fabrication"[1] fail to appreciate the character of the Brown Book and the circumstances in which it was compiled. It was necessary for Münzenberg and his contributors to stick closely to the facts and to produce as much concrete information as possible because they relied on the effects of documentary evidence. The claim made in the anonymous preface to the book, which came in fact from Münzenberg's pen, that "every statement in this book is based on documentary material" was not simply invented, even though it was somewhat misleading. Apart from official German announcements the "documentary" material consisted primarily of reports by refugees—political or Jewish—from Germany, or of information from Communist sources, and there was little opportunity to examine these stories and to produce historically impeccable documentation. It was only because Münzenberg's office was a meeting point for German refugees and because he had such good connections that this collection of contemporary reports could be assembled at all. Under Münzenberg's leadership many helpers were soon busily gathering evidence. Otto Katz was in charge of the research and more and more material accumulated in his hotel room in the Rue St. Roch where he lived with his wife Ilse. Numerous volunteers appeared with some piece of news, or some seemingly revealing document. Münzenberg looked in almost daily. It took days and nights to sift through the mountains of material. In addition to information on the Reichstag fire the Brown Book was also to contain reports on the general terror in Germany. Gustav Regler, in his autobiography, writes of these weeks:

> Our office was like an island on which many shipwrecked individuals found safety . . . After their fashion they all collaborated on the Brown Book.[2]

Münzenberg rightly emphasized in his introductory remarks that the Brown Book was a communal effort.

As a collection of contemporary accounts by Hitler's opponents in Germany and in exile the Brown Book—only about a third of it dealt with the Reichstag fire—was not only the most comprehensive work of its kind but in some respects continues to be of historical value even today. It was this aspect of the Brown Book that accounts for its propa-

[1] Cf. the comments on the Brown Book in Fritz Tobias, op. cit., p. 206 et seq.
[2] Gustav Regler, Das Ohr des Malchus, Cologne 1958, p. 215.

gandistic impact because there was much less manipulation of the facts than many critics believed in their imaginative overestimate of the "Münzenberg headquarters."

The account of the Reichstag fire which was in fact subsequently proved wrong in many respects may serve as an example. Münzenberg and his helpers began by asking the questions that the general public had asked ever since the day of the fire. Was van der Lubbe, the arrested culprit, an agitator or a misled victim? Who profited politically from the fire? And they "found" the same answer: van der Lubbe could not have perpetrated this crime unaided (this was also the conclusion subsequently reached by the German court). It was inevitable that suspicion should fall on the National Socialists. Münzenberg appreciated the great propaganda potential of this material. Therefore he lost little time over scruples or doubts. His main concern was to collect details and to present a convincing account of what had happened.

Otto Katz, together with a Dutch journalist, visited the Netherlands to investigate van der Lubbe and his family, his friends and his political associates. Much of the information he published on this subject in the Brown Book was correct; it has since been incorporated into numerous biographies of van der Lubbe, usually without any acknowledgement of the source. Some of the information and arguments with which Katz returned from Holland led to severe criticism of the Brown Book and of Katz personally. Katz wanted to establish that van der Lubbe was a homosexual and had previously had contacts with leading National Socialists with similar inclinations. If he could prove this his claim that van der Lubbe was a tool of the SA would be strengthened. Dutch friends of the accused at once produced a so-called "Red Book"[1] claiming that the Brown Book's allegations about van der Lubbe's homosexuality were untrue. Instead they stressed that van der Lubbe belonged to the small, strongly anarchist orientated group of "Soviet Communists of Holland" through whom he had come into contact with Berlin friends belonging to the *Allgemeine Arbeiter-Union*. In connection with the *Spiegel* series on the Reichstag fire these circles later produced a description of van der Lubbe as a man who, when he appeared in Berlin, gave the impression of a fanatic, who thought that there was a "revolutionary situation" and who held the view that the masses were merely waiting for a signal to strike.[2]

Another hypothesis of the Brown Book was the assertion that the fire-raisers had come in through a subterranean passage connecting the Reichstag building with the nearby residence of the President of the

---

[1] *Roodboek, Van der Lubbe en de Rijksdag Brand*, Amsterdam 1933.
[2] A. Weiland in a letter to the author.

Reichstag, Hermann Göring. This story had not been invented by Münzenberg. The correspondent of the *Wiener Allgemeine Zeitung*, Willi Frischauer, had wired to his paper a bare two hours after the start of the fire:

> There can be little doubt that the fire which is at this moment destroying the Reichstag was started by paid agents of the Hitler Government. It seems that the fire raisers used a subterranean passage linking the Reichstag with the Palais of its President, Minister and Reich Commissioner of the Prussian police, Hermann Göring.[1]

He had come to the same seemingly logical conclusion as the Brown Book did later. These and other assertions were based on very few facts. "We had", writes Arthur Koestler, "to rely on guesswork, on bluffing, and on the intuitive knowledge of the methods and minds of our opposite numbers in totalitarian conspiracy."[2]

Like Koestler and most of world, Münzenberg was basically convinced that the National Socialists had a hand in the Reichstag fire. For this reason he dared to base details of the "evidence" in the Brown Book on inspired guesswork. There is nothing to support the supposition that Münzenberg's entire Reichstag fire campaign was a determined piece of Communist fabrication, that he knowingly made false accusations against the National Socialists. It is equally true, however, that the Brown Book helped to perpetuate the theory of National Socialist involvement although all the concrete evidence that has so far been advanced in support of this theory has proved unsound.

The first Brown Book was reprinted several times within a short space of time. It also appeared in Britain, the United States, France, Czechoslovakia, Holland, Sweden, Denmark, Finland, Latvia, Poland, Rumania, Spain and the Soviet Union. A special German edition was published by the Universum Bücherei in Basle because Switzerland had banned the import of the book from France. The size of the Brown Book's various editions is sometimes exaggerated. Parts of the book were indeed published by the press all over the world and it is not known how many copies the Russian edition ran to. But the German and French editions, published by the *Editions du Carrefour*, did not exceed 25,000 copies and it is unlikely that translations in a further twelve countries, including Greece and Palestine, accounted for more than 70,000 copies.

The Brown Book was distributed in Germany in two illegal versions

[1] Willi Frischauer, *Ein Marschallstab zerbrach. Eine Göring-Biographie*, Ulm 1951, p. 100 *et seq.*
[2] Arthur Koestler, *The Invisible Writing*, London 1954, p.198.

under Reclam's Universum-Bücherei covers, one disguised as *Hermann und Dorothea* and the other as *Wallenstein*. On 25 October 1933 the Württemberg Ministry of the Interior announced the confiscation of a hundred copies of this illegal edition.

5. *The London Counter-Trial*

The IVth Senate of the *Reichsgericht* in Leipzig fixed the start of the trial for 21 September 1933. Apart from van der Lubbe the accused were the German Communist Ernst Torgler and the Bulgarians Georgi Dimitroff, Blagoj Popoff and Wasil Taneff. Torgler was chairman of the Communist Reichstag faction and head of the official KPD election committee. On the evening of 27 February he had left the Reichstag building at 8:15 with the Communist deputy Wilhelm Koenen. When the reports appeared in the National Socialist press the following morning accusing him of fire-raising he went with his lawyer, Kurt Rosenfeld, to the police presidium to prove that he had an alibi for the preceding evening; he was immediately taken into custody.

Dimitroff, Popoff and Taneff had been arrested on 9 March while lunching at the Bayernhof, a Berlin restaurant where they sometimes met. A waiter by name of Helmer, a National Socialist it was rumored, had reported these "suspicious foreigners" conversing in their mother tongue—which sounded confusingly like Russian—to the police. Of the three Bulgarians, only Dimitroff, the most colourful figure at the trial, had had a varied and adventurous past; the other two were obscure party officials. Dimitroff had early played an important role in the Communist Party of Bulgaria. When the group around Zankoff had come to power in a coup in June 1923, the Bulgarian Communist Party, the strongest workers party in the country, had remained neutral. The ECCI had disapproved of this attitude. Radek and Zinoviev sent the Bulgarian Communist Wasil Kolaroff to Sophia to convey the ECCI's view that the Bulgarian party should organize with the utmost speed an armed rising against the Zankoff Government. Blagoeff, the founder and leader of the party, and the party secretary, Lukanoff, refused on the grounds that there was no "revolutionary situation." However, a revolutionary committee set up under the leadership of Dimitroff and Kolaroff expressed itself in favour of implementing Moscow's directives. Arrests of Communist officials caused the revolutionary committee to panic. A premature start was made on 22 September with the result that the rising—inadequately prepared—collapsed a day later. There followed a wave of persecutions, arrests and death sentences. The Bulgarian Communist Party collapsed and the leaders of the rising fled abroad. Dimitroff was active in the headquarters of the Bulgarian Communist Party in exile until 1929 when he was removed from the party leadership for "conciliatory, rightist tendencies." Since then he had been used by the Comintern as an emissary and had become head of its West European Bureau. His main task was to maintain links with the Communist Parties in the Balkan countries, most of which were operating in semi-legality. That Göring's police had made a serious blunder in linking him with the Reichstag fire on the basis of an unsubstantiated denunciation was to become clear in the course of the trial.

In Moscow in the summer of 1933 Münzenberg discussed with the Comintern what further steps should be taken in the campaign against the forthcoming Reichstag fire trial. Efforts had already been made to send pro-Communist foreign lawyers to defend the accused in Leipzig. Although the National Socialist authorities had refused to admit these lawyers the Comintern plan had given Münzenberg an idea. Why not set up a commission of internationally known lawyers, submit to them the existing defence material and if possible present them with a number of witnesses for the defence. They would thus be able to stage a sort of counter trial which would be all the more effective since the lawyers involved could not be accused of open membership in the Communist Party. The idea was a brilliant one which was used again in many Communist campaigns and which has long since become part of the stock in trade of Communist propaganda methods.

The Comintern leadership agreed to Münzenberg's proposal. He was given the necessary powers and the financial means to set up Reichstag fire investigation commissions in several Western countries. In Britain the Marley Committee proved a suitable basis of operations. A number of prominent British lawyers were quickly enlisted; Sir Stafford Cripps, the future Chancellor, declared his readiness to make the opening speech; D. N. Pritt, a lawyer who was frequently consulted in international legal disputes took the chair. From the United States came Arthur Garfield Hays, a well-known champion of the Civil Liberties movement and one time counsel for Sacco and Vanzetti, from Sweden Georg Branting, son of the first Socialist Prime Minister, Hjalmar Branting, from France the famous criminal lawyer Moro-Giafferi and Gaston Bergery, from Denmark Dr. Wal Huidt, from Holland Dr. Betsy Bakker-Nort and from Belgium Dr. P. Vermeylen. The President of the Swiss *Nationalrat*, Johannes Huber, had agreed to be present but was prevented from doing so by pressure of parliamentary work. Several of these personalities had previously taken part in Münzenberg's campaigns. Münzenberg himself did not appear. As was so often the case, his work was done for him by reliable helpers; Louis Gibarti visited

America and enlisted A. G. Hays. From Paris Otto Katz pulled strings in Britain. Of the jurists, Münzenberg relied particularly on Georg Branting. He had met the reserved Swede in Paris with Olof Aschberg. Branting was a Socialist deputy and a pacifist by conviction. Even in 1933 he saw in the National Socialists' recent rise to power a new threat of war. He did not know the Soviet Union nor had he ever had any personal contacts with the Bolsheviks but he regarded them as the only power strong enough to guarantee the peace. A close relationship grew up between Branting and Münzenberg. Branting was a quiet, dreamy man who was amused by Münzenberg's ceaseless activity and by his determination to have all or nothing. But at the same time he was impressed by Münzenberg's uncompromising, aggressive attitude. Like so many dreamers he was fascinated by the man of action.

The counter trial took place in London from 4 to 19 September. The final communiqué of the commission which amounted to a verdict, if an unofficial one, was published the day before the opening of the Reichstag fire trial at Leipzig. When the accused were led into the courtroom in Leipzig on 20 September 1933 several hundred foreign newspapers had already published the London verdict which absolved the Communist accused from all guilt.

The Nazi rulers had responded nervously even to the announcement of the London counter trial. Berlin knew exactly who was pulling the strings and the entire German press denounced the counter trial as "Marxist propaganda." The fiercest attacks were directed against Münzenberg. Under the heading "One of the Perpetrators of the Reichstag Fire" the Berlin and North German edition of the *Völkischer Beobachter* of 21 September 1933 carried a column on the "life story of the Communist capitalist Münzenberg." In National Socialist propaganda fashion the article sought to blacken Münzenberg's character, but at the same time it reluctantly presented him as an extremely clever and successful agitator. "The rogues" of the former Communist group in the Reichstag, the article said in perfect Nazi jargon,

> included a busy little man who was forever dashing to and fro. The pinched, impudent features, the slanting, crafty eyes and the sardonic lines at the corners of a tight-lipped mouth revealed the arrogant cynic: not an intellectual giant, but a cunning individual endowed with a truly Jewish business sense.[1]

---

[1]It is noteworthy that the depiction of the *Jewish* Communist agitator Münzenberg even found its way into the international biographical archives (the Munzinger Archives) where it is said (no. 36/57 of 7 September 1957) (!) that Münzenberg was "the son of Jewish parents."

The article did not deal with the Brown Book, it was concerned mainly with Münzenberg's role before 1933 as head of an assortment of enterprises concerned with the press, publishing and pacifist and humanitarian propaganda. In this realm he ruled "like an Asian despot," like a merciless slave driver. "Münzenberg was a ruthless dictator and his jovial, somewhat casual manner hid a coolly calculating, plotting brain to which any means were justified in pursuit of his sinister ends."

Four days later, on 25 September 1933, the *Völkischer Beobachter* reported "from abroad" a piece of news which was either based on misinformation or freely invented: it claimed that the office of the Dutch Prosecutor General had issued a warrant against Münzenberg for a fraud "which Münzenberg is said to have committed on 25 February in the Dutch frontier village of Glauenburg" (Münzenberg had never been to this place and was at the time still in Germany). On 1 October 1933 the *Kölnische Zeitung* carried a report taken from the Dutch pro-Nazi paper *Telegraaf* on the activities of the German Communist leader Münzenberg:

He has gathered together the collection of deliberate lies about Germany known as . . . the Brown Book and initiated the judical farce in London. *Telegraaf* now proves that he is also behind the 'League against Imperialism and Colonial Oppression' and that he tries with the aid of apparently humanitarian organizations to incite coloured colonial peoples against European colonial administrations.

It is grotesque that Münzenberg as publisher of the Brown Book has found admirers among the political and cultural élite of Europe, among those, that is, against whom he actively foments hatred on the part of coloured peoples in the Far East.

The Nazis were indeed irritated by Münzenberg's ability to find an echo among "the political and cultural élite of Europe." Where calumnies failed they resorted to lies. At the start of the counter trial the National Socialist Eckart-Verlag published a book by Adolf Ehrt entitled *Bewaffneter Aufstand* (Armed Rising). It contained material allegedly found in searches at the Karl Liebknecht house, the KPD party headquarters, and revealed the Communists as "terrorists and fire-raisers." This work was solemnly handed over to the entire foreign press before the start of the Leipzig trial.

On 9 August 1933 Ernst Torgler, awaiting trial in Moabit prison, asked the well-known lawyer, Dr. Sack, to defend him. Sack was a member of the NSDAP and had made a name for himself in the Weimar Republic as an excellent defence counsel. His reputation was somewhat dubious as he acted primarily for members of the Right, at the *Feme* murder trials, at the trial of the Rathenau murderers and later at the trial of the Ulm Reichswehr officers. On 8 September, Sack met Branting and Hays in Paris. From the discussion it emerged that he had not come to Paris just to discuss the evidence for Torgler's defence but to discover how far the preparations for the London counter trial had advanced and what the plans of the investigation commission were. Münzenberg did not put in an appearance at these discussions. His place was taken by Otto Katz who introduced himself to Sack and his two assistants as an Austrian journalist by the name of Breda. In his book *Der Reichstagsbrand-Prozess* Sack referred to Katz as an "alleged Austrian journalist." The members of the investigation commission naturally refused to show Sack any of their material. If he wished to know their arguments, let him come to London as an observer. Sack knew that even his trip to Paris had enhanced the importance of the investigation commission and that a visit to London would further increase the commission's standing. But in his view this body, unlike the Marley Committee, was one of the organizations

> which wanted to be regarded as an objective body, which "for the sake of justice" concerned itself with discovering the truth about the Reichstag fire . . . It was, however, strange and in the history of the nations unique that a group of private individuals should come together independently to investigate a trial pending at the highest court of a foreign sovereign state and thus to interfere in the supreme judicial authority of a foreign state . . . Suspicion might also have been aroused by the mysterious manner in which the commission was formed. But its membership, composed of lawyers from every country under the sun, seemed to offer a guarantee for practically useful and objective work.[1]

Sack's main concern was no doubt to inform himself on the mood abroad and to counteract the "émigré campaign" against the German Government and its responsibility for the Reichstag fire.

Before the London meetings started a group from the investigation commission had visited Holland and questioned sixteen witnesses. Their enquiries concerned van der Lubbe's personality, his political attitude and the world in which he moved. In its report the group noted that van der Lubbe had been a member of the Communist Youth or of the Dutch Communist Party until his expulsion on 5 April 1931, that he was a "supporter of individual action and individual terror," that he had opposed the trade unions and the workers parties as being unrevolutionary and reformist. The report described van der Lubbe as moving in a world of anarchist and asocial elements. The political accent of the report lay in the emphasis which it placed on van der Lubbe not having

[1]Dr. Sack, *Der Reichstagbrand-Prozess*, Berlin 1934, p. 111 *et seq.*

been a member of the Communist Party at the time of the fire.

On 15 September the meeting of the "International Juridical Investigation Commission on the Reichstag Fire" was opened by Sir Stafford Cripps in the Law Society's hall in London. In his opening speech he emphasized that it was the commission's task to collect all the available material for the defence of the accused Communists and to hear above all those witnesses who could not go to Leipzig because of the danger of arrest. In this context Cripps quoted a German newspaper article demanding the death sentence for defence witnesses. He underlined that none of the lawyers present belonged to the party of those accused in Leipzig; in the name of the other members of the commission he explicitly dissociated himself from documentation such as the Brown Book which the commission would examine but which it had had no part in preparing. Cripps described the forthcoming Leipzig trial as a political trial in the widest sense of the word. There had been a fire in the Reichstag building and the Communists were accused of starting it. But there were rumours about other causes of the fire and it was even claimed that the National Socialists themselves had set it. For these reasons it had been desirable to set up a juridical commission which would scrutinize all available material outside Germany and which if necessary would investigate the allegations about other causes of the fire. Naturally no trial, in the proper meaning of the word, could take place outside Germany.

This opening address was a masterpiece of thoughtful legal formulation. It had no connection with rabble-rousing and propaganda and it gave the London counter trial an atmosphere of factuality and integrity which justified the world-wide attention paid to this venture. Sir Stafford meant what he said. For him it was a matter of examining with extreme objectivity facts which because of political conditions inside Germany could not be examined at the trial proper. Although Sir Stafford may have been unaware of the political purpose of the counter trial, this purpose showed itself repeatedly during the five day proceedings. The main aim of the counter trial like that of the Brown Book was to direct the attention of the world to conditions inside Germany although by different and less controversial means.

After Sir Stafford's welcome address D. N. Pritt, King's Counsellor and future Labour M.P., took the chair. Even at that time Pritt had pretty close links with the Soviet Government. Münzenberg had met him at the end of 1933 when Pritt passed through Paris on his way to the Middle East where he acted as defence counsel for the Soviet Government in an international legal dispute. The extent of the links between Pritt and Moscow was revealed in 1936 when Pritt was admitted as an "observer" to the show trial of Zinoviev, Kamenev and the others. After his return to Britain he published articles and gave lectures praising the "fair" way in which this eerie trial had been conducted by the Soviet judiciary. Later he produced a pamphlet justifying the Moscow trials.[1] The commission's chairman and the opening speaker therefore belonged to very different breeds.

A number of prominent Social Democrats put in an appearance at the London counter trial, among them Paul Hertz, Albert Grzesinski and Rudolf Breitscheid. Georg Bernard also gave evidence. He concentrated on the political situation before the Reichstag fire and emphasized that in his opinion there had been no Communist threat, that the Communists could derive no benefit from the Reichstag fire, whereas the fire offered the National Socialists a welcome opportunity to rigorously eliminate the parties of the left and to intimidate their right wing coalition partners. Breitscheid shared this view.

The Social Democratic Reichstag deputy Dr. Hertz said in his deposition that the day after the fire he had tried to enter the SPD's private room in the Reichstag building but that he had been refused admission. The officials who barred his way had said that only National Socialist deputies were permitted to enter their private rooms. A few days later he was allowed back into the SPD's room. On this occasion he had inspected the burnt out interior of the Chamber. He had noticed that the corridor at the front of the Chamber had shown no traces of the fire although it was situated next to the badly burned Plenary Chamber. He stated that in his opinion the fire had started in the closed off parts of the Reichstag, in the press rooms and the press galleries to which only visitors with special passes were admitted. Albert Grzesinski, the former Berlin police president, testified that no signal for a full-scale emergency was given, a procedure otherwise automatic in the case of fires in government buildings.

Communist witnesses were also questioned. The Reichstag deputy Wilhelm Koenen who, like his colleague Torgler, was charged with responsibility for the fire but who had escaped arrest by fleeing abroad, described how he had spent the afternoon of 27 February in the Reichstag building and had left with Torgler half an hour before the discovery of the fire. Other Communist witnesses who had probably come to Britain without proper papers gave evidence in private. Dimitroff's sister and a Yugoslav Communist gave evidence that Georgi Dimitroff had been in Munich on the evening of the Reichstag fire.

No sooner had the proceedings started than the German embassy in London protested to the British Government. But the British Govern-

---

[1] After the Second World War Pritt was a member of the "World League of Democratic Jurists," one of the many Communist front organizations. He was made an honorary citizen of Leipzig, was a frequent guest of Ulbricht and a founder member of a "German-British society" in the German Democratic Republic.

ment pointed out that the activities of the commission and its meetings were of a purely private nature.[1] On the first day of the counter trial Dr. Sack arrived in London to keep an appointment with Branting and Gallagher. On this occasion Sack provided some information, hitherto unknown to the members of the commission, on the course of the fire and also on the security arrangements for the Reichstag buildings. From Berlin Sack had issued an invitation to Branting and Gallagher to attend the Leipzig trial. Branting refused but the two American lawyers, Gallagher and Hays, accepted.[2]

On the eve of the Leipzig trial, Pritt announced the result of the London commission's investigations in a final communiqué. The "counter trial," although more cautious and restrained in its conclusions, had by and large come to the same view as the first Brown Book from which Cripps had disassociated himself at the opening of the trial. This was a triumph for Münzenberg but it also shows how great the impact of the Brown Book had been. The communiqué read:

> The Commission concluded on the investigations which it has made:
> That van der Lubbe was not a member of the Communist Party.
> That no connection whatsoever could be traced between the Communist Party and the burning of the Reichstag.
> That the accused Torgler, Dimitroff, Popoff and Taneff ought to be regarded not merely as innocent of the crime charged, but also as not having been concerned with or connected in any manner whatsoever, directly or indirectly, with the burning of the Reichstag.
> That the examination of all possible means of ingress and egress to or from the Reichstag made it highly probable that the incendiaries made use of the subterranean passage leading from the Reichstag to the house of the President of the Reichstag.
> That the happening of such

[1] Ernstgert Kalbe, *Freiheit für Dimitroff*, (East) Berlin 1963, p. 94.
[2] See also *The Times* reports of 14–19 September 1933.

a fire at the period in question was
of great advantage to the National
Socialist Party.

That for these reasons and
others, grave grounds existed
for suspecting that the Reichstag
was set on fire by, or on behalf
of, leading personalities of the
National Socialist Party.[1]

6. Withdrawal or Defeat

At the end of March 1933 when Münzenberg had just installed himself in the Hotel Jacob he received a telephone call from Madrid. At the
other end of the line he heard the voice of Heinz Neumann, incoherent
with excitement. Even in Spain, Neumann had not stopped thinking
about developments in Germany and in long letters he had implored
his friend Hermann Remmele to resist the demands of the Muscovites
whom he disrespectfully described as "the gang". The news from Germany was a bitter blow to him. Neumann was intelligent enough to
understand that the KPD had collapsed. But what had happened to the
people with whom he had worked? Through the international Comintern network he had finally gathered that Münzenberg had escaped to
Paris.

Münzenberg, like Neumann, was convinced that the German working class and above all the KPD had suffered a devastating defeat. We
all felt that we were to some extent to blame for this catastrophe. The
party's many calls to fight the Fascists had been shown up as empty
phrases. When the moment of final confrontation arrived the field was
left to the National Socialists without a struggle. No preparations had
been made for the likely eventuality of a ban of the Communist Party
or for the protection of individual officials who were particularly at risk
because of their work. Provisions had been made only for a small circle
of Politburo members who were in constant contact with the party
organization. All the others had been left to their fate. Officials who for
years had attacked the Nazis at public meetings or in articles and pamphlets and whom the Nazis had threatened to kill were forced to go
underground unaided or to escape as best they could. If there was no
one willing to shelter a wanted person this person's only hope was to
flee abroad. The party apparatus had collapsed. Peter Maslowski for
instance who in August 1933 was still drifting about illegally in Berlin

[1] *The Times*, 21 September, 1933.

finally found his name on one of the Hitler Government's first lists of persons deprived of their civil rights.

The arrest of Ernst Thälmann on 3 March 1933 had paralysed the party leadership. In case of his arrest, a successor had in fact been nominated—John Schehr, a member of the Politburo. In March 1933 Schehr went to Moscow to attend the meeting of the ECCI presidium and in April he returned illegally to Germany via Prague. He brought with him the resolutions relating to the German Communists in which the ECCI asked for the united front with the Social Democratic workers to be continued in order to bring down the Fascist dictatorship by means of an armed rising. *Humanité* of 1 April commented:

> The establishment of an open fascist dictatorship which destroys the masses' democratic illusions and thereby reduces the influence of Social Democracy will hasten Germany's progress towards the proletarian revolution.

From Prague the German Central Committee issued a resolution on events in Germany designed to silence all critics of the party line:

> The victory of the counter-revolutionary party of Fascism has temporarily forced the working class and its party to withdraw. But only capitulators and opportunists can say that the working class has been beaten in the struggle against Fascism, that it 'has lost a battle' and 'suffered a defeat.'[1]

This long-winded resolution, drafted in the best "party Chinese," criticized the mistaken policy of the Neumann group in 1931 and never even suggested that the KPD's suicidal struggle against the SPD and its ambivalent attitude towards the Nazis might have contributed to the party's "temporary withdrawal." The party leadership successfully silenced the discussion among émigré party members on the causes of the catastrophe. The KPD had not suffered any defeat, it had merely made a strategic withdrawal into illegality. Anyone who refused to accept this palpable nonsense was expelled from the party "for profound lack of faith in the power of the working class." Most Communists acquiesced and kept their peace. Münzenberg also remained silent in spite of all inner reservations. In Berlin he had frequently used *Rote Fahne* as an alibi for his critical attitude. He now made the same use of its successor, the monthly journal *Unsere Zeit*, which was published (with Abusch as editor-in-chief) by Editions du Carrefour from 1933 to 1935. Sauerland and Feistmann, two editors who loyally toed the line, were made to expound the semi-official party point of view. In April

---

[1] *Rundschau* (Basle), 2 June 1933.

1933, in the first number which appeared abroad, Münzenberg himself contributed an article savagely attacking the Social Democrats for basically approving of Hitler's foreign policy statement in the Reichstag on 23 March. In the issue of 15 June 1933 the editors admonished several readers who had protested against the continued use of "social fascism" as an insult. Sauerland told his readers:

> The expression social fascism is correct. We regard as our greatest task the struggle against capitalism and fascism, the struggle also against their supporters, whether it is the Social Democrats or the illusion of bourgeois democracy, of parliamentarianism or of pacifism.

In 1935 Sauerland went to Moscow to work for the Comintern. As a loyal young theorist he was given a friendly reception and he and his wife were installed on the second floor of the Hotel Lux where fairly important persons were accommodated. One night in 1937—at the same time as Remmele and Neumann—he was arrested. He disappeared in a Soviet camp.

7. Unease in Moscow

On 5 June 1933 the Comité contra la Guerre et le Fascisme organized a congress in the Salle Pleyel in Paris. This meeting was a continuation of the Amsterdam Peace Congress of August 1932. The Amsterdam congress had been openly organized by Münzenberg. In Paris he could now be active only behind the scenes as he was not permitted to interfere in the work of a French body. The organizers at first tried to hold the congress in Copenhagen or Prague but met with opposition from the governments concerned. The congress was aimed primarily against German Fascism. More openly than at Amsterdam the meeting at Paris was run by the Communists so that even to the Russians this "movement" lost much of its value as a supra-party instrument. The attitude of the non-Communists was illustrated by the example of Gaston Bergery who with his *Front Commun* had disassociated himself even from the Amsterdam congress and who now voiced stronger and less equivocal reservations about the meeting in the Salle Pleyel.

After the Paris Congress Münzenberg visited Moscow. He did not exactly look forward to the trip, even though during the few months of his stay in Paris he had in fact achieved considerable successes. The campaign against the Hitler government had reached sensational proportions with much discussed publications like the Brown Book. Further Münzenberg had been able to enlist on behalf of the Communist cause a number of new influential sympathizers. But all this could not disguise the fact that his relationship with Moscow had undergone a decisive change. In Berlin he had been a factor in the political life of the country, with a solid organization and with the German Communist Party behind him. This basis had gone. Now he was a refugee of whom there were legions in Moscow from every country in the world. Then there was the confused struggle within the German party leadership. Heinz Neumann continued to be in the crossfire of serious public attacks and Münzenberg was counted among Neumann's friends.

In the past as an official visitor he had gone to Moscow by air or by rail several times a year. Now there were difficulties even over the technical preparations for the trip. The French police must not discover that he was visiting Moscow. The route through Germany was barred and he was not allowed into most of the countries through which he could have made a detour. The best route was via Copenhagen, Stockholm and Helsinki to Leningrad. The best passport in those days was a Swiss one which enabled the holder to travel everywhere without a visa. Although the Comintern had a passport organization which supplied important officials with suitable papers Münzenberg did not think much of these documents. In his opinion one never knew where the papers came from. With the help of reliable Swiss friends we therefore acquired "genuine" Swiss papers by a very simple method: one Swiss friend applied for a passport. He was requested to bring a photograph when he came to collect the document. Instead of fetching the passport himself he sent his wife with Münzenberg's photograph. In all good faith the official at the passport office stuck Münzenberg's photograph into her husband's passport and stamped it without asking any questions.

With the growing chaos in Europe in the thirties Swiss authorities could not fail to become aware of these tricks and put an end to them. For various reasons therefore we tried to undertake journeys such as this one as discreetly as possible. But even on the stormy crossing from Dunkirk to Esbjerg we ran into other German Communists. One of them, a former member of our Berlin publishing house, recalls his discussion with Münzenberg on board ship. Münzenberg spoke of the days when he had been in charge of the Youth International and had visited Moscow as its leader. With bitterness he described the intrigues and struggles behind the scenes which had finally led to his dismissal. Subconsciously he was probably under the influence of the far greater disappointment over the Soviet Union's German policy in recent years. For a disciplined Communist it was impossible to mention this matter and therefore he suddenly remembered long forgotten conflicts.

In the six months which had passed since Münzenberg's last visit to Moscow the catastrophic food situation had somewhat improved. Although people still looked pale and emaciated it was at least possible to obtain proper rye bread instead of the soggy, cloying stuff which in the starvation winter of 1932/33 had passed as bread. The Russian friends whom we visited spoke of nothing but the fulfilment of the plan or the crisis in the countryside. What was happening in Germany seemed a long way away. Seemingly people in Russia were hardly affected by events there.

In Moscow there were topics which could be discussed only with people in whom one had complete confidence. Among these was the fate of the fallen leaders. Short shrift was made of any sign of opposition. Although Zinoviev and Kamenev had returned from banishment after humbly admitting the errors of their ways they lived in complete seclusion and without political contacts on a dacha near Moscow. On 20 June 1933, shortly before our arrival, Klara Zetkin had died. Her body lay in state in the trade union house where crowds filed past her coffin. One of her sons, sitting in seats reserved for special guests, suddenly saw among the crowd a familiar figure shuffling past with his head bowed. He recognized Zinoviev, hurried to him and took him back to sit among the guests of honour. Zinoviev broke down completely; after he had somewhat recovered his composure he said that in the country where he lived with Kamenev he had the greatest difficulty in finding enough to eat. They had acquired a cow but it was impossible to find fodder for the animal.

One day we received an invitation from an old acquaintance who had worked with Münzenberg during the hunger relief campaign. When we arrived Eiduck, a bald, broad-shouldered man, was in the midst of his second breakfast which consisted of an enormous beefsteak with pickled cucumbers. This opulence—so strikingly different from conditions everywhere else—showed that he belonged to the chosen, namely the GPU, who could buy what they wanted at "closed" shops. We drove with him for an hour and a half to the vicinity of Shelkovo where they were building a canal between the Kljasma and the Moskva, a section of the Moskva-Volga canal. The enormous building site was surrounded by a high barbed-wire fence dwarfed at intervals by guard towers. We visited a small group of barracks at the farthest end of the deep trench. Apparently we were in one of the countless "work camps." From there we had a view of the entire area. Hundreds of people rushed up and down the steep slope, shovelling sand into flat baskets which they carried to the top. There were no technical appliances, no crane, no dredger, no lorry. The entire vast canal bed which descended to a depth of at least one hundred and eighty feet had apparently been dug out by hand. Eiduck, the *nachalnik* of this camp, proudly told us how many cubic feet of earth had been moved by this primitive method. In answer to our question about the prisoners, he indifferently explained that they were kulaks who had refused to join *kolkhozy*. As we stood in the big square outside the barracks one of the prisoners approached, bowed low and began to talk insistently to Eiduck. We did not understand a word but the subservience with which the man put his business was painful to behold. Münzenberg looked at the teeming mass of humanity and commented beneath his breath that this reminded him of the building of the pyramids by the pharaohs. He was depressed by the reality of "socialist reconstruction." He said less and less while Eiduck, the old Bolshevik, the worthy civil war fighter promoted to concentration camp supervisor, proudly showed us his camp.

Münzenberg spent most of his time in the *mokhovaya*, the Comintern building, with the leading officials in charge of so-called "mass labour." Here it was decided to establish a committee in Paris to work for the liberation of Thälmann. Here budgets for all plans for the immediate future were prepared. The last word in financial matters rested with Piatnitsky; technical co-operation between the Comintern in Moscow and Münzenberg's staff in Paris was in the hands of his old friend Mirov-Abramov, the head of the department for international liaison (*Otdel mezhdunarodnoi svyatzi*, or OMS). Mirov-Abramov's office was on the top floor of the Comintern building. He gave a wicked grin when he saw our Swiss passports which he handed on to the police. His department had gained in importance since the end of the twenties when the secret Comintern organization and certain espionage sections were detached from the diplomatic missions in the most important countries. OMS covered the entire globe, its leading members were highly intelligent men, devoted to the Communist cause and expertly trained in conspiracy. Mirov-Abramov could rely on them in every way.

OMS was responsible for technical questions that were of the greatest importance to the Comintern: the courier service, the secret telegraphic links between Moscow and the major cities of the world and the smuggling of propaganda material, people, money or arms from one country into another. Mirov-Abramov made use of a number of different persons. Foreign Communists who happened to be in Moscow or Russian officials travelling abroad were called upon to transport mail or money. These doings were known to Münzenberg; he did not object to them but he was not particularly eager to be of service. After his secretary had spent some months in Moscow becoming acquainted with the Comintern's methods, Münzenberg often preferred to delegate this part of his work to Schulz. It was he who was in touch with the OMS representatives whom he met regularly, in Berlin almost always in cafés where he handed them confidential papers and accounts. Schulz was also in charge of the illegal cash books for Münzenberg's various congresses. Maxim Gorki stopped over in Berlin while on one of his visits to Italy. Münzenberg and Schulz called on him. Gorki had brought a large sum in dollars which, if memory serves me right, was intended for the Amsterdam Peace Congress. The old man was no easy courier: he insisted on having the entire sum counted out before accepting a receipt.

Mirov-Abramov's representatives in Paris were two Poles. The one who was in charge was small and short-sighted and looked like a Jewish doctor. The other was a tall, younger man who was apparently responsible for technical details. Münzenberg sometimes met with one or the other of these two, always at the same hour and the same place, towards evening in the quiet Rue Montparnasse. More often, however, it was Hans Schulz or his wife who went to these rendezvous. Occasionally Schulz, to simplify matters, even accepted letters for sympathetic French organizations. I was always amazed at the speed with which the OMS people brought replies to Münzenberg's queries. Their telegraphic communications apparently were excellent. They felt so safe in Paris that the four of us occasionally met socially in the evening. Once I drove the men in our little Ford to a small workers restaurant outside Paris which Münzenberg knew. There we had an excellent meal and then walked in the shelter of the night, Münzenberg exchanging views with the older man while I had a less political conversation with the other. I had no idea who these two were, whereas they probably knew everything about Münzenberg and myself.

Some of the other OMS activities were less idyllic. In 1933 a school, called "Eighth International Sports Base," was opened in the vicinity of the Moscow suburb of Podlipki. The mysterious complex of buildings was protected by a double fence which was patrolled day and night by military guards with dogs. This was an espionage school directed by Mirov-Abramov. About eighty students of both sexes lived in modern surroundings; the teaching quarters had installations in every room for Morse code training and they were equipped with laboratories and workshops. The complex also had an administrative building, an assembly room with a restaurant, flats for about ten permanent teachers, domestic quarters with a nursery, big greenhouses and in a distant corner a comfortable house for the political leaders—the so-called Comintern dacha.

Candidates were nominated by Communist Party leaders from all countries and accepted by Mirov-Abramov after careful scrutiny.[1] He

---

[1] A participant of the 1933/34 course of 'Eighth International Sports Basis' gives the following breakdown of the nationality of pupils and teachers in his year: USA: 6 male (m), 2 female (f) pupils, 1 teacher (t); Britain: 3 m, 4, f, 1 t; Spain: 3 m, 3 f, 1 t; Sweden: 4 m, 3 f; China: 4 m; Germany: 1 m, 3 f, 1 t; Czechoslovakia: 3 m, 1 f; France: 2 m, 1 f,

proved an excellent psychologist. He invited the candidate into his office and asked whether he wished to make himself available for important cadre work in order to participate actively in the fight against Hitler and Fascism. Every good Communist longed to be a member of the "cadres" so the candidate felt flattered. After several meetings Mirov-Abramov asked the candidate to sign the written conditions for this "training"— which he almost always did—thereby totally committing himself to the Soviet espionage system. The trainees had to change their names and promise never to reveal their true identities, not even to their colleagues. During the training they had to break off all links with friends, were never allowed to leave the school alone, and were not permitted to take photographs or to talk to anyone about the school and their curriculum. The betrayal of secrets was punishable by death.

The candidates selected were young, unmarried, intelligent people with a special gift for languages or for technical matters. The financial direction of the school was the responsibility of Abramov's wife Lola who kept a special eye on English and French speaking pupils. Unsuitable candidates were eliminated by continual examinations. The curriculum was large and varied, it included languages, geography, history, Morse code and the decoding of messages. Trainees were taught to construct radio transmitters and receivers with simple materials, and learned to use them by contacts with radio amateurs all over the world. The technical examinations were conducted, in the presence of senior international party members and all pupils, by the head of the organization, Professor Gläser, who was then about forty years old. After completion of their studies some of the pupils, chosen by Mirov-Abramov personally, were given further arduous training at an army sports camp and finally sent to recuperate at a sanatorium in the Crimea. They then went out into the world for the OMS.[1]

It was very noticeable that this stay in Moscow severely tested Münzenberg's patience. He tried to end it as quickly as possible. There was constant friction also with the Russian IAH representatives. All disputes with the Russian authorities were postponed from one visit of Münzen-

2 t; Finland: 2 m, 1 f; Bulgaria: 1 m, 1 f; Poland: 1 m, 2 f; Norway: 2 m, 1 f; India: 2 m; Yugoslavia: 2 m, 1 f; USSR: 1 m, 1 t; Hungary: 1 m, 1 f; Switzerland: 1 m, 1 f; Belgium, Holland, Paraguay, Venezuela: 1 m each; Austria, Italy, Korea: 1 f each; Austria 1 t; Lithuania: 1 m, 1 f; Mexico: 2 m; Denmark: 2 m.

[1] When Mirov-Abramov was removed from Comintern work in 1935 and arrested in 1937 several of his ex-students who happened to be in Soviet Russia shared his fate. Like their former chief they were accused of spying for numerous countries. Others who were not arrested were held to their written undertaking. In the war some of them were parachuted with radio equipment into Germany. The cases that became known were those of Heinz Koenen, son of the Reichstag deputy Wilhelm Koenen, Else Koehler and Katja Niederkirchner, all of whom were caught by the Gestapo and shot.

berg's to the next in the hope that with his political weight and his connections he would set everything right again. With the collapse of the republic in Germany the Moscow IAH office had lost its *raison d'être*. Moreover the GPU intrigued ever more actively against the special status which the foreign IAH workers still enjoyed. There were anonymous reports accusing the foreigners of working unsupervised, of smuggling in things from abroad and of other misdemeanours. As the police régime became stricter and suspicion of all foreigners grew it seemed inevitable that the time would come when the Moscow office could no longer be maintained. This development depressed Münzenberg and his mood improved only when he was in the train to Leningrad on his way home.

8. New Countries, New People

After his return from Moscow at the end of August 1933 Münzenberg's depression vanished, and he threw himself into his work. In the few months of its existence the *Editions du Carrefour* had made great progress. The world-wide success of the first Brown Book determined the future output of the firm.

Between 1933 and 1937, before Münzenberg was forced to terminate his association with the *Editions du Carrefour* because of his break with the Comintern, he was responsible for the production of about fifty German pamphlets and books—an impressive list—many of which were translated into French or English. After the Brown Books, each of which was followed up with a supplement, there came more political literature in 1934. The output included a collection of thirty-three biographies from the Third Reich, *Naziführer sehen Dich an* (Nazi Leaders Look at You), written by Walter Mehring but published anonymously; Walter Schönstedt's novel *Auf der Flucht erschossen* (Shot While Trying to Escape); the *Weissbuch über die Erschiessungen des 30.Juni* (White Book on the Shootings of 30 June); a political novel by Gustav Regler, *Im Kreuzfeuer* (Under Cross-fire), published on the occasion of the forthcoming Saar plebiscite; and a book of almost five hundred pages documenting Hitler's secret rearmament which, to make it more effective, was ascribed to the English journalist Dorothy Woodman. In the same year Editions du Carrefour published *Lieder, Gedichte und Chöre* by Bertolt Brecht and Hanns Eisler, and Egon Erwin Kisch's political novel *Eintritt verboten* (No Entry). The documentation on the Third Reich was continued in 1935 with *Das braune Netz* (The Brown Net) which described the work of National Socialist

agents abroad, and with a further volume on the secret rebuilding of
the German air force. The firm also published Paul W. Massing's concentration camp novel *Schutzhäftling 880* (under the pseudonym Karl
Dillinger), a collection of Dimitroff's letters and notes from the period
of his detention and the Leipzig trial edited by Alfred Kurella, Anna
Seghers' novel *Der Weg durch den Februar*, Bodo Uhse's *Söldner und
Soldat* (Mercenary and Soldier), and other works.

The most important publications in 1935 included the first comprehensive account of Nationalist Socialist persecution of the Jews, *Der
gelbe Fleck* (The Yellow Patch), for which Lion Feuchtwanger wrote
the preface, Fritz Lieb's book on the struggle of the Confessional
Church, *Christ und Anti-Christ im Dritten Reich*, and documentation
by Berthold Jacob on *Das neue deutsche Heer und seine Führer* (The
new German Army and its leaders). Among the authors published in
1936 were Louis Aragon and André Malraux. As part of the wider
struggle against "Fascism" the *Editions du Carrefour* brought out documentation on Japan which concluded the anti-Comintern pact with
Hitler that year, and also on National Socialist intervention on behalf
of Franco in Spain. The Spanish Civil War greatly influenced the firm's
output in 1937. At Münzenberg's suggestion Arthur Koestler wrote
"The Black Book on Spain" denouncing Fascist barbarities. The actual
title, *Menschenopfer unerhört*, was taken from a Goethe quotation, a
suggestion which Otto Katz had made.[1] In 1937 Münzenberg made his
most significant personal contribution to anti-Fascist literature, the
book *Propaganda als Waffe*, a comprehensive analysis of National Socialist propaganda of which more will be said later.

The titles of these books speak for themselves. Rarely has the programme of a publishing house been directed with so much determination towards a single aim. Together with the Social Democratic publishing house Graphia in Carlsbad, the *Editions du Carrefour* was
undoubtedly the most active centre of anti-fascist German émigré literature in those years.

Apart from seeking to arouse opinion abroad by constantly providing
information about conditions in Germany, an attempt was now also
made to reach the Germans themselves. Cleverly hidden in fashion
journals, material was sent to reliable addresses in Germany. In all
thirteen informative pamphlets were sent across the frontiers by this
method in 1933 and 1934.

The Berlin Gestapo observed in March 1933 that "the flood of anti-
German leaflets and pamphlets which are being distributed in Ger-

---

[1]Cf. Arthur Koestler, *The Invisible Writing*, p. 333.

many and abroad" stemmed from Münzenberg; the report added "that they [Münzenberg's men] clearly have good connections in Germany."[1]

Münzenberg had few links with the French Communists. He had been told by the authorities not to interfere in internal French questions and these included the party policy of the French Communist Party. Moreover, the French Communists jealously saw to it that Münzenberg did not influence mass organizations or individual sympathizers beyond the degree envisaged by the Comintern. But he remained in touch with Marcel Cachin, Vaillant-Couturier and others who were members of the *Comité contre la Guerre et le Fascisme* and continued to belong to the Communist group of this organization. His friendship with Henri Barbusse continued until the writer's death.

Even more important was the exchange of views with people from other camps, with left wing bourgeois politicians and French Socialists. From his Swiss years Münzenberg knew the Socialist Salomon Grumbach who, although a member of the right wing of the SFIO (Section Française de l'Internationale Ouvrière), for reasons of French military policy advocated an alliance between the USSR and France. Grumbach's circle of acquaintances extended from Pierre Laval to right-wing Socialists and he introduced Münzenberg to some of their representatives. In the years to come they actively supported Münzenberg in his work in France.

Münzenberg had known the head of the press office at the Quai d'Orsay, Pierre Comert, in Berlin. Now he renewed that acquaintance and there developed between him and Comert, who was sympathetically disposed towards all German refugees, a friendship which—an unusual phenomenon in France—even resulted in visits to Comert's home. Through Comert, Münzenberg met other Radical Socialists: Henri Laugier, who always accompanied his friend Yvon Delbos as *chef de cabinet* whenever the latter took charge of a ministry, Gaston Palewski who later became Secretary of State under Georges Mandel, Pierre Cot, the dramatist Jean Giraudoux and others. Laugier knew many writers and artists, including Braque and Léger.

Olof Aschberg was one of the friends from the old days whom Münzenberg met again in Paris. Years ago he had made his second home in Paris where he was the centre of the Swedish colony. He immediately took charge of Münzenberg and of many other German refugees. In one of his properties in the forest of Compiègne his wife Siri set up a home for German refugee children, and Münzenberg was a welcome

[1]Microfilm, *Institut für Zeitgeschichte*, MA 699, p. 9461 *et seq.*

guest at his large country house at La Brevière and also at his town house on the Place Casimir Périer.

At Lucien Vogel's, Münzenberg met Marcel Rosenberg who was First Secretary at the Russian embassy in Paris. Telegrams were sent through him to Moscow in the early days in Paris although he was more cautious and restrained in his contact with Communists than his Berlin colleague Alexandrovsky. We needed all our persuasive powers to get him to have our "fighting fund" brought to Paris from Berlin by diplomatic courier. But it arrived and was handed over to Münzenberg.

The turbulent year 1933 had exhausted Münzenberg, he needed rest and intended to relax for a fortnight on the Côte d'Azur. Months before we had shipped the limousine of the Berlin days on a Soviet ship to the Moscow IAH office as a welcome present. For the equivalent of five hundred marks we now bought an antique Ford and at the beginning of February 1934 set out on our first journey across France. At Roquebrune on the Riviera, Münzenberg tried to enjoy the early spring. But the anxious times and the daily news from Germany allowed us no rest. We heard that the Nazis had shot four leading Communist officials "while trying to escape" en route from one prison to another: John Schehr, Thälmann's representative, Eugen Schönhaar, a friend and colleague of Münzenberg's from the Stuttgart days, and Steinfurth and Schwarz.[1] With Schehr's death and Thälmann's arrest the group around Thälmann in the German party leadership was for all practical purposes immobilized. When, on top of this, Münzenberg heard about violent clashes in Paris he returned to Paris immediately.

The men acquitted in the Reichstag fire trial were still in prison and Münzenberg did his utmost to ease their situation. He appealed to his friends in Zurich, Fritz Brupbacher and Dr. Minna Tobler, to insist that a Swiss doctor who would "not let the fascists pull the wool over his eyes" be sent to Germany to examine Dimitroff who, according to German reports, had fallen ill and could not be released. At the same time the Communists started a world-wide campaign for the release of Ernst Thälmann whose safety was feared for after the brutal murder of Schehr and the others.

With the help of pro-Communist organizations and individuals in the United States, Gibarti had arranged for a "counter trial" on the London model to be held in New York on 2 July by the "World Aid Committee

[1]Alfred Kattner, one of Thälmann's loyal assistants, had been arrested with him. After his release from concentration camp nine months later he began to betray Communist officials to the Gestapo. Thereupon the illegal Communist organization decided to get rid of Kattner; a member of the workers' rifle club cycled to Kattner's flat in Nowawes near Potsdam, shot him dead and got away. As a reprisal the Gestapo shot these four leading Communist officials.

for the Victims of Hitler Fascism." The verdict of the Leipzig court had
been passed long ago but beyond trying to discover what had really
happened on 27 February 1933 the main attention of the New York
gathering was focussed "on the lack of legal safeguards, on the iniqui-
tous court established in Germany under the name of people's court,
on the persecution of all anti-fascists . . . on the Thälmann trial and on
other anti-fascist trials."[1] The opening address was to be given by New
York's popular mayor, La Guardia, and the most famous of all defence
counsels, Clarence Darrow, had agreed to act as chairman.

A so-called "Thälmann week" had been held in New York before the
start of the counter trial, with a mass demonstration in Central Park.
This seems to have been one of the factors which persuaded the German Ambassador, Luther, during his visits to Berlin to urge that Germany should do something to avoid losing the last vestiges of American
respect.

Münzenberg, for whom Gibarti had organized a lecture tour in the
United States, was given an entry visa on condition that he abstain from
all public activity. He travelled with the Social Democratic Berlin lawyer Kurt Rosenfeld and the British Labour M.P. Aneurin Bevan. I accompanied him on his first trip across the Atlantic. The news of the
blood bath of 30 June reached us at sea and filled us with the hope that
the brown despots would slaughter each other.

Our experiences in America genuinely amazed us. The authorities of
this "country of capitalism" put not the slightest obstacle in the way of
Münzenberg, the Communist. He spoke at public meetings in New
York, Chicago, Cleveland, Milwaukee, Detroit, Boston and Washington
and also at many German workers' clubs and holiday camps. The biggest rally was held in Madison Square Garden, New York. During our
four week visit, our American friends told us, the German embassy in
Washington protested continuously against Münzenberg's public ap-
pearances. Another who looked askance at Münzenberg's meetings was
Gerhard Eisler, the secret Comintern emissary to the American Communist Party, who was worried by Münzenberg's success with representatives of the American middle class. Previously Eisler had bitterly
resisted Gibarti's successful efforts to gain the support of New York's
mayor for Thälmann's liberation campaign. Eisler maintained that La
Guardia's support was damaging to Thälmann's cause.

The main purpose of Münzenberg's visit was to raise money for the
relief committee and this he did. We returned to Europe with a substantial sum. The visit was a success also from the propaganda point of view.
After his arrival in Paris, Münzenberg said in *Gegen-Angriff*[2] that the

[1] *Der Gegen-Angriff* (Paris), 1934, No. 26 (now available in the Westfälisch-Niederrhein-
ische Institut für Zeitungsforschung, Dortmund).
[2] *Der Gegen-Angriff*, 1934, No. 34 (22 August 1934).

campaign for Thälmann's liberation had become a "popular movement" in America. Once again he had succeeded in winning the intellectuals for his cause. An appeal signed by Sinclair Lewis, Malcolm
Cowley, Granville Hicks and other famous writers, journalists and
scientists said:

> We demand the immediate cessation of every form of torture and perse-
> cution of people with different political views in Hitler Germany and the
> liberation of all political prisoners, particularly Ernst Thälmann, from the
> Nazi dungeons.[1]

Münzenberg observed with surprise in the autumn of that year that
he had not been to Moscow for over twelve months. A fact which had
escaped him in the continuous activity of the first year in Paris was
suddenly brought home to him: he had ceased to exert himself on behalf
of Soviet Russia, he was no longer engaged in campaigns for the Comintern. He was still a Communist and this was clear from his speeches and
articles but his entire political activity now centred on one issue: the
struggle against Hitler Germany.

In October 1934, world attention had turned to Spain where under
Lerroux a new government had been formed which included some
avowed opponents of the republic. When Conservative Gil Robles became a member of the cabinet the Socialists decided to call for a general
uprising, an appeal which was heeded only by the mining province of
Asturias on the northern coast. The government had got wind of the
preparations, mobilized police units and the Foreign Legion against
Asturias and the Asturian rising collapsed within ten days. The retribu-
tion of the Guardia Civil was like a bitter foretaste of the horrors of the
civil war. The leader of the rebels, Gonzalez Pena, an official of the
miners' union, was betrayed, arrested and sentenced to death. The
entire world was shocked. Münzenberg exerted himself on behalf of the
prisoners and a British investigation commission, which included Ellen
Wilkinson and the Earl of Listowel, was sent to Madrid. Because of
persistent international protest Pena's death sentence was commuted
to life imprisonment. In 1936 the Socialists elected him to the Cortes
as deputy for Asturias and he thus regained his freedom. The abortive
revolt brought the first wave of Spanish political refugees to Paris and
Münzenberg met many of them. The Comintern and the USSR now
also turned their attention to Spain where the Communists had hitherto
had almost no influence. On the anniversary of the October Revolution
in 1934 a large delegation of Asturian miners was invited to Moscow as
proof of Soviet Russia's concern with the affairs of the Spanish workers.

[1] Ibid.

It was at this time that Alvarez del Vayo re-established contact with Münzenberg whom he had known in Berlin where he had worked for a Latin American paper. Del Vayo was Socialist, an educated polyglot who had always shown much sympathy for Soviet Russia. He invited Münzenberg to visit Spain and at Christmas 1934 we went to Madrid and then with del Vayo to Malaga. The strange beauty of southern Spain, the acres of flowers around Torremolinos where we spent Christmas could not hide the incredible poverty and the social unrest everywhere. In the early summer of 1935 Münzenberg paid a second visit to Madrid accompanied by a member of the International Red Cross, Maike Schorr, this time to attend conferences with Communist organizations and to meet Socialist, pro-Russian politicians.

During these months Münzenberg developed appendicitis. He was operated on by a Communist doctor, Dr. Rouquès, at a private clinic in Paris. During the Spanish civil war Roquès, a pleasant and capable surgeon, was in charge of a medical mission for wounded Spanish refugees. After the war he became personal physician to the ailing French party leader, Thorez, whom he accompanied on his visits to Moscow. Münzenberg's operation lasted several hours but passed off successfully. Soon he was well enough, although still weak, to resume his work. One weekend we visited the Loire, near Nevers. A travelling circus had set up its tent in a village. A woman called us from a caravan. She spoke German and offered to read our palms. Münzenberg sat down with her. To our amazement she described in detail the operation which he had just had. Suddenly she stopped and stared at Münzenberg. Then she continued hesitantly, and predicting a gloomy future warned him to be very careful. We made light of these prophecies and forgot the curious interlude.

9. Everything for Unity

In France an unexpected rapprochement took place in 1934 between the Communists and the Socialists. On 6 February 1934 when paramilitary Fascist organizations held a big rally in the Place de la Concorde with the intention of storming the parliament and bitter clashes occurred, the Socialists vainly appealed for united action by all workers organizations. At that time the French Communist Party still pursued the objective of a "united front from below," i.e. it bitterly opposed the Socialist party leaders and the reformist trade unions. Then suddenly, in the summer of 1934, Moscow ordered the French party leadership to suggest to the Socialists a "pact for united action."

The French Socialists' leader, Léon Blum, saw the turnabout as a

Russian attempt to establish better relations with the League of Nations and to make the French Communist Party—hitherto hopelessly isolated and, after the loss of the German party, the strongest party in the Comintern—a factor in the political life of France. But more was at stake: the Russian predictions about the future of the National Socialist régime had been proved fatally wrong. Hitler was firmly in the saddle, the opposition had been broken and everything and everybody in Germany were forced into conformity. Hitler was taking a more active line in foreign policy, he turned ostentatiously away from the Soviet Union and wooed Great Britain by presenting himself as a peace advocate and opponent of Bolshevism. In the East he sought to achieve a rapprochement with Marshal Pilsudski's Poland. These were warning signals which Moscow could not afford to overlook. The Russians tried to re-establish contacts with the West, Litvinov worked for better relations with France, he took steps to bring about Russia's admission to the League of Nations and in May 1935 succeeded in concluding a Franco-Russian pact of mutual assistance with the Flandin Government.

In July 1934 the leaders of the two French workers parties concluded a "united action pact" and this agreement, like the first steps towards an amalgamation of the reformist CGT *(Confédération Générale du Travail)* with the Communist CGTU *(Confédération Générale du Travail Unitaire)*, was warmly welcomed by the French workers.

But the Russians went further—and that was the novel aspect of this policy—they wanted the French Communist Party to draw into the united action the lower middle classes, craftsmen, shopkeepers and officials—the groups which in Germany and Italy had formed the core of the fascist forces. In terms of party politics this meant the establishment of contacts with the leftist bourgeois party of the radical Socialists. These tactics represented a complete break with Lenin's doctrine of the role of the Communist Parties. Even before the October Revolution, Lenin had managed to stop any attempt to bring about a coalition between the Russian Socialists and the leftist bourgeois parties. The leaders of the reformist parties were bitterly attacked in the Comintern for entering into coalitions with bourgeois parties. In 1928, during a discussion on the new party programme of the Austrian Socialists, Otto Bauer said that cooperation between the classes became necessary at times when democracy, the republic, was quite seriously threatened. He was severely taken to task in *Communist International* for this attitude. His critic argued that the threat to democracy and the republic could come only from a revolutionary crisis. In such a situation the choice was limited to bourgeois or proletarian dictatorship. Thereby any coalition between the working class parties and the Capitalist parties was automatically ruled out.

The Radical Socialists continued to view the Communists with the utmost reserve; but when they saw at a local council election what advantages in votes and seats the Socialists and the Communists derived from their election agreement and when the French Communist Party finally, at Stalin's behest, from one day to the next abandoned its traditional anti-militarist propaganda the leaders of the Radical Socialists decided to join the new grouping. The Socialists agreed to this widening of the united front to the right as a counterweight to the powerful influence of the Communists and thus the "popular front" was formed.

The expression *Front Populaire* was invented by Albert Vassart, the French representative at the Comintern, to describe the new tactics of the French Communists. He hoped the expression would lessen the impact of the French Fascists' national front propaganda. At first the Russians objected to the name because the Russian translation recalled the *narodnaya Volya*, the great workers and peasant parties of pre-revolutionary Russia. A Russian philologist was asked for advice and held that there was a basic difference between *Front Populaire* and *narod; Front Populaire* meant "a front which the people join", it did not mean "going out to the people." Thereupon *Front Populaire* was approved.

Popular front tactics required joint action by the Communists and the leaders of the other, mostly Socialist, workers' parties, i.e. the Communists' "class comrades." After the formation of this "united front from above" the left would be able to approach the bourgeois parties, agree with them on electoral arrangements or coalitions and form a so-called popular front. Those tactics were to be employed in situations where the Communists were too weak and too isolated to gain power unaided.

The German refugees followed these happenings with interest. The election campaign for the plebiscite on the future fate of the Saar, fixed for 13 January 1935, had begun. The Hitler Government effectively used the slogan "Home to the Reich"; the Social Democrats opposed the union of the Saar with Nazi Germany; the Communists wanted "a Red Saar in Soviet Germany"—an objective which also meant union with Germany. Influenced by the negotiations between the two French workers parties on a united front the leaders of the German Communist Party in exile changed their original line and decided to support the *status quo*. Münzenberg's IAH set up a children's home near Saarbrücken and IAH officials, together with several hundred KPD officials who had fled to the Saar, helped with the election campaign. From the start Münzenberg had been strongly opposed to the expression "Red Saar." He sent Hans Schulz to Moscow with letters to Bela Kun suggesting ways of improving this phrase. Bela Kun was supposed to submit these proposals to Stalin and the Russian Politburo but he was not even given an audience. Schulz returned without having achieved anything, but as usual the Comintern used him as a courier and gave him letters and money to take back to France.

The combined efforts of the Social Democrats and the Communists failed to swing the plebiscite in their favour. Four hundred and seventy-seven thousand votes were cast for unification with Germany and only forty-eight thousand against. Although a return of Germans to Germany seemed the natural solution it was depressing to see the enthusiasm with which the Saar population welcomed the National Socialists. After the plebiscite several thousand Saarlander and all German refugees left the Saar for France. In Paris the Socialist leaders of the Saar, Max Braun, August Kirschmann and others, continued to maintain close contact with the Communist refugee groups.

10. "The Congress of the New Tactical Reorientation"

At the end of February 1934, Dimitroff arrived in Moscow after his release from a German prison. He was fêted as the "victor of Leipzig" and he, Popoff and Taneff were ceremoniously received by Stalin. He was put in charge of the Comintern. One year later he presided over the last world congress of this organization.

We arrived in Moscow in July 1935 after an absence of almost two years. There had been a noticeable improvement in economic conditions since our last visit in the summer of 1933. The official party slogans exuded optimism: "Life is happy, life is gay." The dictator had proclaimed that people must be cared for like flowers. The *Insnab* shops where foreigners only could buy food on presentation of ration cards had been closed. Everything was obtainable on the free market at very high prices which the ordinary Soviet citizen could not pay. As in the NEP days one could go into a restaurant and order all sorts of specialities. This year the salaries of party officials and other dignitaries had been substantially increased so that some of them now earned thirty times as much as the ordinary worker. If there was no more hunger, there were crass social differences for all to see.

Behind this façade there was a curious sense of unease. The murder of the Leningrad party secretary, Sergei Kirov, on 1 December 1934 had given Stalin a welcome excuse to take action against anyone who had allegedly deviated from whatever happened to be the party line of the moment. The Kirov murder, Krivitsky later wrote with bitterness, had been as useful to the dictator as the Reichstag fire to the National

Socialists.[1] The first half of 1935 had brought numerous arrests; that year the former opposition leaders, Zinoviev and Kamenev, had been sentenced to several years imprisonment after a trial from which the public had been excluded. A number of foreign Communists had also fallen victim to the wave of arrests: the Hungarian Communist L. Magyar, a noted economist at Eugene Varga's Moscow Institute of Economics, had visited Paris in 1932 and 1933 as a Comintern representative and worked with Münzenberg. After his return to Moscow he had published various studies on the Chinese revolution at the Institute. It was rumoured that he had been arrested on charges of being a Trotskyist, and several members of the Institute were now engaged in expunging his name from the Institute's annals. Erich Wendt of the "Association of Foreign Publishers in the USSR", the man who was later to issue passes on behalf of the Ulbricht government, had been arrested. It was not until 1947 that he returned from Siberia where he had edited a village paper for ex-patriated Volga Germans. At the same time another member of the publishing firm, Otto Unger, a co-founder of the Youth International, was arrested and vanished forever. After the first big wave of arrests in Leningrad, the Leningrad GPU offered to organizations in Moscow at bargain prices furniture confiscated from arrested persons.

Alarming news—such as the circumstances of the death of Max Hölz who was said to have been murdered by the GPU in a boat on the Oka —was passed on in whispers. Were those who had been arrested rightists or conciliators? The things that were happening were most disquieting but no one suspected that this was the eve of the Great Purge. One day I was sitting with Sophie Liebknecht and Susanne Leonhard outside the Hotel Metropole where chairs and tables had been placed on the pavement in French fashion. The two women were bitterly disappointed by life in the Soviet Union, by Stalin's policy, by everything connected with Russia. Jokingly I warned them that if they talked like this it would not be long before they were arrested—a joke which soon afterwards became a bitter reality as far as Susanne Leonhard was concerned. This growing insecurity weakened still further the confidence of foreign Communists, already considerably undermined by Russian totalitarianism. A Swiss Communist living in Moscow at the time said that Hugo Eberlein had complained to Piatnitsky that everyone treated him like a leper and that he had no wish to hold office any more. Thereupon Piatnitsky had taken him by the arm and walked with him through the corridors of the Comintern building to the *stolovaya* —the refectory—where he had tea with him. The fact that Piatnitsky

[1]Krivitsky, *I Was Stalin's Agent*, p. 186.

(no one knew that his hour would come soon) had bestowed this honour on Eberlein sufficed to make the latter's stock rise again with the Comintern.

The IAH's hour had also now struck. The persecution mania which Stalin had systematically fostered with continual references to alleged threats of war and the danger of spies had developed into xenophobia. The IAH office, which was staffed mostly by non-Russians who had been joined by many refugees from Germany, was regarded by the GPU as an irritating foreign body. Münzenberg had ceased to work for the IAH after 1933. When the Russian Central Committee decided to close down the IAH he did not quarrel with the decision but regarded it as a loss of prestige. A Swiss, Karl Hofmeyer, who had vanished shortly before from an Italian prison where he had served seven years of a fifteen year prison sentence for illegal activity was appointed liquidator of the IAH in Russia. The examination of the organization's financial situation revealed that *Meshrabpom* had substantial assets. Hofmeyer asked Moskvin, representative of the CPSU(B) in the Comintern, what he should do with these assets. Moskvin shrugged his shoulders and finally asked another Comintern colleague by name of Brandt to take them over. In France, Czechoslovakia, Austria and several other countries where the IAH organizations continued to function they were amalgamated with International Red Aid.

During those days of complex negotiations, Münzenberg repeatedly came into contact with a man whose name was to be associated a decade or so later with a period of rigorous persecution of all liberal tendencies in Communist countries: Andrei Zhdanov. Zhdanov impressed Münzenberg as a powerful personality, he behaved like a despot and was totally Russian. He was completely ignorant of the world outside Russia—at the time Münzenberg informed him about the situation in Spain.

In this atmosphere of general insecurity the Seventh World Congress of the Comintern began in July in the Moscow Palace of Nobles. Dimitroff announced the new line which thereby received official sanction: united front from above, joint action with the Socialist parties, participation and assistance in the formation of governments of the united front or of the anti-fascist popular front. No more radical change from Comintern policy of the past seven years could be imagined. Belatedly it was realized that "in our ranks there existed a tendency to adopt a general approach to fascism without taking into account the concrete peculiarities of the fascist movement in various countries and mistakenly to consider all reactionary measures on the part of the bourgeoisie as fascism and even to look upon the entire non-Communist camp as fascist." This, Dimitroff observed in retrospect, had resulted "not in strengthening but in weakening the anti-fascist opposition".[1] But Manuilsky, in a talk on the Seventh World Congress to Moscow and Leningrad party activists, denied some of these accusations. To the objection that the Communists had not organized the united front before and were organizing it now he replied: "If the Communists did not organize it earlier it is because the Social Democrats rejected the propositions that were put to them."[2]

Das Banner der revolutionären Einheit (The Banner of Revolutionary Unity), a journal of the Socialist Workers Party, was at the time distributed illegally in Germany. In an undated number published after the Seventh World Congress of the Comintern under the heading "Whither is the Comintern Drifting?", it commented that years ago anyone who had dared to make demands such as Dimitroff would have been "expelled as an opportunist, a renegade, an enemy of Communism, a hireling of the bourgeoisie and a counter-revolutionary."[3] Trotsky described Dimitroff's speech as "a document of theoretical and political self-renunciation."[4] But the congress gave Dimitroff the customary fifteen minute ovation during which Manuilsky called out: "Long live the loyal, trusted comrade-in-arms of the great Stalin, the helmsman of the Comintern, comrade Dimitroff."[5]

Münzenberg accepted the new line with mixed feelings. For years he had advocated joint campaigns with the Socialists and the left wing bourgeois parties, and time and again his efforts had been frustrated by inflexible and unrealistic decisions. During all those years Moscow had never wanted genuine links with reformists or leftist bourgeois. Such efforts as were made were merely designed to draw individuals into the Communist camp. Münzenberg was too familiar with Soviet conditions not to realize who was behind this new line which Dimitroff now proclaimed to be the only one that could save the party. Münzenberg probably doubted its durability, but it was certainly more in line with his wishes and ideas than the ultra left wing directives of past years. He returned to Paris with Dimitroff's order to pursue the new line there and to work for collaboration with the Social Democrats and the representatives of the bourgeois German refugees.

After his departure and after the end of the Seventh Congress about fifty German Communists met at the so-called "Brussels Party Conference" held in the autumn of 1935 near the Russian capital. There the KPD leaders in exile, district secretaries who were working illegally in

---

[1] *Rundschau* (Basle), No. 66 of 19 November 1935.
[2] *Ibid.*, No. 67 of 21 November 1935.
[3] Copy in the possession of the author.
[4] L. Trotsky, *Stalins Verbrechen*, Zurich 1937, p. 126
[5] *Rundschau*, No. 66 of 19 November 1935.

Germany and some leading officials living as refugees in Moscow, sought to "explain" the defeat of the Communists in Germany. Not one of those present dreamt of criticizing the tactics of the Comintern. Scapegoats had already been found: the "Neumann group" was held responsible for the policy towards the National Socialists. This group included another member of the Politburo, Hermann Remmele, who supported Neumann.

Apart from a few young members sent to Germany from the Lenin School the assembled officials were members of the old Thälmann party leadership. But Ernst Thälmann was in a German prison and John Schehr, who was regarded as Thälmann's successor, had been shot by the National Socialists "while trying to escape." Now another successor must be found. The conference was preceded by weeks of in-fighting from which Ulbricht and Pieck had emerged as victors. They were supported by Dahlem, Ackermann, Merker, Wehner (pseudonym: Funk), Mewis, Dengel and others, while Thälmann's closer friends, like Florin, Schubert, Schulte, Kippenberger and Kreutzburg were pushed aside. With the exception of Florin they later, together with Neumann and Remmele, became victims of the Great Purge and were liquidated in Soviet prisons and camps.

In spite of his known links with Neumann and in the face of strong resistance from Ulbricht, Münzenberg was re-elected to the Central Committee of the KPD which at that time consisted of fifteen people. Herbert Wehner comments:

> Münzenberg's election was supported by Pieck on behalf of the ECCI so that Münzenberg who did international work would remain linked with the German party and would have a certain standing (as it was said).[1]

Wilhelm Pieck's task at the "Brussels Conference" was to condemn the policy of the KPD in 1932. It was wrong "that the KPD had fought the Prussian Government of Braun and Severing, that it had failed to see the imminent threat of the fascist terror reign and that it had thereby been prevented from pursuing a truly broad united front policy focussed above all on the defence of democratic rights and freedoms." Now the most important task was "the establishment of the popular front." The "Brussels Manifesto" said: "The German popular front fights for a democratic republic, it is not a manoeuvre designed to deceive the parties to it."[2] The reactions of the Second International towards the new Communist tactics were varied and contradictory. Its executive decided to leave the individual parties a free hand in their

[1] H. Wehner, *Erinnerungen* (unpublished MS, 1957).
[2] *Rundschau* (Basle), December 1935.

relations with the Communists and thereby gave its blessing to united front campaigns in France, Spain, Austria and Italy. But the executives of the Scandinavian, Belgian, Dutch and British parties refused outright to cooperate with the Communist parties of their countries. The executive of the Socialist Party in exile in Prague took the same line. The main concern of the KPD leadership, however, was to establish contacts with the Prague party executive because without the latter's collaboration the attempts to establish a united front remained fragmentary.

On 10 November 1935 the KPD Central Committee approached the SPD Executive in Prague in a secret letter which did not have the purely propagandist purpose of previous "open letters."[1] The Communists expressed a wish for joint discussions about the establishment of a united front. They said that the present situation called for such a move. The joint agreement should cover assistance to political prisoners, exchanges of view on the most suitable methods of conspiratorial work, protection against informers and an appeal to officials in Germany to organize collaboration with Communist underground workers. The Communists suggested that the two party leaderships should issue a joint statement on the struggle against the Hitler dictatorship and the reestablishment of the lost freedoms, and also create a liaison commission to be responsible for joint activity. The letter referred to the statements made by Dimitroff who was described as "the popular hero beloved of all anti-fascists", announced that the Central Committee had appointed its members Walter Ulbricht and Franz Dahlem as its representatives and asked the SPD executive to nominate two representatives.

On 23 November 1935 the two Communists met with Social Democrats Hans Vogel and Friedrich Stampfer in Prague for over three and a half hours. Vogel refused to issue a joint statement. He said that the Social Democrats working illegally in the Reich were opposed to a united front with the Communists because they had no faith in assurances that the Communists wanted to fight for the restoration of democracy. He felt that a joint declaration would drive Socialist sympathizers in Germany to the right by creating the impression that the Socialists had gone over to the Communists. The party executive itself also strongly doubted the sincerity of the sudden Communist respect for democratic rights and freedoms. Hitherto a united front had merely been a slogan in the fight against the SPD. Vogel wondered whether the united front was not a new Communist ruse. And he asked what would happen once the bourgeois and democratic freedoms were re-established in Germany with the help of the united front.

[1]The letter and the protocol and documents referred to below are in the SPD archives in Bonn.

Ulbricht did not reply to Vogel's objections and reservations. He restricted himself to an account of the decisions of the Seventh World Congress. His reply to the question about what would happen after the bourgeois and democratic freedoms had been re-established was:

> The people shall decide freely what form of government it wishes to have.
> If it does not wish for soviet power then a national assembly shall decide.

Vogel observed that his party's objections did not prevent collaboration between the two parties on certain occasions, but a prerequisite was absolute loyalty and the Communists would have to prove this loyalty by deeds. He suggested a "non-aggression pact," analogous to the pact concluded by the French Socialists and Communists in July 1934. Ulbricht and Dahlem rejected such a pact on the grounds that they must be free to attack those Social Democrats who rejected the united front. Franz Dahlem described the exchange as pleasant. He said that the KPD and the SPD were the only true resistance forces in the Reich, that all the rest were "jelly-fish." He added: "If the people do not want Soviets we are ready to respect the popular will." He also reported "that the comrades in the Communist leadership who had objections to the united front have been removed. The new leadership which was elected by the party conference will carry out the Comintern's decisions." He too asked for a joint statement in which "our comrades in Germany are invited to come to terms with each other." When Walter Ulbricht pulled a statement from his pocket and read "that on the basis of their exchanges of view the two party leaderships call upon their supporters in the Reich to come together to discuss various of the tasks listed in the declaration." Stampfer and Vogel protested and refused to sign any public declaration. Vogel told the Communists sharply that if they wanted to say anything at all they should say that an exchange had taken place and had finished with a negative result.

On 2 December 1935 Ulbricht sent the Prague party executive a long letter with an account of the discussions as he had understood them and announced that this "protocol," a kind of leading article full of attacks on the SPD party executive, would be sent to KPD officials. Thereupon the Prague party executive published its account of the negotiations.[1]

While these exchanges were taking place the Communists were making energetic attempts to capitalize on the general sentiment in favour of a united front and a popular front. Every possible means was used —cunning and persuasion, financial offers and, as happened in Antwerp, bodily attacks on Social Democratic officials to persuade the SPD

---

[1] *Neuer Vorwärts*, No. 130 of 8 December 1935.

abroad to participate in joint campaigns. The Communists main concern was to infiltrate their people into the Social Democratic network in the Third Reich. But Ulbricht failed in his most important endeavour, to persuade the Prague SPD executive to take joint action.

11. The German Popular Front Committee in Paris

Immediately after his return from Moscow, Münzenberg set about establishing contacts with Socialists and representatives of the bourgeois emigration. In the autumn of 1935 he again took up the threads of his last attempt, made in February 1933 in Berlin, to bring together Hitler's enemies in various parties and groups. In contrast to the French popular front movement the German emigration offered no mass basis. It was entirely a question of establishing contacts with the representatives of various parties and groups and with individuals, with refugees who were in touch with groups in the Third Reich which they could influence or whose papers and journals they could make the focal point for like-minded persons.

Münzenberg quickly collected a group of refugees prepared to set up a "Committee for the Establishment of the German Popular Front." The founding meeting was held on 6 February 1936 at the Hotel Lutetia in Paris. One hundred and eighteen people attended, including many German writers, among them Heinrich and Klaus Mann, Emil Ludwig, Lion Feuchtwanger, Ernst Toller and Ludwig Marcuse. The journalists who participated included Leopold Schwarzschild, Victor Schiff, Georg Bernhard. Of the Social Democrats Rudolf Breitscheid, Albert Grzesinski, Erich Kuttner, Alexander Schifrin, Paul Hertz were there, as well as representatives of the Saar Socialists. Other political groups such as the Socialist Workers' Party and the Internationaler Sozialistischer Kampfbund were represented, as were many intellectuals and academics without party allegiances. Apart from Münzenberg, Communist officials at the Hotel Lutetia included Franz Dahlem, Hermann Matern, Peter Maslowski and Alexander Abusch.

A meeting had been held on 1 February, under the chairmanship of Breitscheid, between the Marxist parties, the SPD, the KPD, the Socialist Workers' Party and the "Revolutionary Socialists"; Münzenberg made a statement at this meeting—about which a participant later sent a report to the Social Democratic party executive in Prague—which greatly impressed those present. He said that he wanted it to be understood that the popular front would be based on complete freedom of belief and conscience, that the Communists' past policy had been wrong and that henceforth there must be a German policy. In short "he made a confession which enormously impressed our comrades, it was as if the Comintern was saying this," wrote the observer,[1] while Herbert Wehner from his standpoint at the time condemned Münzenberg's utterances for "opportunist lack of principle."[2]

The gathering at the Hotel Lutetia constituted itself as a committee and drew up a joint manifesto which was agreed to and signed by everyone present. Heinrich Mann had a major share in drafting the manifesto which read:

> Over one hundred representatives of the free German middle classes and the German workers of all political shades assembled at a meeting in early February 1936, three years after the start of the present German régime, unanimously conclude their survey and exchange of views as follows:
>
> *They note:*
>
> 1. That the present German Government has undermined the country's economic and social position by wastefulness, rearmament, the destruction of foreign trade and the reduction in the purchasing power of money. Under this régime the situation must get progressively worse.
>
> 2. That, by its un-German system of arbitrary action and force, of the suppression of freedom of conscience and of the personal enrichment of the rulers, the present German Government has filled almost all Germans, the direct beneficiaries of the system excepted, with a deep and united desire to end this terror and to restore the most elementary human rights.
>
> *They declare and demand:*
>
> 1. That at present the restoration of these elementary rights shall have precedence over everything else. That the various parties and groups shall be asked to come together and, without abandoning their programmatic aims, concentrate their entire energy on the realization of the following universally valid and fundamental postulates: freedom of opinion, expression, research and teaching, freedom of religious belief and practice, freedom of the individual, respect for the sacredness of human life, legal security and equality before the law, responsibility and removability of the highest state organs, control of public income and expenditure, eradication of corruption and of parasitic party rule.
>
> 2. That each group and all individuals who consider these elementary demands to be their own shall solemnly be asked to regard themselves as comrades-in arms and allies of every other group which is known to make the same demands, and they shall be called upon to act accordingly; that it is their duty, transcending all class, group and party barriers, in every situation to seek and cultivate each other's friendship and to offer each other assistance and protection.

[1] Anonymous report in the SPD Archives, Bonn.
[2] H. Wehner, *Erinnerungen, op. cit.*

3. That this attitude becomes a sacred duty at a time when the present German Government's intensified military, economic and political preparations for war increase the danger that the programme of annihilation and conquest spelt out in *Mein Kampf*—as authoritative a book today as ever—will be carried out. In the face of this horror which threatens Germany itself and the rest of the world with destruction those assembled stress that the occurrence or non-occurrence of disaster may depend on whether and to what degree the opposition among the German people spreads and unites. All groups and all individuals who follow this appeal to unite will help preserve Germany and the German nation and thereby other countries and other peoples from annihilation by a new world war. *They resolve:*

To invite the committee to ask suitable experts to prepare a platform on which all opposition groups can agree. That it shall be the task of this body to submit a programme which shall be the basis for a Germany of freedom and of peace, of morality, of cleanliness and of law, and of a strong, self-assured democracy of the working people in town and country protected from misuse by powerful economic forces.[1]

It was probably largely because of Münzenberg's long acquaintance with such tactics and because those whom he wooed had confidence in him that of the various efforts to establish a united front or a popular front only his was successful. Kurt Kersten describes the German popular front committee set up in the Lutetia as the committee which in the years after 1933 united the greatest number of different political groups and personalities among the German emigration:

In some sense he could for a while regard himself as the true representative of the political German emigration even if the Social Democratic party executive declined to join officially.[2]

Communists and fellow travellers, Social Democrats, members of the Socialist Workers' Party, writers, artists, bourgeois journalists, observers for Catholic trade unions, intellectuals with and without party allegiances came together. Under the impact of the successes of the French popular front these heterogeneous forces believed that they could overlook the differences between them in order to speak as a united opposition for a Germany condemned to silence.

The events in France had their effect on Münzenberg too. Although the French Left's successes in domestic policy were indisputable, Münzenberg was anything but optimistic. Nevertheless he continued to

[1] *Das Neue Tagebuch*, Vol. 4, No. 7, 15 February 1936, p. 151 *et seq.*
[2] Kurt Kersten, *Das Ende Willi Münzenbergs*, in *Deutsche Rundschau* (Stuttgart), Vol. 83, May 1957, p. 489.

campaign assiduously for new friends because in his opinion the German refugees needed to justify their existence as political émigrés by uniting in the struggle against the threatening catastrophe. A mood of "in spite of everything" emerges clearly from a letter written to his friend Brupbacher on 17 April:

> Work continues with varying success. By and large things are not very successful and regrettably the diagnosis which we made when we walked the historic pavement of the classic revolution (1934) seems to have come true . . . In spite of it one labours on because it is after all better than to stand aside and to do nothing.[1]

It had not taken Münzenberg long to appreciate that it was not only a question of Hitler's victory in Germany but that the warning call *Hitler ante portas* must go out to Germany's neighbours. He therefore welcomed Russia's new foreign policy, not only because it was in the interest of the anti-fascist struggle but because, in spite of the criticism building up within him, he was not yet prepared to break with Moscow.

The French successes led Rudolf Breitscheid and other Social Democrats with connections with the SPD party executive to collaborate with the popular front committee and other campaigns for unity. Breitscheid was very friendly with Léon Blum and his group. It seemed useful to him to go part of the way with the Communists. Breitscheid believed in the possibility of reaching agreement with the Communists on united action against aggression and approved of the new Soviet policy of collective security. He and Münzenberg quickly became close friends. This did not mean, however, that he allowed himself to be taken in tow by the Communists. He always remained a critical observer and never abandoned his links with the SPD executive in Prague.

Soon after its foundation the Lutetia committee embarked on a variety of activities. It set up a press service, *Deutsche Informationen,* published jointly by the Social Democrats and the Communists and financed discreetly by the Communists. The publishers and editors of the bilingual organization were Heinrich Mann, Rudolf Breitscheid, Max Braun and Bruno Frei. A joint refugee committee was set up under the chairmanship of Albert Grzesinski to advise German refugees and to help them in their negotiations with the French authorities. In June 1936, with Breitscheid as chairman, this committee held a conference with the motto: "A popular front for a common emergency and a common struggle." On 15 February 1936 Breitscheid had informed the

[1]In the Archives of the International Institute for Social History, Amsterdam.

Prague party executive that he would go to a meeting in Ghent and Antwerp to discuss political prisoners in Germany; the meeting had been convened by the "Thälmann committee" of which he was a member. He promised to make sure that the committee changed its name.[1] German émigrés everywhere established popular fronts which published their own programmes. In Buenos Aires a popular front committee was set up by refugees on 29 June 1936; another in Uruguay described the popular front simply as the union of all Germans in Uruguay opposed to Hitler.

12. New "Peace Fighters": the RUP

The biggest and most lasting success of the Communist united front policy was probably the amalgamation of the reformist CGT with the Communist CGTU. It took place in March 1936 in Paris, and as a result many leading positions in the big joint organization were opened to the Communists. The president, Léon Jouhaux, who was anything but pro-Communist, was now assisted by the Communist Frachon as vice-president. The Russian trade unions made the most of this development. Their president, Shvernik, paid several visits to Paris and proposed to the French a new world-wide peace offensive. With the support of a mass movement, which had not yet acquired the odium of a purely Communist organization like the *Comité Mondial contre la Guerre et le Fascisme*, backing could at the same time be given to the "indivisible peace" thesis propounded by Litvinov to the League of Nations.

Once more Münzenberg assisted behind the scenes in the preparations for this last Russian "peace offensive" before 1939. During a short visit to Moscow in May 1936 he was informed about the character of the new campaign. In contrast to the Amsterdam Pleyel movement the initiative on this occasion came not from the Comintern but from the Soviet trade unions. The secretary of the new venture was Louis Dolivet, a clever young journalist from Transylvania, who was reputated to have no party allegiances, but had for years worked with the Communists, first on Barbusse's journal, *Monde,* and later in the *Comité Mondial contre la Guerre et le Fascisme.* The new peace movement, named *Rassemblement Universe pour la Paix* (RUP), set up its headquarters in the Rue de Bourgogne, near the French Chamber. Distinguished personalities were quickly enlisted in support of the RUP: pacifists such as Lord Robert Cecil, who became its chairman, and Philip Noel-Baker; Socialists such as S. Grumbach who advocated closer political links with Soviet Russia; fellow travellers such as the then

[1]Letter in the SPD Archives, Bonn.

French Minister of Aviation, Pierre Cot, who became head of the French section of the RUP.

Münzenberg's first task was to inform the Communist group of the *Comité Mondial* that it would not be running the new campaign, that other forces would be mobilized to do so and that it must persuade its notable supporters to collaborate in the new venture. Grudgingly but obediently the Communists bowed to Moscow's orders and on 6 June 1936 an "open letter to all friends of peace" was published, signed by Paul Langevin, Norman Angell, Francis Jourdain, André Malraux, John Dos Passos and Sherwood Anderson. The letter said that Japan was pursuing its conquest of China and Mongolia, and that Italy had annexed Abyssinia. The committee reported it was working unceasingly for peace. Other groups had the same "deep urge to use all their energies to co-ordinate the forces of peace." The "open letter" concluded with an urgent appeal to "all friends of 'indivisible peace' " to send large delegations to the RUP and to participate in the preparations for the congress.[1]

The RUP congress which met on 7 or 8 September 1936 in Brussels was even more extravagantly staged than the Amsterdam congress four years previously. The organizers had invited all organizations the world over to attend—provided they favored peace and strengthening the League of Nations. So that it could not be said that this was a "red congress" the Communists announced in advance that they would not raise the subject of Fascism and anti-Fascism nor refer to the events in Spain where since 15 July a steadily expanding civil war was being fought between Fascist and anti-Fascist forces. The organizers succeeded in bringing together about five thousand-five hundred delegates with "proper mandates" at Brussels[2] where they demonstrated for "peace through the League of Nations," for "collective security and indivisible peace" and listened to noncommittal peace appeals by French politicians, English pacifists, Belgian Socialists and a few prominent Communist speakers. Münzenberg did not make a public appearance at the congress; he was simply one of several liaison men working for the Russians. In the midst of the preparations for this congress, in the second half of August, the first public trial of Zinoviev, Kamenev and other old Bolsheviks ended in Moscow. Death sentences were passed and the accused were executed immediately. During this period Münzenberg ran into the Dutch ex-Communist and co-founder of the Comintern, Sneevliet on a street in Brussels. Sneevliet blocked his path shouting: "Cain, where is thy brother Abel-Zinoviev?" Silently and

---

[1]Open letter of 6 June 1936, Archives of the International Institute for Social History, Amsterdam.
[2]*Rundschau* (Basle) of 10 September 1936.

profoundly depressed by what was happening in Moscow Münzenberg went his way.

Immediately after the end of the Brussels conference one hundred and fifty Communist delegates arrived in Paris for a plenary meeting of the *Comité Mondial* at which Münzenberg, representing the secretariat, gave an account of the congress. The report revealed his inner reservations about the Brussels venture, which had shown up "the true character of the threat of war" but had drawn only "very general conclusions."[1] Representatives of the Russian trade unions established themselves in the RUP office and from that base pursued their softening up of non-Communist French politicians and trade unionists. The RUP was given a broad social basis by Olof Aschberg who set up in his rooms on the Place Casimir Périer, the Cercle des Nations, a sort of political and cultural salon where French and foreign visitors met informally for small and large conferences or purely social occasions.

13. The Break with Moscow

The Spanish civil war, now in its third year of bitter fighting, offered the anti-Fascist forces everywhere a chance to prove themselves as the defenders of freedom and democracy—or so they thought. Germany had been lost to the Fascists without an armed conflict. In Spain the outcome of the struggle was still open, despite the superiority of Franco's forces, because the majority of the people were behind the Republican government. Even before the establishment of the International Brigades, volunteers from many European countries, as well as refugees, including several from Münzenberg's office, were offering their services. As early as the end of July, Münzenberg had formed a "Committee for the War Relief of Republican Spain" which, particularly in Britain, began to provide aid at once. In collaboration with the Republican ambassador in Paris, Fernando de los Ríos, and later with the wife of his successor, Socialist politician Luis Araquistain, a campaign to help Spanish children was organized at the instigation of the Swedish trade unions and with generous financial support from them. From the Ile de France to the Spanish frontier we rented about twenty houses which were made into homes for several hundred refugee children from the combat areas near the French frontier. Aschberg and Branting persuaded the Swedish trade unions to make monthly contributions towards the upkeep of these homes. Among the volunteers who called on Münzenberg to express their preparedness to go to the Spanish front was Arthur Koestler. But Münzenberg thought that he could make

---

[1]Protocol in the Archives of the International Institute for Social History, Amsterdam.

better use of him in other ways. When he learned that Koestler had a press pass as correspondent of the *Pester Lloyd* Münzenberg suggested that he go as a reporter to Franco's camp at Seville because Germany and Italy had just begun to give Franco military aid. Before Koestler set out he was given his instructions by Münzenberg and Katz. Katz also gave him money to buy clothes and invited him to an opulent meal at a Czech restaurant. But to Koestler it seemed like the condemned man's last meal. In Spain he collected the material for his first book on the civil war *(Menschenopfer unerhört)* which was published in 1937 in German and French by the *Editions du Carrefour.*[1]

During these hectic weeks Münzenberg received a call from the Comintern to come to Moscow. Before that, in the summer of 1936, Moscow had sent the old, trusted Czech Communist, Bohumil Smeral, who was totally under the Comintern's thumb[2] to Paris to "collaborate" with Münzenberg and, about the same time, Münzenberg had been pressed to stay in Moscow and to work in the Comintern's Agitprop section. Münzenberg had said neither yes nor no at the time and now because of the events in Spain he considered the proposal outdated. He regarded himself as indispensable in Paris. This feeling was due in large part to the knowledge that for years he had occupied a special position within the Communist movement—a position he had originally come to hold because of Lenin's encouragement. It was in

[1]The second visit to the Spanish front for which Koestler set out on 22 January 1937 he made mainly as a reporter for the London *News Chronicle*. In *A Spanish Testament* (London, 1937) he gave an account of his detention in a Franco prison awaiting the execution of the sentence of death passed on him.
[2]Bohumil Smeral had been one of the most respected leaders of the Czech Socialists under the Hapsburg monarchy. At the age of 30 the gifted speaker became editor in chief of the *Prager Tagblatt* and a member of the Vienna Reichsrat. During the First World War he belonged to the right wing of the Social Democrats and fought for Austria-Hungary. He broke with the Czech Social Democrats in 1918 when he opposed the setting up of a Czech state, the Balkanization of central Europe and advocated a federalist solution, co-operation with the Austrian Socialist Party and the creation of large economic areas. In March 1919 he visited Moscow where he stayed for six months; he returned to Prague a friend of Lenin and a convinced Bolshevik. In Czechoslovakia he succeeded in persuading a large number of Socialists to join the Communists. In May 1921 he founded the Czechoslovak Communist Party which in November 1921 was joined by the Sudeten German Communists. Smeral disagreed with Lenin's view about a Bolshevik cadre party; to friends he remarked that such parties were useless for Central Europe, that they would lead to the atomization of the workers' parties, to the formation of sects. At the Second Comintern Congress the Czechoslovak delegation under his leadership still tried to resist Moscow's influence but the Bolsheviks had already sent their stooges Rakosi and Alpari to Czechoslovakia to convert leading officials there with threats and promises to the Russian point of view. In 1923 Smeral's role as party leader ceased; in 1924 he was called to Moscow and in 1925 on Comintern orders he emigrated voluntarily to Moscow. Henceforth he was not allowed to interfere in Czech affairs, thereby committing political suicide. He undertook a number of major political missions for the Comintern in Morocco, Palestine, Outer Mongolia and finally in Paris. He died in Moscow in 1942.

this mood that he went to Moscow in October 1936.

If Münzenberg had hoped that the wave of arrests would end with the murder of Zinoviev and Kamenev he was quickly disillusioned: the extermination of most Russian party members from the revolutionary period and of many foreign Communists had only just begun. People were bewildered. They could not understand what was happening. They wracked their brains to remember any deviations from the party line of which they might have been guilty and of which they could now be accused in the "Great Purge". They looked for witnesses to defend them and denounced each other without hesitation in order to escape themselves. No one dared to visit us in the newly built Hotel Moskva; after all we might be among the damned.

When Münzenberg tried to make an appointment with Radek he was told by a former colleague—under the seal of secrecy—that Radek had just been arrested and with him Piatakov and other leading officials who only recently had been among Stalin's keenest supporters and most loyal collaborators. These were indeed alarm signals. At the Comintern, Togliatti—whose Comintern pseudonym until 1944 was Ercoli—was standing in for the Secretary General Dimitroff and for Manuilsky both of whom were on holiday. Münzenberg was told to hand over his organization in Paris to Smeral and begin work in the Agitprop section of the Moscow Comintern. Münzenberg reported on the activities connected with the Spanish Civil War and on the pressure of public opinion on Soviet Russia to provide the hard-pressed Spanish Republicans with arms. Like other members of the League of Nations the Soviet Government had signed the non-intervention clause which prohibited arms deliveries to either protagonist in the civil war.

While these discussions were in progress Münzenberg was invited to present himself to the International Control Commission. The model for this organization, the Control Commission of the Soviet party, had originally been set up to keep an eye on the integrity of party members. Under Stalin, however, the Commission became an instrument for tracking down deviators and incipient opposition and was used to interrogate party members preliminary to expulsion and arrest. The International Control Commission fulfilled the same function for foreign Communists working in the Comintern.

Münzenberg was called before the ICC to answer for "a lack of revolutionary vigilance." He was accused of having employed a Liane Klein, whose father was said to be a Franco spy and who received information about Münzenberg's Paris activities from his daughter. At first Münzenberg treated this accusation as a joke, calling the whole affair "flea killing." Liane had worked as a shorthand typist in the Berlin office of the League Against Imperialism; in 1933 she came to Paris of her own accord and for a time—again as a shorthand typist—worked in one of Münzenberg's offices. In 1935 she had left and joined her father who was living in Majorca. She had never dealt with confidential papers. But the ICC persisted and when Münzenberg was called for a second and third interrogation on the same affair he understood that the case of Liane was only a pretext to deal with him personally. There were innumerable other ways of preparing a noose for him. The countless activities which he had planned and carried out in the no man's land between legality and illegality, his connections with personalities of every political shade, all this would provide ample material to finish him. Now he had only one idea: to leave Moscow as quickly as possible and await events in Paris.

Then came the decision of the CPSU(B) to support the Spanish Loyalists. On 15 October 1936 Stalin sent a telegram to the leader of the Spanish Communist Party, José Diaz, openly announcing this assistance. At the same time he gave a secret order, circulated at once among officials, that arms and volunteers were to be sent to Spain. This was the sheet anchor. Münzenberg told Togliatti that he must return to Paris to see through the campaigns for Spain which he had started and which included the procuring of arms. Having done this, he said he would then come back to Moscow, answer any further questions from the ICC and start work in the Agitprop section. He succeeded in convincing Togliatti that it was essential for him to return at once; Togliatti in turn advised the cadre department that Münzenberg should be allowed to go back and we were informed that approval had been given for our departure.

Heinz Neumann who was living with my sister in the Comintern Hotel Lux came to say goodbye. After months of interrogation by the ICC he had been relieved of all political functions and was working as a translator in the association of foreign publishers. He broke down when we took our farewell; we knew that we would never see each other again.

We arrived at the agreed time in the evening at the station but nobody came to hand us our passports with the exit visas and the tickets. Downcast we returned to the hotel. That night we did not sleep, waiting for the knock of the NKVD. But the night passed and the next morning Münzenberg stormed into Togliatti's office and made a great scene. This worked and Togliatti telephoned the police in Münzenberg's presence; we received our papers and tickets and departed the same day.

We stopped for a few days in Denmark, enjoying our freedom and the autumn woods around Fredericia. In the Baltic our small ship ran into a storm and for forty-eight hours battled from one German lighthouse to another. After the hectic days in Moscow, Münzenberg had recovered his equanimity. He would never return to Moscow. Now he must continue to live and work without the support of the Comintern, indeed he was likely to work against it.

Upon his arrival in Paris, Münzenberg began to demand final reports, balance sheets and accounts for all committees and publishing houses under his control. They were handed over to Smeral who certified them in documents signed by both men. As Münzenberg knew that he was only beginning his clash with the Comintern he arranged for copies of the transfer documents and accounts to be kept in a safe place. Friends deposited them in the safe of a Catholic press service. When the Gestapo entered Paris the Catholic fathers burned the contents of the safe.

Smeral had copied the documents in his best copperplate handwriting and deposited them with the Paris branch of the KPD or the Comintern. At the beginning of the war, when all émigrés were interned in French camps, the archives of these organizations were stored in several trunks in the hotel room of the writer Friedrich Wolf. There they fell into the hands of the Gestapo. At his trial by the people's court, Münzenberg's former collaborator, Josef Füllenbach, was shown Smeral's documents as evidence of his treasonous activity.

Instead of starting work in Moscow, Münzenberg now put himself under the care of Dr. Le Savouret and spent some weeks in the physician's small sanitorium in Chaténay-Malabry, a property which had once belonged to the poet Chateaubriand. Dr. Le Savouret was married to a daughter of Plekhanov and moved in Russian Menshevik circles in Paris. Shortly before he had met Bukharin when the latter visited Paris to give a lecture to the Society of Friends of Soviet Russia. Le Savouret said that it was painful to listen to Bukharin. He seemed troubled, kept closely to his text and delivered parts of his lecture in a voice so low as to be inaudible. Le Savouret was with him when Bukharin received a telegram from Moscow asking him to interrupt his visit and to return immediately. Le Savouret implored him to remain in Paris. But, white as a sheet and with a trembling voice, Bukharin explained that he must go although he knew exactly what fate awaited him in Moscow.

While Münzenberg was staying with Dr. Le Savouret who had confirmed that his patient was suffering from a slight cardiac neurosis, the second great show trial took place in Moscow in January 1937. Now it was Karl Radek's turn to face the court whose verdicts had been decided long before the start of the trial. Like other prominent men accused before him, Radek confessed to ridiculous crimes which Münzenberg knew he had never committed. What physical and psychological tortures had preceded this gruesome comedy? It was not only news and rumours that reached him from Moscow, people turned up who had been personally affected by events in Russia, ghostly figures whom he had once known well and who had changed in a terrible way.

One day, Mirov-Abramov's wife Lola came to see us. Apparently she was on a secret mission. She lived in the Russian embassy and addressed us as though we were strangers, anxiously avoiding all personal topics. Mirov-Abramov, whom she did not mention, worked in the Soviet Foreign Office and was arrested soon afterwards. On his way to Moscow the Russian ambassador to Madrid, Marcel Rosenberg, stopped in Paris. Münzenberg visited him at the Russian embassy. It was the last time that he entered this building. He tried to discuss Spain with Rosenberg. He told him of his clashes with the KPD leadership and tried to explain to him why he did not want to work in Moscow in the Comintern. Rosenberg sat there looking at him without interest. He moved like an automaton and his face was of a sickly, greenish hue: he was visibly marked by the death which awaited him at home. He replied in monosyllables and avoided all comment, apparently afraid of the microphones that were hidden in the embassy's reception rooms.

Meanwhile the ICC extended its field of activity. It sent spies from Moscow to Paris. Münzenberg's secretary, Hans Schulz, was interrogated by Grete Wilde, an emissary from Moscow, because in 1934 he had attended a memorial celebration of the Youth International at the German club in Moscow where some critical comments had been made. In the spring of 1937, Leo Flieg was also called to Moscow. Münzenberg and other friends implored him not to go. He assured them quietly that he had nothing to blame himself for and that he would not refuse to. After his arrival he was arrested. And soon afterwards we received a postcard from Moscow informing us of Heinz Neumann's arrest.

14. *The Popular Front Collapses*

"In a state of profound depression which he knew how to hide"[1] Münzenberg opened on 10 April 1937 in a hall in the rue Cadet in Paris what was to be the first and only conference of the German popular front. About three hundred Western European delegates of every political shade attended. Heinrich Mann spoke on the resistance movement, Rudolf Breitscheid on foreign policy and Münzenberg on the tasks of the popular front which he wanted to see expanded into a politically active organization. Kersten reports:

> In a big speech ... Münzenberg advocated the unification of all anti-Hitler forces, demanded frankness particularly on the part of the Communists and expressed criticism of any narrow-minded, calculating policy that

[1]Kurt Kersten, *Das Ende Willi Münzenbergs, op, cit.,* p. 490.

could only undermine confidence. Heinrich Mann thanked Münzenberg ostentatiously for his frank words.[1]

Behind the scenes Ulbricht had intrigued actively against Münzenberg's continued participation in popular front work. He was accused of being too involved with the Social Democrats, Breitscheid and Braun, and of describing Ulbricht's policy in the popular front as that of a wolf in sheep's clothing.

Although the German emigration's attempts to establish a popular front had considerable support and were apparently unanimous it was evident that the movement was already disintegrating. The bourgeois group of progressive liberals around Leopold Schwarzschild and *Das Neue Tagebuch* had disassociated themselves from this experiment in the preceding months.

In spite of his critical attitude towards the SPD and his open rejection of Communism, Schwarzschild had at first joined the popular front committee. He and his collaborators had been of the opinion that Münzenberg—without being committed too closely to the Communist Party line—was ready to serve the interests of German anti-fascism. Another reason why they had welcomed the popular front was that they were convinced that Hitler was preparing for war and that a constitutional programme for the period after his fall—for the "Fourth Reich"—was required.

Das Neue Tagebuch had welcomed the popular front manifesto of February 1936 and the popular front committee established at that time as a "serious, restrained and possibly for that very reason confidence-inspiring beginning" that could ensure that the Hitler régime would one day be succeeded not by a vacuum and chaos but by a force prepared to take over from the existing system without replacing it by "another terror". But this could only be achieved "by procuring the widest possible theoretical agreement beween sections and classes of profoundly differing traditions and by achieving an assimilation of their ideas to a point where liberals and members of the *Stahlhelm*, Communists and Catholics, tradesmen, workers and peasants can join forces in practical work."[2]

Apart from Schwarzschild another representative of the bourgeois-liberal, and in particular the German Jewish, emigration to take an active part in the discussions of the popular front committee was Georg

[1] *Ibid.*, p. 490 *et seq.*
[2] *Das Neue Tagebuch* (Paris), Vol. 4 (1936); No. 7 of 15 February 1936, p. 151 *et seq* and also No. 14 of 11 April 1936, p. 345 *et seq* (text of and commentary on the declaration of the Politburo of the KPD of 23 March 1936 which explicitly endorsed the popular front manifesto of February 1936).

Bernhard, the editor of the *Pariser Tageblatt*. Along with their popular front activities Bernhard and Schwarzschild had each prepared a draft constitution for the post-Hitler "Fourth Reich". Printed on thin paper and illegally distributed in Germany by the KPD (0) the booklet was entitled *Materialen zur Volksfront*.[1] The two drafts contained several interesting proposals. Both authors thought that a limited period of transition was needed to eradicate the traces of Nazi rule. They demanded drastic measures against lawyers and officials who had cooperated in illegal laws and measures. Bernhard insisted that the number of professional civil servants be considerably reduced and that all basic industries and all large estates be nationalized. Schwarzschild wanted the freedom of the daily press in the "New Reich" to be safeguarded by a senate composed of a handful of elected "qualified publicists" and also made proposals on how to prevent financially powerful pressure groups from influencing election propaganda.

In the spring and summer of 1936, Schwarzschild and Münzenberg had organized a number of working conferences in an attempt to agree on a draft acceptable to the Communists. This proved impossible—the Communists were not prepared to commit themselves to any programme that limited their freedom of manoeuvre. Least of all were they prepared to accept the ideas of European integration and future social and economic reorganization contained in Bernhard's and Schwarzschild's drafts. The negotiations were finally broken off without anything having been achieved.

Schwarzschild had observed in *Das Neue Tagebuch* as early as October 1936 that, as an attempt to establish a truce and an alliance between the French Communists and the bourgeois, the popular front policy in France had achieved less than had been expected from it.[2] At the end of 1936 he commented publicly on the negative lessons to be drawn from the experiences of the German popular front committee in Paris of which he was no longer a member:

> The German version of the popular front experiment has shown, and that was indeed its most instructive result, that the idea of adding together old established groups and thereby obtaining a sum greater than each represents individually has proved illusory. The total came to less not to more than the individual parts . . .
> Everyone was obsessed by the determination if possible to exploit every other [group] without giving away any of his own advantages. Nobody seriously wanted to think about new programmes or unification and whenever an important point arose there was a tendency to ignore it

[1]Copy in the possession of the author.
[2]*Das Neue Tagebuch*, Vol. 4, No. 44, 31 October 1936, p. 1041 *et seq.*

altogether or to escape into ambiguous and therefore meaningless set formulas . . .

Nothing came [of the popular front attempt] except the occasional appeal the content of which was dictated by the need of these groups to stay within the sphere of generally acceptable, and obvious formulas. The fact that they are graced by a few illustrious names whose holders, in spite of a feeling of futility, did not actually want to go so far as to withhold their support contributes little . . .

It has become clear that this work cannot succeed if it is dominated by these individual groups . . .[1]

After Münzenberg had withdrawn also from the popular front committee work, the conflicts between the Communists and other members of the committee became more marked. During his last visits to Moscow, Münzenberg had tried in vain to warn against a policy which would merely alienate the other popular front partners and prevent any united action on the part of the German anti-fascists. He had submitted a plan prepared jointly with other Communist representatives of the Paris popular front group. But the Comintern was no longer interested in the German emigration's efforts to achieve unity or to establish a popular front. For Ulbricht and the KPD leaders in Paris the popular front committee was merely a welcome basis from which to approach Social Democratic groups in the Reich and to set up Communist controlled "popular front friendship circles" abroad. Thereupon the Social Democratic members of the committee ceased to collaborate. The Socialist Workers Party also withdrew from the popular front. At the popular front conference in April 1937, the Socialist Workers Party had openly expressed its indignation at the Moscow trials and the execution of the old Bolsheviks. Meanwhile the Soviet security service had extended its activities to Spain where Mark Rein, the son of the well-known Menshevik, Abramovich, had been kidnapped and never found. When the Socialist Workers Party publicly denounced this flagrant breach of the Spanish popular front policy the Communist *Deutsche Volkszeitung*, published in Prague, described the Socialist Workers Party's leaders as Trotskyites who had tried "to discuss with the Spanish Partido Obrero de Unificación Marxista (POUM) how to achieve victory more effectively for Hitler and Mussolini."[2]

The popular front committee became less and less active. In the autumn of 1938 the Communists tried once more to revive it by holding a meeting, although the Social Democratic members and many other personalities had already resigned. The president of this meeting, Heinrich Mann, by then an out-and-out Communist, expressed his readiness

[1] *Das Neue Tagebuch*, Vol. 4, No. 52, 26 December 1936, p. 1231 *et seq.*
[2] *Deutsche Volkszeitung* (Prague) 8 July 1937.

to serve on future occasions and issued invitations to so-called "popular front discussions." He proposed that three known Communists, Felix Boenheim, Alfred Kantorowicz and Hermann Budzislawski, run the committee. When he invited the non-Communists present to join the committee they refused on the grounds that the organization was Communist dominated. Thus ended the German Communists' attempt, which had been decisively influenced by Münzenberg, to unite the German émigrés into a politically effective popular front movement. Münzenberg was anything but surprised by these developments.

In November 1939 he observed retrospectively in his journal, *Die Zukunft*, that as early as the middle of 1936 the Comintern abandoned the resolutions of the Seventh World Congress and, taking its cue from an article by Stalin on the theme "There is a Class Question", adopted a "new orientation towards pure party politics and total party rule." In their efforts to disguise this turn the representatives of the Communists had been compelled to continue "playing at the popular front" and to let credulous democrats and intellectuals advocate a "democratic popular front". All the "Thomas Mann committees", "Heinrich Mann committees" or "action committees of the German opposition" had only been crude deception manoeuvres. Münzenberg was conscious of this and worried by it while he was still trying to save the German popular front; then the day came when his party comrades left nothing to be saved.

Even Heinrich Mann became aware of this situation and in the course of 1937 repeatedly attacked the KPD leadership in exile for deviously undermining the popular front. But good will and a most praiseworthy anxiety to preserve the unity of the anti-fascist forces prevailed in the case of this clever writer whose politics were swayed by his emotions rather than by his intellect. His attitude towards topical political questions was one of childish naivety, making him defenceless against Communist efforts to associate him with their cause. Those who knew him were not surprised that these efforts were always successful.

Münzenberg and Heinrich Mann were attached to each other. The writer admired the politician's inexhaustible vitality while Münzenberg was drawn to the older man who, though politically naive, committed himself out of a strong sense of responsibility. It was easy moreover to make friends with the open-minded, easy-going *bon vivant* Heinrich, who unlike his brother Thomas was not in the "least bit" pompous. I frequently accompanied Münzenberg on his visits to Heinrich Mann at his summer house in Briançon, the little Alpine town on the slopes of Mont Cenis, or in his fourth floor flat in Nice where he lived, surrounded by canaries, with his future wife Nelly.

The friendship between the two men continued until the Communists could no longer bear to see Heinrich Mann on such intimate terms with the renegade Münzenberg. Wilhelm Pieck visited Nice and persuaded Heinrich Mann to dissociate himself from Münzenberg. Mann's links with the Communists were already so firm that he lacked the strength to insist on remaining friends with an excommunicated person. In a weak letter which reeked of bad conscience he observed that "things must be allowed to take their course."[1]

15. The German Freedom Party

From the start bourgeois German politicians had refused to take part in the popular front committee. It was from this quarter that the German Freedom Party emerged; it was not, as was later claimed, one of Münzenberg's brain children. The first suggestion came from Otto Klepper, the last Prussian Minister of Finance before the Papen coup, who at the beginning of 1936 had returned from China where he had been financial advisor to Chiang Kai-shek. From New York and then from Paris, Klepper had called for a new movement directed at the real "soft underbelly of National Socialism," the "suppression of freedom."[2] Klepper was in touch with Brüning's former press chief, Dr. Karl Spiecker, whose political associates included Father Muckermann, the publisher of the journal Der Deutsche Weg in Holland, and Prelate Poels. They all were in touch with politically like-minded elements in Germany who had suggested early in 1937 that the refugees who agreed with Klepper's ideas should form an organization and support their friends inside Germany with illegal propaganda.

Early in 1937, strictly in accordance with the rules of conspiratorial activity, the "German Freedom Party" (DEP) was established and publication of "freedom letters" was begun. The first of these letters, written by Otto Klepper, appeared in March 1937. It began with a programmatic statement: "What is the German Freedom Party and what are its aims?" It described itself as a "fraternal league of determined women and men who have but one task: to serve Germany, who know only one happiness in life: to help the German people and who have only one aim: to fight for freedom."[3] The German Freedom Party existed for those who wanted a constitutional state and who were tired of the tyranny of a partisan police and a partisan judiciary; who wanted

[1]Kurt Kersten, Das Ende Willi Münzenbergs, op. cit., p. 492.
[2]Otto Klepper, Europäische Freiheit, in Das Neue Tagebuch, 26 December 1936, p. 1236 et seq.
[3]Quoted in the judgement of the Second Senate of the People's Court of 8 November 1939 in the case against Georg Walter and Oskar Wagner (accused of 'treasonable' activity for the German Freedom Party); photocopy in the Institut für Zeitgeschichte, Fa 117/9.

the restoration of an honest and expert central and local administration,
who despised the corruption that was beginning to spread at every level
in Germany. The nerve centres of the National Socialist régime, which
were targets of criticism for many Germans also, were cleverly attacked. The style of the freedom letters, devoid as it was of all ideological or party jargon, was most effective.

In all, seventy-five "freedom letters" were issued up to the eve of the
war, each dealing with a particular topic and addressed to different
selected groups in Germany.

In the course of 1937 it had become clear that Münzenberg had
broken with the Communists. Klepper and Spiecker invited him to
work with them. The echo from the Reich was unexpectedly strong. We
learned that there was so much discussion of the "freedom letters" at
the universities, in the army and among youth organizations in Germany that party officials were compelled to take action.

The letters were sent across the German frontier by courier or
through the ordinary mail. Colleagues of Münzenberg's who had remained loyal to him after his break with the party looked after the
production and despatch of the letters, taking care that none of the
Communists who continued to come and go was given a chance to look
at them. For a time the illegal material—freedom letters and leaflets—
was sent to Berlin in the French embassy's diplomatic bag. Münzenberg's colleagues also experimented with letting off balloons near the
frontier to carry the material onto German territory. The worried Gestapo suspected that commercial pilots were involved in the plot but
could prove nothing.

The material was taken to Berlin from an office set up at Karl Emont's
house in Eupen near the Belgian-German frontier. One day the house
was broken into and ransacked. Although the culprits were never found
we had no doubt at the time that this was the work of the Communist
secret service. The KPD leadership in exile had not remained unaware
of the activity of the Freedom Party. It tried to persuade the non-party
popular front committee to condemn the Freedom Party: the attempt
failed. A tribunal under the chairmanship of Heinrich Mann announced
that there was no reason for the committee to fight the Freedom
Party and that if anything it helped the popular front if opposition
to Hitler was fomented inside Germany from as many sides as
possible. The Freedom Party was greatly harmed when the KPD
organ, *Deutsche Volkszeitung*, in its Paris edition of 17 October 1937
gave details of the Freedom Party's organization and of Karl Emont's
distribution service of the freedom letters, thereby providing helpful

information for the National Socialist investigators.[1]

For a few months in 1938 the Freedom Party even had at its disposal a shortwave transmitter which operated from a fishing vessel cruising outside the two mile limit in the Channel. But as this resulted in political complications with the host countries it became necessary to stop the transmissions.

The German Freedom Party and the freedom letters had occupied the attention of Third Reich authorities and party officials since the spring of 1937.[2] On 1 May 1939, the chief of the security police sent a fifteen--page confidential report on the German Freedom Party—based on recent Gestapo investigations—to various departments.[3] In some respects the Gestapo showed itself well informed while in others it was groping in the dark, making do with often inaccurate guesswork. The report said that recently "about ten different propaganda sheets in the form of German freedom letters [were once more] . . . distributed in Germany through the post or through illegal importation."

While the postal dispatch "has for long time been arranged almost exclusively from Copenhagen and some other cities in Denmark the smuggling of the leaflets continues to be organized by a former trade union secretary in Eupen." The author of the report who was anxious to find the "men behind the scenes" and to discover the organizational structure of the DFP named among its leaders Willi Münzenberg, Heinrich Mann and Karl Spiecker and also, mistakenly, Social Democrats Max Braun, Hermann Rauschning and Otto Strasser.

The Gestapo's information on the financing of the DFP was inaccurate or vastly exaggerated. Particularly misleading was a diagram attached to the report presenting the small group as a firm with a "Paris office" and with close links with British and French politicians as well as with other German émigré groups.

In 1939 the Gestapo captured two members of the Freedom Party. One of them, Georg Walter, a relative of Emont, who before 1933 had been a member of the Stennes opposition in the NSDAP and after 1935 had been in touch with the opposition in Germany, was caught on courier duty. In prison, awaiting trial, he tried twice to commit suicide. Walter's capture resulted in further arrests. At the trial by the People's Court the two accused were found guilty of treason and sentenced on 8 November 1939 to ten and four years imprisonment respectively.

[1] Cf. verdict of the People's Court against Walter and Wagner (see footnote 1, p. 298), p. 13.

[2] Cf. The article *"Die Freiheitspartei"* in *Das Neue Tagebuch*, Vol. 5, No. 16 of 17 April 1937.

[3] A copy is contained in the documents of the Reich Commissioner for the reunification of Austria and the German Reich; microfilm in the Institut für Zeitgeschichte, Ma 145/1, p. 10437 *et seq.*

16. The "Münzenberg Case"

As soon as Münzenberg returned to Paris in 1936 the first fantastic rumours about him began to circulate. The stories had started, while he was still in Moscow, with a report in the Paris *Matin* which was immediately taken over by the *Frankfurter Zeitung*. The item claimed that Münzenberg and Hugo Eberlein had been arrested in Moscow. As Moscow's "paymaster" in Western Europe, Münzenberg was said to have been accused of not keeping silent about these payments.[1] But he had returned. It seemed clear that a decisive change had occurred in his already uneasy relations with the Comintern. But what change? As he himself remained silent the others indulged in speculation. A Russian émigré in Paris, Miliukov, claimed in his paper to know in 1937 that Münzenberg had put aside a large sum of Comintern money which he was unwilling to hand over until the release of his friend "Sauerfeld" arrested in Moscow—presumably meaning Kurt Sauerland who had in fact been arrested in 1937. Münzenberg's own appearance in Moscow was also said to depend on granting this condition.[2] The non-Communists must have had strange ideas about the Comintern and the NKVD if they thought that such a piece of horse trading would be possible.

A few days later a Swiss paper claimed that Münzenberg "by virtue of having been treasurer-in-chief of the European Comintern still disposed of vast sums." Therefore he could easily "to the peaceful end of his days praise the Soviet paradise from the shores of the Riviera." The paper added that Münzenberg was toying with the idea of emigrating to America and that the man favoured to succeed him was—Walter Ulbricht.[3]

Münzenberg was unperturbed by these rumours. He withdrew and began to work on a book which he had long planned. Kurt Kersten who had just moved from Prague to Paris assisted him in the preparations for *Propaganda als Waffe* (Propaganda as a Weapon). It was Kersten who collected the extensive material from National Socialist sources on which the book was based. *Propaganda als Waffe,* a thorough analysis of National Socialist propaganda methods, also provided an insight into Münzenberg's personal views on the laws and demands of propaganda. Here he was in his very own sphere.

The book which appeared in 1937 opens with the observation:

[1] *Frankfurter Zeitung*, 31 October 1936.
[2] *Posliedniye Novosti* (Paris), 27 July 1937.
[3] *Neue Baseler Zeitung*, 26 July 1937.

> The National Socialist German Workers Party has made greater use of propaganda than any other political, economic or religious movement hitherto.

Münzenberg was quick to appreciate that propaganda was the first and last word of National Socialism, that it occupied a novel central, but at the same time ambivalent, position in the Hitler movement: on the one hand it was a rationally calculated tool, equipped with "every refined method of large scale twentieth century advertising";[1] on the other hand—unlike the Socialist concept of propaganda which originally implied the propagation of ideas and therefore had a basically instructive character—it replaced a non-existent theory and ideology so that in the end "politics becomes a means of propaganda" and not vice versa.[2] In particular, Münzenberg attempted to explain the relation between the nature of National Socialist propaganda and the brutalities of the régime. This type of propaganda—which could not convey the intellectual content of ideas because there were no ideas—was unthinkable without force and found its logical supplement in the coercive tools of the Nazi organization. National Socialist propaganda, which was mainly a demonstration of determination and always served the purpose of self-assertion, was characterized by violence, by the aggressive negation of reality.

> The Hitler movement is not interested in actually changing conditions but only in making them appear different to the masses.[3]

Münzenberg continued: "Hitler is primarily and above all a propagandist."[4] He had come to power through propaganda.

> Hitler made no attempt to enlighten the masses whom he sought to attract. He encouraged their apathy and obstinacy, their petty hatred, their envy, their vindictiveness, their spiritual resentment—feelings and ideas which had dominated Hitler himself since the days of his youth and which tormented him continuously until he seemed at times possessed by a thirst for revenge. He sought to transfer to others whom he assumed to nurture similar emotions the feelings that burned like poison within him; these feelings he wanted to bring out, to magnify, to release and to activate. This was and is the essence of the propaganda methods which he employs when dealing with these masses.[5]

[1] W. Münzenberg, *Propaganda als Waffe*, Paris/Basle 1937, p. 12 *et seq.*
[2] *Ibid.*, p. 20.
[3] *Ibid.*
[4] *Ibid.*, p. 17.
[5] *Ibid.*, p. 37.

Münzenberg recognized the effectiveness of certain myths, legends and Utopian hopes which were cleverly exploited by National Socialist propaganda: Goebbels' never-ending appeal to the feelings of "the little man", the myth about Hitler as "saviour" and divinely appointed *Führer*, the National Socialist phrase about the "national community." But he rightly regarded the aura of triumphant confidence as the determining factor, the direct and indirect appeal to atavistic feelings and the desire to be the victor, the top dog. He saw the entire Hitler policy as designed to preserve feelings of superiority, and illusions.

If the illusion is destroyed the system collapses. This vital illusion, the prerequisite for Hitler's power can, of this Hitler and his followers are convinced, be produced only by propaganda. Hence more and more propaganda, agitation and myths.[1]

Münzenberg's clear-sighted analysis of National Socialist propaganda indirectly constituted a criticism of the failure to realize its effectiveness and suggestiveness. Münzenberg—undoubtedly attracted to some extent by Goebbels' technique—came in the end to the conclusion that National Socialist propaganda could only be checked by a determined "counter-propaganda offensive."

A prerequisite for the whole of the anti-Hitler struggle is of particular and topical importance on the propaganda battle field: attack, attack and again attack.[2]

Georgi Dimitroff was quoted three times in *Propaganda als Waffe*, on each occasion in connection with the struggle against fascism. Stalin was given a hearing only once but was described as the "great leader of the Soviet Union and the architect of the world's first socialist state." The Stalin quotation related to the threat of war. The quotations were chosen carefully, dealing as they did with problems on which Münzenberg knew himself to be in agreement with the Soviet point of view. Altogether this book, written in the critical year in which he broke with his old comrades in arms, contained not one word against the Soviet Union. The German Communists, on the other hand, were not mentioned. They were no longer allocated a place in this review of the forces of propaganda warfare.

Not surprisingly the KPD press strongly attacked *Propaganda als Waffe*. Münzenberg was accused of over estimating the importance of National Socialist propaganda and of badly underestimating the effectiveness of Communist propaganda. He was said to have done grievous

[1] *Ibid.*, p. 20.
[2] *Ibid.*, p. 281.

damage to Communist Party policy and thus to the struggle against fascism.

This was not the first public attack on Münzenberg. He had already been criticized for Berthold Jacob's book *Das Neue Deutsche Heer und seine Führer* (The New German Army and its Leaders), published in 1936 by the *Éditions du Carrefour*. Jacob had produced a very informative account of the growth of the new German army by studying the German press and specialist military journals, by scrutinizing personnel lists and reports of troop movements and other materials. His guesses about the probable plans of operation of this young, powerful army proved well-founded. As early as the spring of 1936 Jacob predicted the blow against Prague, "certain to succeed in view of Czechoslovakia's unfortunate situation," and he also foresaw the attack on Poland which he thought would lead to a fourth partition of Poland between the Russians and Hitler. Such prophecies were not at all approved of by the Communists. Their attacks were directed against Münzenberg who published these speculations about the role of Soviet Russia in a future war at the very moment when Soviet Russia was trying at the Brussels "World Peace Congress" to convince the world of its good will and loyalty to the League of Nations.

These were at first the only indications of any differences between Münzenberg and the Communist Party. The real attacks started in the autumn of 1937. Until then the KPD leadership in exile remained quiet and ignored Münzenberg's activities among the members of the popular front and in the Spanish committees. Perhaps they still thought that he might visit Moscow and disappear there forever, or else they wished to avoid open attacks because they feared his popularity and his influence among German refugees of all political shades. The attack finally began in the popular front committee. In a circular to the Communist group in the committee, the Communists said that proceedings had been started against Münzenberg because without the party's knowledge he had been having talks with right-wing bourgeois circles, an initiative which was not in the interest of unification in the struggle against Hitler. This circular was followed by another in which it was claimed that certain circles around Spiecker intended to join forces with capitalists, right-wing Catholic leaders and Reichswehr generals and push the KPD out of the popular front. Finally on 27 October all Communist members of the popular front committee were notified that Münzenberg had been expelled from the Communist Party.

The Comintern's files on the "Münzenberg case" seemed to have been closed. The waves of arrests in 1937 and 1938 had almost immobilized this organization. It was true that summons continued to arrive calling Münzenberg to Moscow. Without refusing outright he managed to think up new excuses on each occasion. Krivitsky confirms that Dimitroff wrote reassuring letters to Münzenberg: new important tasks awaited him in Moscow. The NKVD—according to Krivitsky—sent an agent by the name of Belitsky to Paris to convince Münzenberg that he need have no fears. "Who decides your fate?" Belitsky was said to have argued, "Dimitroff or the NKVD? And I know that Yezlov is on your side."[1] But Münzenberg did not fall into the trap.

In May 1938 Louis Gibarti returned to Paris from the United States. Before his departure Earl Browder, the leader of the American Communist Party, had told him that he must not speak to the traitor Münzenberg. As soon as he got back he naturally had a meeting with the "traitor" on the terrace of the Café Viel. Münzenberg showed him a letter from Dimitroff couched in very friendly terms, saying that the affair must be settled. Dimitroff went on to say that he had the fullest understanding of the difficulties that existed in Paris, and they must talk things over.

Gibarti thought that nothing much could happen to Münzenberg; he might be relieved of his functions but after a while he would be allowed to go on with his work. Münzenberg disagreed. He thought he would be shot like the others and that ten years later it would be said that a big mistake had been made. With a smile he said that he preferred to forgo the trip.

Many of his friends were anxious to find a *modus vivendi* between him and the Russians. Münzenberg was by no means uninterested in these efforts, he regarded them as a delaying manoeuvre which gave him a respite. On 12 July 1938, for example, Count Karolyi approached Romain Rolland about the differences between Münzenberg and the Comintern. He said that he knew nothing about the background except that Münzenberg had shown "a lack of discipline" by refusing to go to Moscow. Karolyi complained bitterly that these differences had recently led to a distinct slackening in anti-Hitler activities, on the occasion of Austria's *Anschluss* for example. "All of us who know what he has done this year and in past years realize that it will not be easy to replace a man of his calibre. With his untiring activity, his tremendous dynamism and his initiative he has done much for the party." Karolyi continued, saying that Marcel Cachin was of the same opinion and that he had promised to write to Dimitroff to plead for Münzenberg. The charmingly naïve letter finished with the remark that after much persuasion Münzenberg had agreed to send a telegram to the Comintern expressing his willingness to come to Moscow.[2]

[1]Krivitsky, *I Was Stalin's Agent*, 1939, p. 62.
[2]Photocopy of Karolyi's letter in the possession of the author.

This communication probably resembled the telegram which Münzenberg sent to Moscow on 21 July 1938 after the American journalist Louis Fischer, with whom he was on friendly terms, had called on him at Dimitroff's behest:

> Am prepared to travel at once if visit can be organized so that I am back in Paris by mid-July.[1]

The same delaying purpose was served by letters of which copies were found in France after the war and subsequently published.[2] The pathetic style of these letters, most unusual in correspondence between senior Communist officials, leads one to suspect that Münzenberg was less concerned with ensuring that the originals reached their destination than that copies were circulated among well meaning friends.

In March 1938 Münzenberg had written to Brupbacher that he was preparing to make a change, a change in a formal relationship which for a long time had been neither political nor in any way practical.[3] This was the first indication of the circular sent to his friends in the autumn of 1938 in which he spelt out his break with the Communists.[4] Münzenberg justified his break with the KPD in detail and with care:

> . . . because conditions in Germany and the worsening of the international crisis demand the use of every individual my political past, my socialist sense of responsibility and my temperament demand that I part from an organization which makes political work impossible for me.

Münzenberg avoided all emotional outbursts, all attacks on former comrades in arms or on the new party leadership. He merely dealt factually with a policy which he had realized to be false and irreconcilable with his political intentions and objectives. In conclusion he noted that his attitude towards the Soviet Union had not changed.

It is perhaps surprising that he continued to hide his real opinion of Stalin's purges, that he never even mentioned them. His behaviour can only be understood in the context of the situation at the time. Having always had a party, an organization behind him, Münzenberg was now alone. He felt too weak, too isolated to attack Stalin in public. He was afraid that he would suffer the fate of other deserters. In July, Ignaz Reiss, a Pole who had been a Communist from the very start and who

[1]Copy in the possession of the author.
[2]Günther Nollau, *Die Internationale,* Cologne 1959, p. 320 *et seq.*
[3]From the correspondence of Fritz Brupbacher, Archives of the International Institute for Social History, Amsterdam.
[4]Copy in the possession of the author.

for years had occupied a senior position in the foreign department of the Soviet military espionage service, had broken with Moscow and in an open letter had accused Stalin of murdering the author of the October Revolution. On 4 September 1938, Reiss was murdered by GPU agents near Lausanne. Others who had broken with Moscow were persecuted and denounced. Even in 1937, Münzenberg was being watched by the Communist secret service, his mail was intercepted, he received threatening letters and he feared that knowing too much about internal Russian affairs his life was in danger.

Added to this there was the general attitude of Western socialists and left-wingers. Most of them were still not prepared to break with Soviet Russia. From de Brouckère to Otto Bauer they regarded the USSR as their ally in the fight against fascism. If it was Münzenberg's objective to gather around him as many dissatisfied Communists as possible he needed to manoeuvre with great caution. Moreover, in spite of everything he was convinced that the Soviet Union was an indispensable ally whom it was a tactical mistake to attack.

Much more explicit was a statement of the reasons for his leaving the KPD which Münzenberg made in a letter to the party and which was published on 10 March 1939 in *Zukunft*. Here are some paragraphs of this remarkable statement:

> It is with difficulties that I part from an organization which I have helped to found and to form. After becoming a member of the Socialist movement in 1906 as a young factory worker I was one of the first German Socialists who in 1915 joined Lenin and the movement for which I have worked not without success for almost twenty-five years.
>
> A two year conflict with the present-day leadership of the Communist Party over decisive political and tactical issues, including the party's aims, questions arising out of the united front with our Socialist comrades, popular front policy, methods of propaganda, basic concepts of internal party democracy and the party's attitude towards the individual member has brought home to me that within the present-day party organization it is impossible to solve these problems, to restore members' elementary rights and to adopt a policy that takes account of the changes which have occurred since 1933.
>
> The contradictory policy of the party which in empty phrases refers to new tasks without basically changing its fighting methods or the form and language of its propaganda, the absence of any clear ideas of the requirements of a 'democratic people's republic,' combined with an unwillingness to abandon single party dictatorship, the ambivalent united front policy which postulates the creation of a united workers party while continuing the old 'tactics' condemned by the Seventh World Congress of the Communist International, all this has made it impossible to create

among socialists and democrats that confidence in the party without which unity is impossible. But how can a party be politically active with success if its closest allies have no confidence in it?

. . . The workers party must support the basic principles of the classic workers movement, the inviolability of internal party democracy and the right of all members to share in decision making.

If it is true that, in spite of all motorization and mechanization of the machine of war, in the last resort war is decided by men alone, it is also true that the proletarian revolution can only be won by men, and by men who are convinced that the ideas which their own experience has given them are correct, who by the exercise of *voluntary* revolutionary discipline endure great suffering and sacrifice and who by their example in the hour of decision carry the masses with them to victory. The revolutionary war will not be won with regimented and bullied dead souls . . .

I believed that these political principles could be recognized by the Communist Party, that it would at least be possible to discuss them freely and publicly. I was mistaken. After a conflict of over two years I appreciate that this is impossible. It is made impossible by a form of organization which has little in common with that of the original party, by a powerful bureaucratic machinery which dominates party life and by a leadership which in spite of all defeats since 1933 considers itself infallible and irreplaceable.

I am parting company with this leadership and its organization but I do not part company with the hundreds perhaps thousands who arbitrarily, without reason, without trial, without the possibility of defence were illegally dismissed, 'sacked' and expelled by faceless authorities. I do not part from the thousands with whom I have fought since 1906, first in the Socialist and later in the Communist movement, and who today soldier on illegally in Germany together with the young cadres that are born in the daily battle. I have not changed my attitude towards the Soviet Union, the first country to build socialism, the great guarantor of peace and the most important ally in the struggle for a new Germany and its reconstruction, the country to which I devoted my activities in 1921 and subsequent years.

I do not intend to set up a group within the party, nor to restrict my activity to one group. I shall continue, as before, to devote all the resources at my disposal to establishing a great, all embracing united party and to creating a broadly based, powerful popular movement strong enough to overthrow the Hitler system and to create a new Germany. Thus I retain the place which I chose in 1906, first at the side of Karl Liebknecht, then at the side of Rosa Luxemburg, Klara Zetkin and in 1915 at the side of Lenin, the place in the ranks of the fighters of revolutionary socialism.

The KPD leadership described Münzenberg's explanation as "a theoretical fabrication" which would not deceive anti-fascists "either today or in the future." In two successive statements on the "Münzenberg case," first by the KPD and then by the ICC of the Comintern, published in the Comintern journal *Rundschau*[1] in March and April 1939, Münzenberg was blamed for the failure of the popular front movement. The KPD Central Committee said that "among left-wing Social Democrats" he had appeared in a "leftist guise", and "in direct contravention of KPD policy" had encouraged "the slogan about the struggle for socialism", thereby "consciously [driving] the nascent popular front movement into a sectarian cul-de-sac." Among "bourgeois democratic Catholic opponents of Hitler" on the other hand he had appeared "in a right-wing guise", as the "sensible Communist", and had "consciously [fostered] suspicion of the KPD's policy and leadership."

Compared with this confused mass of contradictory accusations the ICC's indictment was somewhat more precise. The ICC stated that Münzenberg had belonged to the outlawed Neumann group, parting company with it in 1932 "in words" only. So as to comply with all formalities, the ICC confirmed Münzenberg's expulsion from the Central Committee of the KPD. Two years after the expulsion had been announced in party circles and six months after Münzenberg's resignation the same number of *Rundschau* finally announced the decision of the Central Committee of the KPD, that Münzenberg had been "expelled from the ranks of the KPD."[2]

It has been claimed that the years in France were Münzenberg's happiest. This is only partly correct. It may have been true of the time before 1936 when he discovered a new country, its people and the beauties of its landscape. Moreover, after 1933 the struggle against Hitler became the preoccupation to which he devoted himself body and soul. If in the past it had been possible to accuse him of political cynicism, there was increasingly less reason to do so after 1933. The clever tactician, the experienced propagandist, had become a man with a mission. After his break with Moscow, after the pressure of party discipline had been lifted from him, he may at times have felt less hemmed in. But in quiet moments his thoughts turned to events in Moscow where Stalin had staged the execution of Bukharin and Rykov, once Lenin's closest collaborators, and a few months later liquidated the Red Army command, officers many of whom had had a substantial share in the victory of the October Revolution and the successes of the civil war.

Towards the end of 1939 Münzenberg and Kurt Kersten sat in an old restaurant by Strasbourg cathedral. Münzenberg reminisced about the work of the Bolsheviks in Switzerland and remarked sadly that he

---

[1] *Rundschau* (Basle), 28 March and 13 April 1939.
[2] *Ibid.*, 13 April 1939.

would soon be the last survivor of the Zimmerwald Left who had met in Kienthal. But he did not allow such moments of melancholy to defeat him; on the contrary he sought to overcome them by more intense activity. At the time of his talk with Kersten he had already founded his new journal, *Die Zukunft* (The Future), the most ambitious venture of the last years of his life.

17. Otto Katz-André Simone's Transformations and End

Münzenberg's break with the Comintern meant a break also with some long standing collaborators who obeyed Comintern orders. Before coming to the last part of Münzenberg's life we might therefore look more closely at at least one of these men who for years was an active if controversial assistant of Münzenberg's, Otto Katz.

The two men's association went back to 1924 when Münzenberg's newly founded publishing house produced its first books. Münzenberg was anxious that they should be reviewed not only in the Communist press but also in the two leading political journals of the left, *Weltbühne* and *Tagebuch*. It was my task at the time to establish the necessary connections and therefore I called at the editorial offices of *Tagebuch*. A young man in immaculate bourgeois dress received me with the utmost politeness. His name was Otto Katz. He seemed amused by my efforts to interest him in our Communist publications. But he promised to see that our books were reviewed in *Tagebuch*. Soon afterwards he telephoned and invited me to a cup of coffee. At this rendezvous he deployed all his charm. He played his trump card by putting his hand into his pocket and pulling out his party card: he had been a member of the KPD since 1922.

When Erwin Piscator opened his own theatre at the Nollendorfplatz in Berlin in 1927 Katz left *Tagebuch* to become Piscator's administrative director. In this position he could give ample proof of his diplomatic skills and persuasive powers. It was not always easy to deal with such complicated personalities as Bela Balasz, Johannes R. Becher, Bertolt Brecht, Alfred Döblin, Wilhelm Herzog, Leo Lania, Walter Mehring, Ernst Toller and Kurt Tucholsky, whom Piscator wanted to organize into a writers collective on the Russian model. But problems of this kind Katz solved with great calm and a friendly smile.

The venture failed in spite of Piscator's genuine artistic determination and in spite of Otto Katz's diplomatic accomplishments and business skills. In September 1929 the theatre was forced to close its doors for the last time. It is evidence of Piscator's humanitarianism that he was worried about his director's future. He recommended him to Münzenberg who found him a niche in *Universum-Bücherei*. Although Katz successfully popularized the firm's products, he had frequent clashes with Münzenberg. Katz had very bourgeois habits, he spent more money than he earned in the publishing house and he was still so preoccupied with the liquidation of the Piscator theatre that he frequently failed to put in an appearance at the *Bücherei* for days on end. He was not popular with the rest of the staff. Although always correct and friendly, he was arrogant. Piatnitsky, moreover, told Münzenberg not to employ such "bourgeois elements." But Münzenberg ignored all criticism because he liked Katz who was quick to see Münzenberg's points, who was imaginative, entertaining, witty and loyal.

At the end of 1930, misfortune befell Otto Katz. The fiscal authorities held him personally responsible for arrears in entertainment taxes for the Piscator theatres. Unless he could raise over one hundred thousand marks he would go to prison. In desperation he asked Münzenberg for help. Otherwise, he said, he would commit suicide. Münzenberg removed him from the authorities' clutches by sending him to Moscow to work in the *Meshrabpom* film section. From the end of 1930 to the spring of 1933 Katz lived and worked in the *Meshrabpom* house in Moscow. In spite of his bourgeois habits he adapted himself with surprising speed to the spartan life in Moscow. When we met him there in 1930 and 1932 he was a changed man. He was serious, determined and reserved. Whatever he thought about the hardships of daily life in Russia, about the incipient Byzantinism in the Kremlin, he kept to himself. The current slogans came readily to his lips; he had become a loyal official of the régime.

In 1933 Münzenberg sent for Katz to assist him in Paris. He was a member of Münzenberg's Paris staff until 1937. He acted as secretary to the Marley committee and visited Britain and the United States to collect money for the Comintern. In Hollywood he charmed German émigré actors, directors and writers. Katz had an extraordinary fascination for women, a quality which greatly helped him in organizing committees and campaigns. He had little personal political ambition and always needed a political mentor. He was loyal to Münzenberg and was honoured by the trust which Münzenberg had in him.

At the beginning of the Spanish civil war Münzenberg and the Spanish Foreign Minister, Alvarez del Vayo, set up a news agency, *Agence Espagne*, in Paris. Its purpose was to provide the French press with news and comment from the Republican Government. Katz took charge of this agency and henceforth signed his articles and other publications with the pseudonym André Simone. From the start *Agence Espagne* was under strong Communist influence which increased even further in 1937 after Münzenberg's break with the Comintern. Before long, Paris political circles came to look upon the agency as a tool of the Russians. Katz-Simone paid substantial sums to French journalists to print pro-Soviet and pro-Communist articles.

When Münzenberg broke with the Comintern all German Communists living in Paris—but above all those who had worked with him—were asked to disassociate themselves from him and to make a written declaration to that effect. Katz obeyed these orders. When Münzenberg was slandered, Katz remained silent and carefully avoided him. Nevertheless the Comintern continued to view him with suspicion. The liquidator of Münzenberg's Paris enterprises, the Czech Smeral, interrogated Katz-Simone on Moscow's orders to check his loyalty.

Katz-Simone travelled for *Agence Espagne* between Paris, Barcelona and Valencia in 1938. Denoël, the Paris publishers, brought out a book edited by him, *Hitler in Spain,* the material for which had been collected by the Russian secret service in Franco-held territory. At *Agence Espagne* he was in close touch with two journalists who were both old friends of the Soviet Union; Emile Buré of *L'Ordre* and Geneviève Tabouis of *Oeuvre* published everything that Katz-Simone gave them by way of secret information. After the collapse of the Spanish Republic he went for a time to the United States and then worked in the Paris office of the Czech Government in exile under its leader, Hubert Ripka. There he came for the first time in close contact with Czech Communists who were employed in the same office.

After the Hitler-Stalin pact and the outbreak of the Second World War Katz-Simone remained at first in Paris. There chance led in November or December 1939 to a last meeting with Münzenberg at which I was present. At a small café in Montparnasse they suddenly came face to face. Münzenberg showered Katz with mockery and scorn asking him whether he was fighting for Hitler, Stalin's ally, or for the Beneš government which Hitler had expelled. Katz paled and without saying a word left the café.

Apart from a brief stay in the United States, Katz-Simone spent the war years in Mexico where he acted as unofficial adviser on foreign policy to Lombardo Toledano, the Stalinist trade union leader. At the same time Katz-Simone worked as a journalist, a façade cleverly covering his real activities. He executed several obscure orders from Moscow passed on to him by Umansky, the Soviet Union's chargé d'affaires in Mexico. Equipped with a new Czech diplomatic passport, he travelled early in 1946 via New York, London and Berlin to Prague. His friend Clementis found him a place in the press department of the Czech Foreign Ministry. He had reached the summit of his Communist career.

But the years of unquestioning devotion were of no avail to Katz-Simone. Moscow remembered the time when he had worked with

Münzenberg or was associated with his organizations. More than ten years after Münzenberg's death, Stalin presented an account of Katz–Simone's activities in which the Münzenberg association was emphasized. Katz–Simone was one of the fourteen accused in the 1952 show trial staged by Stalin who wanted to nip in the bud any stirrings of independence among the Czech party leadership and at the same time rid himself of several leading members of the Soviet espionage service from the pre-1945 days. At the behest of the prosecution Katz-Simone described himself as a "Trotskyist Titoist traitor and enemy of the Czech people in the service of American imperialism."[1]

Katz-Simone's self-condemnation reads like a posthumous attack on Münzenberg. He said that in 1937 he and the Trotskyist Münzenberg had begun "to collaborate on the same noxious Trotskyist lines. This collaboration consciously damaged the KPD because we established links with hostile bourgeois and capitalist elements . . . we undermined the KPD from within. To this end I worked with Münzenberg until 1932. . . . In Paris from 1933 to 1937 I continued my collaboration with Münzenberg on Trotskyist lines. Münzenberg negotiated behind the KPD's back with obdurate enemies, with right wing Socialists who refused to cooperate with the Communists. He was in touch with other anti-Communist groups among the German emigration . . ."

Invited by the prosecuting counsel to sum up his character, Katz-Simone said in his final speech,

> "I regard myself as a criminal, I am a Jew. I stand before the court a traitor and a spy."

And he concluded by asking for the severest possible punishment.

His wish was granted. In the early hours of 3 December 1952 Otto Katz-Simone together with ten other accused was led to a dimly lit gallows in a Prague prison yard and hanged.

18. A Platform for the German Opposition

The report, to which reference has already been made, by the security police chief of 15 May 1939 on "popular front type opposition among German émigrés" initiated by the German Freedom Party, said that a "supra-party opposition paper", Die Zukunft, had appeared for the first time in mid-October 1938 in Paris. "By highlighting political and economic conditions in Germany and using vague humanist theo-

---

[1]This and subsequent quotations are taken from Der Slansky-Prozess, Prague 1953, p. 253 et seq.

ries about equality, freedom and justice [it wanted] to impress on public opinion that the collapse of the Third Reich was inevitable and imminent". The report continued:

> According to various concurring accounts—in part from opponents of the German Freedom Party—*Die Zukunft* is run by the Communist Münzenberg who was mentioned earlier as one of the leading lights of the German Freedom Party. Having been expelled by the KPD from the Central Committee for his high-handed and bourgeois popular front policy which was disapproved of by the Comintern he is now trying to repeat the unsuccessful experiment of a "German popular front in Paris" without the KPD.[1]

Arthur Koestler later said of the same venture in which he took a leading part:

> The idea was to publish an independent, German-language weekly paper which, apart from anti-Nazi propaganda, would work for the *rapprochement* of various groups in exile and develop a programme for the day when the Nazi régime was no more.[2]

What the Gestapo described as "empty phrases" was a serious matter to the men who joined the publisher of *Die Zukunft*. It was concern for Germany's fate after the end of the Nazi régime which inspired the weekly's name. Fourteen days before the publication of the first number of *Die Zukunft*, the Third Reich achieved its greatest triumph yet. On 29 September the Prime Ministers of Britain and France, Chamberlain and Daladier, handed over the Sudetenland to Hitler. The British and the French people rejoiced to hear that Hitler had no further territorial claims and that a battle for peace had been won. Only a few French voices were raised denouncing the Munich agreement as a devastating defeat for the democracies and as an invitation to Hitler to continue his annexation policy. When the aeroplane bringing the French delegation back from Munich arrived over Paris and great crowds could be seen at the airport Daladier enquired as to the meaning of the demonstration. To his surprise he learned that the multitude had assembled to welcome him for saving the peace.

During these days of despondency Münzenberg happened to meet Jawaharlal Nehru. The Indian politician had been visiting his wife in a sanatorium in the Black Forest. Both men realized that the Munich

[1]Microfilm, Institut für Zeitgeschichte, MA 145/1, p. 10451 *et seq.*
[2]Koestler, *The Invisible Writing*, p. 406.

agreement meant war. Nehru wanted to return to India where he was likely to be interned by the British. He welcomed the prospect because he would thereby be absolved from taking sides.

Lengthy preparations had been necessary before the first number of *Die Zukunft* could appear. The financial requirements, which thanks to low production costs in France at the time were very modest, needed to be met for some time to come. Münzenberg approached his rich friend, Olof Aschberg and French politicians from among the Freemasons, who provided the necessary funds. Arthur Koestler edited *Die Zukunft* at first. When he came to concentrate more on other literary activities, the Catholic journalist Werner Thormann was called upon to assist him and for a while the two men worked together. The first number had listed numerous contributors of every political shade with the exception of the Communists: Thomas and Heinrich Mann, Stefan Zweig, Joseph Roth, René Schickele, Arnold Zweig, Lion Feuchtwanger, Alfred Döblin, Alfred Kerr, Rudolf Olden, Alexander Schifrin, Max Beer, E. J. Gumbel, Manès Sperber, Max Hodann, and among non-Germans Duff Cooper, Wickham Steed, Paul Boncour, Carlo Sforza, Francesco Nitti, Georges Bidault, Yvon Delbos, Ignazio Silone, Luigi Sturzo, Edmond Vermeil, H. G. Wells, Kingsley Martin, Herbert Morrison, Philip Noel-Baker, Henri de Kerillis and others.

Die Zukunft also became the mouthpiece of the "Friends of Socialist Unity" (Münzenberg group) which was active more in the field of propaganda than of organization, and which advocated a reformed German unity party of the working class. What Münzenberg demanded in the name of the "Friends of Socialist Unity"[1] was the union of "all honest anti-Nazi workers" into a "revolutionary unity party of the working class" with a guaranteed "right of self-determination" within the party and with complete independence from the Third and the Second International as well as a basic preparedness to enter into alliances with all "honest democratic forces in Germany" outside the working class.

From the start much space was taken up in *Die Zukunft* by discussion on Germany's eventual constitution. As late as 5 January 1940 in a leading article entitled "Democracy and Dictatorship" Münzenberg demanded a completely new approach to these questions:

> The masses do not like the sound of democracy or dictatorship. 'Democracy' reminds everyone in Germany of Weimar and 'dictatorship' of Hitler and Stalin . . . The new Germany must be neither a repetition of the Weimar democracy nor a one party state on the Stalinist model. The economic, social and constitutional basis of a new Germany must depend

---

[1] Cf. for example his article *Für die Einheitspartei der deutschen Arbeiter* (Towards the Unity Party of the German Workers) in *Die Zukunft*, Vol. II, No. 40 of 6th October 1939.

on the actually prevailing national and international situation, taking fully into account the sum of the experiences of all the changes and revolutions of the eighteenth, nineteenth and twentieth centuries . . .[1]

Beyond the limited horizons of the German emigration, *Die Zukunft* sought to address itself to politically interested circles in Britain and France. A special Anglo-German number with contributions by leading British politicians was produced under Arthur Koestler's editorship; a Franco-German *Zukunft* followed and led to the foundation of a *Union Franco-Allemande* which was joined by Jean Giraudoux and other politicians and publicists of note. At the beginning of 1939, Münzenberg founded the Friends of *Zukunft*, a group of contributors and interested readers who met for political discussions and who sought to provide refugees in Paris with an intellectual focus by organizing a number of cultural events. The same objective was served by the political writings which were produced by the Sebastian Brant publishing house in Strasbourg.[2]

The Gestapo offices in Münster which through a liaison agent, "No. 49", specialized in following the activities of German refugees in Paris, reported in July 1939 on the "great efforts" being made by the Münzenberg group to make *Die Zukunft* the mouthpiece of the entire opposition and noted:

> Although this paper has not been appearing long it is thanks to Münzenberg's skill that it has become the leading paper of the emigration and of the German opposition in general.[3]

Meanwhile the Western democracies had suffered one defeat after another: in March 1939 the military resistance of the Spanish Republic collapsed, thousands of Spanish Republicans fled to France and were interned in the camp at Gurs. Münzenberg founded a committee, "People in Distress", which took charge of these civil war victims. Hitler annexed Bohemia and Moravia on 15 March; Slovakia became an "independent state" dependent on Germany. Czechoslovakia had ceased to exist. As soon as the Sudetenland was occupied, German and Austrian refugees tried to leave Czechoslovakia. An appeal was made to the High

[1] *Die Zukunft*, Vol. III, No. 1 of 5 January 1940.
[2] In 1938/39 Sebastian Brant issued: E. J. Gumbel, *Freie Wissenschaft* (Free Learning) (1938); Fritz Sternberg, *Die Deutsche Kriegsstärke* (German Military Strength) (1938); Kurt Kersten, *Unter Freiheitsfahnen, Kalender der Zukunft für 1939* (Under the Flags of Freedom. Calendar of *Zukunft* for 1939); Max Werner, *Der Aufmarsch zum Zweiten Weltkrieg* (Preparations for the Second World War) (1939), Max Werner, *Sozialismus, Krieg and Europa* (Socialism, War and Europe) (1939).
[3] Microfilm, Institut für Zeitgeschichte, MA 644, p. 7738 *et seq.*

Commissioner for Refugees at the League of Nations, and Britain gave entry visas to several hundred political refugees. The KPD leadership in exile managed to infiltrate a reliable man into the refugee commission. He made certain that British visas were given to all Communists while opposition members, Trotskyists or members of groups which the Communists disliked, were stopped from getting visas. Those who failed to escape through Poland fell into the hands of the advancing Gestapo.

Even after leaving the KPD, Münzenberg did not attack Stalin at once. The refugees still regarded Soviet Russia as the country that would fight on the side of the anti-fascists when the military confrontation came. Münzenberg criticized the policy of the Western powers which had led to Munich because "it was a European policy without the Soviet Union" and said that even after Hitler's fall there must be a policy of alliance with Russia, a view which was firmly rejected by Kurt Geyer in *Neuer Vorwärts*.[1] Geyer reminded his readers that in the Weimar Republic the slogan "Alliance with the Soviet Union" had led the KPD onto the side of the counter revolution and that however critical one might be of the attitude of the Western democracies towards Germany one must not forget that it had been the policy of the Soviet Union which had contributed most to the victory of the counter revolution.

Shortly after the fall of Czechoslovakia, the Soviet Foreign Minister, Litvinov, was replaced by Molotov and more warnings were heard predicting Stalin's swing to Hitler. Stalin had made a speech at the Eighteenth Party Congress of the CPSU on 10 March 1939 but the significance of it did not become clear to the world until five months later. It was a statement of complete neutrality, with not one word against fascism:

> We stand for peace and want to strengthen our relations with all countries. We shall follow this line as long as these countries wish to have the same relations with us and do not harm the interests of our country.[2]

In May 1939 Münzenberg gathered together a group of opposition Communists and Socialists who called themselves the "Friends of Socialist Unity in Germany" and who were in close touch with two other groups, the "Working Committee of German Socialists" and the "Revolutionary Socialists of Austria." The debate on the impending war and its consequences continued unabated among political émigrés. Leopold

[1] *Die Zukunft*, Vol. II, No. 19 of 12 May 1939 and *Neuer Vorwärts* of 21 May 1939.
[2] Cf. A. Rossi, *Deux Ans d'Alliance Germano-Soviétique*, Paris 1949, p. 19 *et seq.*

Schwarzschild gave his view on "the day after" when Germany was defeated and Hitler overthrown and demanded that the victors should establish a form of "education administration" before there could be a new civil service and a new government. Other writers advocated a partition of Germany. Emil Ludwig argued that there was no other Germany, that all Germans were National Socialists. *Die Zukunft* commented on these views; it strongly attacked Schwarzschild's ideas, advocated the preservation of Germany's national unity and described Emil Ludwig's ideas as "racialism in inverted commas."

19. The Russian Stab in the Back

As a few observers of the political scene had predicted a bombshell exploded in the second half of August: on 19 August 1939 Stalin concluded a trade agreement with Germany which the Communist press of France hailed as a "new victory" because it proved that Hitler must bow to the superiority of the Soviet Union. On 23 August the German-Soviet non-aggression pact was signed. Münzenberg's reaction to this event sounded like a *cri de coeur*.[1] The "ally" had joined the enemy and the enormity of the step made him forget all anxiety about his own safety which had hitherto stopped him from attacking Stalin. In *Zukunft* of 28 August 1939, Münzenberg protested the Soviet "betrayal." He accused Stalin, the man who had "hitherto claimed to lead the fight against fascism" of having shown the chief fascist power the way to safety. It was no more possible to argue about the fact that the Hitler-Stalin pact increased the threat of war than about the realization that it had been for considerations of power politics alone that both Hitler and Stalin had surrendered all their theories and reversed their ideological positions. He described the pact as a "disgusting spectacle." At the moment it was of no interest who would in the end be the deceived or the deceiver.

On 1 September Hitler's armies crossed the frontier into Poland and on 3 September, Britain and France declared war on Germany. The world was on fire in Poland and the Soviet Union marched at the side of its arch enemy. Molotov broadcast an explanation of Russia's invasion of eastern Poland.

> The Soviet Government sees it as its duty to extend a helping hand to its Ukrainian and Bielo-Russian brothers in Poland, to liberate the Polish people from the unhappy war and to give it the opportunity of leading a peaceful life.[2]

[1] *Die Zukunft*, Vol. II, No. 34, 28 August 1939.
[2] *Die Welt* (Stockholm,) No. 2, 23 September 1939.

Molotov omitted saying that in a secret clause of the pact with Germany demarcation lines were drawn between the spheres of interest of Germany and the Soviet Union and that Finland, Estonia, Latvia, eastern Poland and Bessarabia had been allocated to Russia.

There was no holding Münzenberg now. The accumulation of suppressed knowledge flooded the pages of *Zukunft* with pungent criticism. On 22 September he denounced the "Russian stab in the back." In the last few years political circles and particularly the workers movements of all countries had wondered what was happening in Russia. In recent weeks a clear, terrible answer had been given to that question. Whatever Stalin might pretend his intentions to be the attack on Poland had no place in the democratic peaceful policy of a socialist state.

> The old ideology, the principles of collective security and the socialist and international doctrines which have been laboriously upheld merely to deceive, are dead and buried in Stalin's Russia.

The article finished:

> Peace and freedom must be defended against Hitler and against Stalin, victory must be won over Hitler and Stalin and the new, independent unity party of the German workers must be forged in the struggle against Hitler and against Stalin . . .
>
> For years a kept press has agitated and slandered, has spread hundreds of infamous lies, has cast suspicion on thousands of brave workers. No number of *Volkszeitung* has appeared without repeating a hundred times: "Down with the criminal, down with the traitor."
>
> Today millions rise up in every country, point to the East and cry out: "You, Stalin, are the traitor!"

Subsequently Münzenberg also wrote openly about the crimes of the "Great Purge" which had decimated the Russian Party, dealt a death blow to the Comintern and ruined millions of people living in Russia, Russians as well as foreigners. In the spring of 1940 Münzenberg arranged for the posthumous accusation of the "Hero of the October Revolution," Fyodor Raskolnikov,[1] who had revealed Stalin's crimes, to be published as "an open letter to Stalin." Raskolnikov said:

> You have slandered, dishonoured and murdered Lenin's old comrades in arms: Kamenev, Zinoviev, Bukharin, Rykov and others of whose inno-

---

[1] Raskolnikov did not return to the Soviet Union from his post as Ambassador in Sofia but moved to France and after his break with Stalin lived as a worker under an assumed name in Nice where in the autumn of 1939 he suffered a nervous breakdown and died.

cence you were fully aware . . . Where is the old guard? It is no longer alive. You, Stalin, have shot it.

The outbreak of the war brought serious changes for German and Austrian refugees in France. The French Government interned all Germans regardless of whether they had shown themselves to be determined anti-fascists or not. Women and men over fifty were at first exempted from this regulation. All foreigners who were described as "undesirable" in the police files, including all known foreign Communists, were taken to the camp at Le Vernet near Toulouse. They included most of Münzenberg's close collaborators. The French police, full of right-wing radical elements, was not prepared to distinguish in its arrests between Stalinists and ex-Communists persecuted by Stalin. The Paris prefecture had kept Münzenberg under constant observation while he worked for the Comintern, keeping watch on the offices which he visited and the hotels in which he lived. The prying had not ceased even after Münzenberg's break with the Communists. This suited the Stalinists who had demanded that "there shall be no right of asylum in the democratic countries for these Trotskyist criminals."[1] Münzenberg tried in vain in the months to come to secure the release of his colleagues. He himself remained at large—he had just completed his fiftieth year—and *Zukunft* continued to appear.

The French Communists were as taken aback by the Hitler-Stalin pact as all anti-fascists, particularly as for weeks they received no directives from Moscow. The Communist deputies voted for the war credits and their party's leader, Maurice Thorez, joined the army. Finally, at the end of September, orders came from Moscow to spread "revolutionary defeatism", which meant sabotaging the war efforts of the democracies and playing into the hands of the enemy. In leaflets produced in abundance everywhere in France the illegal party leadership called for sabotage:

> With all suitable means, using your intelligence and your technical skills you must prevent or delay the manufacture of the means of war or render them useless,

said one of these leaflets, entitled "Daladier, Chamberlain, Mussolini, Franco and Pius XII."[2] The secret organization of the French Communist Party called for the liquidation of all defectors who were opposed

[1]Taken from *Russland und die Komintern*, published by the Internationaler Sozialistischer Kampfbund, London 1942
[2]A. Rossi, *Les Communistes Français pendant la Drôle de Guerre*, Paris 1951, p. 176 *et seq.*

to the new directives and who left the party. Thorez who had deserted from his unit and escaped to Moscow indulged in hate-filled tirades against the "traitors in the stocks." He called them criminals, careerists and police spies and abandoned them to the party for revenge.[1] Even at Le Vernet, loyal Stalinist Communists threatened reprisals against comrades who had turned away from the party after the pact.

The German Communists, with Walter Ulbricht in the lead, also recovered their speech. The German workers, wrote Ulbricht, knew the bankers of London and the two hundred families of France and they realized what a British victory would mean.

Anyone who intrigues against the friendship of the German and the Soviet people is an enemy of the German people and will be branded as an assistant of British imperialism.[2]

The Russian attack on Finland which began on 30 November 1939 produced a new wave of anti-Soviet indignation. In New York Thomas Mann and other prominent German refugees publicly accused Stalin of treason. Thomas Mann returned to the analysis which he had made in the summer of 1939. At the time he had said that National Socialism was the younger brother of Bolshevism, and that both systems were essentially unscrupulous. Heinrich Mann on the other hand, as chairman of a Communist-led "Committee of the German Opposition," issued a lame statement which made no reference to the pact, to the partition of Poland or to the Finnish War. His old friend Münzenberg said bitterly in Zukunft that by his silence Heinrich Mann had "taken the side of Hitler and Stalin" and that for this the German people would one day "take him to task."[3]

Barely a shot was fired at the Western front during these months. On the Rhine, on the Maginot Line and on the Western Wall, the French and the German armies faced each other. The French called this curious prelude to their tragedy the drôle de guerre, the queer war. In February 1940, Münzenberg met the British journalist, Sefton Delmer, who as a war reporter had just returned from a visit to the Maginot Line. He drew a sombre picture of the morale of the troops to whom he had talked. In his opinion the defeatist propaganda of the Communists had fallen on receptive ears and he did not expect this army to offer serious resistance.

After the start of the war the French dramatist, Jean Giraudoux, who had been appointed Minister of Information shortly before, set up a

[1] Die Welt, (Stockholm), 21 March 1940.
[2] Ibid., 6 February 1940.
[3] Die Zukunft, 19 January 1940.

"German freedom station" which broadcast to the German troops and the population in Germany. To the annoyance of the German Communists this station transmitted articles by Münzenberg from *Die Zukunft* addressed to the German workers. From Moscow, Wilhelm Florin attacked the "blackguards of the German freedom station," accusing them of inviting the German workers to sabotage the production of war materials.[1]

On 9 April, Hitler's *Blitzkrieg* continued: the German armies invaded Denmark and Norway and overran both countries within a few weeks. On 10 May, the Saturday before Whitsun, Münzenberg, Julius Deutsch and other friends had gone to visit some acquaintances in La Brevière. There we heard that the German armies had marched into Holland, Belgium and Luxemburg and that their armoured divisions were moving towards the French frontier. We did not know that the end had just begun and that the last number of *Zukunft* had appeared the day before. As soon as we were back in Paris we learned that all German and Austrian citizens who, because of their age or for other reasons, had remained at liberty were to report at a certain camp. Women without children under fourteen were also interned. There was general confusion. From the censored press it was impossible to gather how far the German armies had advanced and where the fronts were. A few days later there was a rumour that German armoured divisions had broken through near Sedan. It seemed wiser to be interned because the inmates of the camps at Paris were sent south. A day or so later I therefore went with Münzenberg to the Stade de Colombes. At the gate I said goodbye to him: it was the last time that I saw him.

Together with thousands of other German women I was sent to the former prisoner of war camp at Gurs in the Pyrenees. When the German army came closer the commandant permitted those women who felt politically threatened—of whom I was one—to leave the camp and to shelter under false names in the surrounding villages. Having tried in vain to establish contact with Münzenberg via an agreed address I succeeded in 1940 in fleeing to Portugal and then to Mexico.

Three days after we parted in Paris, Münzenberg and the internees were sent in groups of hundreds to different camps in the French provinces. Meanwhile the wave of refugees from Belgium, the Netherlands and the north of France had assumed gigantic proportions and now blocked all roads. Münzenberg was sent to the camp at Chambaran, south-east of Lyons, a former French artillery training centre. With fixed bayonets and police dogs the guards took the refugees to the barbed wire enclosed camp where for months internees from the de-

[1] *Die Welt*, (Stockholm), 21 March 1940.

partments around Lyons had been assembled, including National Socialists and Communists who had had sufficient time to establish their organization in this camp as everywhere else.

The internees who were detailed to the 143rd French Infantry Regiment were sent to work in the forests. Münzenberg, however, managed to find more congenial work. He helped to keep the camp commandant's garden in order and worked there with another internee, the Social Democratic trade union official, Valentin Hartig. The two men supplied their friends with lettuce and radishes to add a little variety to the monotonous camp diet which consisted of a daily ration of liver paté and bread. All those who were with him in Chambaran agreed that, given the situation, Münzenberg's mood was good. He had lost none of his energy. Paul Elsas who was in the same hut recalls:

> I had a number of discussions with him. He was one of the few who had not lost his nerve and who was sufficiently far-sighted to see the situation as a whole. In this period he made one or two speeches which were first-class and which brought some consolation to over-anxious souls.[1]

As the rumours about the rapid German advance grew, Münzenberg suggested to Hartig that they should try to escape to Switzerland. He obtained a Michelin map of the district. The internees begged the commandant to send them south. Finally on 20 June at 3 A.M. the order to evacuate the camp was given When the camp administration refused to give the internees their papers there was a revolt. Finally they retrieved the papers themselves. Soon afterwards the column began to move southwards through the dark, lonely landscape. The prisoners had not been marching long when dawn began to break. The day had arrived on which the mystery of Münzenberg's death began.

[1]Letter to the author.

Epilogue

The circumstances surrounding Münzenberg's death remain obscure. Several attempts have been made to throw light on this mystery but none of them has provided a satisfactory explanation. They are mentioned here even though the present author is fully aware that they are based on inadequate evidence which has not been improved by the passage of time. The Communists explained the mystery of Münzenberg's death after their own fashion. As early as November and December 1940 when the news of the discovery of the corpse was announced they put it about that Münzenberg had been murdered by former friends whom he had denounced to the police. This version they spread in the French internment camps, in London and in New York. At the time Geneviève Tabouis gave an explanation in a New York paper which she later repeated in her book *Ils l'ont appelée Cassandre* (New York 1942):

> A few months later the whole of Paris knew that Münzenberg was a police agent who had handed over a list of all German anti-fascists in Paris and who had been responsible for numerous arrests. Later I heard first that Münzenberg had come to a sad end and second that he had managed to escape. Some said that during the war when refugees of all political shades had been interned without distinction he found himself in a camp with several German émigrés for whose arrests he had been responsible. He managed to escape from the camp but a few days later the authorities found him, stabbed to death by his former friends.

Another theory regarding Münzenberg's death is suggested by Kurt Müller's evidence. In 1950 the Communist Bundestag deputy was abducted from West Germany by the East German security service and handed over to the Russians who first sentenced him to death and then to life-long imprisonment. When he was released in 1955 and returned to West Germany he reported that in the course of one of his countless interrogations the name Münzenberg was mentioned and the Russian interrogator said: "He is another one with whom we've got even."[1]

When the body was found the French police assumed suicide. Münzenberg's friends disputed this because none of those interned with him who had been in contact with him in the days before he vanished had noticed any signs of depression. On the contrary, Hans Siemsen wrote

[1] Information given by Kurt Müller to the author.

to me in December 1940: "He was very active and energetic that day and survived the tiring march better than I did . . ." And Valentin Hartig wrote on 26 August 1963:

> Suicide seems impossible to me. I spent days with Münzenberg in the garden. Naturally we spoke about the unhappy events which preoccupied and depressed us. But I noticed absolutely no signs of a despair that might have led to suicide or of any intention to take his own life.

Münzenberg sent a telegram from the camp to me at Gurs encouraging me and expressing the hope that we would soon be reunited.

A mysterious role in this drama which still remains unexplained was played by a red-haired man, aged about twenty-five, who shortly before the Chambaran camp was disbanded insisted with determination and finally with success that he should move into the hut occupied by Münzenberg. Nobody knew him. He had not arrived with the others from Paris but was at the camp when the Paris transport arrived, a fact which has led to the deduction that he must have lived previously in the vicinity of Lyons. The only thing known about his past was what he himself said. He claimed to have spent some time in a German concentration camp as a worker with Communist sympathies and to have fled after his release. His account of the concentration camp life was curiously different from the general one and he claimed that he was not too badly treated.

The young man stuck to Münzenberg in the last days at Chambaran and during the march. It was he who, as Valentin Hartig and Clément Korth confirm, most enthusiastically supported Münzenberg's plan to go it alone. After Münzenberg had gone none of his friends ever saw the young man again. He was not at the camp at Le Cheylard nor later at Marseilles, the rallying point for most of the refugees who had evaded the advancing German troops.

Hans Siemsen remembered having seen Münzenberg wave goodbye to him as he walked across the fields with several companions. None of the eyewitnesses whom I questioned at a later date confirmed this detail. Nothing precise is known about the time of Münzenberg's departure nor about the place nor about the number of his companions. Kurt Kersten, basing himself on Siemsen's account and other evidence, in his description of "Münzenberg's End"[1] regards a Stalinist assassination as the most probable explanation. But there is no valid evidence even for this view.

When I visited St. Marcellin in August 1947 the local police archives

---

[1] *Deutsche Rundschau*, Vol. 83 (1957), p. 484 *et seq.*

contained a report on the discovery of the body, a sketch of the locality and medical evidence to the effect that the cause of death could no longer be established. I was not permitted to examine the report which was read to me. As read, the report stated that a hunting dog belonging to a M. Georges Argoud, a timber merchant from St. Antoine, discovered a body with a piece of wire round its neck in the undergrowth. A card addressed to me, a letter from the P.E.N. Club, an identity card and other papers which could no longer be deciphered were found on the body.

I was told that the papers had been sent to the town hall of the small commune of Montagne where Münzenberg was buried. But no papers were found there. The secretary of the commune, M. Micoud, wrote to me on 18 August 1947:

> I do not have in my possession any objects or papers belonging to Herr Münzenberg. A receipt dated 27 October 1940, signed by the Adjutant of the Gendarmerie of St. Marcellin, is proof of the fact that everything that was kept in the Mairie of Montagne relating to Herr Münzenberg was handed over. The relevant papers and possessions were collected by the Gendarmerie and I can show you the receipt . . .

At a new interview with the police the view was expressed that Münzenberg's possessions had probably been sent to the court. I then called upon M. Argoud, who had found the body. He confirmed the account given in the report. He had immediately telephoned the police who had arrived with a doctor and prepared a report. In his opinion it was impossible to determine the cause of death. The police considered it a case of suicide; there was no post mortem.

I paid yet another visit to the police in the spring of 1951 in the hope of being allowed to read the report. But the report and all related documents had been destroyed. The police divisions kept such papers for a period of ten years only. All that remained was a diary entry with details of daily happenings which devoted ten lines to the discovery of the body. The chief of police said that in the case of an unsolved death —if no relatives can be found—papers and valuables are sent to the nearest court. Enquiries at the Palais de Justice in Grenoble, where all the St. Marcellin files had gone after the end of the war, remained fruitless; no documents on Münzenberg were found.

It seems probable that Münzenberg was the victim of a political murder. Who his assassins were can only be guessed at. The mystery of Münzenberg's death, this unusual end to an unusual life, will remain unsolved until the missing documentation is discovered or new evidence appears.

Index